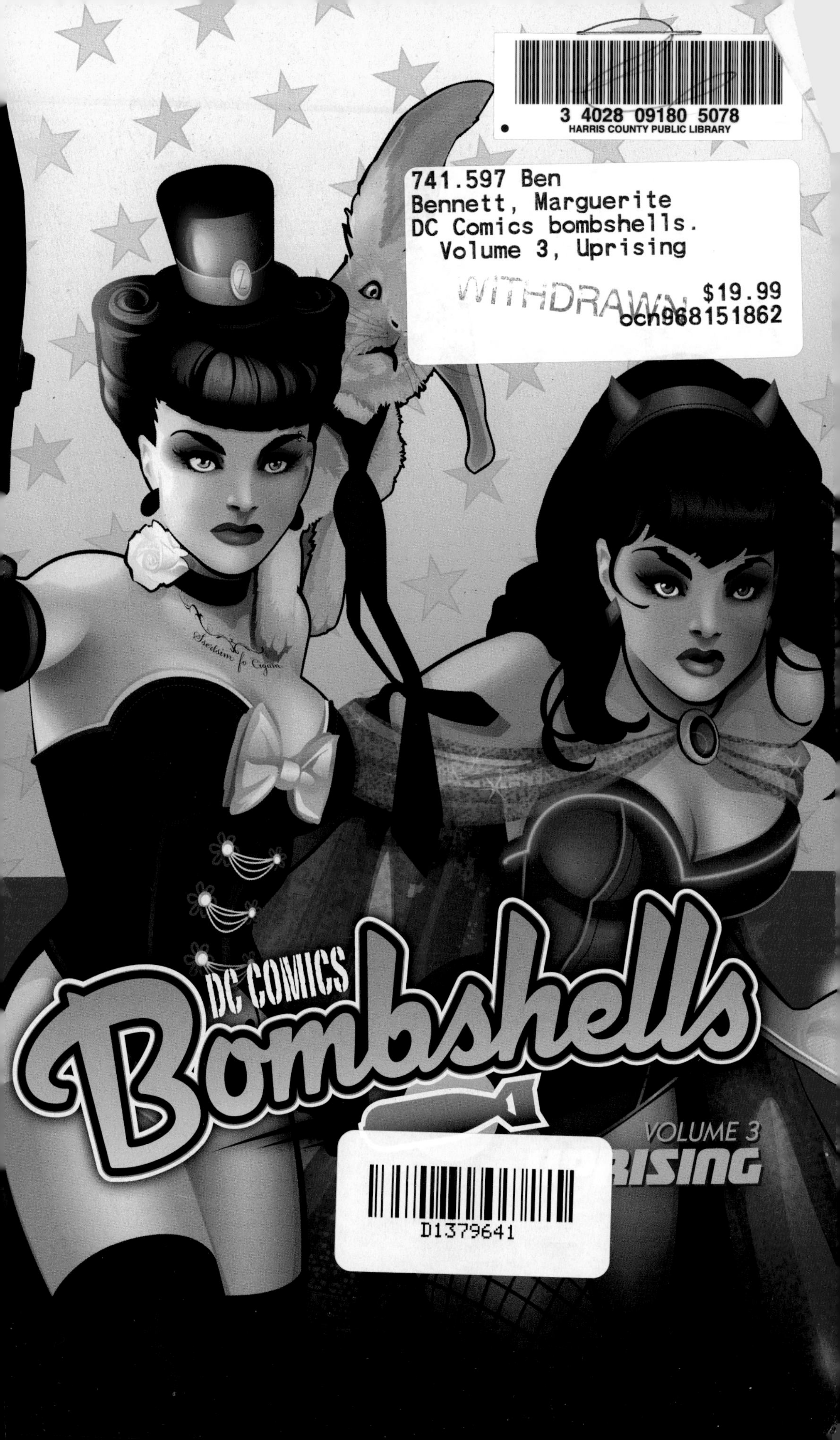
DC COMICS
Bombshells
VOLUME 3
RISING

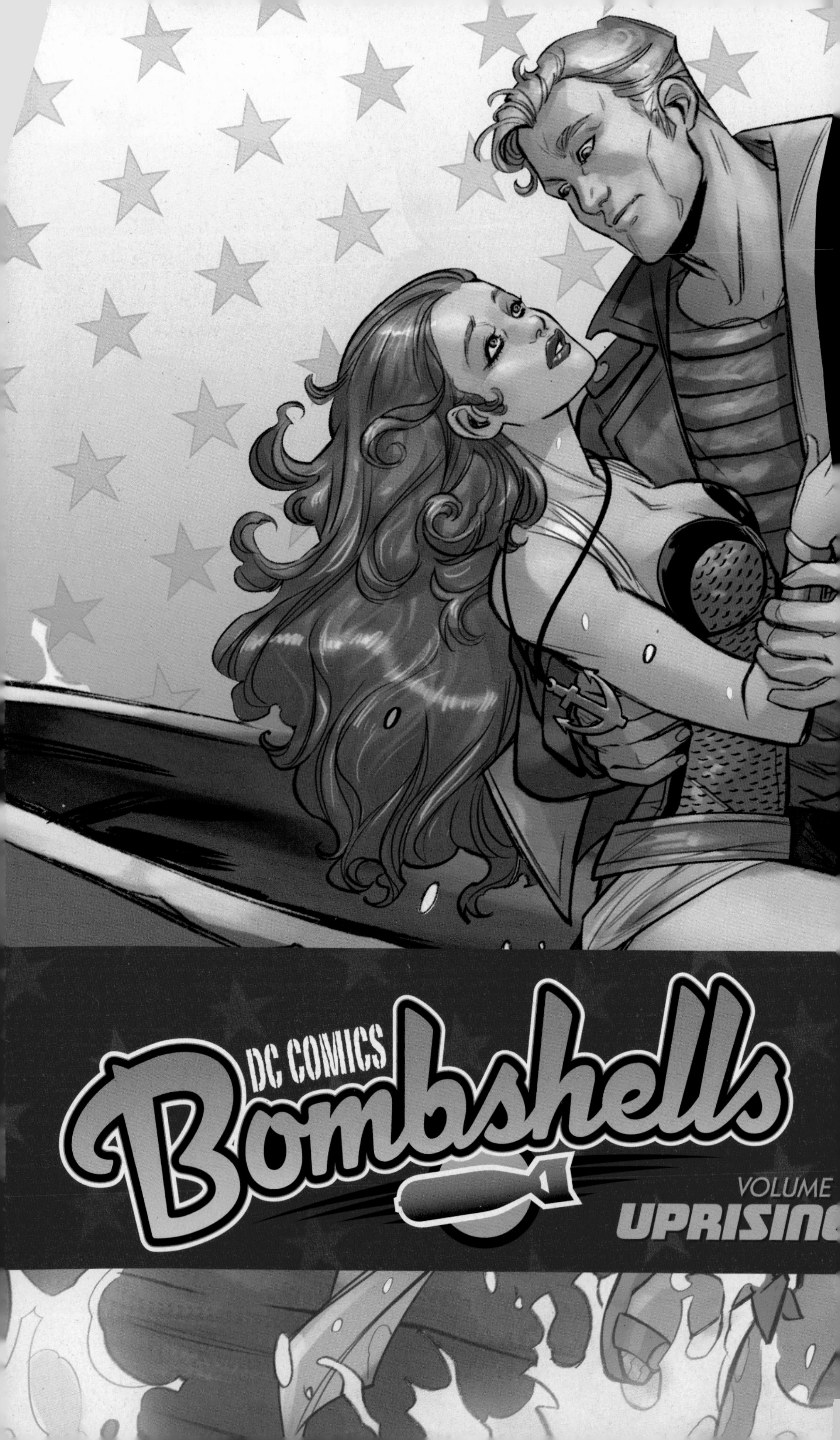
DC COMICS
Bombshells
VOLUME
UPRISING

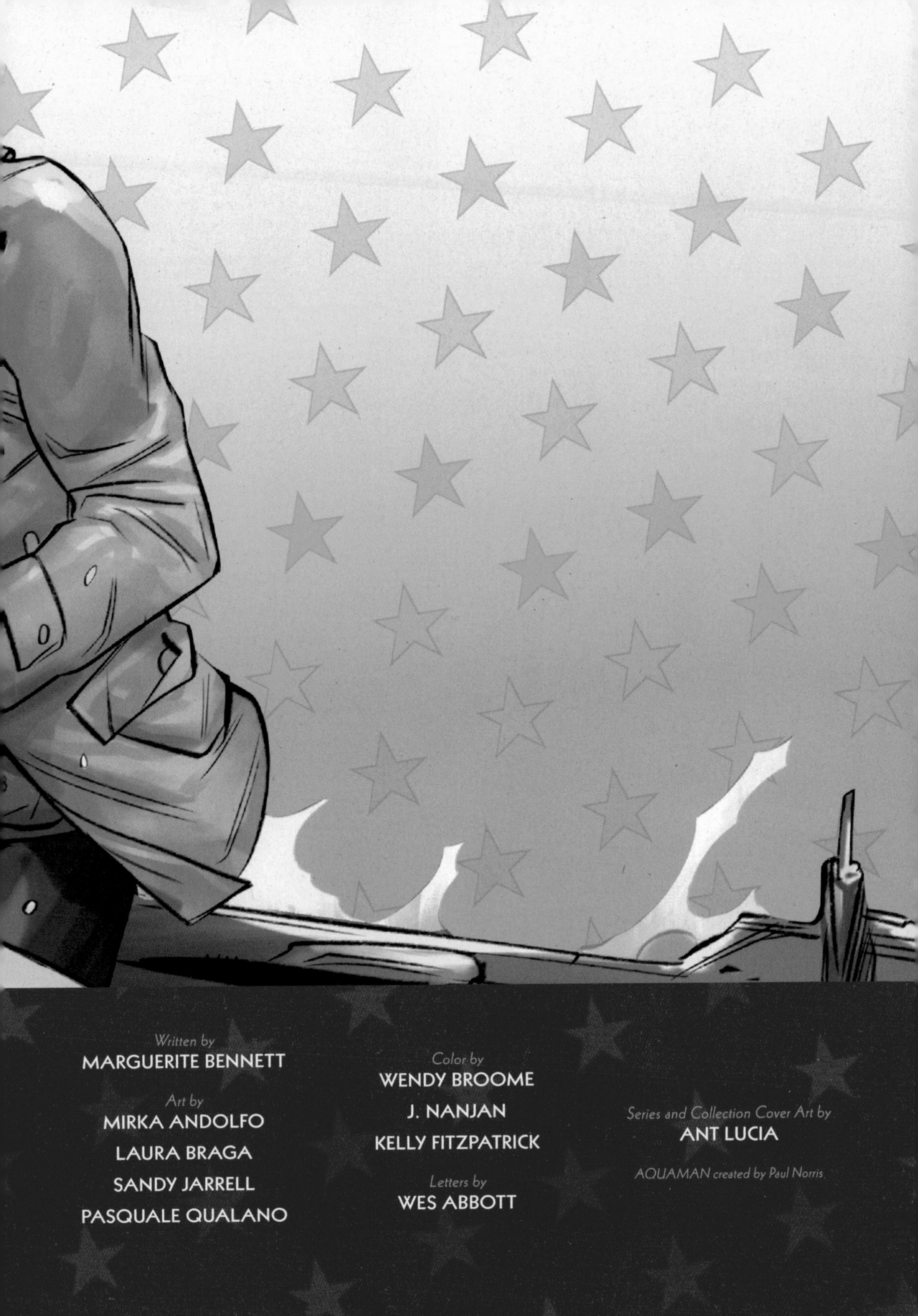

Written by
MARGUERITE BENNETT

Art by
MIRKA ANDOLFO
LAURA BRAGA
SANDY JARRELL
PASQUALE QUALANO

Color by
WENDY BROOME
J. NANJAN
KELLY FITZPATRICK

Letters by
WES ABBOTT

Series and Collection Cover Art by
ANT LUCIA

AQUAMAN created by Paul Norris

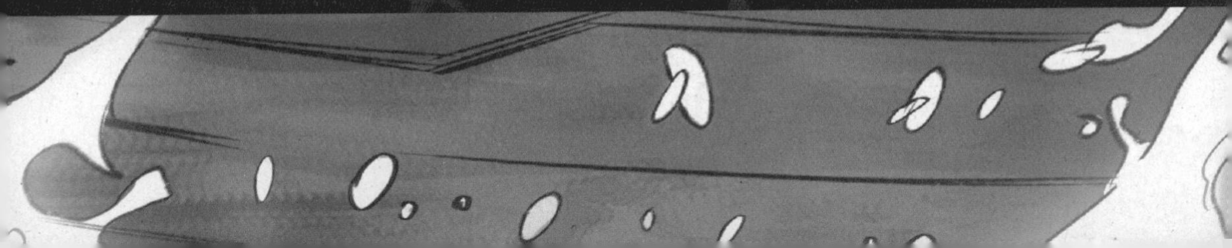

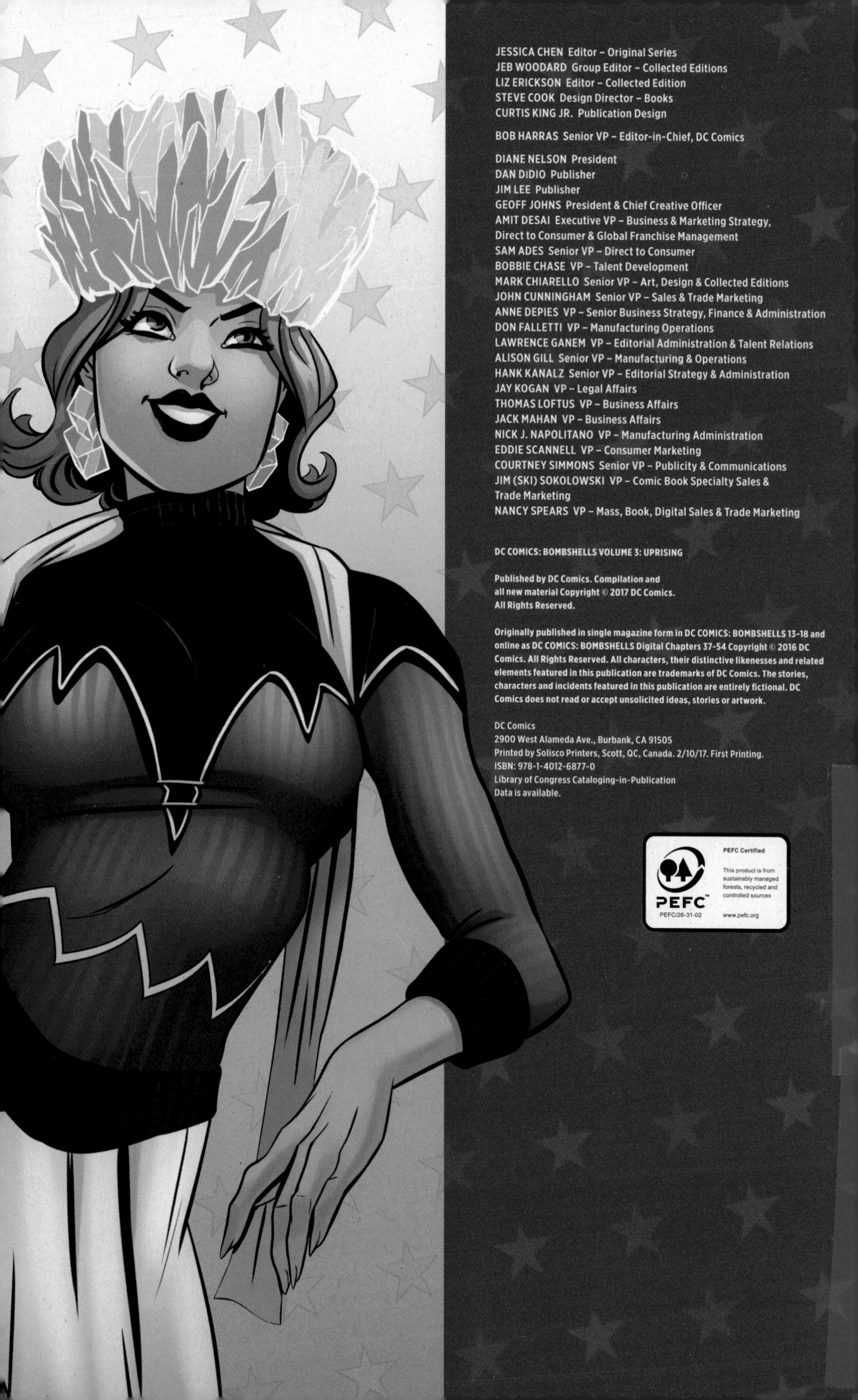

JESSICA CHEN Editor – Original Series
JEB WOODARD Group Editor – Collected Editions
LIZ ERICKSON Editor – Collected Edition
STEVE COOK Design Director – Books
CURTIS KING JR. Publication Design

BOB HARRAS Senior VP – Editor-in-Chief, DC Comics

DIANE NELSON President
DAN DiDIO Publisher
JIM LEE Publisher
GEOFF JOHNS President & Chief Creative Officer
AMIT DESAI Executive VP – Business & Marketing Strategy, Direct to Consumer & Global Franchise Management
SAM ADES Senior VP – Direct to Consumer
BOBBIE CHASE VP – Talent Development
MARK CHIARELLO Senior VP – Art, Design & Collected Editions
JOHN CUNNINGHAM Senior VP – Sales & Trade Marketing
ANNE DEPIES VP – Senior Business Strategy, Finance & Administration
DON FALLETTI VP – Manufacturing Operations
LAWRENCE GANEM VP – Editorial Administration & Talent Relations
ALISON GILL Senior VP – Manufacturing & Operations
HANK KANALZ Senior VP – Editorial Strategy & Administration
JAY KOGAN VP – Legal Affairs
THOMAS LOFTUS VP – Business Affairs
JACK MAHAN VP – Business Affairs
NICK J. NAPOLITANO VP – Manufacturing Administration
EDDIE SCANNELL VP – Consumer Marketing
COURTNEY SIMMONS Senior VP – Publicity & Communications
JIM (SKI) SOKOLOWSKI VP – Comic Book Specialty Sales & Trade Marketing
NANCY SPEARS VP – Mass, Book, Digital Sales & Trade Marketing

DC COMICS: BOMBSHELLS VOLUME 3: UPRISING

DC Comics
2900 West Alameda Ave., Burbank, CA 91505
Printed by Solisco Printers, Scott, QC, Canada. 2/10/17. First Printing.
ISBN: 978-1-4012-6877-0
Library of Congress Cataloging-in-Publication Data is available.

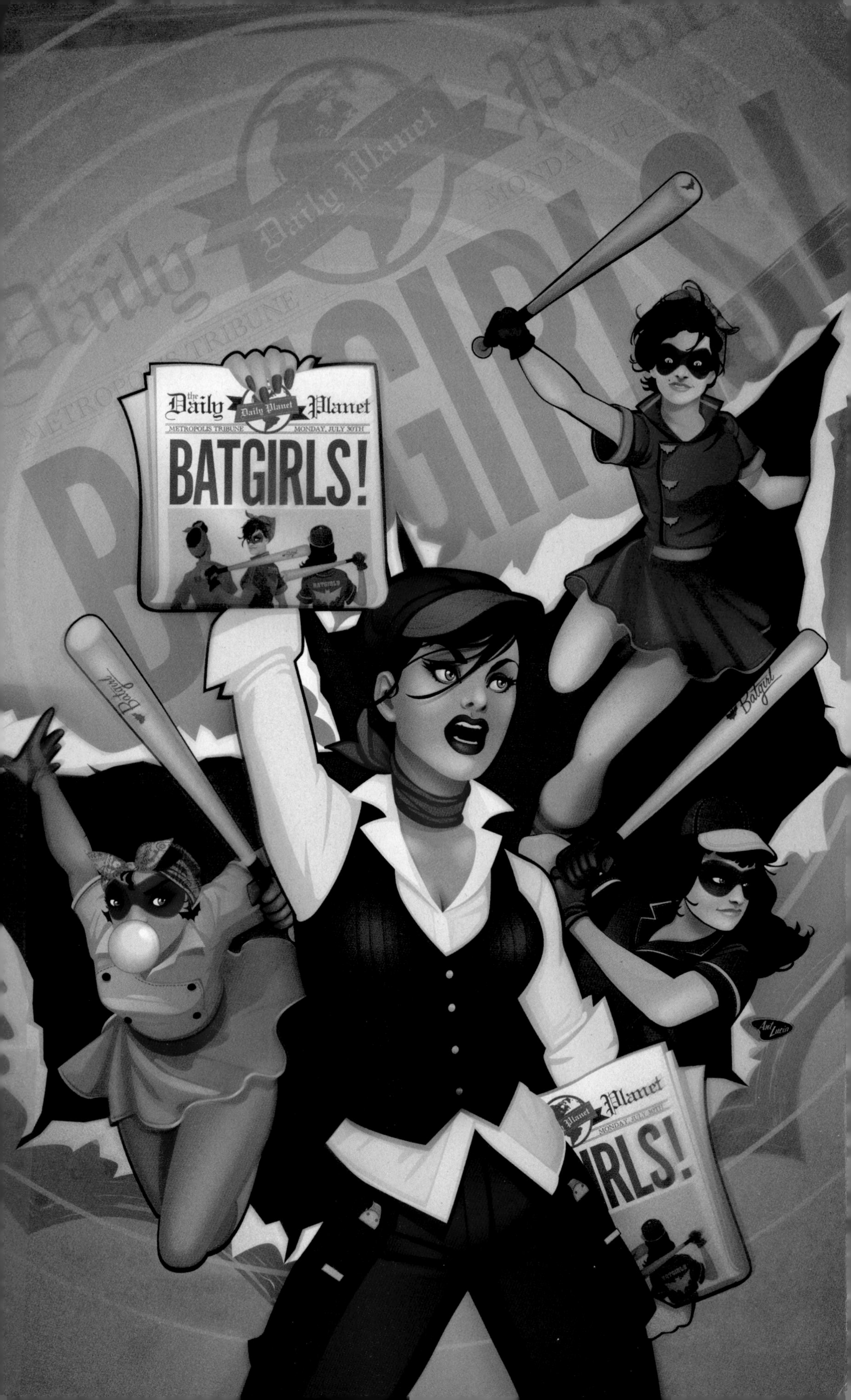
the Daily Daily Planet Planet
METROPOLIS TRIBUNE MONDAY, JULY 30TH
BATGIRLS!
Batgirl
Batgirl
Planet
MONDAY, JULY 30TH
IRLS!
Ant Lucia

BATGIRLS SWING AGAIN!

MARGUERITE BENNETT
Writer

MIRKA ANDOLFO
PASQUALE QUALANO
Artists

WENDY BROOME
Colorist

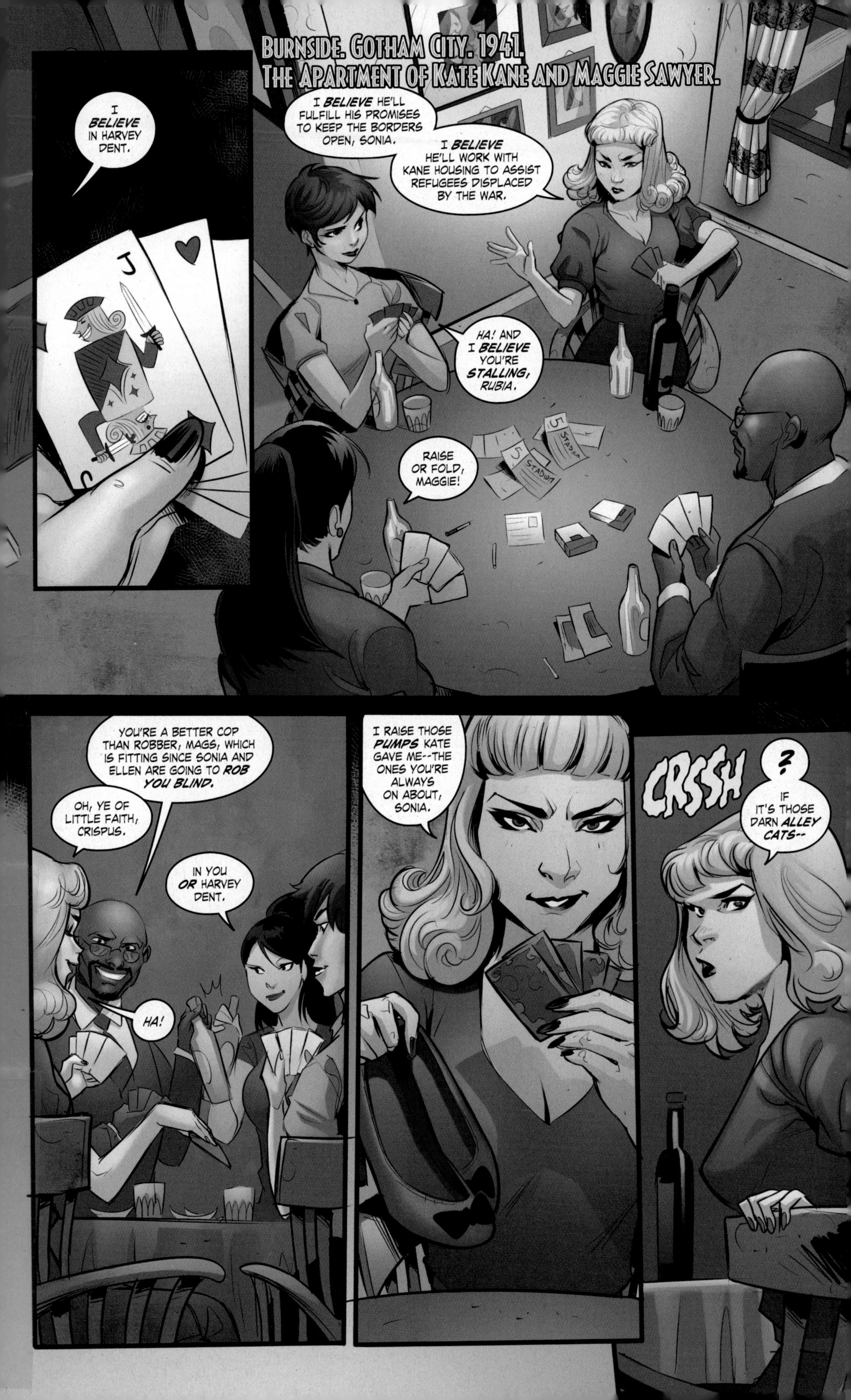
Burnside. Gotham City. 1941.
The Apartment of Kate Kane and Maggie Sawyer.
I BELIEVE IN HARVEY DENT.
I BELIEVE HE'LL FULFILL HIS PROMISES TO KEEP THE BORDERS OPEN, SONIA.
I BELIEVE HE'LL WORK WITH KANE HOUSING TO ASSIST REFUGEES DISPLACED BY THE WAR.
HA! AND I BELIEVE YOU'RE STALLING, RUBIA.
RAISE OR FOLD, MAGGIE!
YOU'RE A BETTER COP THAN ROBBER, MAGS, WHICH IS FITTING SINCE SONIA AND ELLEN ARE GOING TO ROB YOU BLIND.
OH, YE OF LITTLE FAITH, CRISPUS.
IN YOU OR HARVEY DENT.
HA!
I RAISE THOSE PUMPS KATE GAVE ME--THE ONES YOU'RE ALWAYS ON ABOUT, SONIA.
CRSSH
?
IF IT'S THOSE DARN ALLEY CATS--

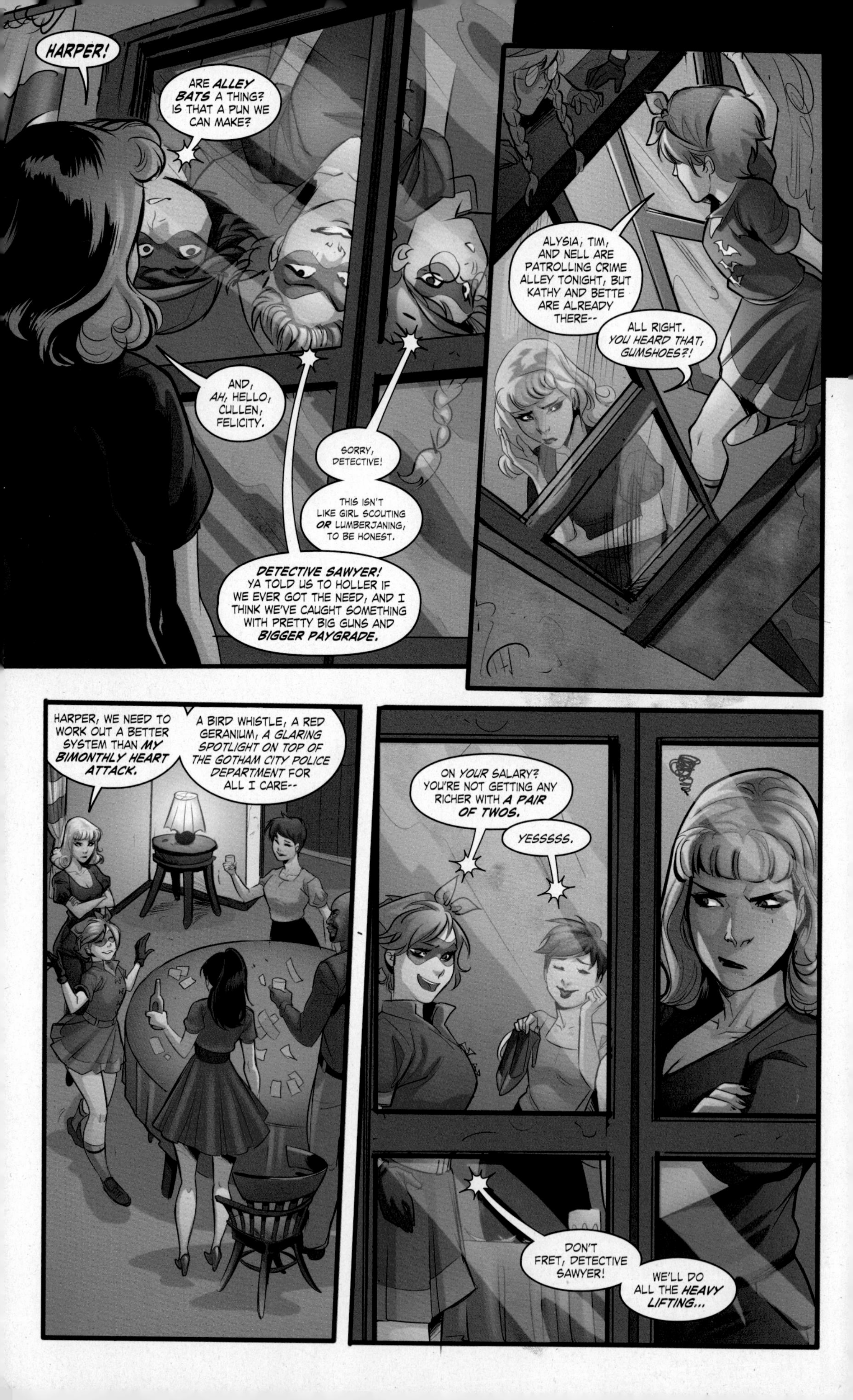
HARPER!
ARE ALLEY BATS A THING? IS THAT A PUN WE CAN MAKE?
AND, AH, HELLO, CULLEN, FELICITY.
SORRY, DETECTIVE!
THIS ISN'T LIKE GIRL SCOUTING OR LUMBERJANING, TO BE HONEST.
DETECTIVE SAWYER! YA TOLD US TO HOLLER IF WE EVER GOT THE NEED, AND I THINK WE'VE CAUGHT SOMETHING WITH PRETTY BIG GUNS AND BIGGER PAYGRADE.
ALYSIA, TIM, AND NELL ARE PATROLLING CRIME ALLEY TONIGHT, BUT KATHY AND BETTE ARE ALREADY THERE--
ALL RIGHT. YOU HEARD THAT, GUMSHOES?!
HARPER, WE NEED TO WORK OUT A BETTER SYSTEM THAN MY BIMONTHLY HEART ATTACK.
A BIRD WHISTLE, A RED GERANIUM, A GLARING SPOTLIGHT ON TOP OF THE GOTHAM CITY POLICE DEPARTMENT FOR ALL I CARE--
ON YOUR SALARY? YOU'RE NOT GETTING ANY RICHER WITH A PAIR OF TWOS.
YESSSSS.
DON'T FRET, DETECTIVE SAWYER!
WE'LL DO ALL THE HEAVY LIFTING...

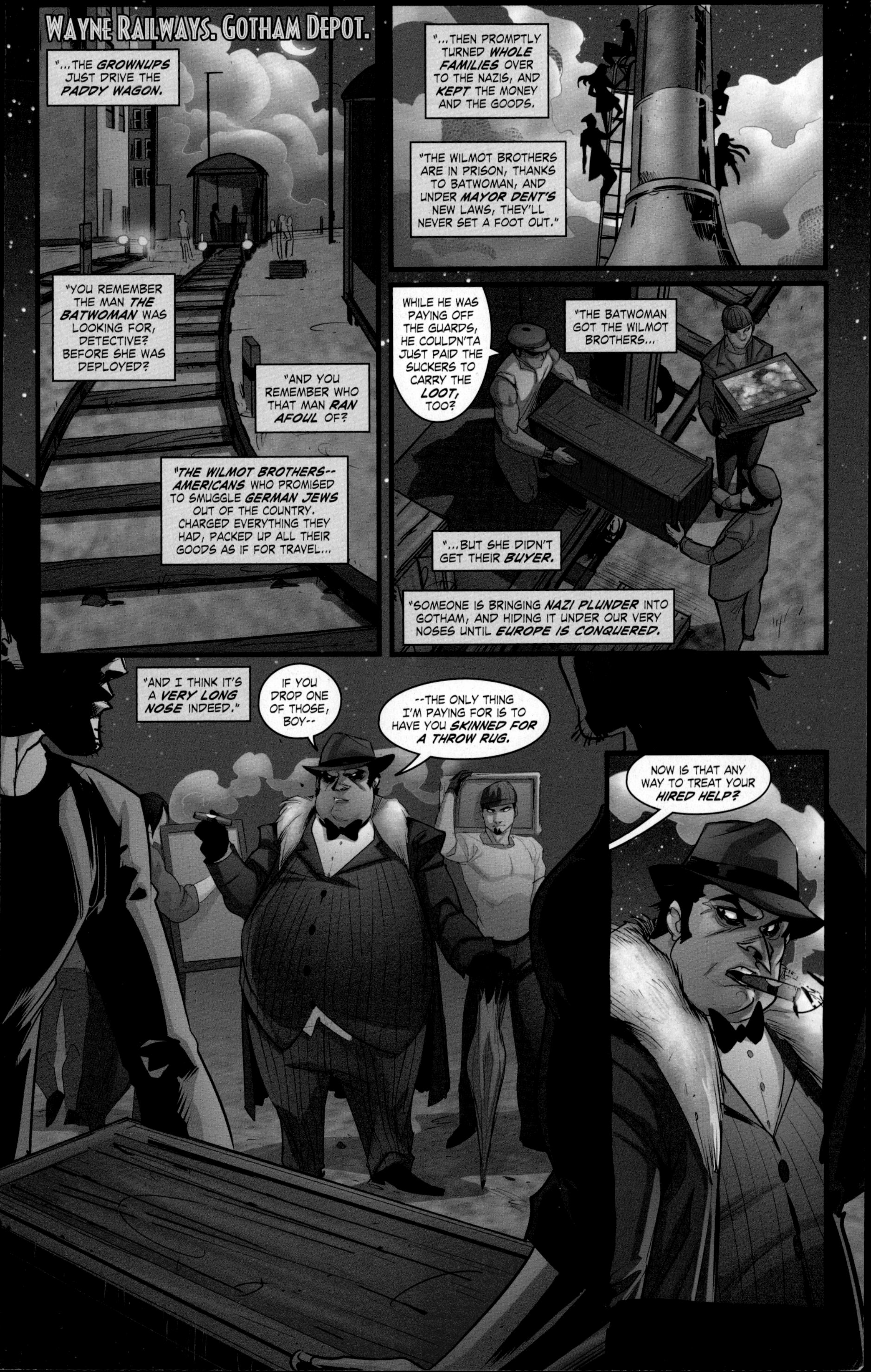
WAYNE RAILWAYS. GOTHAM DEPOT.
"...THE GROWNUPS JUST DRIVE THE PADDY WAGON.
"YOU REMEMBER THE MAN THE BATWOMAN WAS LOOKING FOR, DETECTIVE? BEFORE SHE WAS DEPLOYED?
"AND YOU REMEMBER WHO THAT MAN RAN AFOUL OF?
"THE WILMOT BROTHERS-- AMERICANS WHO PROMISED TO SMUGGLE GERMAN JEWS OUT OF THE COUNTRY. CHARGED EVERYTHING THEY HAD, PACKED UP ALL THEIR GOODS AS IF FOR TRAVEL...
"...THEN PROMPTLY TURNED WHOLE FAMILIES OVER TO THE NAZIS, AND KEPT THE MONEY AND THE GOODS.
"THE WILMOT BROTHERS ARE IN PRISON, THANKS TO BATWOMAN, AND UNDER MAYOR DENT'S NEW LAWS, THEY'LL NEVER SET A FOOT OUT."
WHILE HE WAS PAYING OFF THE GUARDS, HE COULDN'TA JUST PAID THE SUCKERS TO CARRY THE LOOT, TOO?
"THE BATWOMAN GOT THE WILMOT BROTHERS...
"...BUT SHE DIDN'T GET THEIR BUYER.
"SOMEONE IS BRINGING NAZI PLUNDER INTO GOTHAM, AND HIDING IT UNDER OUR VERY NOSES UNTIL EUROPE IS CONQUERED.
"AND I THINK IT'S A VERY LONG NOSE INDEED."
IF YOU DROP ONE OF THOSE, BOY--
--THE ONLY THING I'M PAYING FOR IS TO HAVE YOU SKINNED FOR A THROW RUG.
NOW IS THAT ANY WAY TO TREAT YOUR HIRED HELP?

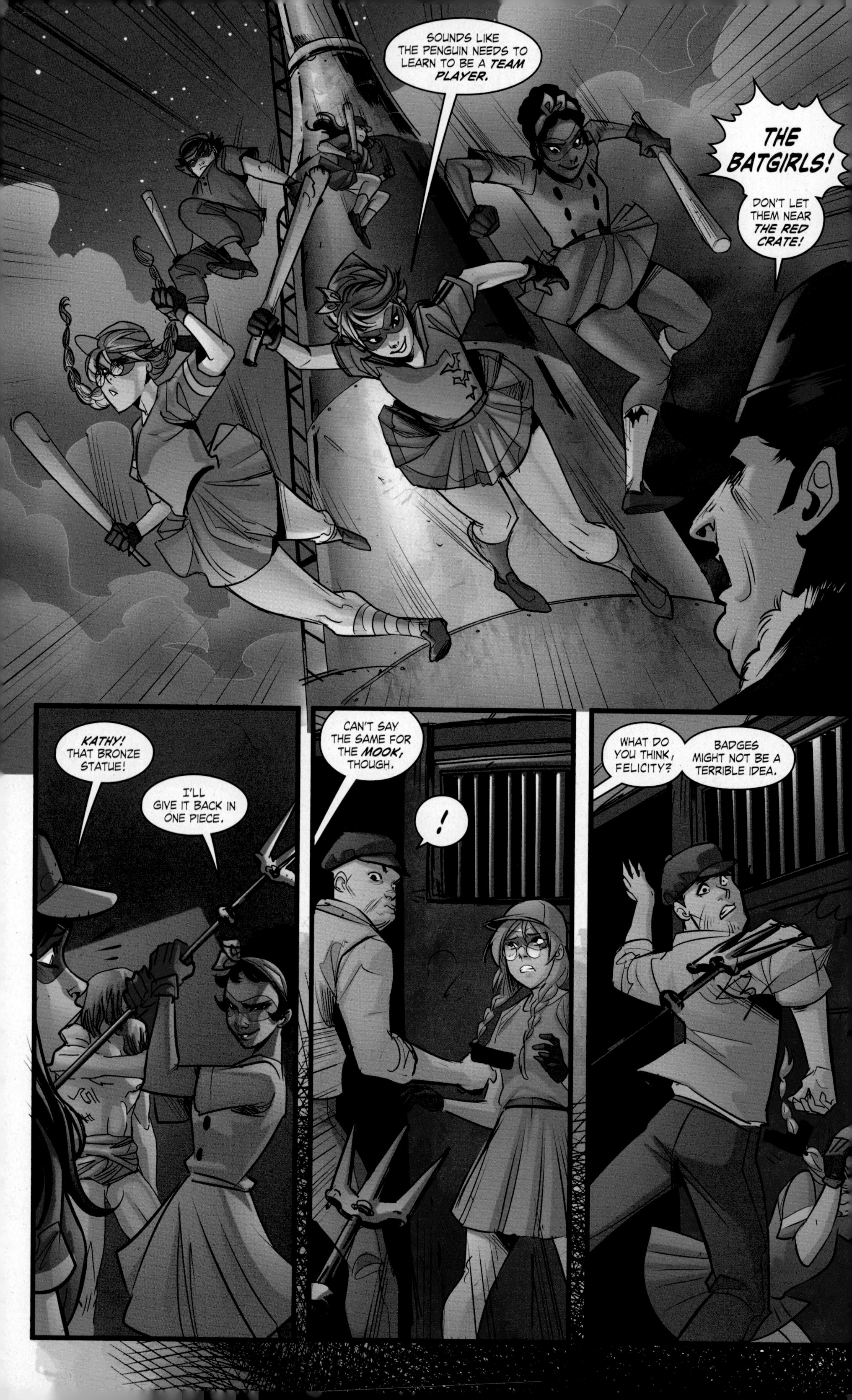
SOUNDS LIKE THE PENGUIN NEEDS TO LEARN TO BE A *TEAM PLAYER.*
THE BATGIRLS!
DON'T LET THEM NEAR *THE RED CRATE!*
KATHY! THAT BRONZE STATUE!
I'LL GIVE IT BACK IN ONE PIECE.
CAN'T SAY THE SAME FOR THE *MOOK,* THOUGH.
!
WHAT DO YOU THINK, FELICITY?
BADGES MIGHT NOT BE A TERRIBLE IDEA.

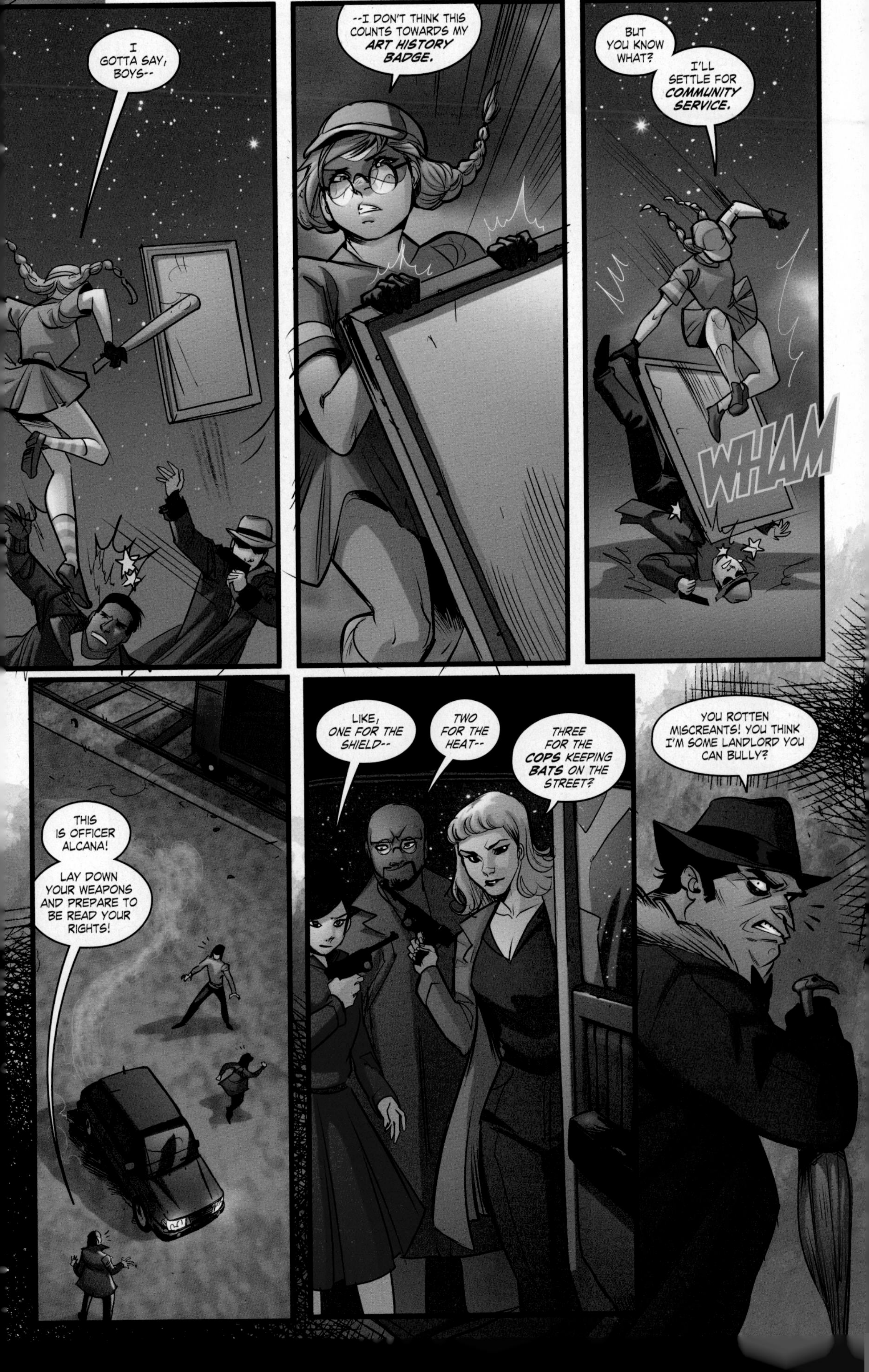
I GOTTA SAY, BOYS--
--I DON'T THINK THIS COUNTS TOWARDS MY ART HISTORY BADGE.
BUT YOU KNOW WHAT?
I'LL SETTLE FOR COMMUNITY SERVICE.
WHAM
THIS IS OFFICER ALCANA!
LAY DOWN YOUR WEAPONS AND PREPARE TO BE READ YOUR RIGHTS!
LIKE, ONE FOR THE SHIELD--
TWO FOR THE HEAT--
THREE FOR THE COPS KEEPING BATS ON THE STREET?
YOU ROTTEN MISCREANTS! YOU THINK I'M SOME LANDLORD YOU CAN BULLY?

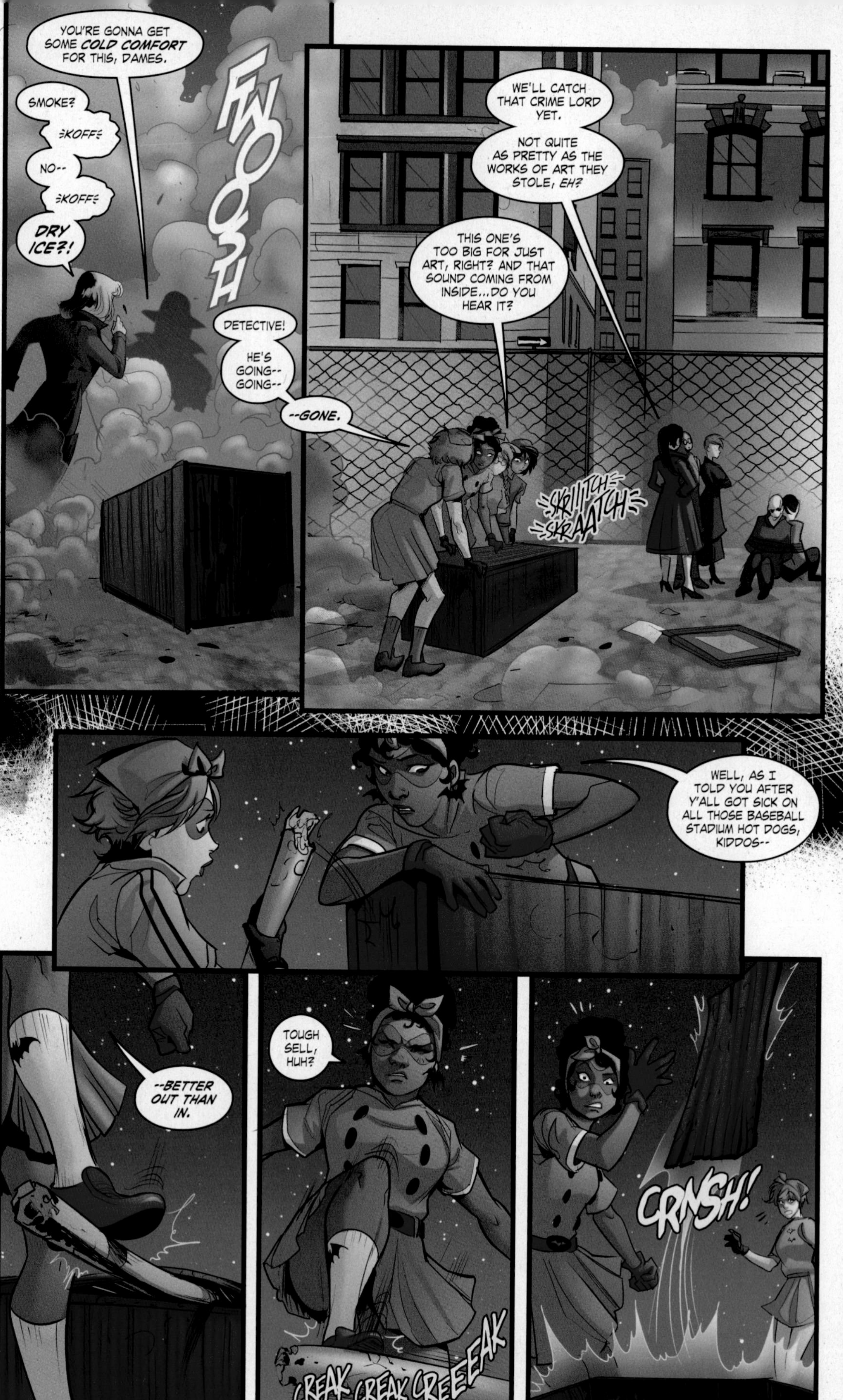
YOU'RE GONNA GET SOME COLD COMFORT FOR THIS, DAMES.
SMOKE?
KOFF
NO--
KOFF
DRY ICE?!
FWOOOSH
DETECTIVE!
HE'S GOING-- GOING--
--GONE.
WE'LL CATCH THAT CRIME LORD YET.
NOT QUITE AS PRETTY AS THE WORKS OF ART THEY STOLE, EH?
THIS ONE'S TOO BIG FOR JUST ART, RIGHT? AND THAT SOUND COMING FROM INSIDE...DO YOU HEAR IT?
SKRIITCH SKRAATCH
WELL, AS I TOLD YOU AFTER Y'ALL GOT SICK ON ALL THOSE BASEBALL STADIUM HOT DOGS, KIDDOS--
--BETTER OUT THAN IN.
TOUGH SELL, HUH?
CREAK CREAK CREEEAK
CRNSH!

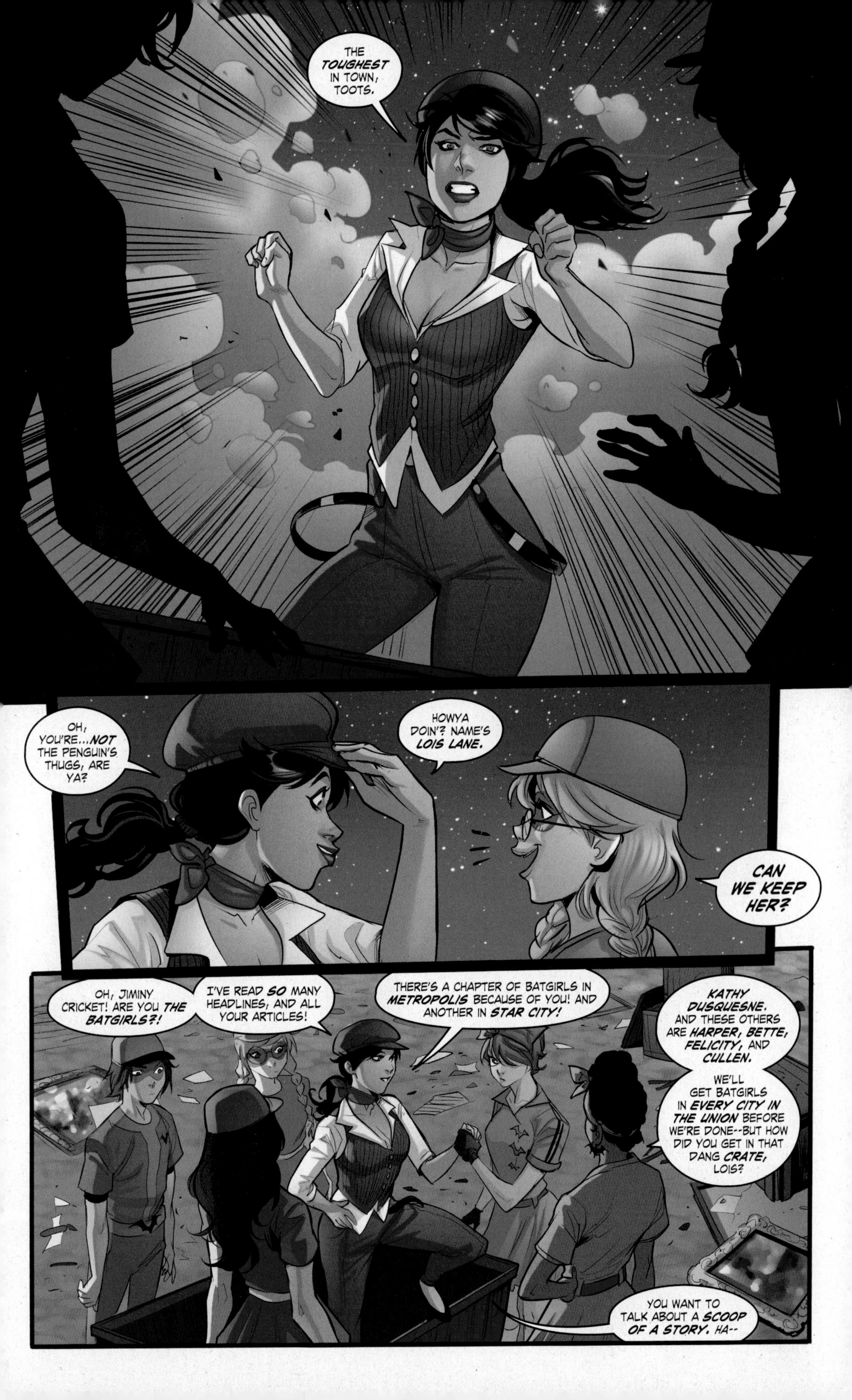
THE TOUGHEST IN TOWN, TOOTS.
OH, YOU'RE...NOT THE PENGUIN'S THUGS, ARE YA?
HOWYA DOIN'? NAME'S LOIS LANE.
CAN WE KEEP HER?
OH, JIMINY CRICKET! ARE YOU THE BATGIRLS?!
I'VE READ SO MANY HEADLINES, AND ALL YOUR ARTICLES!
THERE'S A CHAPTER OF BATGIRLS IN METROPOLIS BECAUSE OF YOU! AND ANOTHER IN STAR CITY!
KATHY DUSQUESNE. AND THESE OTHERS ARE HARPER, BETTE, FELICITY, AND CULLEN.
WE'LL GET BATGIRLS IN EVERY CITY IN THE UNION BEFORE WE'RE DONE--BUT HOW DID YOU GET IN THAT DANG CRATE, LOIS?
YOU WANT TO TALK ABOUT A SCOOP OF A STORY. HA--

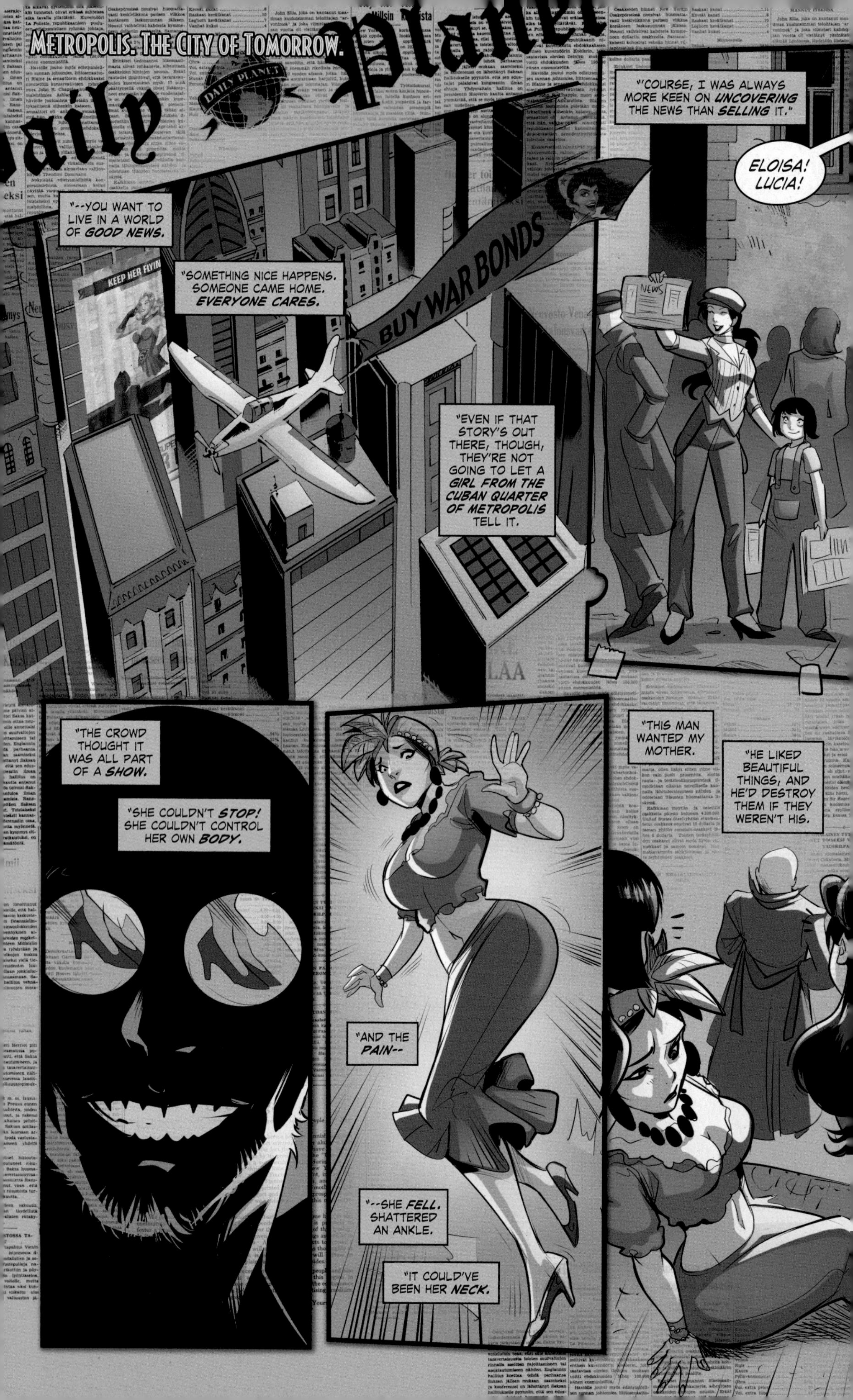
METROPOLIS. THE CITY OF TOMORROW.
DAILY PLANET
"--YOU WANT TO LIVE IN A WORLD OF GOOD NEWS.
"SOMETHING NICE HAPPENS. SOMEONE CAME HOME. EVERYONE CARES.
KEEP HER FLYIN
BUY WAR BONDS
"EVEN IF THAT STORY'S OUT THERE, THOUGH, THEY'RE NOT GOING TO LET A GIRL FROM THE CUBAN QUARTER OF METROPOLIS TELL IT.
"COURSE, I WAS ALWAYS MORE KEEN ON UNCOVERING THE NEWS THAN SELLING IT."
ELOISA! LUCIA!
NEWS
"THE CROWD THOUGHT IT WAS ALL PART OF A SHOW.
"SHE COULDN'T STOP! SHE COULDN'T CONTROL HER OWN BODY.
"AND THE PAIN--
"--SHE FELL. SHATTERED AN ANKLE.
"IT COULD'VE BEEN HER NECK.
"THIS MAN WANTED MY MOTHER.
"HE LIKED BEAUTIFUL THINGS, AND HE'D DESTROY THEM IF THEY WEREN'T HIS.

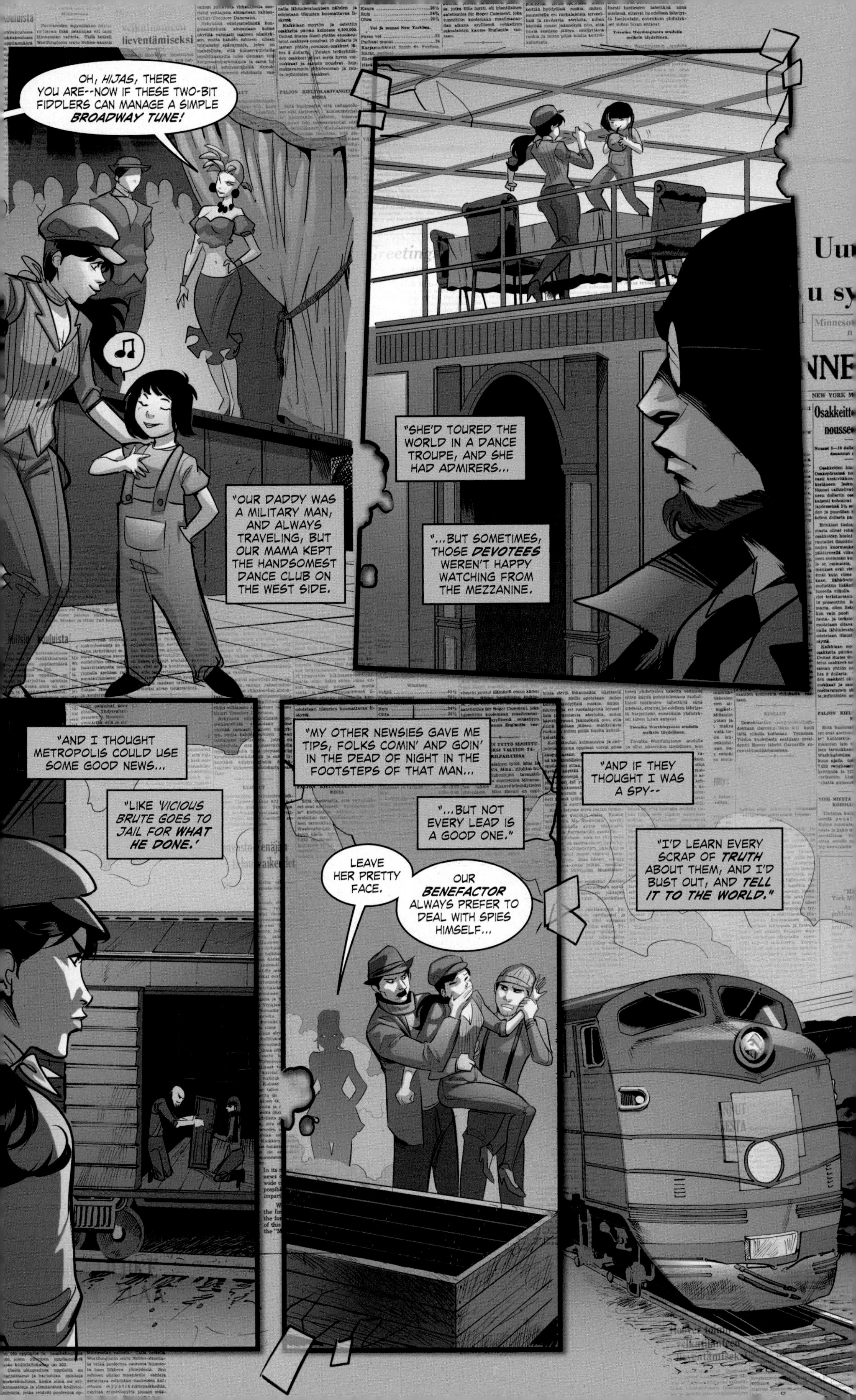

OH, HIJAS, THERE YOU ARE--NOW IF THESE TWO-BIT FIDDLERS CAN MANAGE A SIMPLE BROADWAY TUNE!
"OUR DADDY WAS A MILITARY MAN, AND ALWAYS TRAVELING, BUT OUR MAMA KEPT THE HANDSOMEST DANCE CLUB ON THE WEST SIDE.
"SHE'D TOURED THE WORLD IN A DANCE TROUPE, AND SHE HAD ADMIRERS...
"...BUT SOMETIMES, THOSE DEVOTEES WEREN'T HAPPY WATCHING FROM THE MEZZANINE.
"AND I THOUGHT METROPOLIS COULD USE SOME GOOD NEWS...
"LIKE 'VICIOUS BRUTE GOES TO JAIL FOR WHAT HE DONE.'
"MY OTHER NEWSIES GAVE ME TIPS, FOLKS COMIN' AND GOIN' IN THE DEAD OF NIGHT IN THE FOOTSTEPS OF THAT MAN...
"...BUT NOT EVERY LEAD IS A GOOD ONE."
LEAVE HER PRETTY FACE.
OUR BENEFACTOR ALWAYS PREFER TO DEAL WITH SPIES HIMSELF...
"AND IF THEY THOUGHT I WAS A SPY--
"I'D LEARN EVERY SCRAP OF TRUTH ABOUT THEM, AND I'D BUST OUT, AND TELL IT TO THE WORLD."

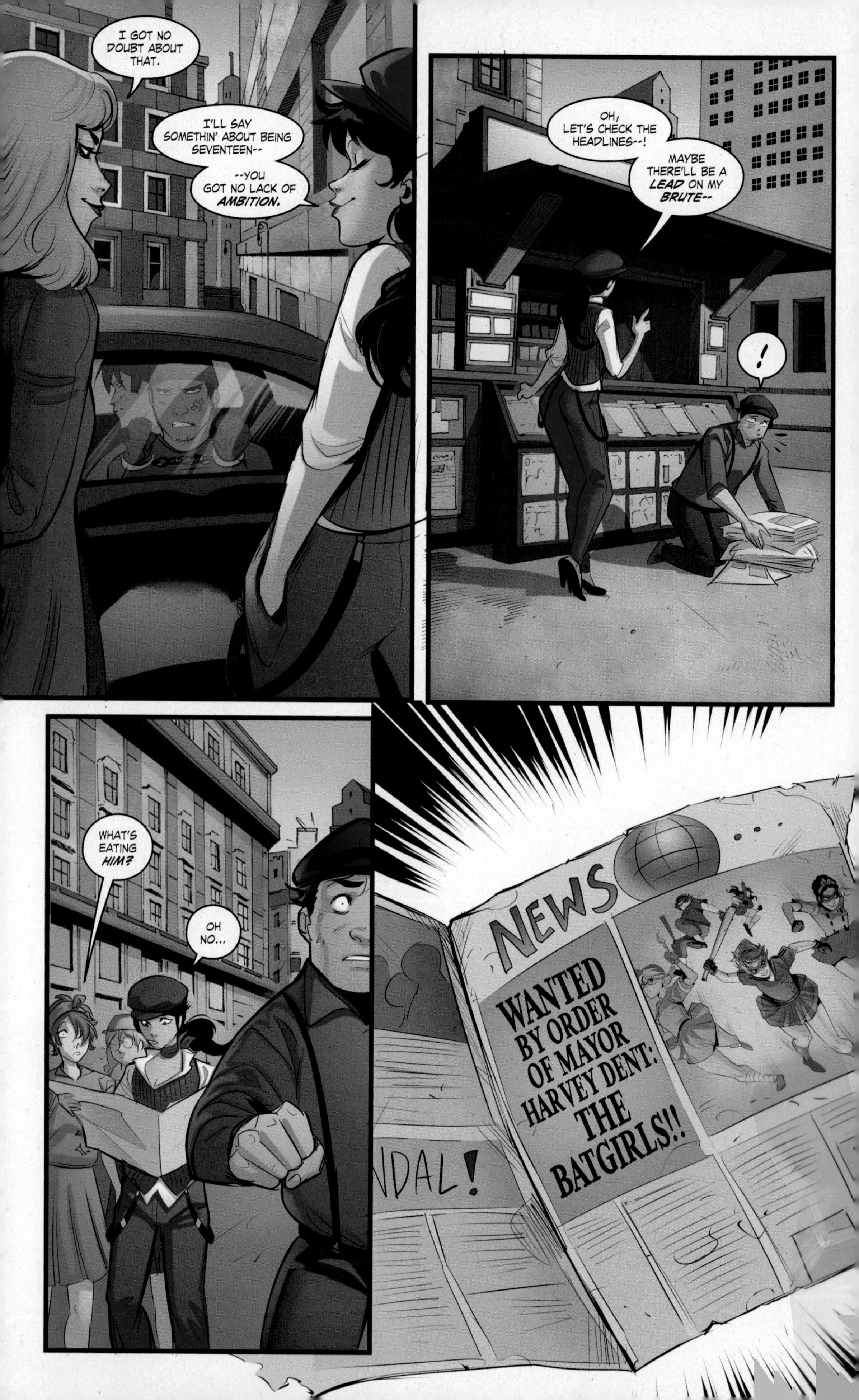
I GOT NO DOUBT ABOUT THAT.
I'LL SAY SOMETHIN' ABOUT BEING SEVENTEEN--
--YOU GOT NO LACK OF AMBITION.
OH, LET'S CHECK THE HEADLINES--!
MAYBE THERE'LL BE A LEAD ON MY BRUTE--
!
WHAT'S EATING HIM?
OH NO...
NEWS
WANTED BY ORDER OF MAYOR HARVEY DENT: THE BATGIRLS!!
NDAL!

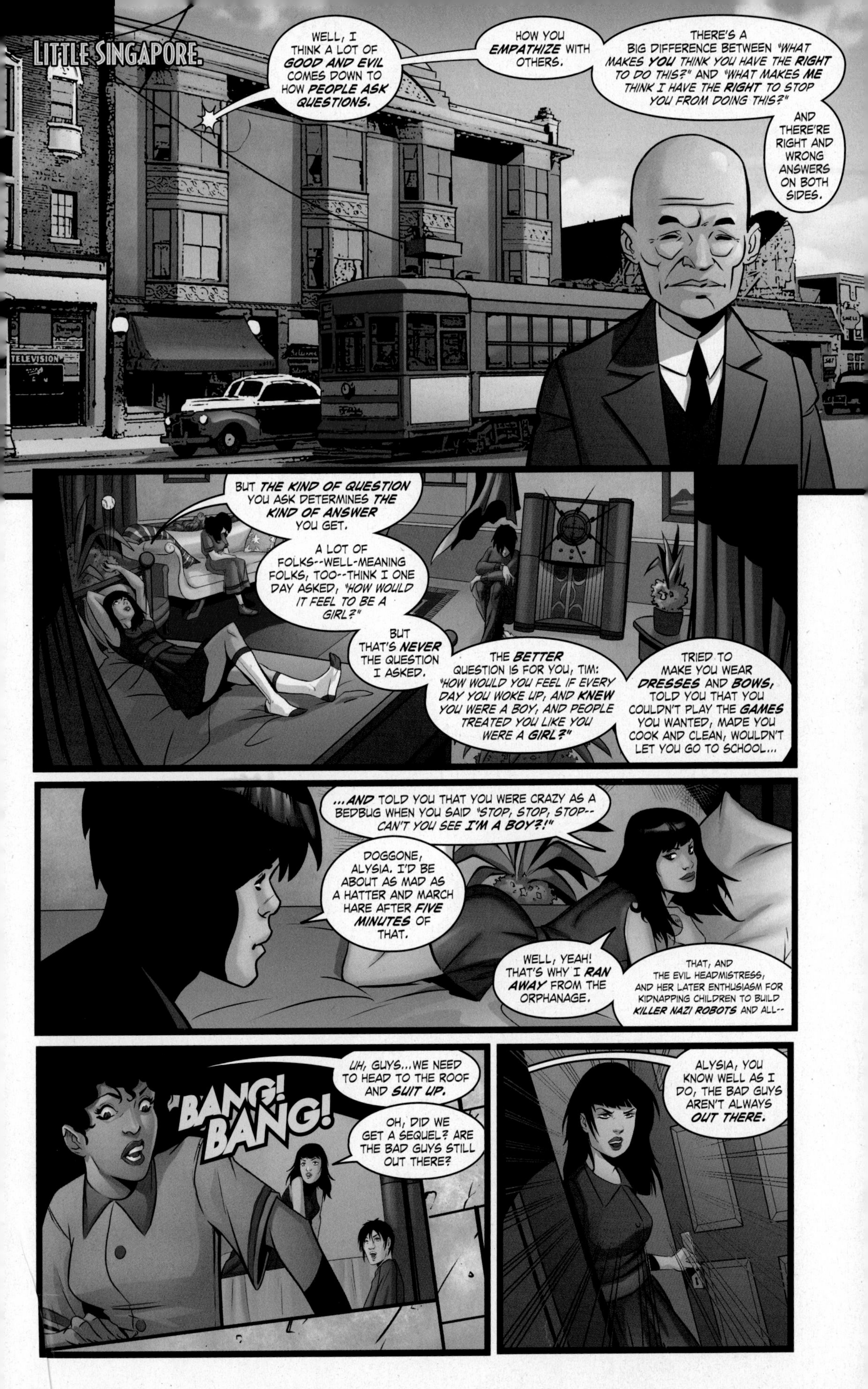
LITTLE SINGAPORE.
WELL, I THINK A LOT OF GOOD AND EVIL COMES DOWN TO HOW PEOPLE ASK QUESTIONS.
HOW YOU EMPATHIZE WITH OTHERS.
THERE'S A BIG DIFFERENCE BETWEEN "WHAT MAKES YOU THINK YOU HAVE THE RIGHT TO DO THIS?" AND "WHAT MAKES ME THINK I HAVE THE RIGHT TO STOP YOU FROM DOING THIS?"
AND THERE'RE RIGHT AND WRONG ANSWERS ON BOTH SIDES.
BUT THE KIND OF QUESTION YOU ASK DETERMINES THE KIND OF ANSWER YOU GET.
A LOT OF FOLKS--WELL-MEANING FOLKS, TOO--THINK I ONE DAY ASKED, "HOW WOULD IT FEEL TO BE A GIRL?"
BUT THAT'S NEVER THE QUESTION I ASKED.
THE BETTER QUESTION IS FOR YOU, TIM: "HOW WOULD YOU FEEL IF EVERY DAY YOU WOKE UP, AND KNEW YOU WERE A BOY, AND PEOPLE TREATED YOU LIKE YOU WERE A GIRL?"
TRIED TO MAKE YOU WEAR DRESSES AND BOWS, TOLD YOU THAT YOU COULDN'T PLAY THE GAMES YOU WANTED, MADE YOU COOK AND CLEAN, WOULDN'T LET YOU GO TO SCHOOL...
...AND TOLD YOU THAT YOU WERE CRAZY AS A BEDBUG WHEN YOU SAID "STOP, STOP, STOP-- CAN'T YOU SEE I'M A BOY?!"
DOGGONE, ALYSIA. I'D BE ABOUT AS MAD AS A HATTER AND MARCH HARE AFTER FIVE MINUTES OF THAT.
WELL, YEAH! THAT'S WHY I RAN AWAY FROM THE ORPHANAGE.
THAT, AND THE EVIL HEADMISTRESS, AND HER LATER ENTHUSIASM FOR KIDNAPPING CHILDREN TO BUILD KILLER NAZI ROBOTS AND ALL--
BANG! BANG!
UH, GUYS...WE NEED TO HEAD TO THE ROOF AND SUIT UP.
OH, DID WE GET A SEQUEL? ARE THE BAD GUYS STILL OUT THERE?
ALYSIA, YOU KNOW WELL AS I DO, THE BAD GUYS AREN'T ALWAYS OUT THERE.

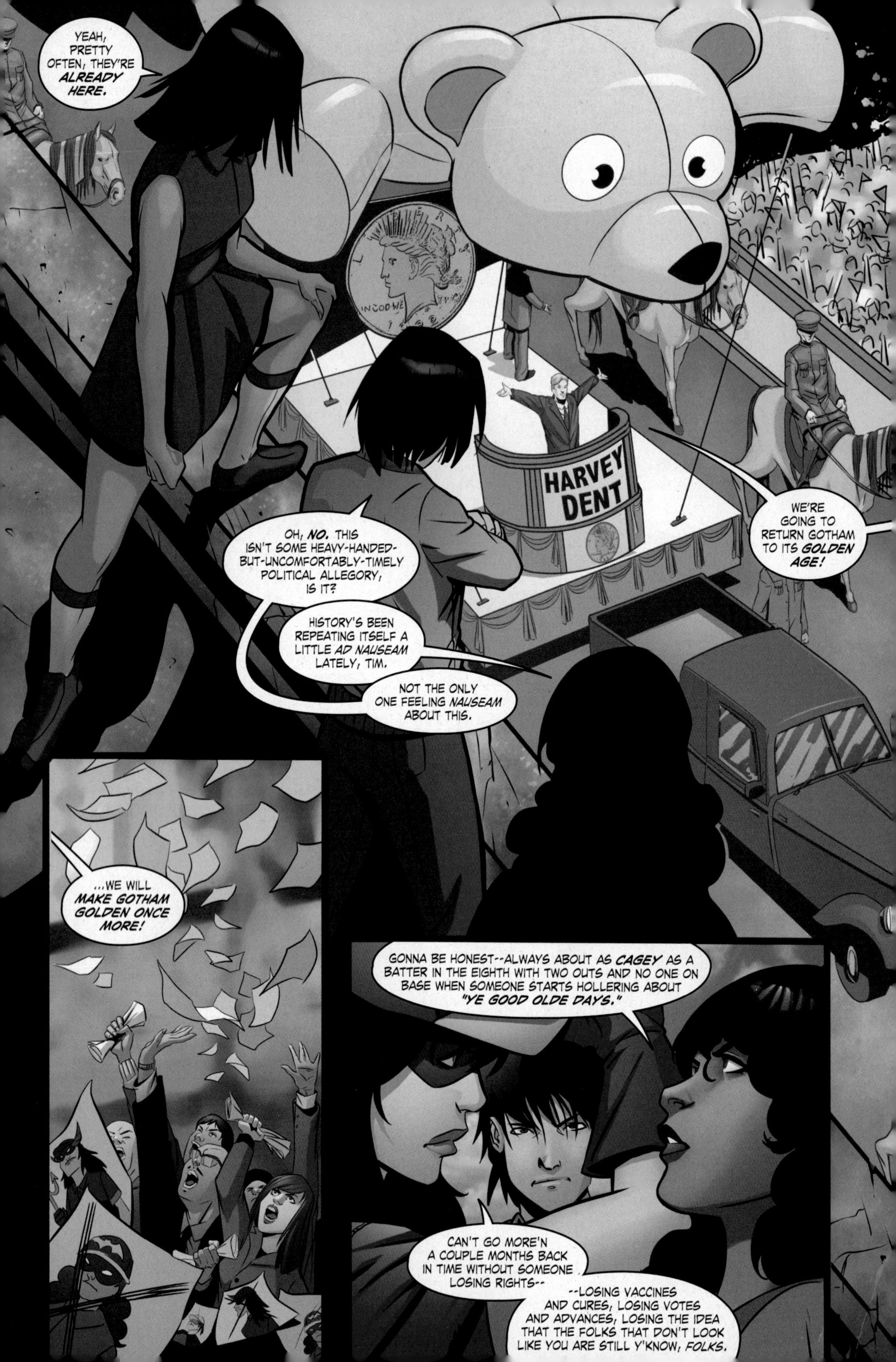
YEAH, PRETTY OFTEN, THEY'RE *ALREADY HERE.*
HARVEY DENT
OH, *NO.* THIS ISN'T SOME HEAVY-HANDED-BUT-UNCOMFORTABLY-TIMELY POLITICAL ALLEGORY, IS IT?
WE'RE GOING TO RETURN GOTHAM TO ITS *GOLDEN AGE!*
HISTORY'S BEEN REPEATING ITSELF A LITTLE *AD NAUSEAM* LATELY, TIM.
NOT THE ONLY ONE FEELING *NAUSEAM* ABOUT THIS.
...WE WILL *MAKE GOTHAM GOLDEN ONCE MORE!*
GONNA BE HONEST--ALWAYS ABOUT AS *CAGEY* AS A BATTER IN THE EIGHTH WITH TWO OUTS AND NO ONE ON BASE WHEN SOMEONE STARTS HOLLERING ABOUT *"YE GOOD OLDE DAYS."*
CAN'T GO MORE'N A COUPLE MONTHS BACK IN TIME WITHOUT SOMEONE LOSING RIGHTS--
--LOSING VACCINES AND CURES, LOSING VOTES AND ADVANCES, LOSING THE IDEA THAT THE FOLKS THAT DON'T LOOK LIKE YOU ARE STILL Y'KNOW, *FOLKS.*

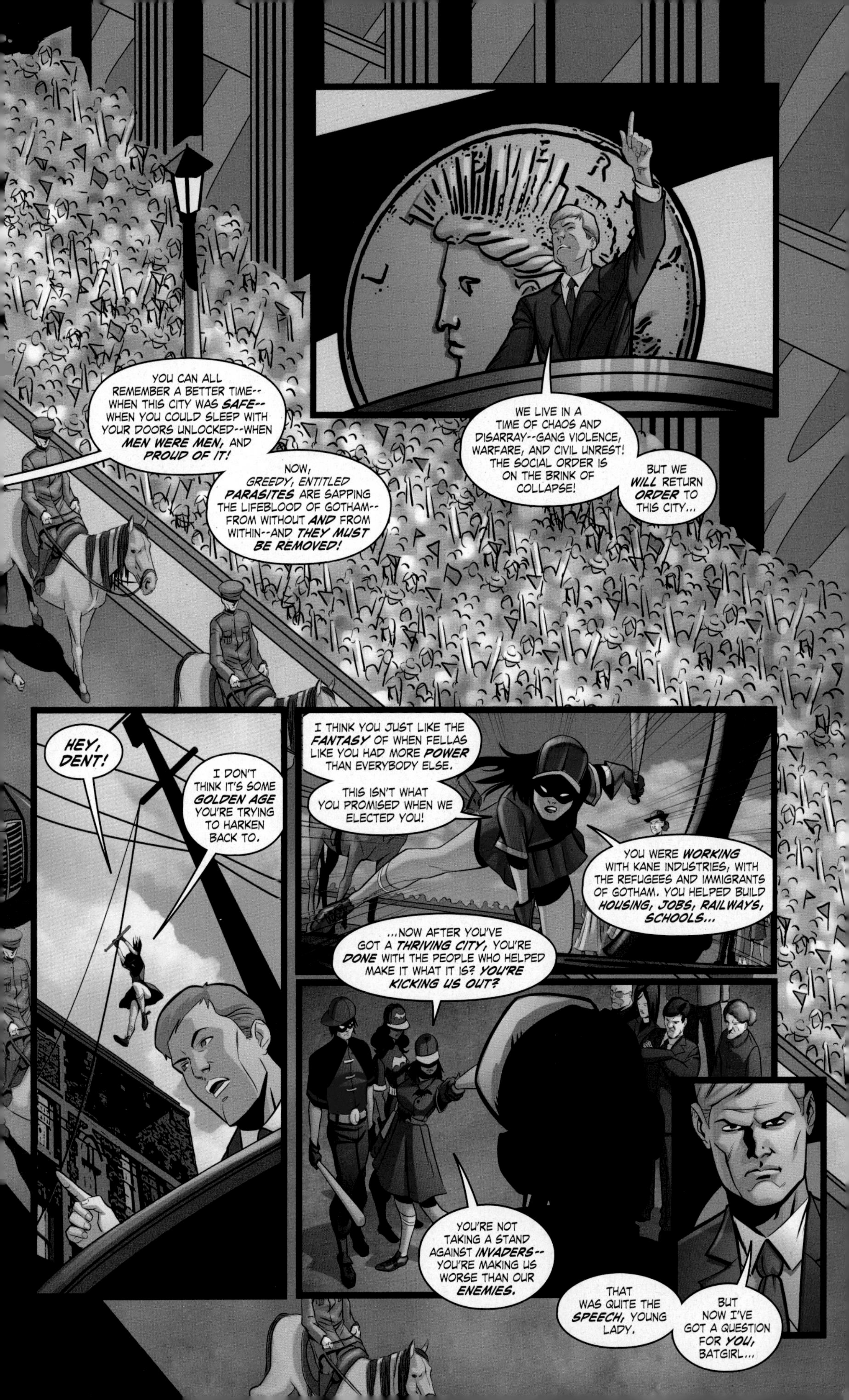

WE LIVE IN A TIME OF CHAOS AND DISARRAY--GANG VIOLENCE, WARFARE, AND CIVIL UNREST! THE SOCIAL ORDER IS ON THE BRINK OF COLLAPSE!
BUT WE WILL RETURN ORDER TO THIS CITY...
YOU CAN ALL REMEMBER A BETTER TIME-- WHEN THIS CITY WAS SAFE-- WHEN YOU COULD SLEEP WITH YOUR DOORS UNLOCKED--WHEN MEN WERE MEN, AND PROUD OF IT!
NOW, GREEDY, ENTITLED PARASITES ARE SAPPING THE LIFEBLOOD OF GOTHAM-- FROM WITHOUT AND FROM WITHIN--AND THEY MUST BE REMOVED!
HEY, DENT!
I DON'T THINK IT'S SOME GOLDEN AGE YOU'RE TRYING TO HARKEN BACK TO.
I THINK YOU JUST LIKE THE FANTASY OF WHEN FELLAS LIKE YOU HAD MORE POWER THAN EVERYBODY ELSE.
THIS ISN'T WHAT YOU PROMISED WHEN WE ELECTED YOU!
YOU WERE WORKING WITH KANE INDUSTRIES, WITH THE REFUGEES AND IMMIGRANTS OF GOTHAM. YOU HELPED BUILD HOUSING, JOBS, RAILWAYS, SCHOOLS...
...NOW AFTER YOU'VE GOT A THRIVING CITY, YOU'RE DONE WITH THE PEOPLE WHO HELPED MAKE IT WHAT IT IS? YOU'RE KICKING US OUT?
YOU'RE NOT TAKING A STAND AGAINST INVADERS-- YOU'RE MAKING US WORSE THAN OUR ENEMIES.
THAT WAS QUITE THE SPEECH, YOUNG LADY.
BUT NOW I'VE GOT A QUESTION FOR YOU, BATGIRL...

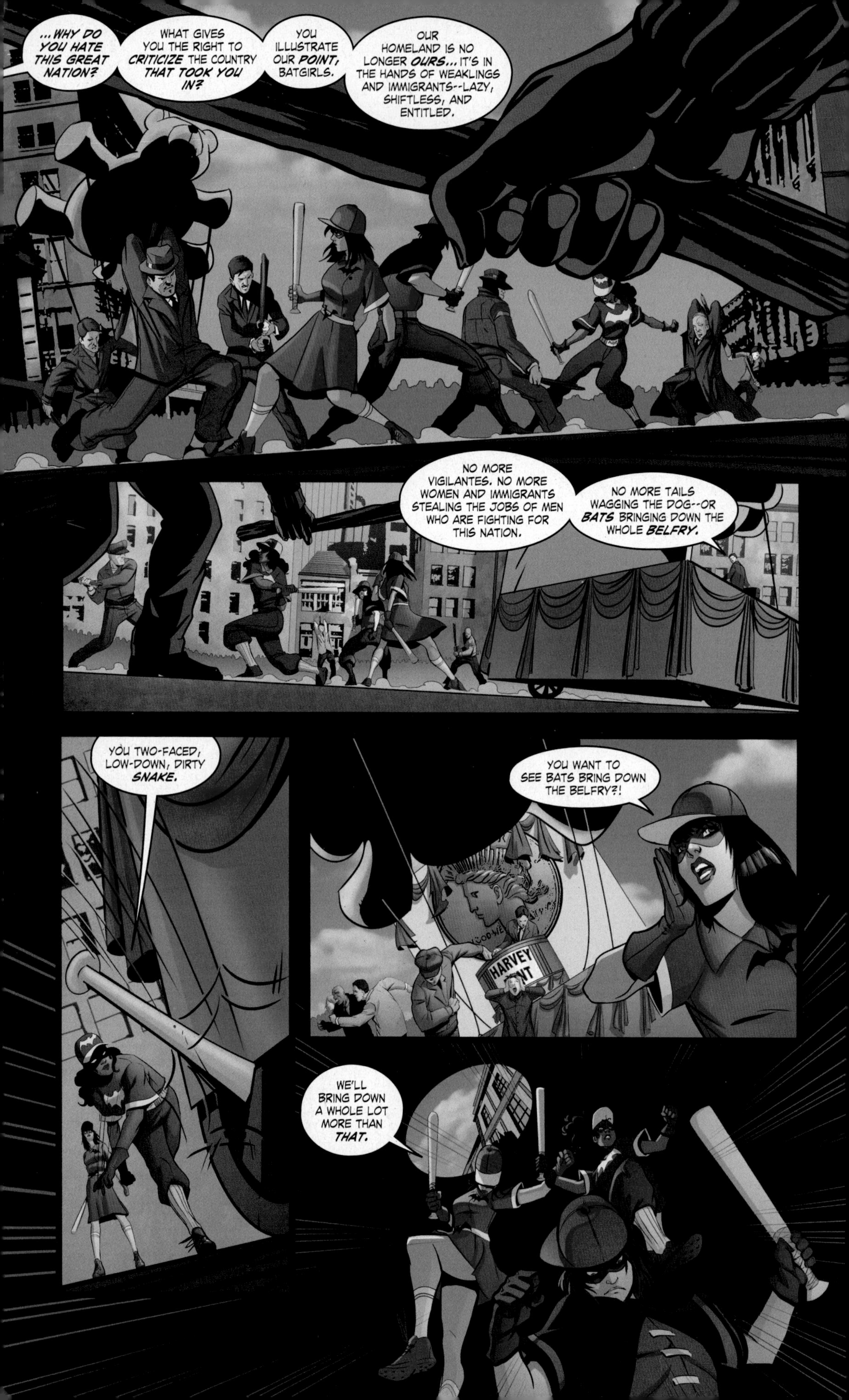
...WHY DO YOU HATE THIS GREAT NATION?
WHAT GIVES YOU THE RIGHT TO CRITICIZE THE COUNTRY THAT TOOK YOU IN?
YOU ILLUSTRATE OUR POINT, BATGIRLS.
OUR HOMELAND IS NO LONGER OURS... IT'S IN THE HANDS OF WEAKLINGS AND IMMIGRANTS--LAZY, SHIFTLESS, AND ENTITLED.
NO MORE VIGILANTES. NO MORE WOMEN AND IMMIGRANTS STEALING THE JOBS OF MEN WHO ARE FIGHTING FOR THIS NATION.
NO MORE TAILS WAGGING THE DOG--OR BATS BRINGING DOWN THE WHOLE BELFRY.
YOU TWO-FACED, LOW-DOWN, DIRTY SNAKE.
YOU WANT TO SEE BATS BRING DOWN THE BELFRY?!
HARVEY
WE'LL BRING DOWN A WHOLE LOT MORE THAN THAT.

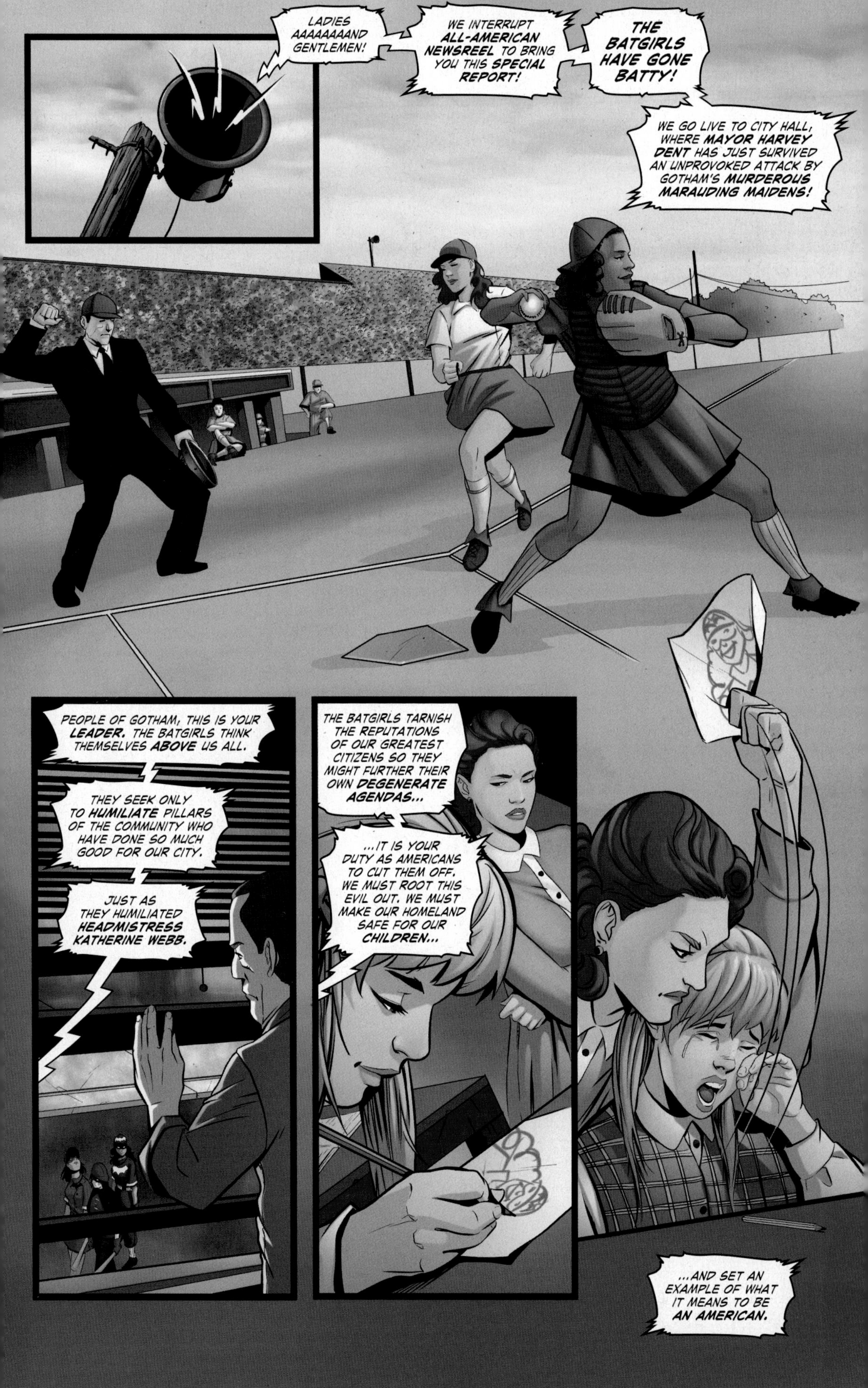
LADIES AAAAAAAAND GENTLEMEN!
WE INTERRUPT ALL-AMERICAN NEWSREEL TO BRING YOU THIS SPECIAL REPORT!
THE BATGIRLS HAVE GONE BATTY!
WE GO LIVE TO CITY HALL, WHERE MAYOR HARVEY DENT HAS JUST SURVIVED AN UNPROVOKED ATTACK BY GOTHAM'S MURDEROUS MARAUDING MAIDENS!
PEOPLE OF GOTHAM, THIS IS YOUR LEADER. THE BATGIRLS THINK THEMSELVES ABOVE US ALL.
THEY SEEK ONLY TO HUMILIATE PILLARS OF THE COMMUNITY WHO HAVE DONE SO MUCH GOOD FOR OUR CITY.
JUST AS THEY HUMILIATED HEADMISTRESS KATHERINE WEBB.
THE BATGIRLS TARNISH THE REPUTATIONS OF OUR GREATEST CITIZENS SO THEY MIGHT FURTHER THEIR OWN DEGENERATE AGENDAS...
...IT IS YOUR DUTY AS AMERICANS TO CUT THEM OFF. WE MUST ROOT THIS EVIL OUT. WE MUST MAKE OUR HOMELAND SAFE FOR OUR CHILDREN...
...AND SET AN EXAMPLE OF WHAT IT MEANS TO BE AN AMERICAN.

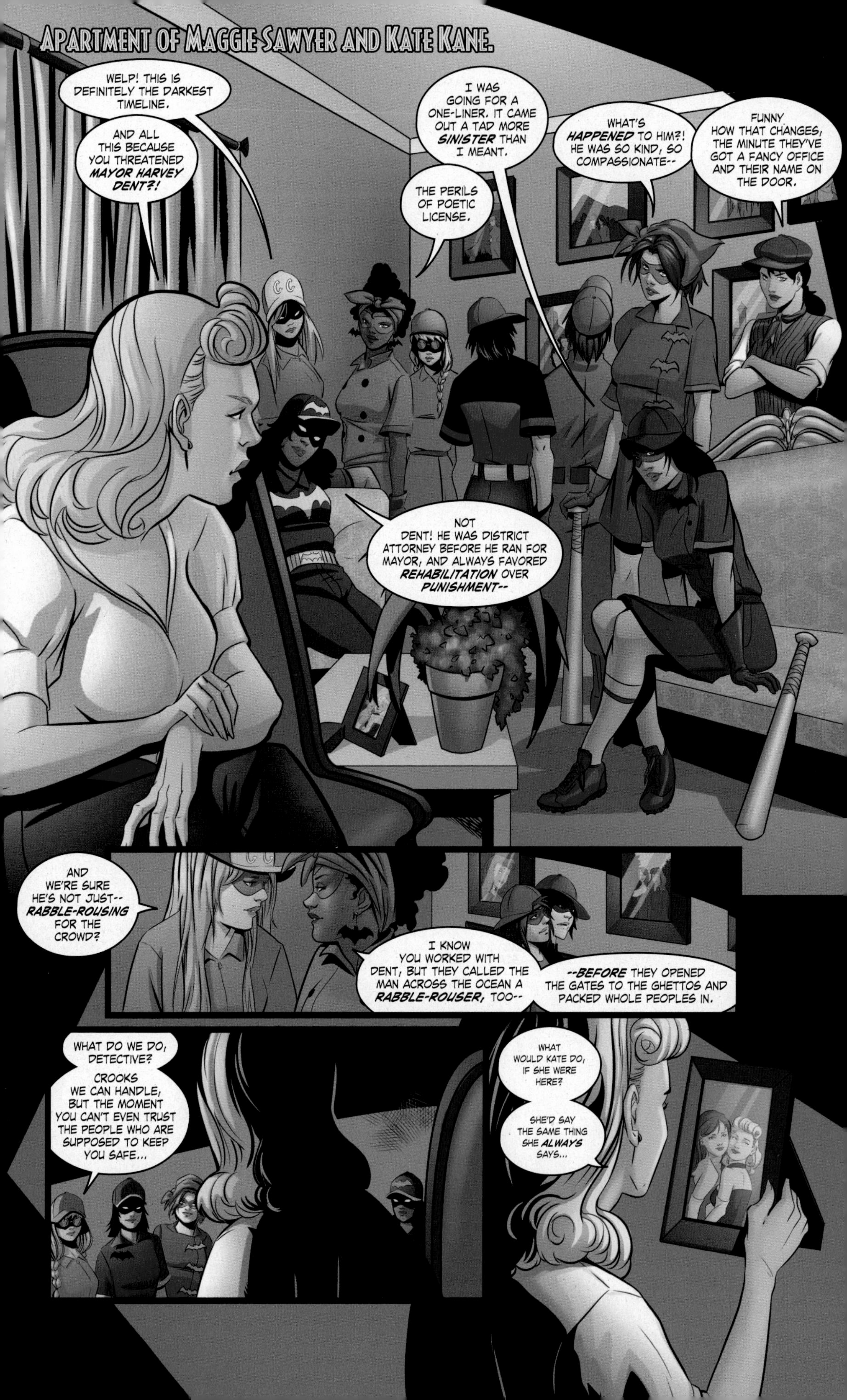
APARTMENT OF MAGGIE SAWYER AND KATE KANE.
WELP! THIS IS DEFINITELY THE DARKEST TIMELINE.
AND ALL THIS BECAUSE YOU THREATENED MAYOR HARVEY DENT?!
I WAS GOING FOR A ONE-LINER. IT CAME OUT A TAD MORE SINISTER THAN I MEANT.
THE PERILS OF POETIC LICENSE.
WHAT'S HAPPENED TO HIM?! HE WAS SO KIND, SO COMPASSIONATE--
FUNNY HOW THAT CHANGES, THE MINUTE THEY'VE GOT A FANCY OFFICE AND THEIR NAME ON THE DOOR.
NOT DENT! HE WAS DISTRICT ATTORNEY BEFORE HE RAN FOR MAYOR, AND ALWAYS FAVORED REHABILITATION OVER PUNISHMENT--
AND WE'RE SURE HE'S NOT JUST-- RABBLE-ROUSING FOR THE CROWD?
I KNOW YOU WORKED WITH DENT, BUT THEY CALLED THE MAN ACROSS THE OCEAN A RABBLE-ROUSER, TOO--
--BEFORE THEY OPENED THE GATES TO THE GHETTOS AND PACKED WHOLE PEOPLES IN.
WHAT DO WE DO, DETECTIVE?
CROOKS WE CAN HANDLE, BUT THE MOMENT YOU CAN'T EVEN TRUST THE PEOPLE WHO ARE SUPPOSED TO KEEP YOU SAFE...
WHAT WOULD KATE DO, IF SHE WERE HERE?
SHE'D SAY THE SAME THING SHE ALWAYS SAYS...

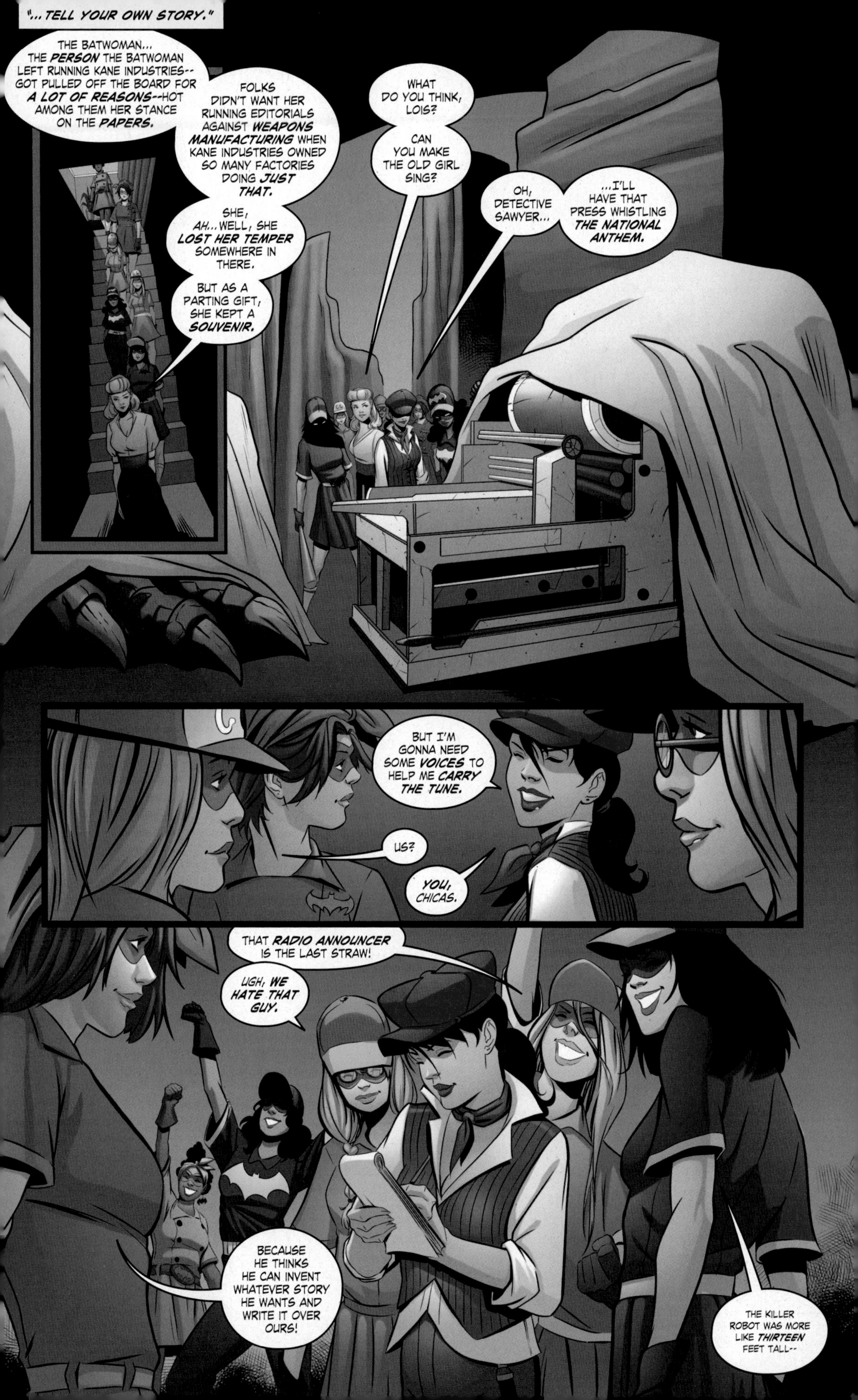
"...TELL YOUR OWN STORY."
THE BATWOMAN... THE PERSON THE BATWOMAN LEFT RUNNING KANE INDUSTRIES--GOT PULLED OFF THE BOARD FOR A LOT OF REASONS--HOT AMONG THEM HER STANCE ON THE PAPERS.
FOLKS DIDN'T WANT HER RUNNING EDITORIALS AGAINST WEAPONS MANUFACTURING WHEN KANE INDUSTRIES OWNED SO MANY FACTORIES DOING JUST THAT.
SHE, AH...WELL, SHE LOST HER TEMPER SOMEWHERE IN THERE.
BUT AS A PARTING GIFT, SHE KEPT A SOUVENIR.
WHAT DO YOU THINK, LOIS?
CAN YOU MAKE THE OLD GIRL SING?
OH, DETECTIVE SAWYER...
...I'LL HAVE THAT PRESS WHISTLING THE NATIONAL ANTHEM.
BUT I'M GONNA NEED SOME VOICES TO HELP ME CARRY THE TUNE.
US?
YOU, CHICAS.
THAT RADIO ANNOUNCER IS THE LAST STRAW!
UGH, WE HATE THAT GUY.
BECAUSE HE THINKS HE CAN INVENT WHATEVER STORY HE WANTS AND WRITE IT OVER OURS!
THE KILLER ROBOT WAS MORE LIKE THIRTEEN FEET TALL--

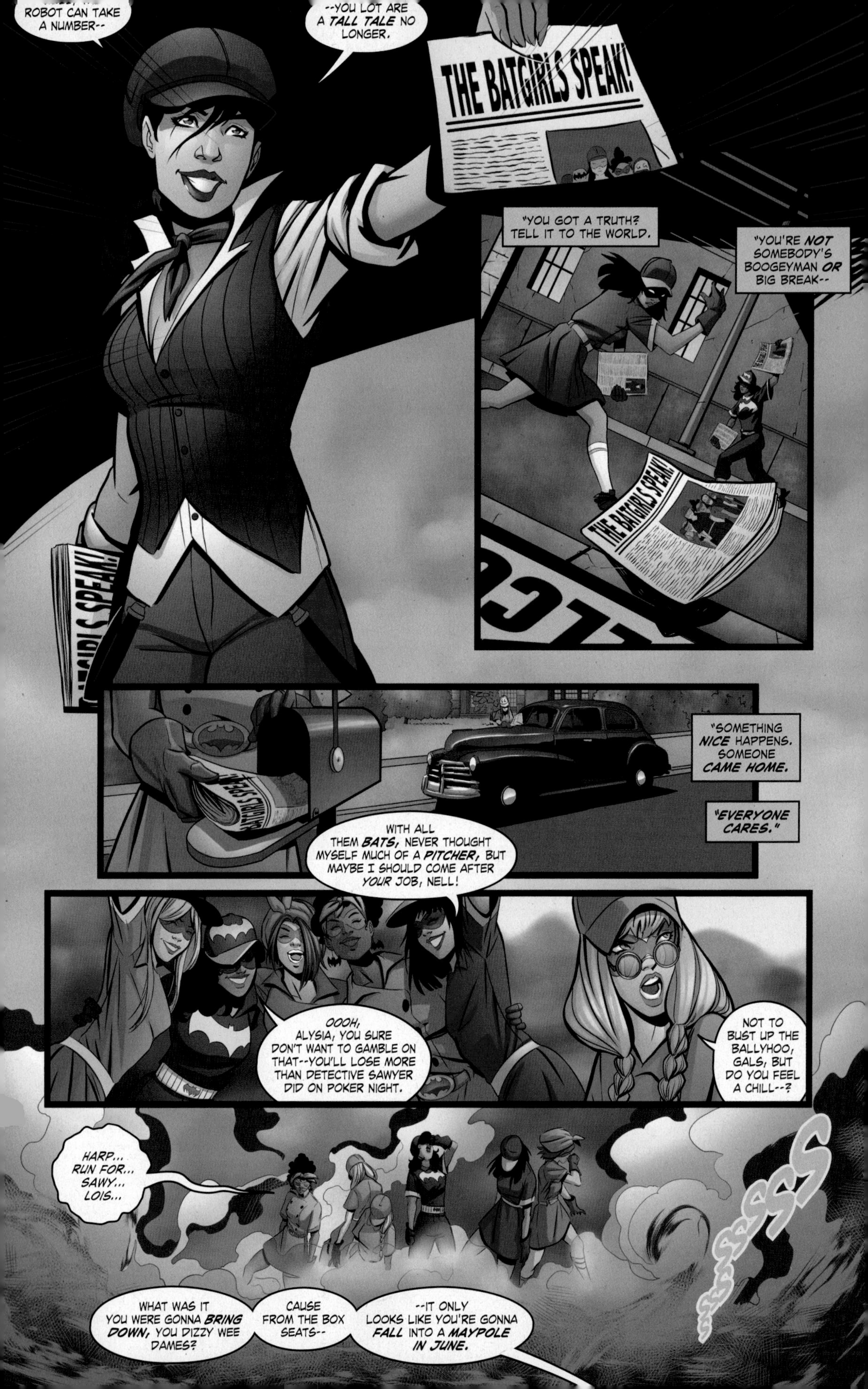
ROBOT CAN TAKE A NUMBER--
--YOU LOT ARE A TALL TALE NO LONGER.
THE BATGIRLS SPEAK!
"YOU GOT A TRUTH? TELL IT TO THE WORLD.
"YOU'RE NOT SOMEBODY'S BOOGEYMAN OR BIG BREAK--
THE BATGIRLS SPEAK!
"SOMETHING NICE HAPPENS. SOMEONE CAME HOME.
"EVERYONE CARES."
WITH ALL THEM BATS, NEVER THOUGHT MYSELF MUCH OF A PITCHER, BUT MAYBE I SHOULD COME AFTER YOUR JOB, NELL!
OOOH, ALYSIA, YOU SURE DON'T WANT TO GAMBLE ON THAT--YOU'LL LOSE MORE THAN DETECTIVE SAWYER DID ON POKER NIGHT.
NOT TO BUST UP THE BALLYHOO, GALS, BUT DO YOU FEEL A CHILL--?
HARP... RUN FOR... SAWY... LOIS...
SSSSSSSS
WHAT WAS IT YOU WERE GONNA BRING DOWN, YOU DIZZY WEE DAMES?
CAUSE FROM THE BOX SEATS--
--IT ONLY LOOKS LIKE YOU'RE GONNA FALL INTO A MAYPOLE IN JUNE.

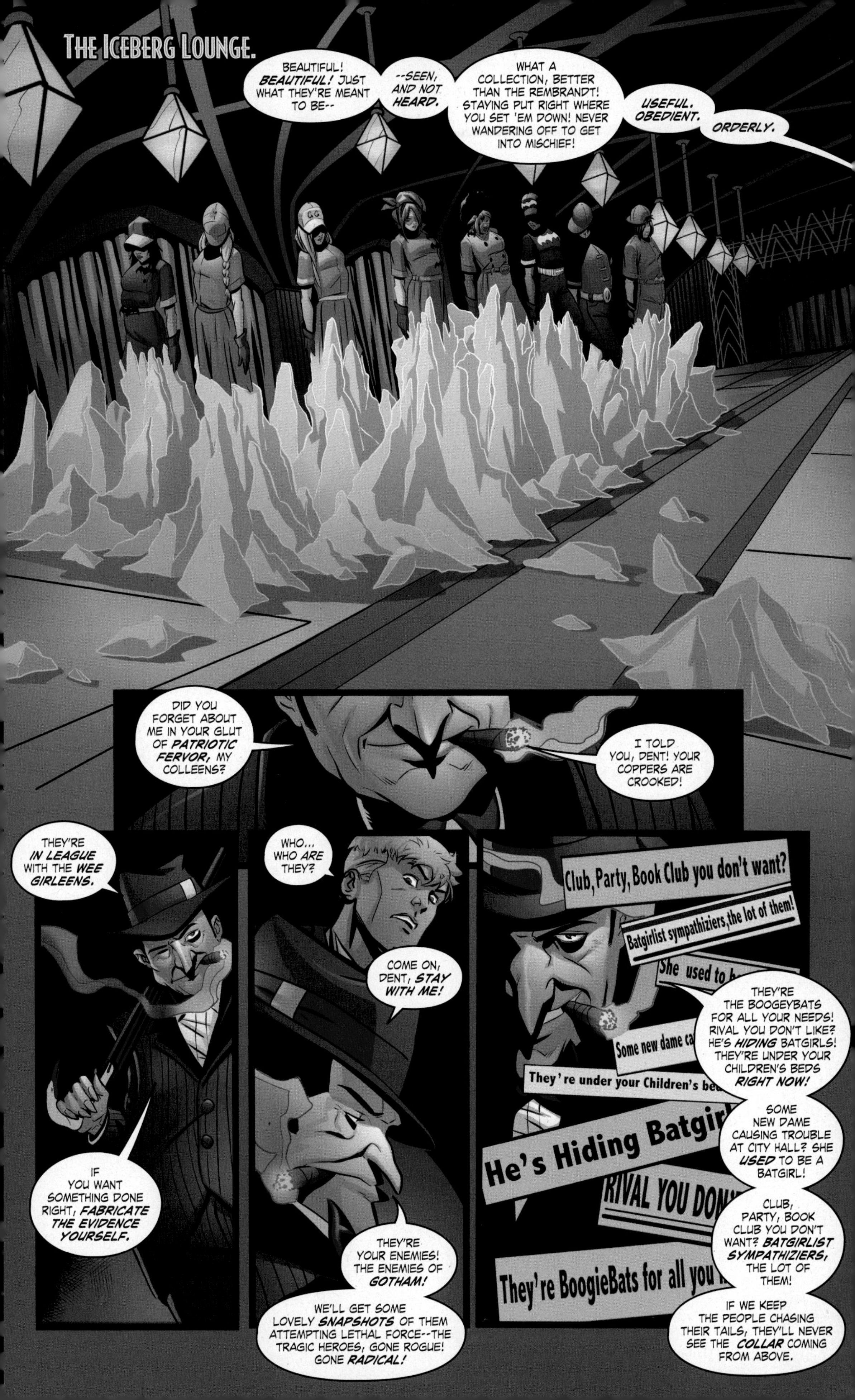
THE ICEBERG LOUNGE.
BEAUTIFUL! BEAUTIFUL! JUST WHAT THEY'RE MEANT TO BE--
--SEEN, AND NOT HEARD.
WHAT A COLLECTION, BETTER THAN THE REMBRANDT! STAYING PUT RIGHT WHERE YOU SET 'EM DOWN! NEVER WANDERING OFF TO GET INTO MISCHIEF!
USEFUL. OBEDIENT.
ORDERLY.
DID YOU FORGET ABOUT ME IN YOUR GLUT OF PATRIOTIC FERVOR, MY COLLEENS?
I TOLD YOU, DENT! YOUR COPPERS ARE CROOKED!
THEY'RE IN LEAGUE WITH THE WEE GIRLEENS.
IF YOU WANT SOMETHING DONE RIGHT, FABRICATE THE EVIDENCE YOURSELF.
WHO... WHO ARE THEY?
COME ON, DENT, STAY WITH ME!
THEY'RE YOUR ENEMIES! THE ENEMIES OF GOTHAM!
WE'LL GET SOME LOVELY SNAPSHOTS OF THEM ATTEMPTING LETHAL FORCE--THE TRAGIC HEROES, GONE ROGUE! GONE RADICAL!
Club, Party, Book Club you don't want?
Batgirlist sympathiziers, the lot of them!
She used to
Some new dame
They're under your Children's
He's Hiding
RIVAL YOU
They're BoogieBats for all you
THEY'RE THE BOOGEYBATS FOR ALL YOUR NEEDS! RIVAL YOU DON'T LIKE? HE'S HIDING BATGIRLS! THEY'RE UNDER YOUR CHILDREN'S BEDS RIGHT NOW!
SOME NEW DAME CAUSING TROUBLE AT CITY HALL? SHE USED TO BE A BATGIRL!
CLUB, PARTY, BOOK CLUB YOU DON'T WANT? BATGIRLIST SYMPATHIZIERS, THE LOT OF THEM!
IF WE KEEP THE PEOPLE CHASING THEIR TAILS, THEY'LL NEVER SEE THE COLLAR COMING FROM ABOVE.

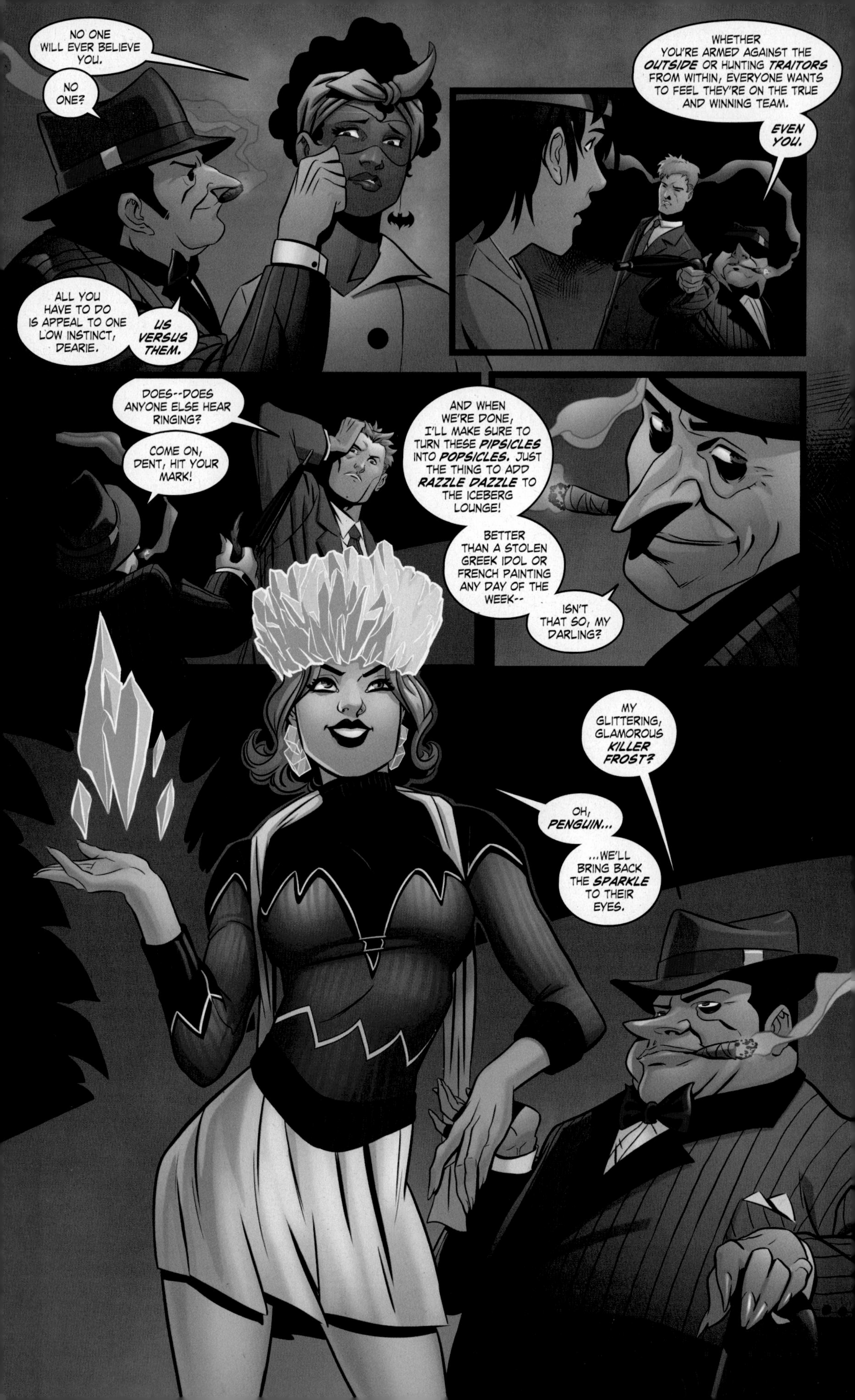
NO ONE WILL EVER BELIEVE YOU.
NO ONE?
ALL YOU HAVE TO DO IS APPEAL TO ONE LOW INSTINCT, DEARIE.
US VERSUS THEM.
WHETHER YOU'RE ARMED AGAINST THE OUTSIDE OR HUNTING TRAITORS FROM WITHIN, EVERYONE WANTS TO FEEL THEY'RE ON THE TRUE AND WINNING TEAM.
EVEN YOU.
DOES--DOES ANYONE ELSE HEAR RINGING?
COME ON, DENT, HIT YOUR MARK!
AND WHEN WE'RE DONE, I'LL MAKE SURE TO TURN THESE PIPSICLES INTO POPSICLES. JUST THE THING TO ADD RAZZLE DAZZLE TO THE ICEBERG LOUNGE!
BETTER THAN A STOLEN GREEK IDOL OR FRENCH PAINTING ANY DAY OF THE WEEK--
ISN'T THAT SO, MY DARLING?
MY GLITTERING, GLAMOROUS KILLER FROST?
OH, PENGUIN...
...WE'LL BRING BACK THE SPARKLE TO THEIR EYES.

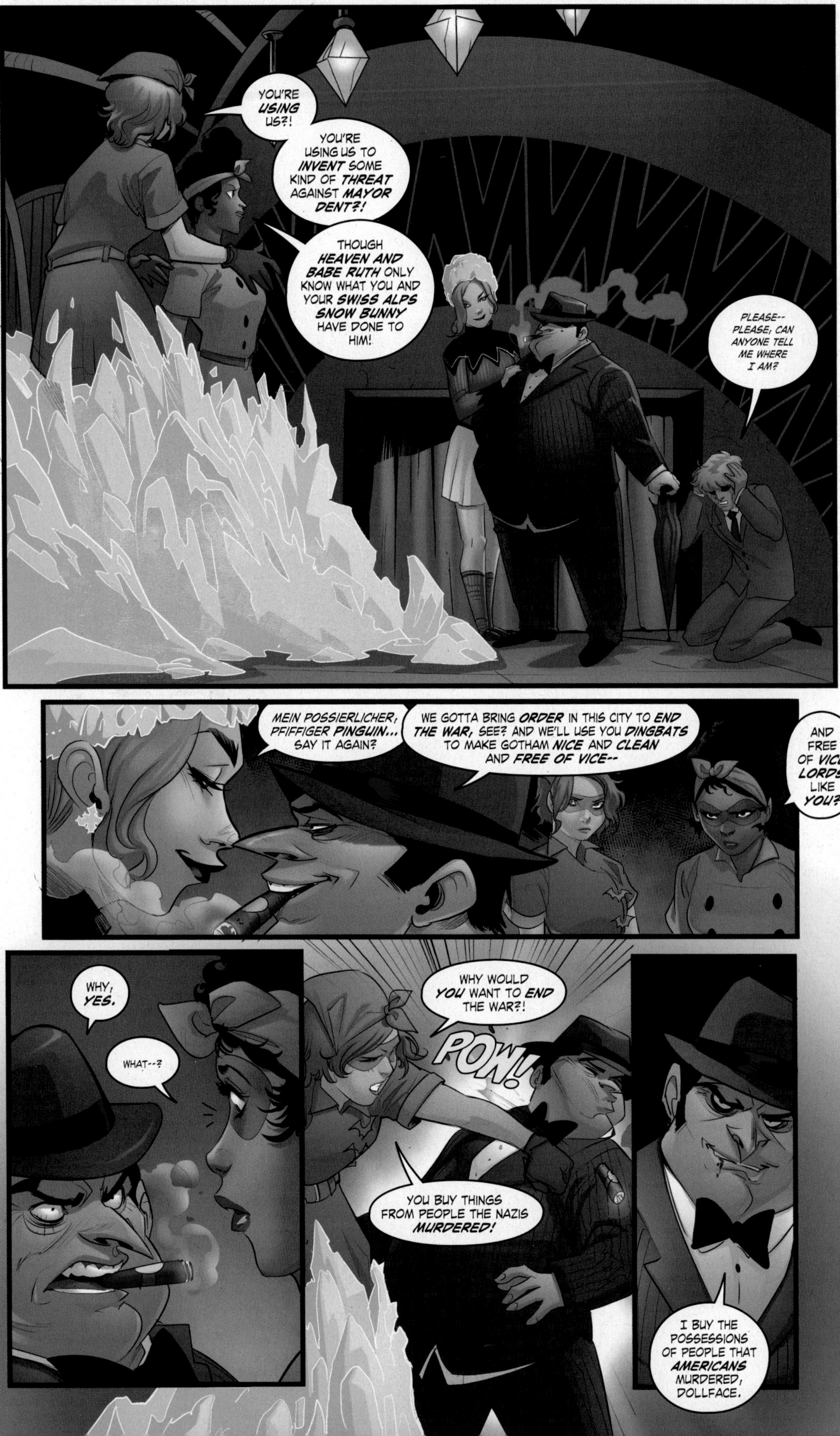
YOU'RE USING US?!
YOU'RE USING US TO INVENT SOME KIND OF THREAT AGAINST MAYOR DENT?!
THOUGH HEAVEN AND BABE RUTH ONLY KNOW WHAT YOU AND YOUR SWISS ALPS SNOW BUNNY HAVE DONE TO HIM!
PLEASE-- PLEASE, CAN ANYONE TELL ME WHERE I AM?
MEIN POSSIERLICHER, PFIFFIGER PINGUIN... SAY IT AGAIN?
WE GOTTA BRING ORDER IN THIS CITY TO END THE WAR, SEE? AND WE'LL USE YOU DINGBATS TO MAKE GOTHAM NICE AND CLEAN AND FREE OF VICE--
AND FREE OF VICE LORDS LIKE YOU?
WHY, YES.
WHAT--?
WHY WOULD YOU WANT TO END THE WAR?!
POW!
YOU BUY THINGS FROM PEOPLE THE NAZIS MURDERED!
I BUY THE POSSESSIONS OF PEOPLE THAT AMERICANS MURDERED, DOLLFACE.

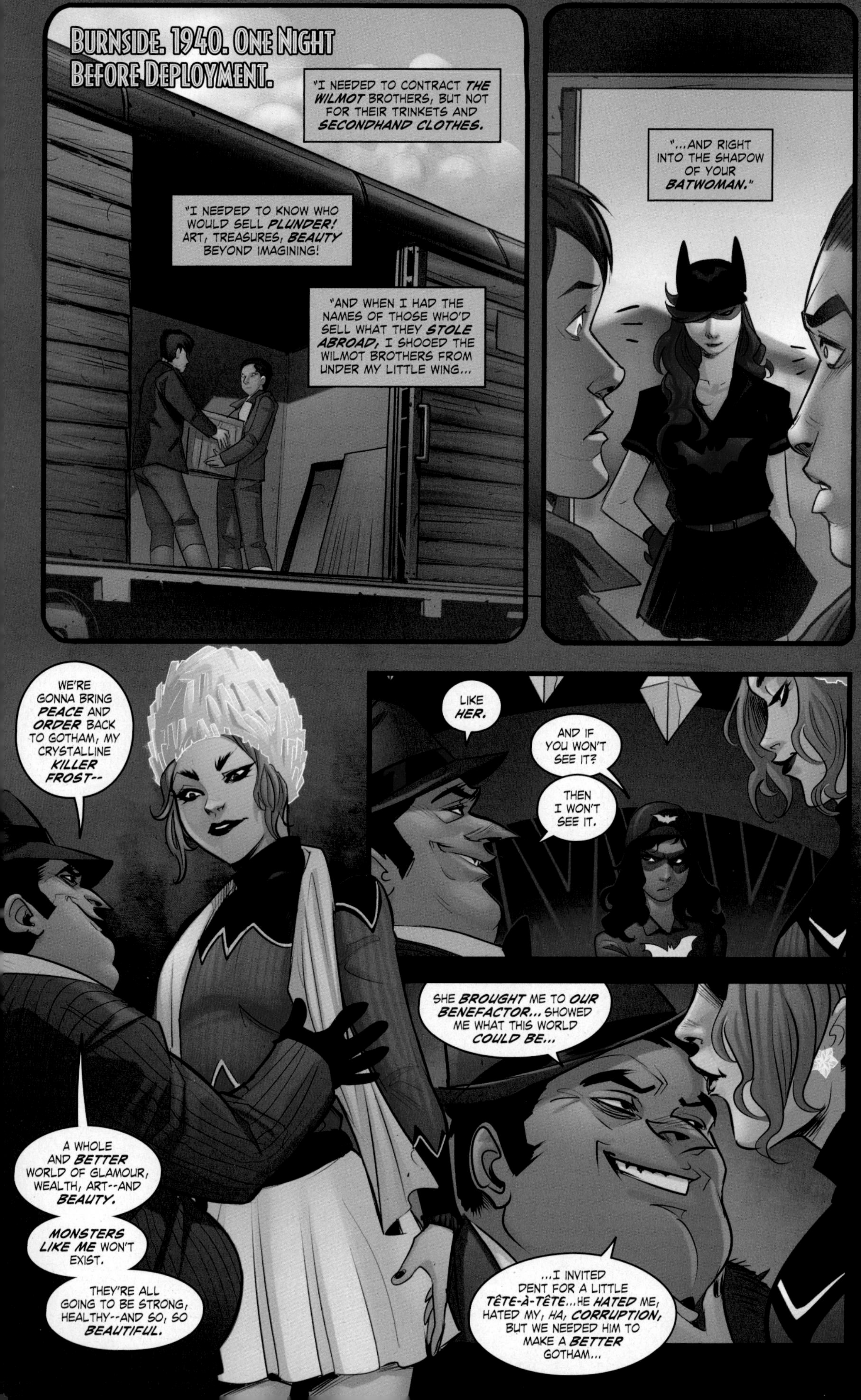
BURNSIDE. 1940. ONE NIGHT BEFORE DEPLOYMENT.
"I NEEDED TO CONTRACT THE WILMOT BROTHERS, BUT NOT FOR THEIR TRINKETS AND SECONDHAND CLOTHES.
"I NEEDED TO KNOW WHO WOULD SELL PLUNDER! ART, TREASURES, BEAUTY BEYOND IMAGINING!
"AND WHEN I HAD THE NAMES OF THOSE WHO'D SELL WHAT THEY STOLE ABROAD, I SHOOED THE WILMOT BROTHERS FROM UNDER MY LITTLE WING...
"...AND RIGHT INTO THE SHADOW OF YOUR BATWOMAN."
WE'RE GONNA BRING PEACE AND ORDER BACK TO GOTHAM, MY CRYSTALLINE KILLER FROST--
LIKE HER.
AND IF YOU WON'T SEE IT?
THEN I WON'T SEE IT.
SHE BROUGHT ME TO OUR BENEFACTOR... SHOWED ME WHAT THIS WORLD COULD BE...
A WHOLE AND BETTER WORLD OF GLAMOUR, WEALTH, ART--AND BEAUTY.
MONSTERS LIKE ME WON'T EXIST.
THEY'RE ALL GOING TO BE STRONG, HEALTHY--AND SO, SO BEAUTIFUL.
...I INVITED DENT FOR A LITTLE TÊTE-À-TÊTE...HE HATED ME, HATED MY, HA, CORRUPTION, BUT WE NEEDED HIM TO MAKE A BETTER GOTHAM...

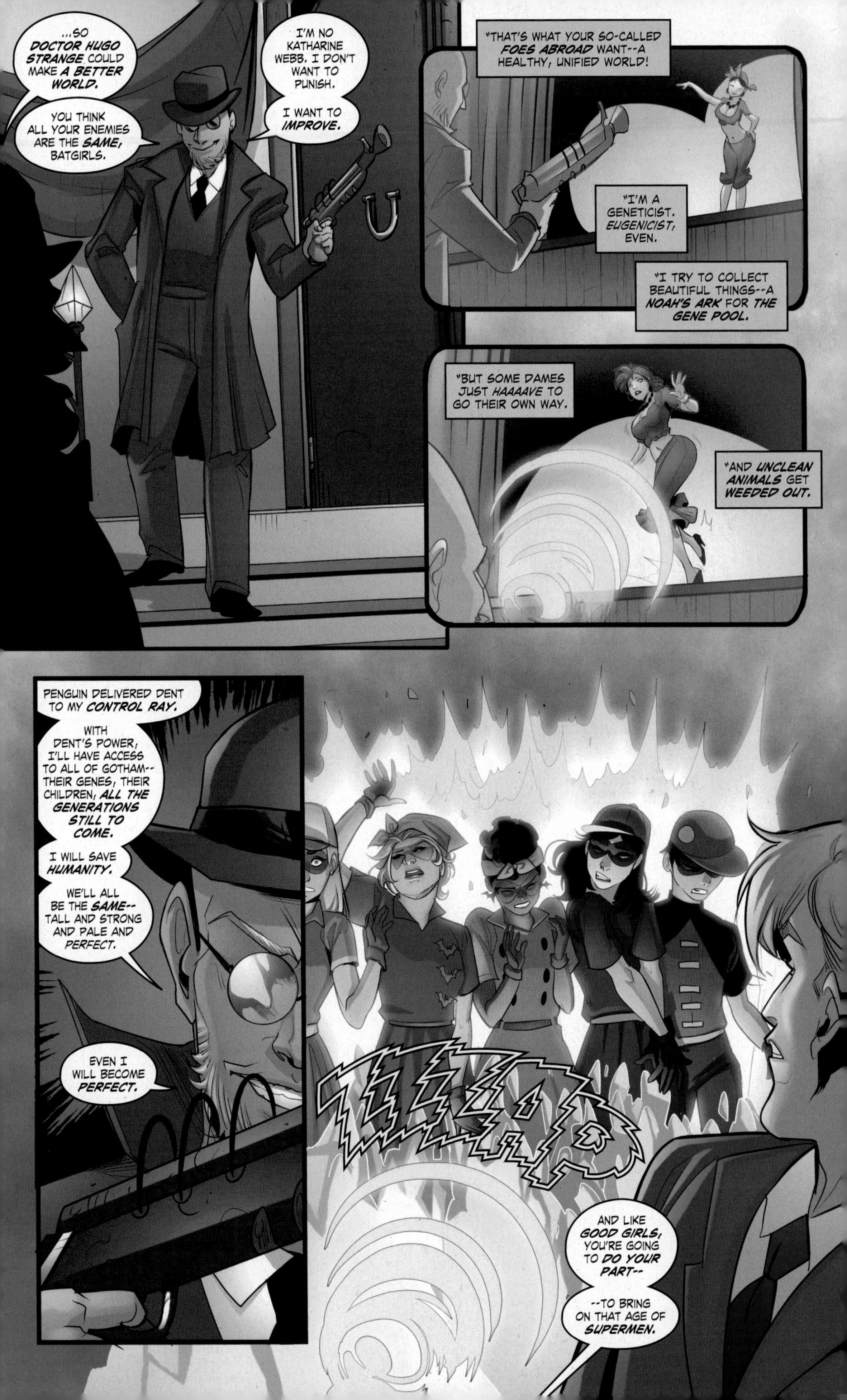

...SO DOCTOR HUGO STRANGE COULD MAKE A BETTER WORLD.
YOU THINK ALL YOUR ENEMIES ARE THE SAME, BATGIRLS.
I'M NO KATHARINE WEBB. I DON'T WANT TO PUNISH.
I WANT TO IMPROVE.
"THAT'S WHAT YOUR SO-CALLED FOES ABROAD WANT--A HEALTHY, UNIFIED WORLD!
"I'M A GENETICIST. EUGENICIST, EVEN.
"I TRY TO COLLECT BEAUTIFUL THINGS--A NOAH'S ARK FOR THE GENE POOL.
"BUT SOME DAMES JUST HAAAAVE TO GO THEIR OWN WAY.
"AND UNCLEAN ANIMALS GET WEEDED OUT.
PENGUIN DELIVERED DENT TO MY CONTROL RAY.
WITH DENT'S POWER, I'LL HAVE ACCESS TO ALL OF GOTHAM--THEIR GENES, THEIR CHILDREN, ALL THE GENERATIONS STILL TO COME.
I WILL SAVE HUMANITY.
WE'LL ALL BE THE SAME--TALL AND STRONG AND PALE AND PERFECT.
EVEN I WILL BECOME PERFECT.
AND LIKE GOOD GIRLS, YOU'RE GOING TO DO YOUR PART--
--TO BRING ON THAT AGE OF SUPERMEN.

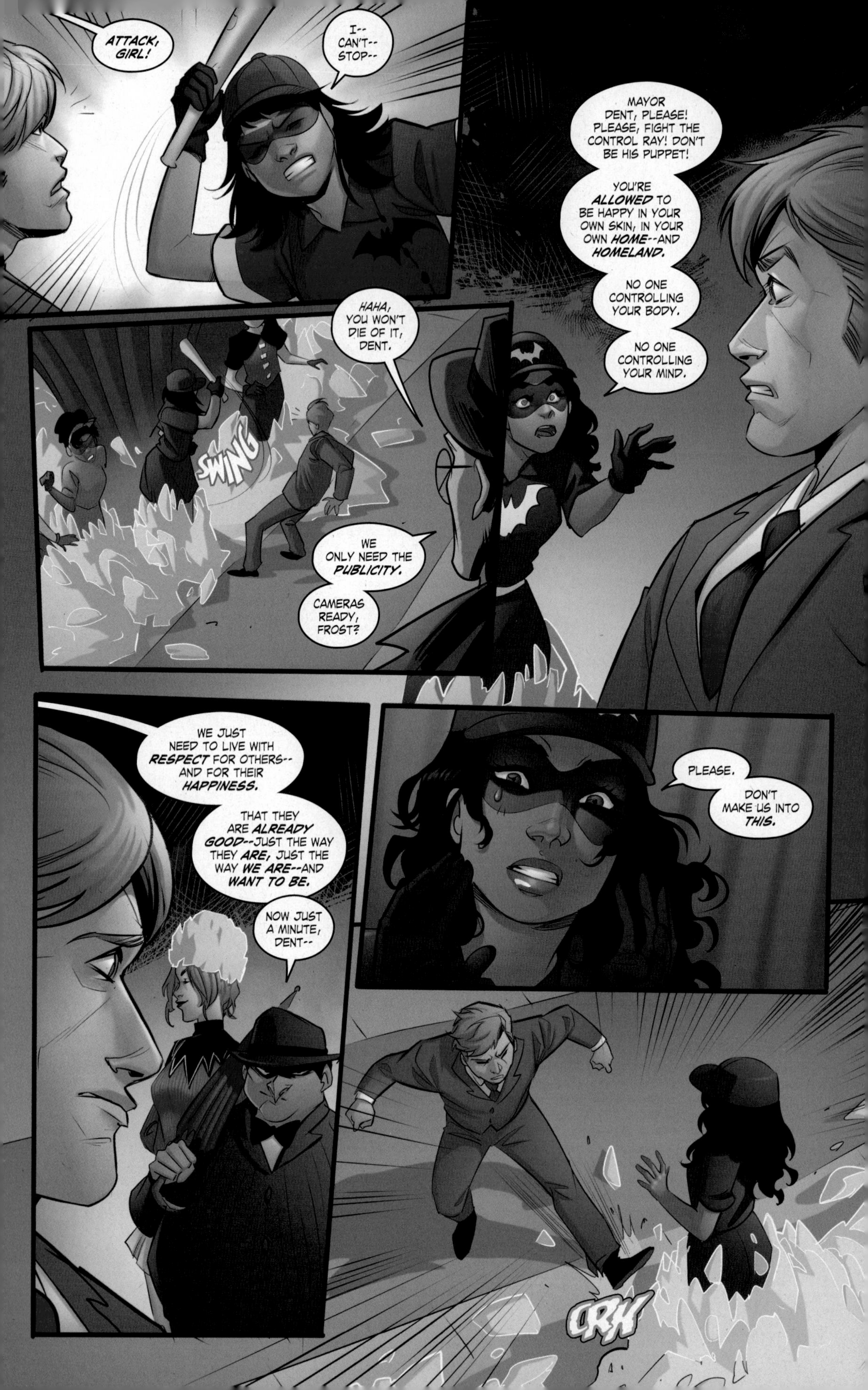
ATTACK, GIRL!
I-- CAN'T-- STOP--
MAYOR DENT, PLEASE! PLEASE, FIGHT THE CONTROL RAY! DON'T BE HIS PUPPET!
YOU'RE ALLOWED TO BE HAPPY IN YOUR OWN SKIN, IN YOUR OWN HOME--AND HOMELAND.
NO ONE CONTROLLING YOUR BODY.
NO ONE CONTROLLING YOUR MIND.
HAHA, YOU WON'T DIE OF IT, DENT.
SWING
WE ONLY NEED THE PUBLICITY.
CAMERAS READY, FROST?
WE JUST NEED TO LIVE WITH RESPECT FOR OTHERS-- AND FOR THEIR HAPPINESS.
THAT THEY ARE ALREADY GOOD--JUST THE WAY THEY ARE, JUST THE WAY WE ARE--AND WANT TO BE.
NOW JUST A MINUTE, DENT--
PLEASE.
DON'T MAKE US INTO THIS.
CRK

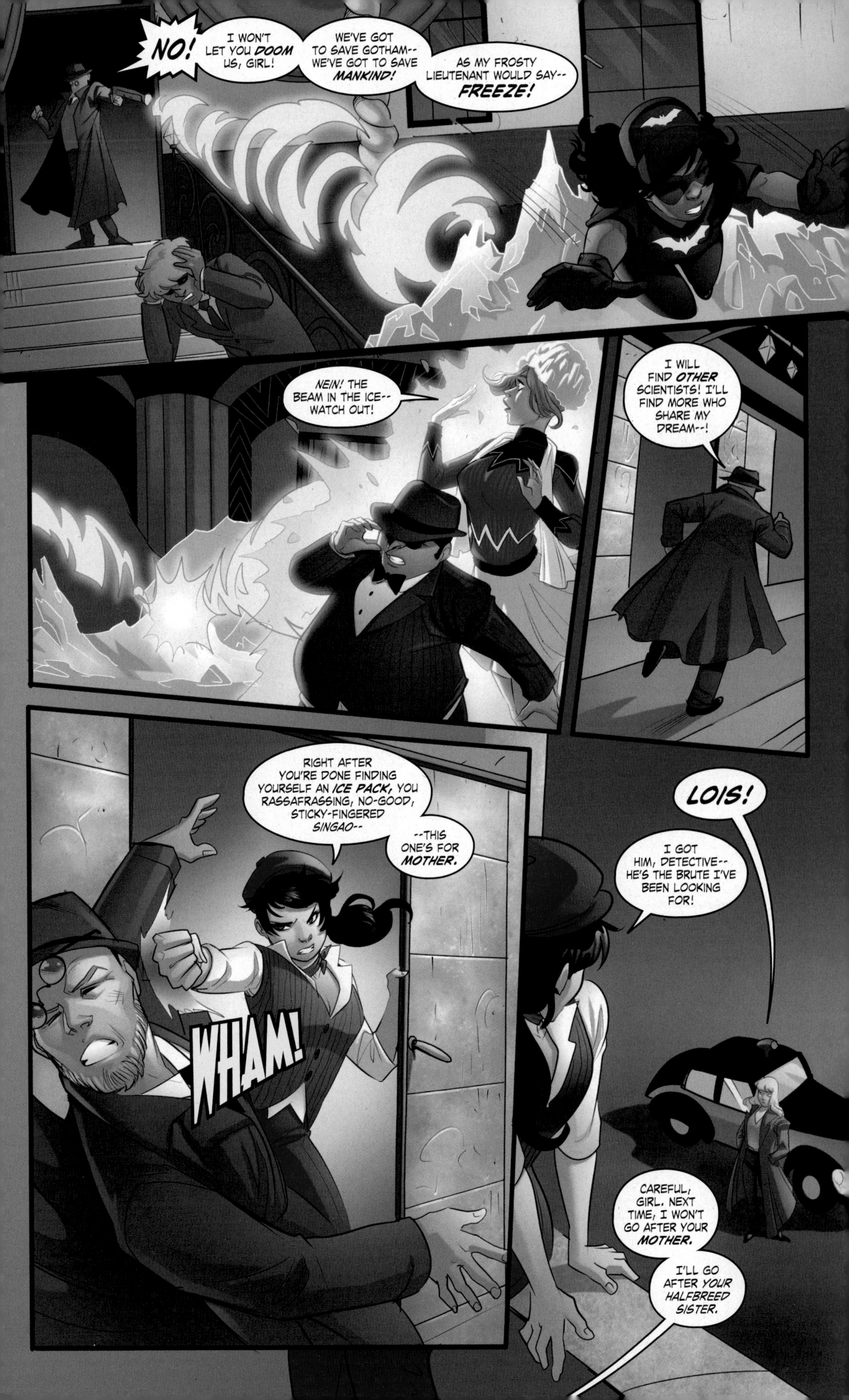
NO!
I WON'T LET YOU DOOM US, GIRL!
WE'VE GOT TO SAVE GOTHAM-- WE'VE GOT TO SAVE MANKIND!
AS MY FROSTY LIEUTENANT WOULD SAY-- FREEZE!
NEIN! THE BEAM IN THE ICE-- WATCH OUT!
I WILL FIND OTHER SCIENTISTS! I'LL FIND MORE WHO SHARE MY DREAM--!
RIGHT AFTER YOU'RE DONE FINDING YOURSELF AN ICE PACK, YOU RASSAFRASSING, NO-GOOD, STICKY-FINGERED SINGAO--
--THIS ONE'S FOR MOTHER.
WHAM!
LOIS!
I GOT HIM, DETECTIVE-- HE'S THE BRUTE I'VE BEEN LOOKING FOR!
CAREFUL, GIRL. NEXT TIME, I WON'T GO AFTER YOUR MOTHER.
I'LL GO AFTER YOUR HALFBREED SISTER.

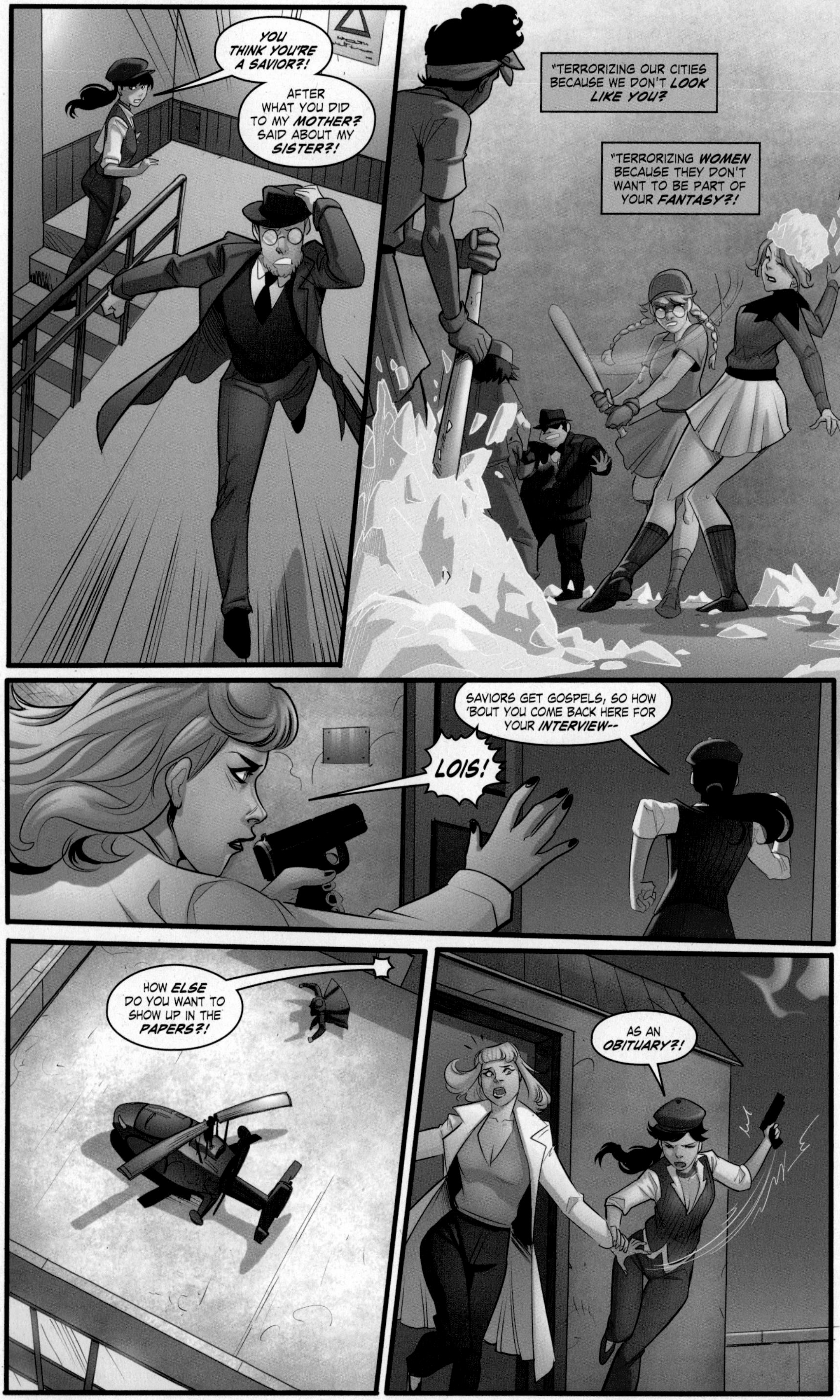
YOU THINK YOU'RE A SAVIOR?!
AFTER WHAT YOU DID TO MY MOTHER? SAID ABOUT MY SISTER?!
"TERRORIZING OUR CITIES BECAUSE WE DON'T LOOK LIKE YOU?
"TERRORIZING WOMEN BECAUSE THEY DON'T WANT TO BE PART OF YOUR FANTASY?!
SAVIORS GET GOSPELS, SO HOW 'BOUT YOU COME BACK HERE FOR YOUR INTERVIEW--
LOIS!
HOW ELSE DO YOU WANT TO SHOW UP IN THE PAPERS?!
AS AN OBITUARY?!

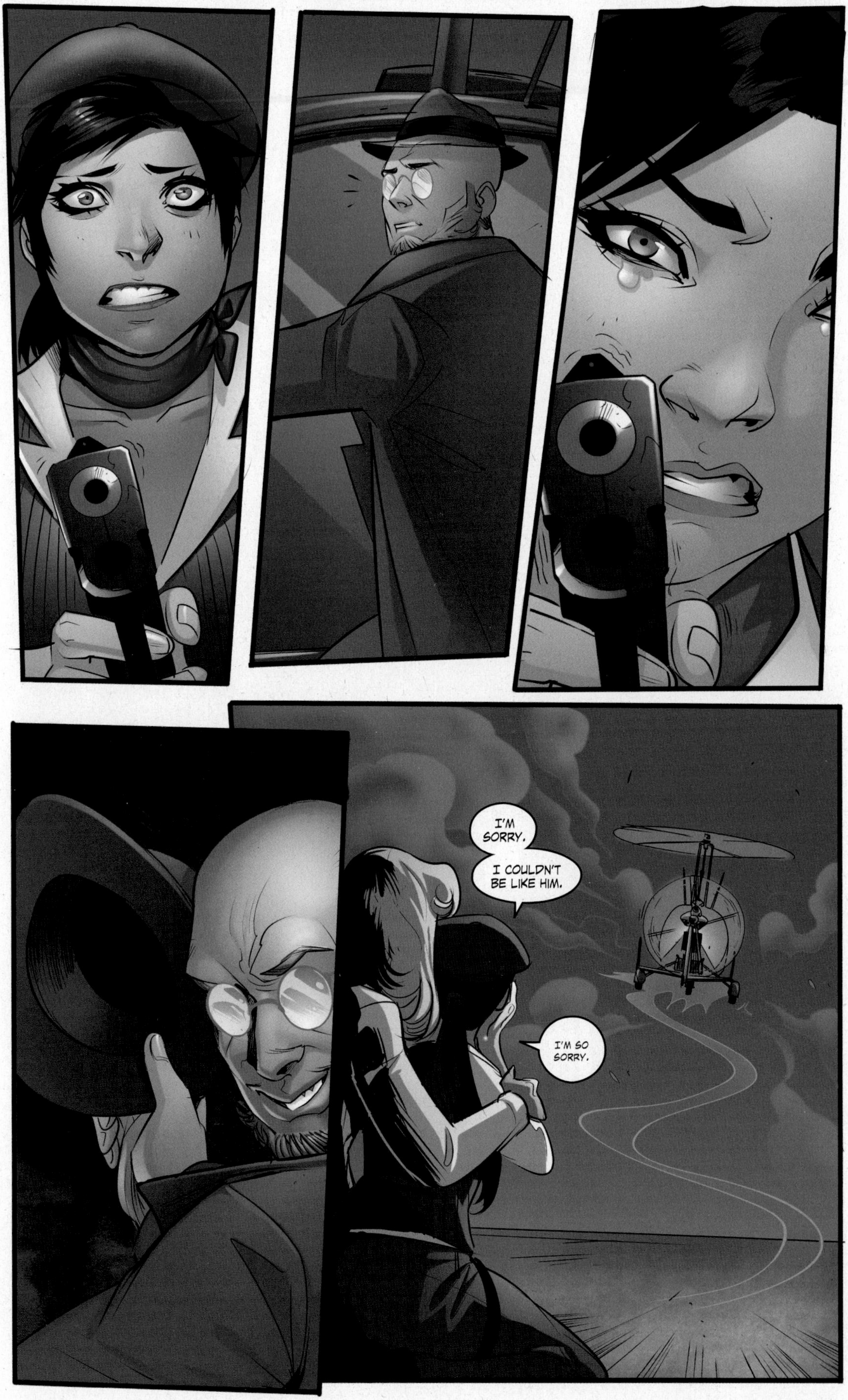
I'M SORRY.
I COULDN'T BE LIKE HIM.
I'M SO SORRY.

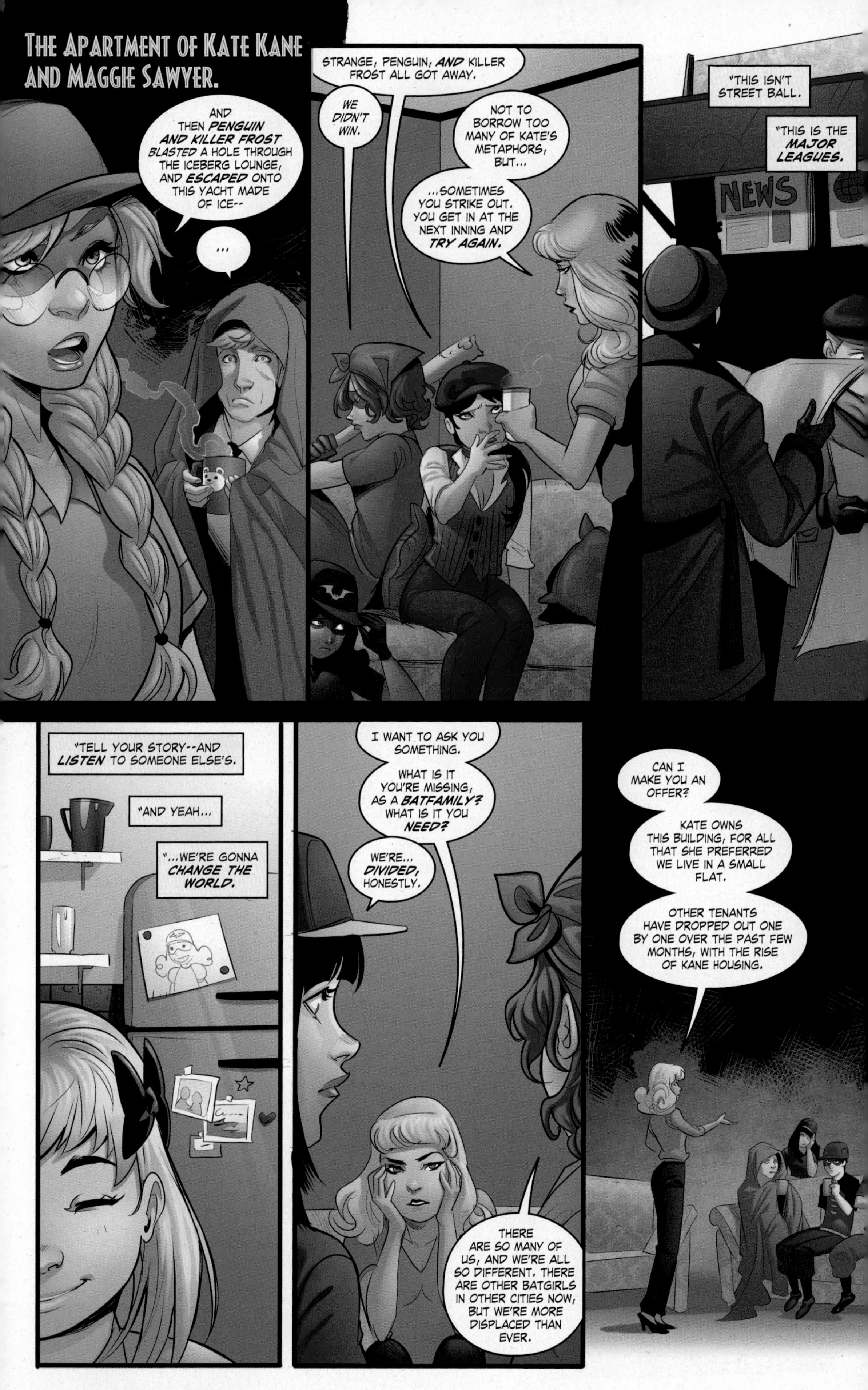

The Apartment of Kate Kane and Maggie Sawyer.
AND THEN PENGUIN AND KILLER FROST BLASTED A HOLE THROUGH THE ICEBERG LOUNGE, AND ESCAPED ONTO THIS YACHT MADE OF ICE--
...
STRANGE, PENGUIN, AND KILLER FROST ALL GOT AWAY.
WE DIDN'T WIN.
NOT TO BORROW TOO MANY OF KATE'S METAPHORS, BUT...
...SOMETIMES YOU STRIKE OUT. YOU GET IN AT THE NEXT INNING AND TRY AGAIN.
"THIS ISN'T STREET BALL.
"THIS IS THE MAJOR LEAGUES.
NEWS
"TELL YOUR STORY--AND LISTEN TO SOMEONE ELSE'S.
"AND YEAH...
"...WE'RE GONNA CHANGE THE WORLD.
I WANT TO ASK YOU SOMETHING.
WHAT IS IT YOU'RE MISSING, AS A BATFAMILY? WHAT IS IT YOU NEED?
WE'RE... DIVIDED, HONESTLY.
THERE ARE SO MANY OF US, AND WE'RE ALL SO DIFFERENT. THERE ARE OTHER BATGIRLS IN OTHER CITIES NOW, BUT WE'RE MORE DISPLACED THAN EVER.
CAN I MAKE YOU AN OFFER?
KATE OWNS THIS BUILDING, FOR ALL THAT SHE PREFERRED WE LIVE IN A SMALL FLAT.
OTHER TENANTS HAVE DROPPED OUT ONE BY ONE OVER THE PAST FEW MONTHS, WITH THE RISE OF KANE HOUSING.

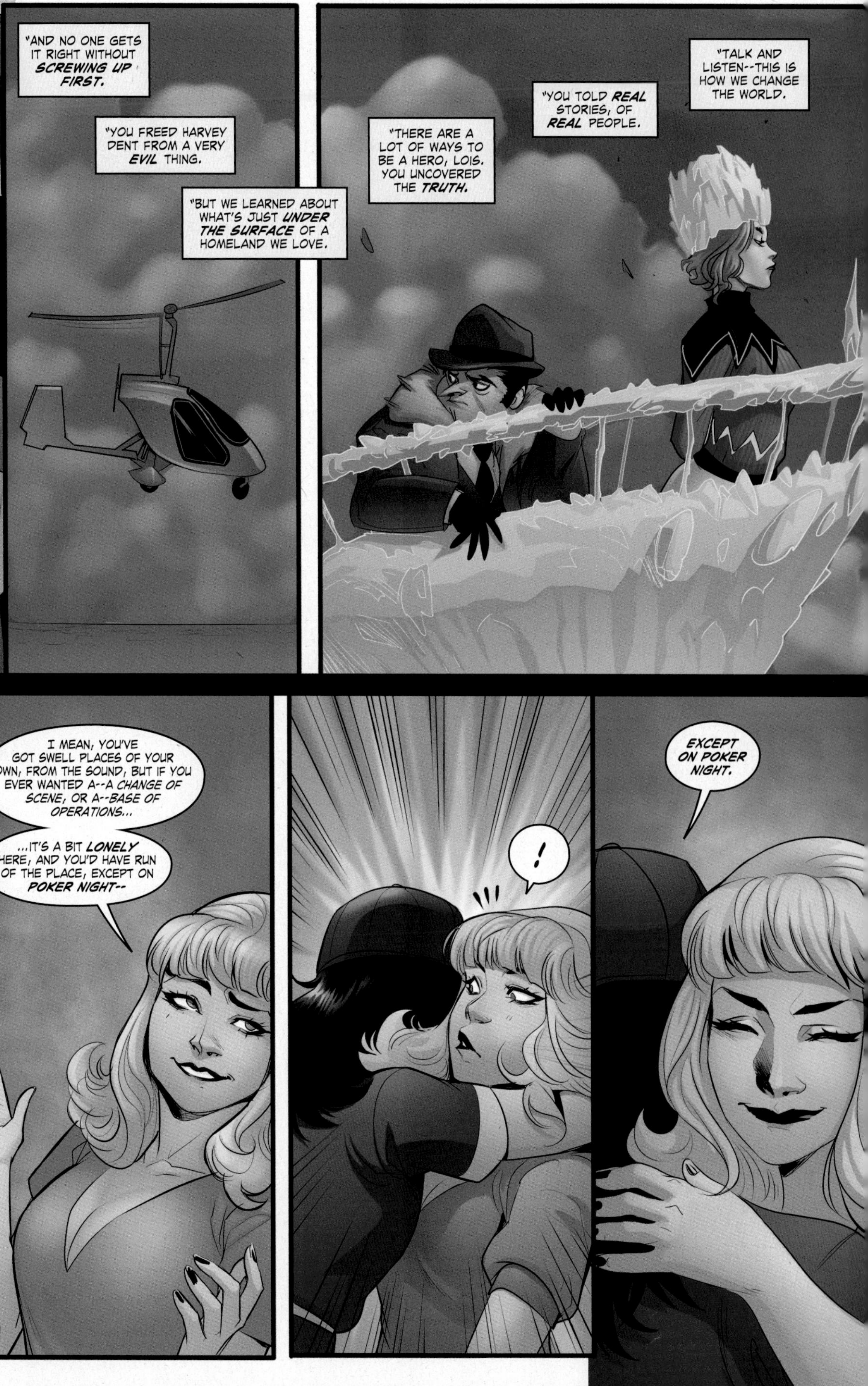
"AND NO ONE GETS IT RIGHT WITHOUT SCREWING UP FIRST.
"YOU FREED HARVEY DENT FROM A VERY EVIL THING.
"BUT WE LEARNED ABOUT WHAT'S JUST UNDER THE SURFACE OF A HOMELAND WE LOVE.
"THERE ARE A LOT OF WAYS TO BE A HERO, LOIS. YOU UNCOVERED THE TRUTH.
"YOU TOLD REAL STORIES, OF REAL PEOPLE.
"TALK AND LISTEN--THIS IS HOW WE CHANGE THE WORLD.
I MEAN, YOU'VE GOT SWELL PLACES OF YOUR OWN, FROM THE SOUND, BUT IF YOU EVER WANTED A--A CHANGE OF SCENE, OR A--BASE OF OPERATIONS...
...IT'S A BIT LONELY HERE, AND YOU'D HAVE RUN OF THE PLACE, EXCEPT ON POKER NIGHT--
!
EXCEPT ON POKER NIGHT.

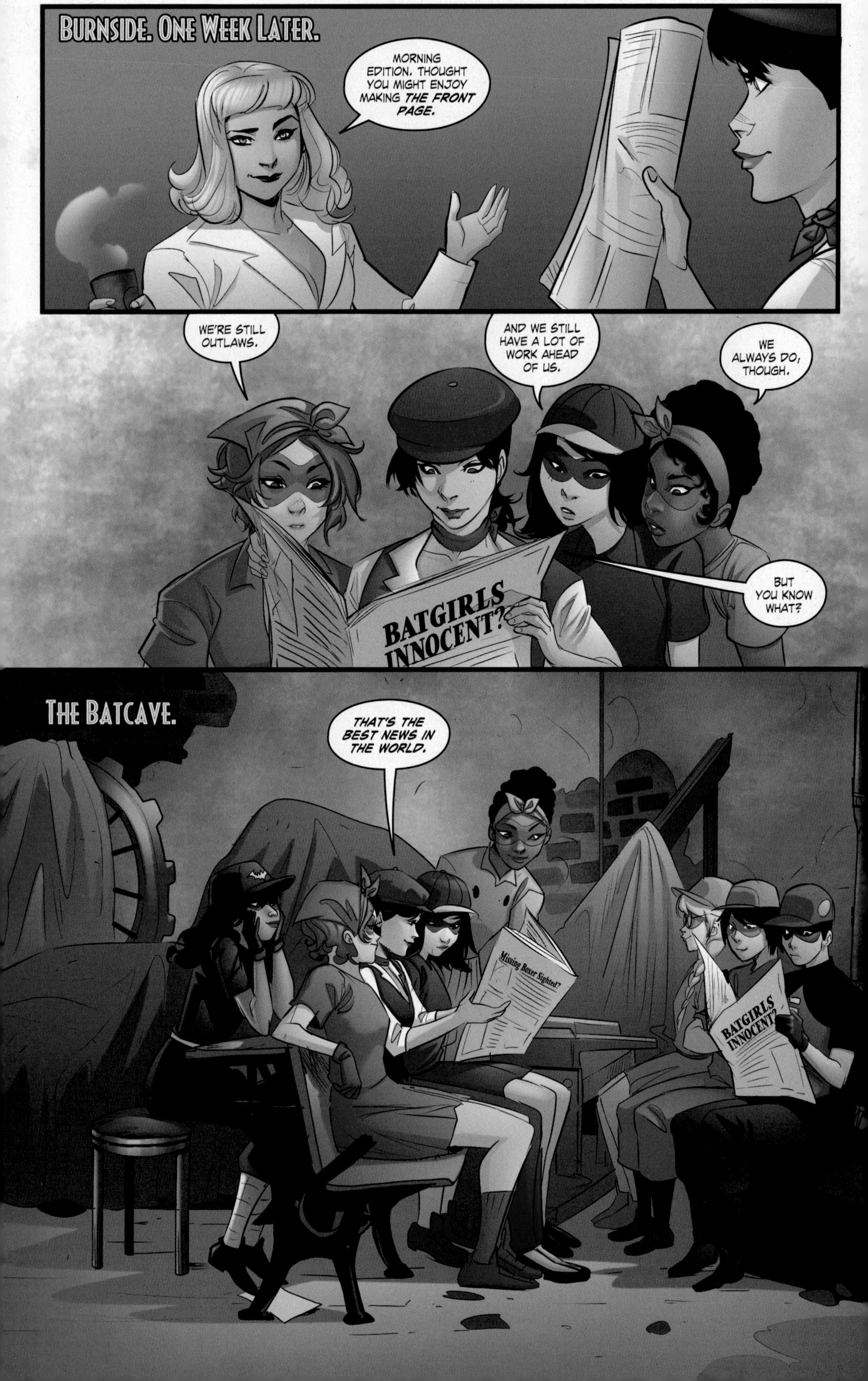
BURNSIDE. ONE WEEK LATER.
MORNING EDITION. THOUGHT YOU MIGHT ENJOY MAKING THE FRONT PAGE.
WE'RE STILL OUTLAWS.
AND WE STILL HAVE A LOT OF WORK AHEAD OF US.
WE ALWAYS DO, THOUGH.
BATGIRLS INNOCENT?
BUT YOU KNOW WHAT?
THE BATCAVE.
THAT'S THE BEST NEWS IN THE WORLD.
Missing Boxer Sighted?
BATGIRLS INNOCENT?

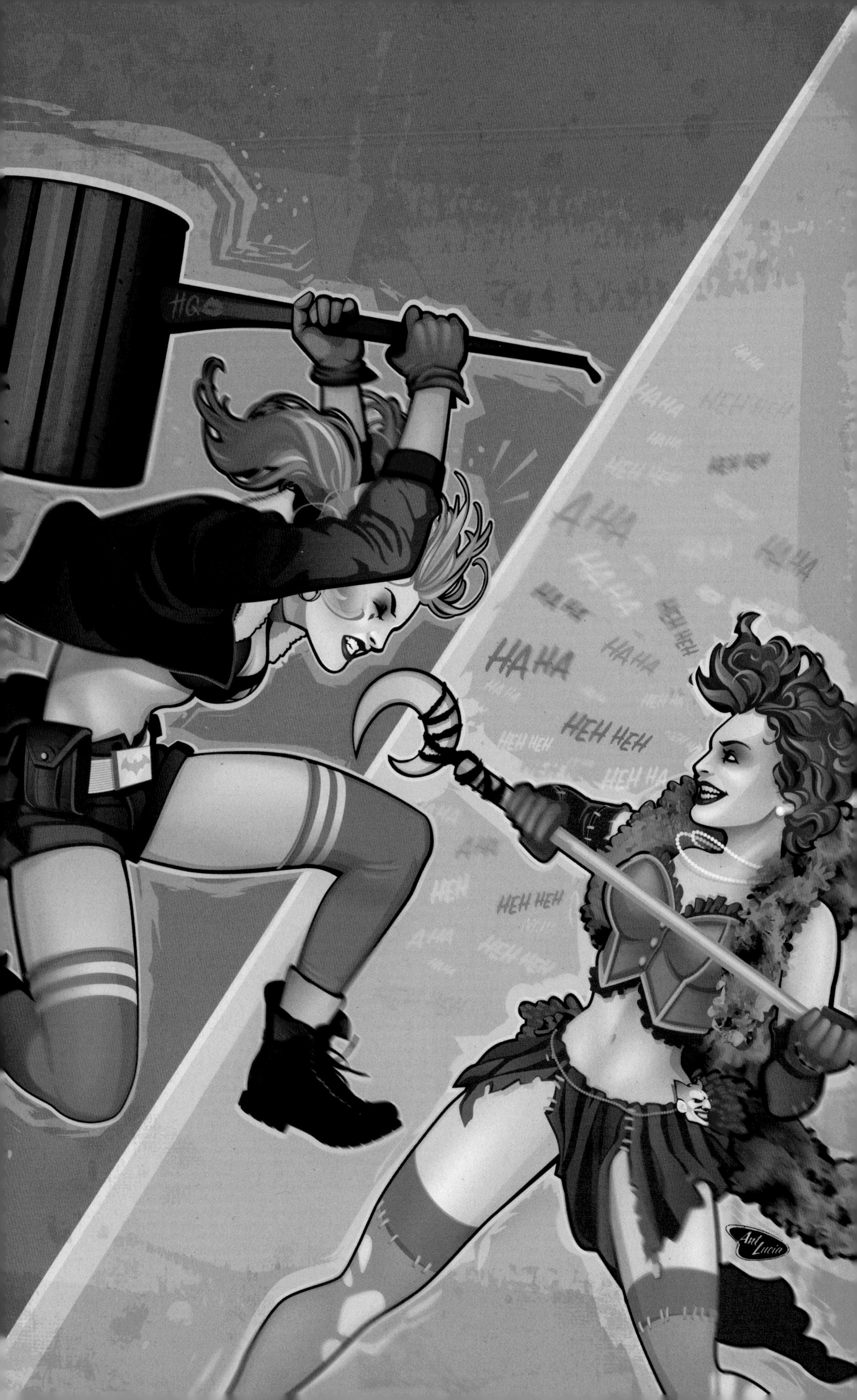
HQ
HAHA
HEH HEH
AHA
HAHA
HEH HEH
HAHA
HA HA
HEH HEH
HEH HA
HEH HEH
Ant Lucia

LOVE STORIES

MARGUERITE BENNETT
Writer

LAURA BRAGA
MIRKA ANDOLFO
Artists

J. NANJAN
WENDY BROOME
Colorists

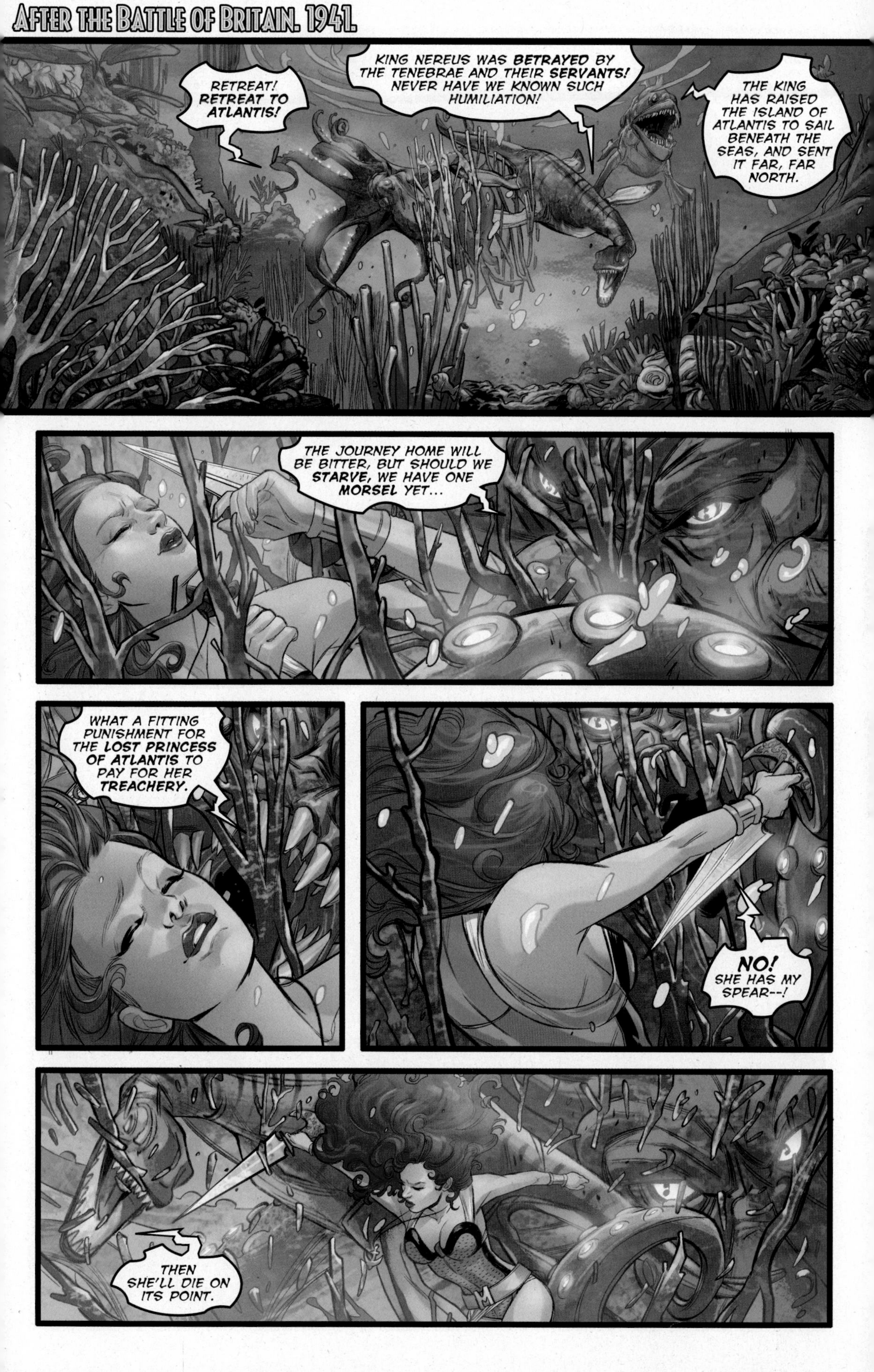

AFTER THE BATTLE OF BRITAIN. 1941.
RETREAT! RETREAT TO ATLANTIS!
KING NEREUS WAS BETRAYED BY THE TENEBRAE AND THEIR SERVANTS! NEVER HAVE WE KNOWN SUCH HUMILIATION!
THE KING HAS RAISED THE ISLAND OF ATLANTIS TO SAIL BENEATH THE SEAS, AND SENT IT FAR, FAR NORTH.
THE JOURNEY HOME WILL BE BITTER, BUT SHOULD WE STARVE, WE HAVE ONE MORSEL YET...
WHAT A FITTING PUNISHMENT FOR THE LOST PRINCESS OF ATLANTIS TO PAY FOR HER TREACHERY.
NO! SHE HAS MY SPEAR--!
THEN SHE'LL DIE ON ITS POINT.

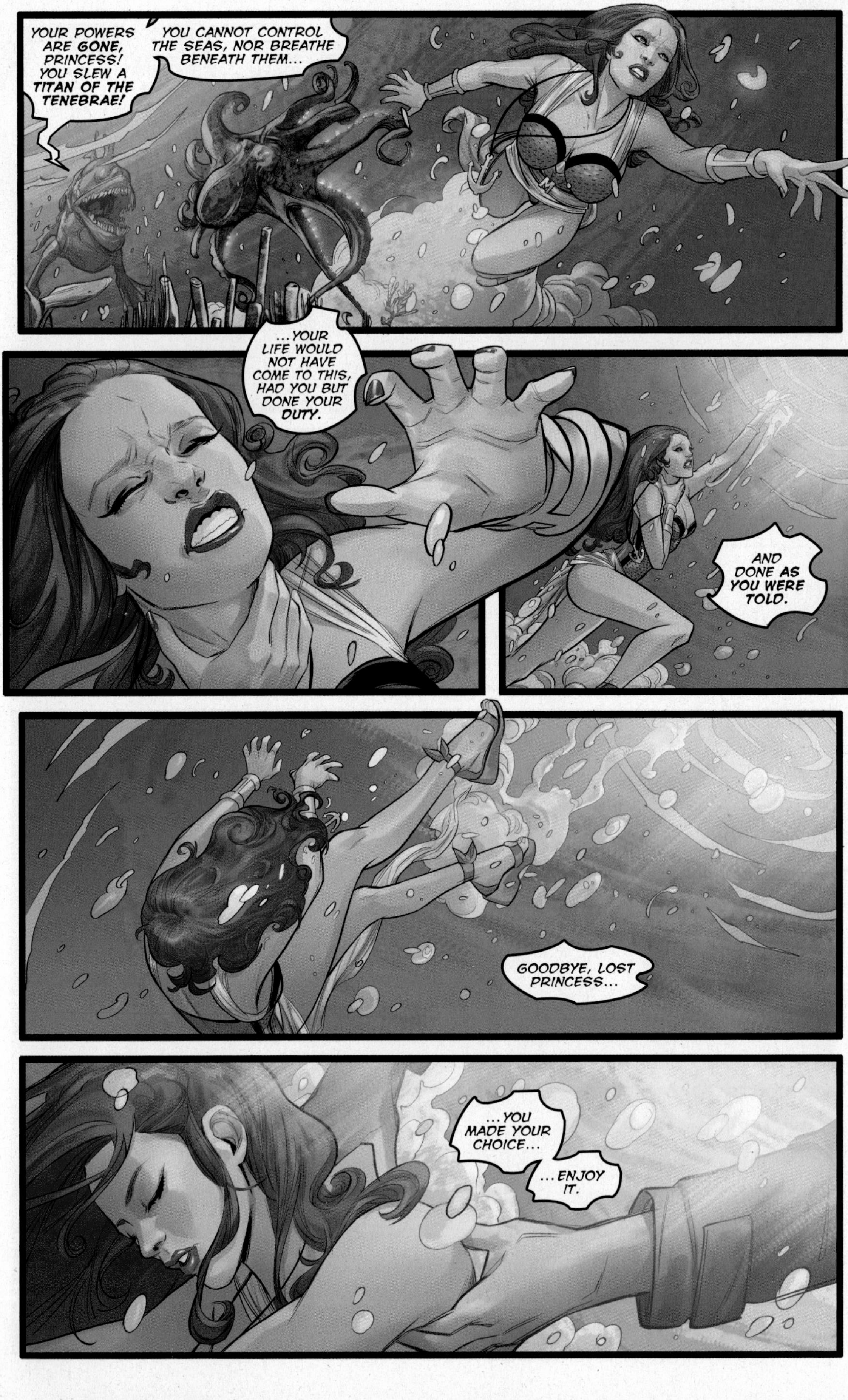
YOUR POWERS ARE GONE, PRINCESS! YOU SLEW A TITAN OF THE TENEBRAE!
YOU CANNOT CONTROL THE SEAS, NOR BREATHE BENEATH THEM...
...YOUR LIFE WOULD NOT HAVE COME TO THIS, HAD YOU BUT DONE YOUR DUTY.
AND DONE AS YOU WERE TOLD.
GOODBYE, LOST PRINCESS...
...YOU MADE YOUR CHOICE...
...ENJOY IT.

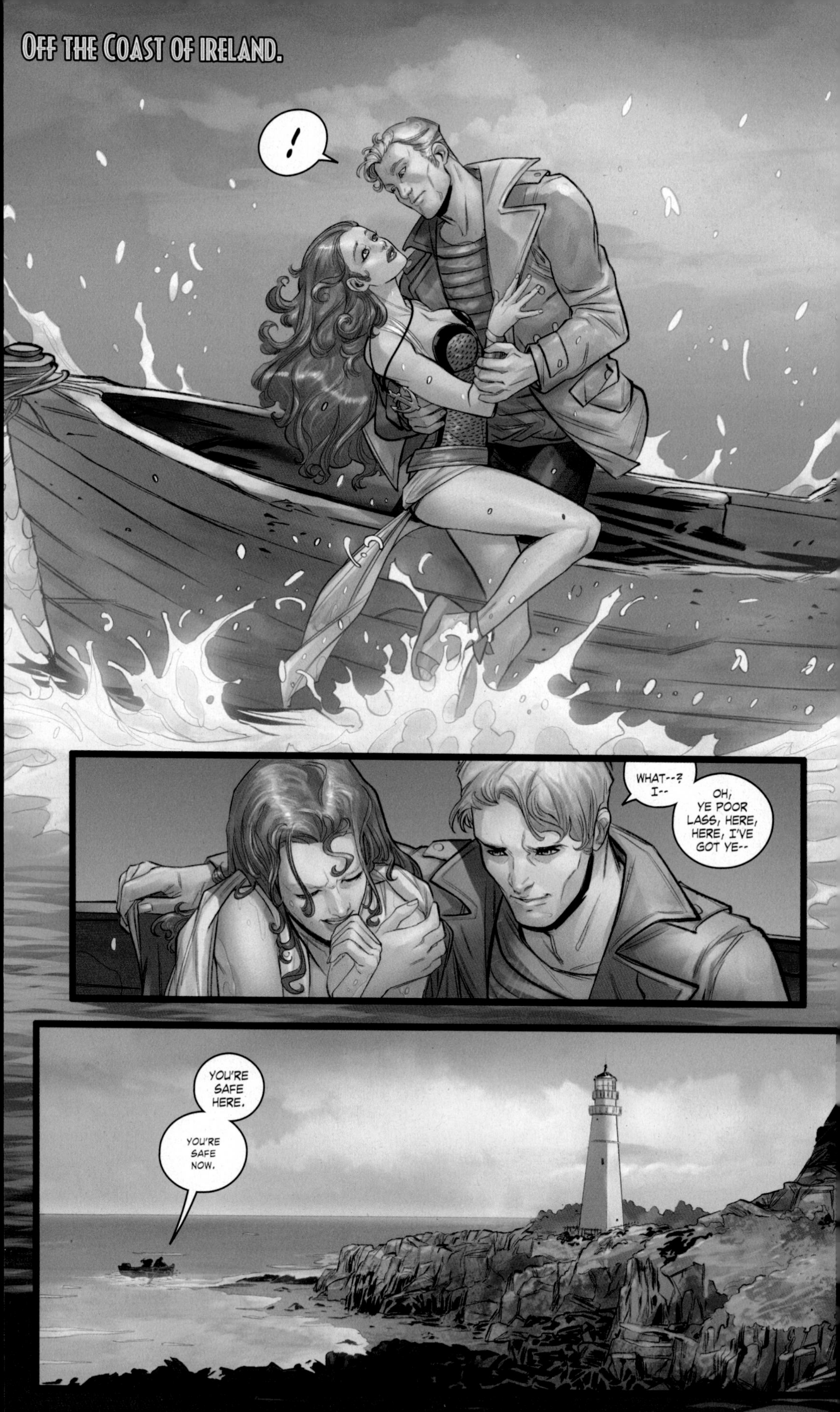
Off the Coast of Ireland.
!
WHAT--? I--
OH, YE POOR LASS, HERE, HERE, I'VE GOT YE--
YOU'RE SAFE HERE.
YOU'RE SAFE NOW.

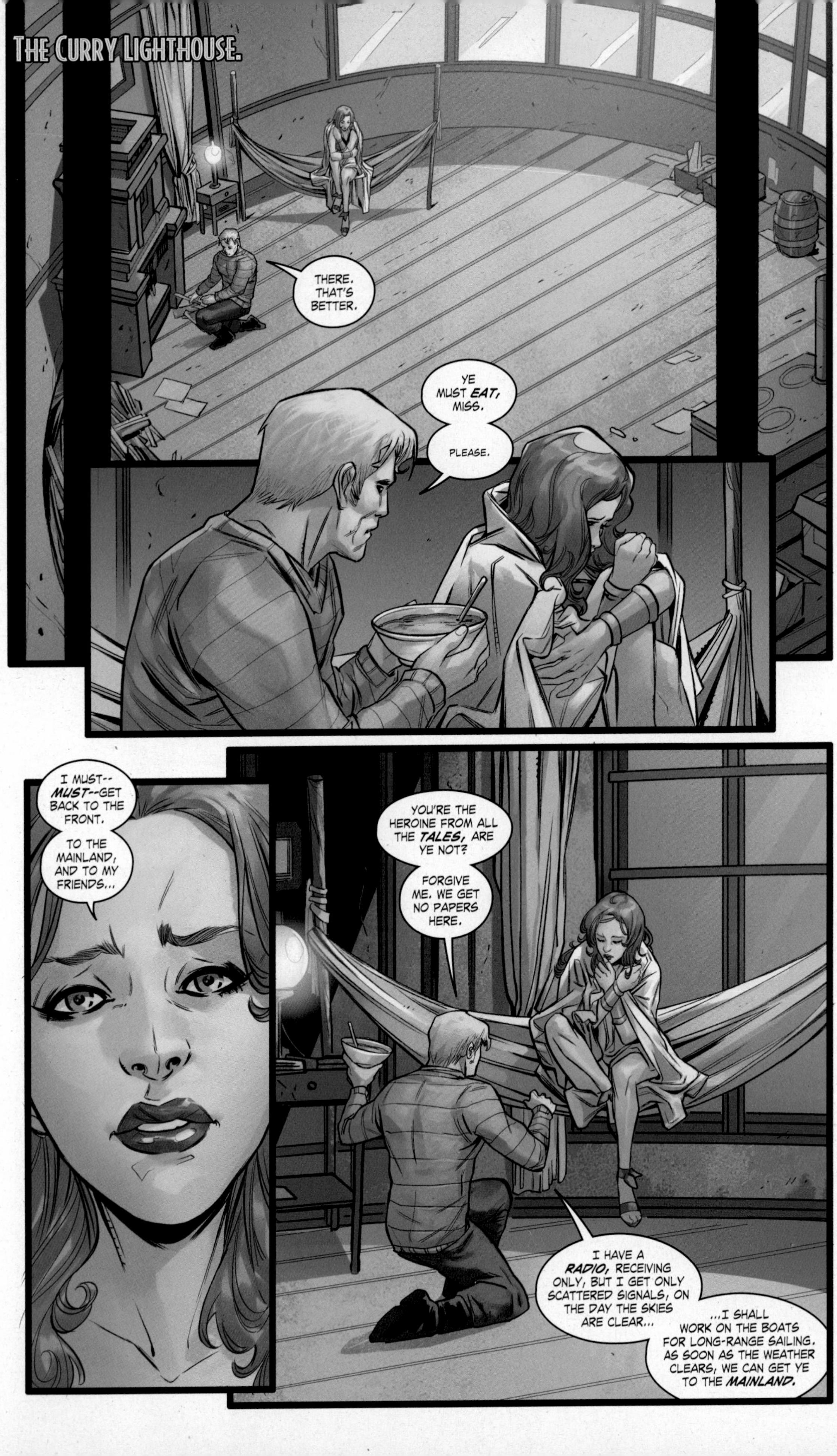
THE CURRY LIGHTHOUSE.
THERE. THAT'S BETTER.
YE MUST EAT, MISS.
PLEASE.
I MUST--MUST--GET BACK TO THE FRONT.
TO THE MAINLAND, AND TO MY FRIENDS...
YOU'RE THE HEROINE FROM ALL THE TALES, ARE YE NOT?
FORGIVE ME. WE GET NO PAPERS HERE.
I HAVE A RADIO, RECEIVING ONLY, BUT I GET ONLY SCATTERED SIGNALS, ON THE DAY THE SKIES ARE CLEAR...
...I SHALL WORK ON THE BOATS FOR LONG-RANGE SAILING. AS SOON AS THE WEATHER CLEARS, WE CAN GET YE TO THE MAINLAND.

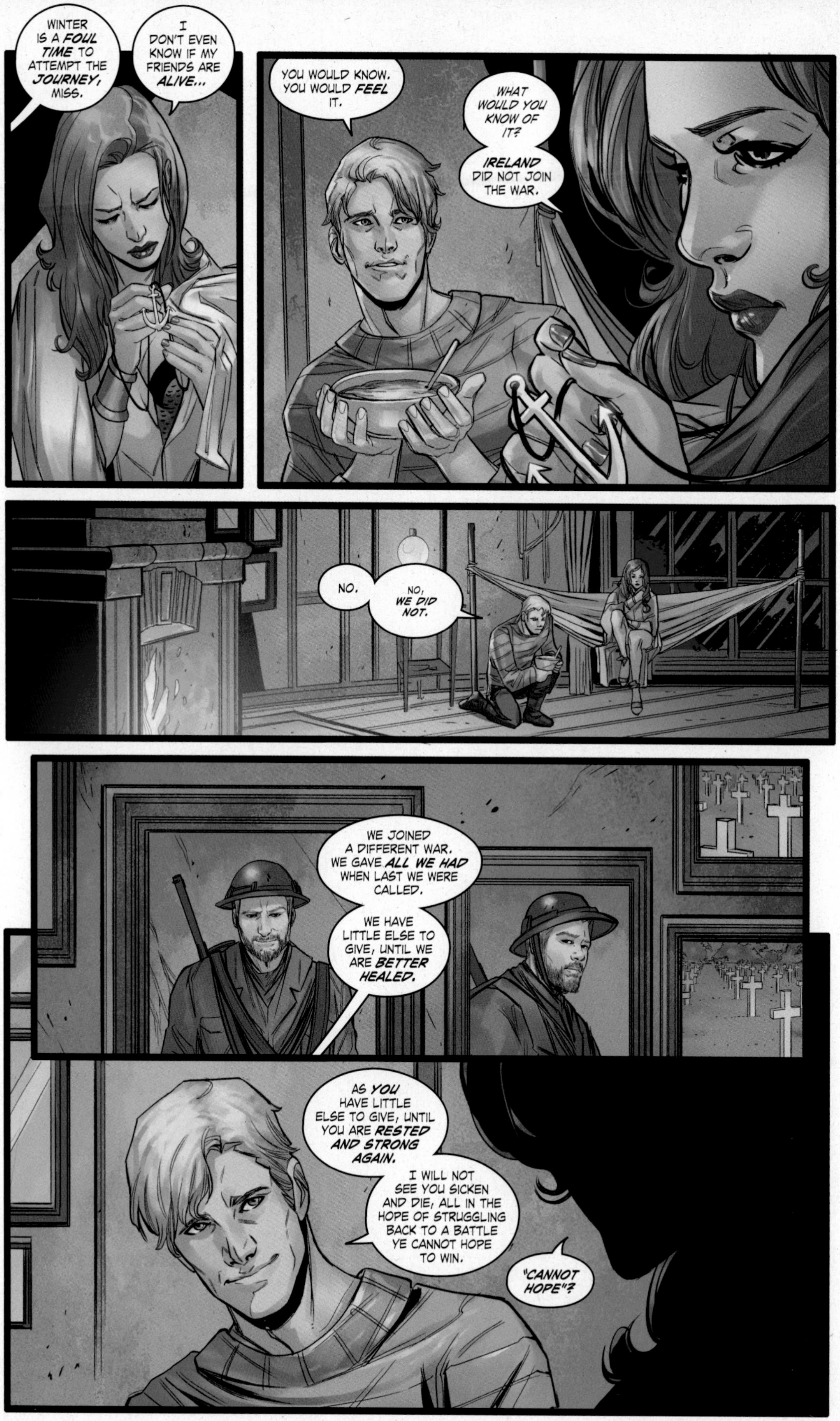
WINTER IS A FOUL TIME TO ATTEMPT THE JOURNEY, MISS.
I DON'T EVEN KNOW IF MY FRIENDS ARE ALIVE...
YOU WOULD KNOW. YOU WOULD FEEL IT.
WHAT WOULD YOU KNOW OF IT?
IRELAND DID NOT JOIN THE WAR.
NO.
NO, WE DID NOT.
WE JOINED A DIFFERENT WAR. WE GAVE ALL WE HAD WHEN LAST WE WERE CALLED.
WE HAVE LITTLE ELSE TO GIVE, UNTIL WE ARE BETTER HEALED.
AS YOU HAVE LITTLE ELSE TO GIVE, UNTIL YOU ARE RESTED AND STRONG AGAIN.
I WILL NOT SEE YOU SICKEN AND DIE, ALL IN THE HOPE OF STRUGGLING BACK TO A BATTLE YE CANNOT HOPE TO WIN.
"CANNOT HOPE"?

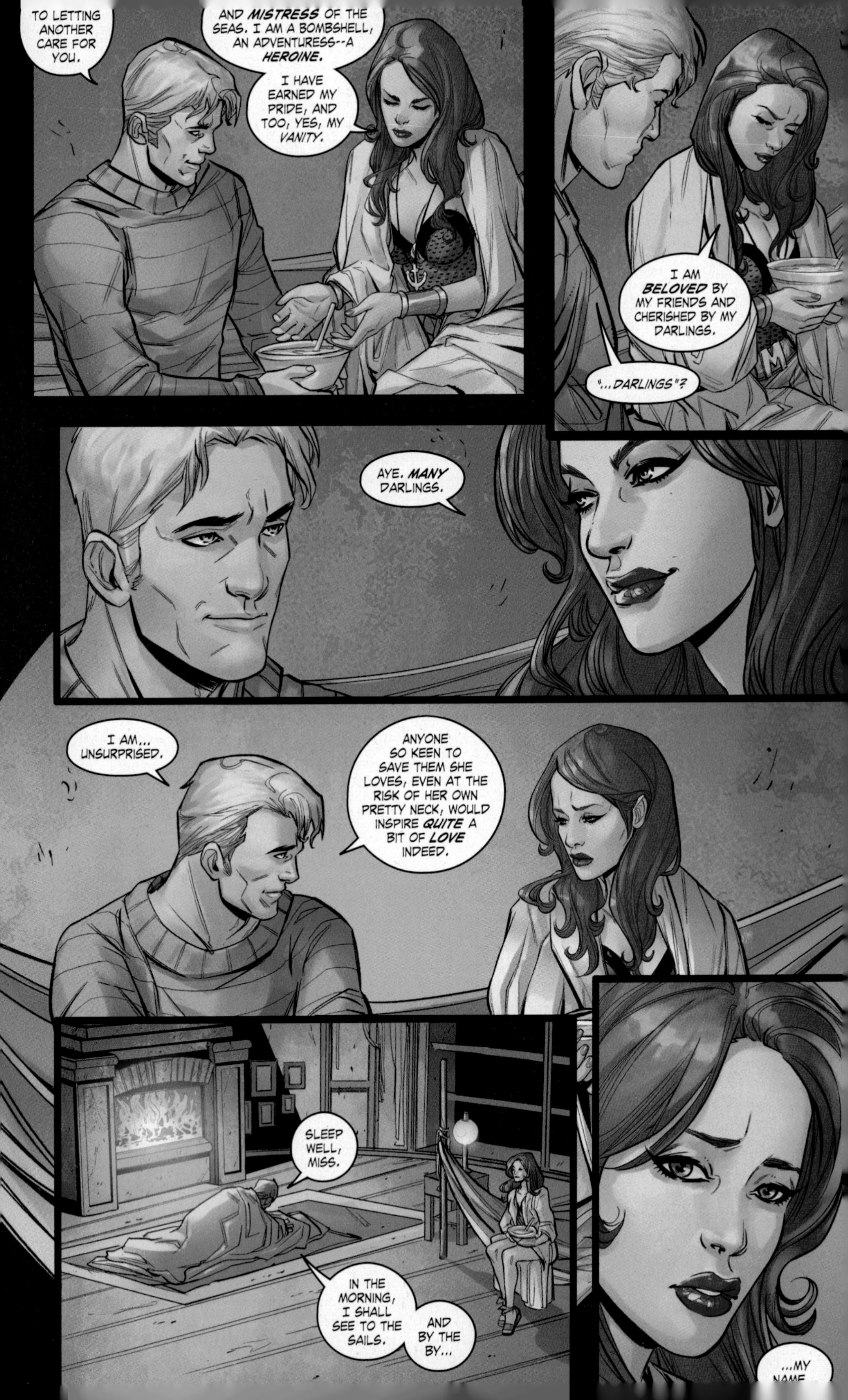
TO LETTING ANOTHER CARE FOR YOU.
AND MISTRESS OF THE SEAS. I AM A BOMBSHELL, AN ADVENTURESS--A HEROINE.
I HAVE EARNED MY PRIDE, AND TOO, YES, MY VANITY.
I AM BELOVED BY MY FRIENDS AND CHERISHED BY MY DARLINGS.
"...DARLINGS"?
AYE. MANY DARLINGS.
I AM... UNSURPRISED.
ANYONE SO KEEN TO SAVE THEM SHE LOVES, EVEN AT THE RISK OF HER OWN PRETTY NECK, WOULD INSPIRE QUITE A BIT OF LOVE INDEED.
SLEEP WELL, MISS.
IN THE MORNING, I SHALL SEE TO THE SAILS.
AND BY THE BY...
...MY

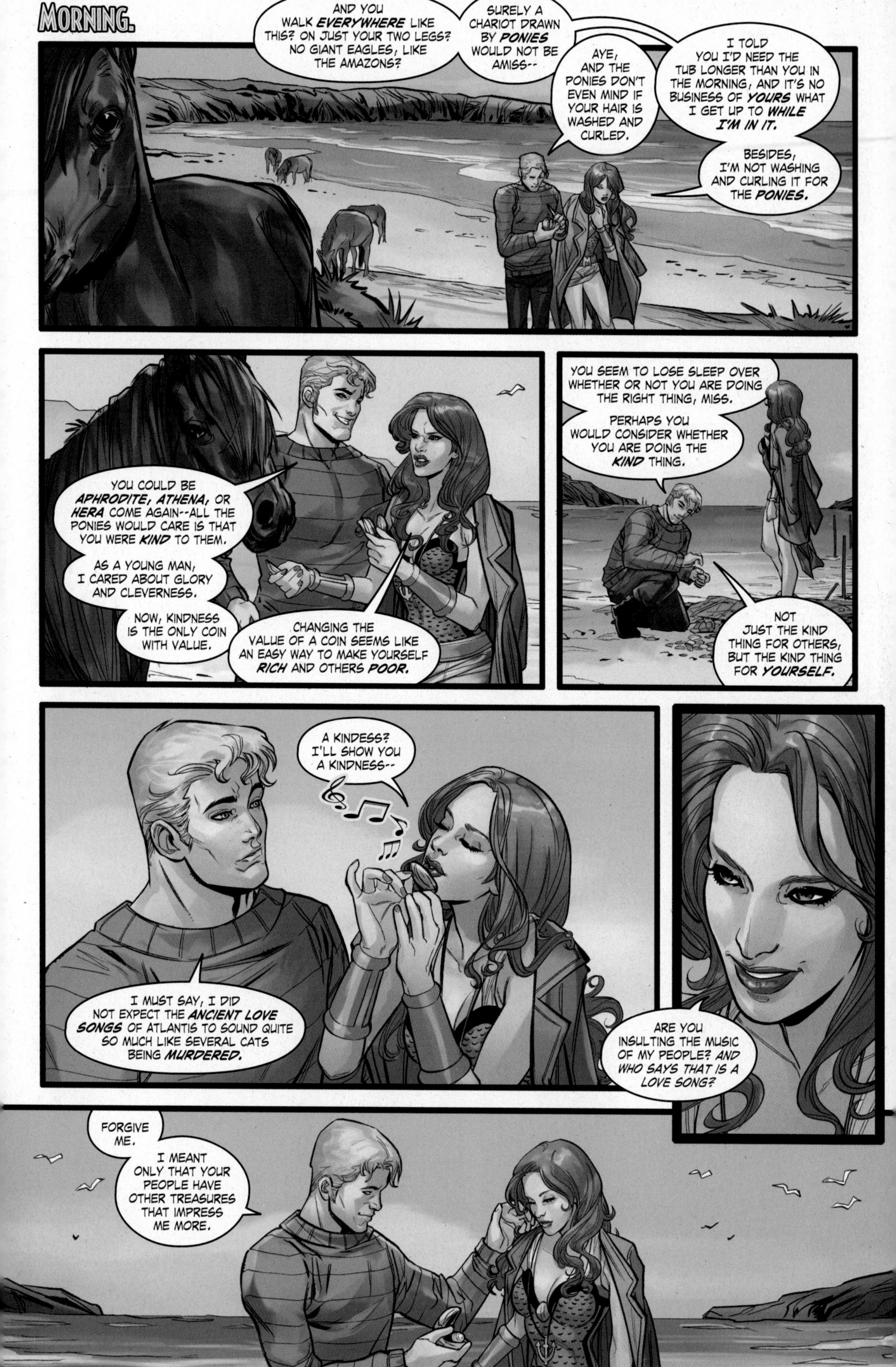
MORNING.
AND YOU WALK EVERYWHERE LIKE THIS? ON JUST YOUR TWO LEGS? NO GIANT EAGLES, LIKE THE AMAZONS?
SURELY A CHARIOT DRAWN BY PONIES WOULD NOT BE AMISS--
AYE, AND THE PONIES DON'T EVEN MIND IF YOUR HAIR IS WASHED AND CURLED.
I TOLD YOU I'D NEED THE TUB LONGER THAN YOU IN THE MORNING, AND IT'S NO BUSINESS OF YOURS WHAT I GET UP TO WHILE I'M IN IT.
BESIDES, I'M NOT WASHING AND CURLING IT FOR THE PONIES.
YOU COULD BE APHRODITE, ATHENA, OR HERA COME AGAIN--ALL THE PONIES WOULD CARE IS THAT YOU WERE KIND TO THEM.
AS A YOUNG MAN, I CARED ABOUT GLORY AND CLEVERNESS.
NOW, KINDNESS IS THE ONLY COIN WITH VALUE.
CHANGING THE VALUE OF A COIN SEEMS LIKE AN EASY WAY TO MAKE YOURSELF RICH AND OTHERS POOR.
YOU SEEM TO LOSE SLEEP OVER WHETHER OR NOT YOU ARE DOING THE RIGHT THING, MISS.
PERHAPS YOU WOULD CONSIDER WHETHER YOU ARE DOING THE KIND THING.
NOT JUST THE KIND THING FOR OTHERS, BUT THE KIND THING FOR YOURSELF.
A KINDESS? I'LL SHOW YOU A KINDNESS--
I MUST SAY, I DID NOT EXPECT THE ANCIENT LOVE SONGS OF ATLANTIS TO SOUND QUITE SO MUCH LIKE SEVERAL CATS BEING MURDERED.
ARE YOU INSULTING THE MUSIC OF MY PEOPLE? AND WHO SAYS THAT IS A LOVE SONG?
FORGIVE ME.
I MEANT ONLY THAT YOUR PEOPLE HAVE OTHER TREASURES THAT IMPRESS ME MORE.

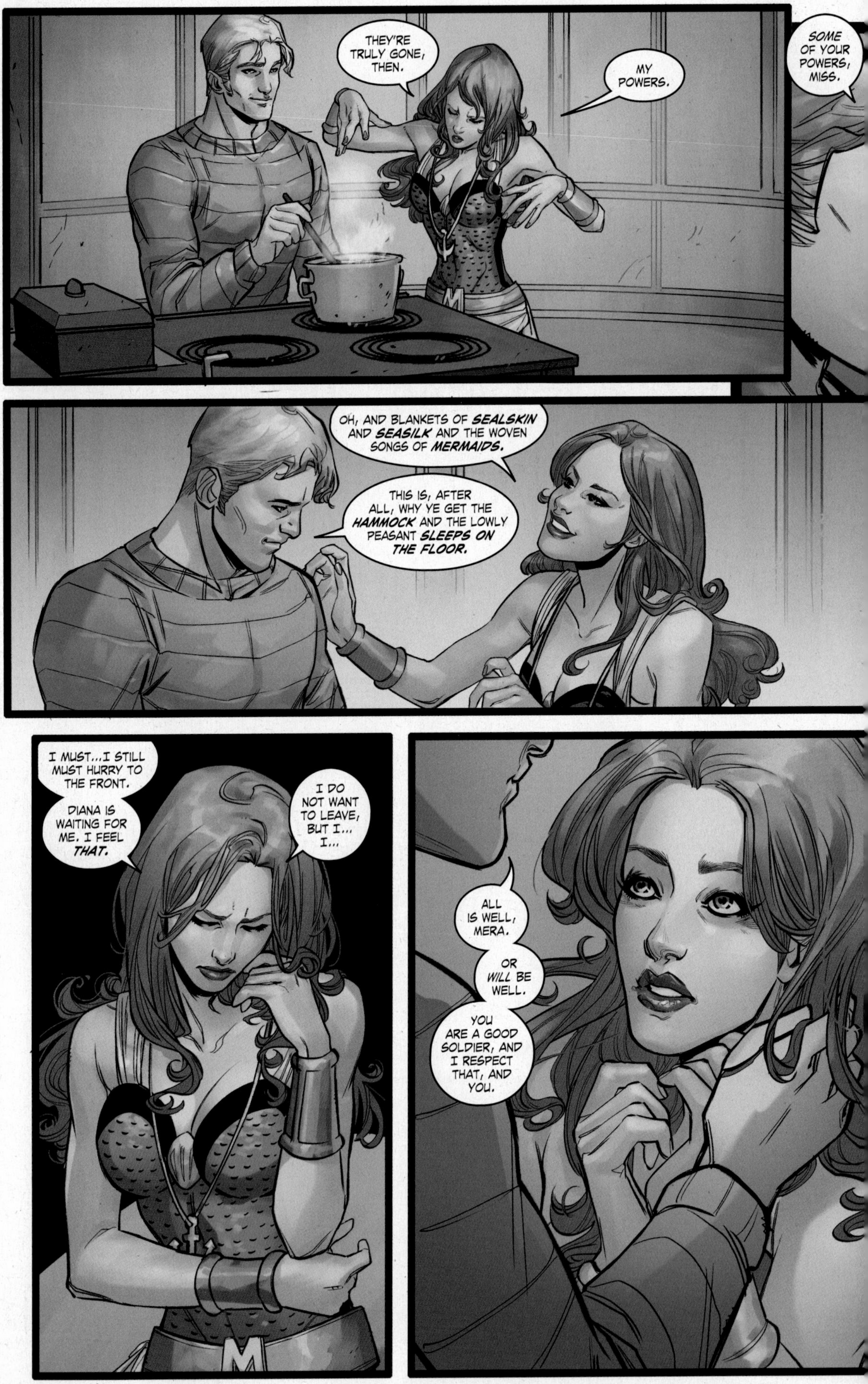
THEY'RE TRULY GONE, THEN.
MY POWERS.
SOME OF YOUR POWERS, MISS.
OH, AND BLANKETS OF SEALSKIN AND SEASILK AND THE WOVEN SONGS OF MERMAIDS.
THIS IS, AFTER ALL, WHY YE GET THE HAMMOCK AND THE LOWLY PEASANT SLEEPS ON THE FLOOR.
I MUST...I STILL MUST HURRY TO THE FRONT.
DIANA IS WAITING FOR ME. I FEEL THAT.
I DO NOT WANT TO LEAVE, BUT I... I...
ALL IS WELL, MERA.
OR WILL BE WELL.
YOU ARE A GOOD SOLDIER, AND I RESPECT THAT, AND YOU.

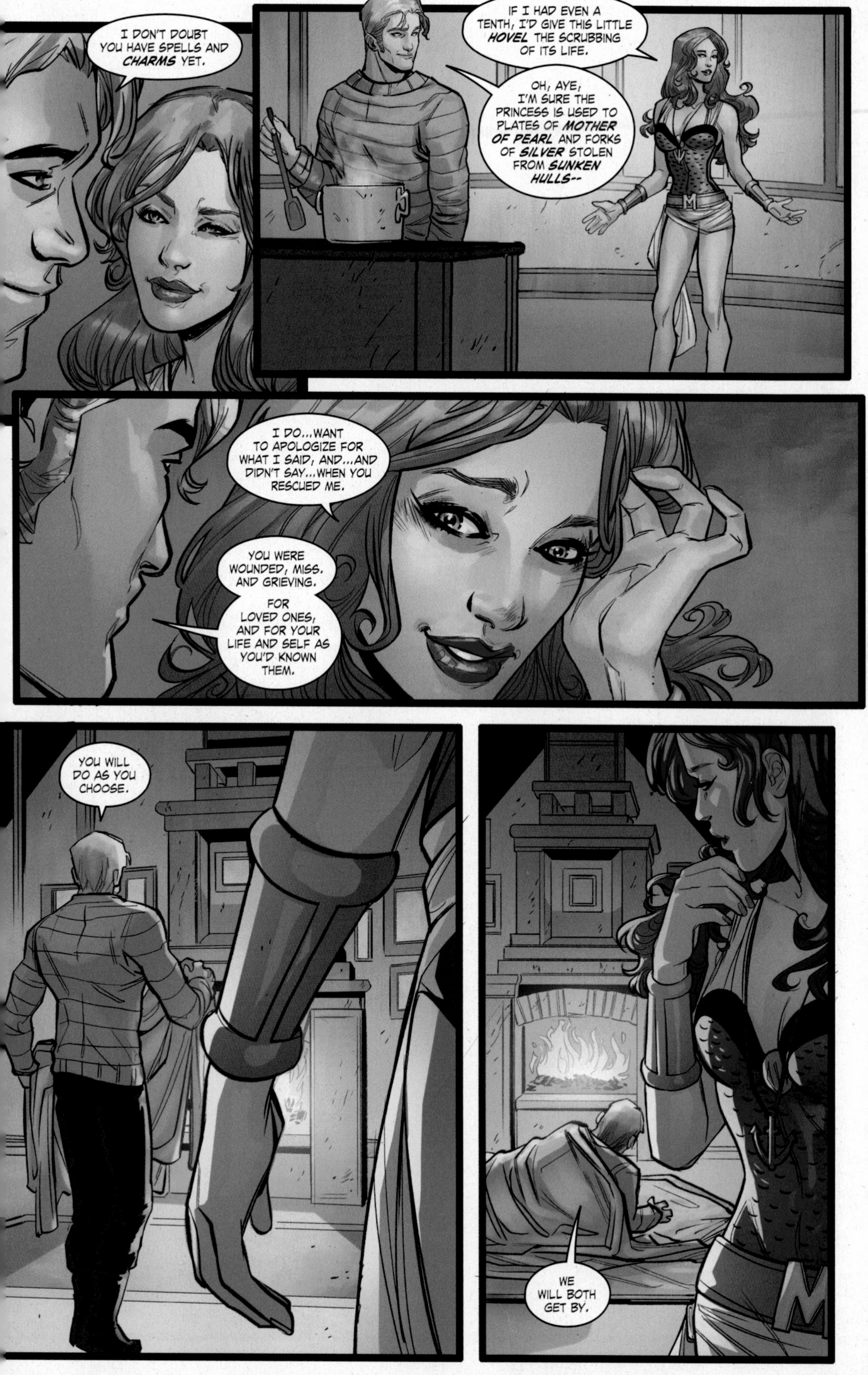
I DON'T DOUBT YOU HAVE SPELLS AND CHARMS YET.
IF I HAD EVEN A TENTH, I'D GIVE THIS LITTLE HOVEL THE SCRUBBING OF ITS LIFE.
OH, AYE, I'M SURE THE PRINCESS IS USED TO PLATES OF MOTHER OF PEARL AND FORKS OF SILVER STOLEN FROM SUNKEN HULLS--
I DO...WANT TO APOLOGIZE FOR WHAT I SAID, AND...AND DIDN'T SAY...WHEN YOU RESCUED ME.
YOU WERE WOUNDED, MISS. AND GRIEVING.
FOR LOVED ONES, AND FOR YOUR LIFE AND SELF AS YOU'D KNOWN THEM.
YOU WILL DO AS YOU CHOOSE.
WE WILL BOTH GET BY.

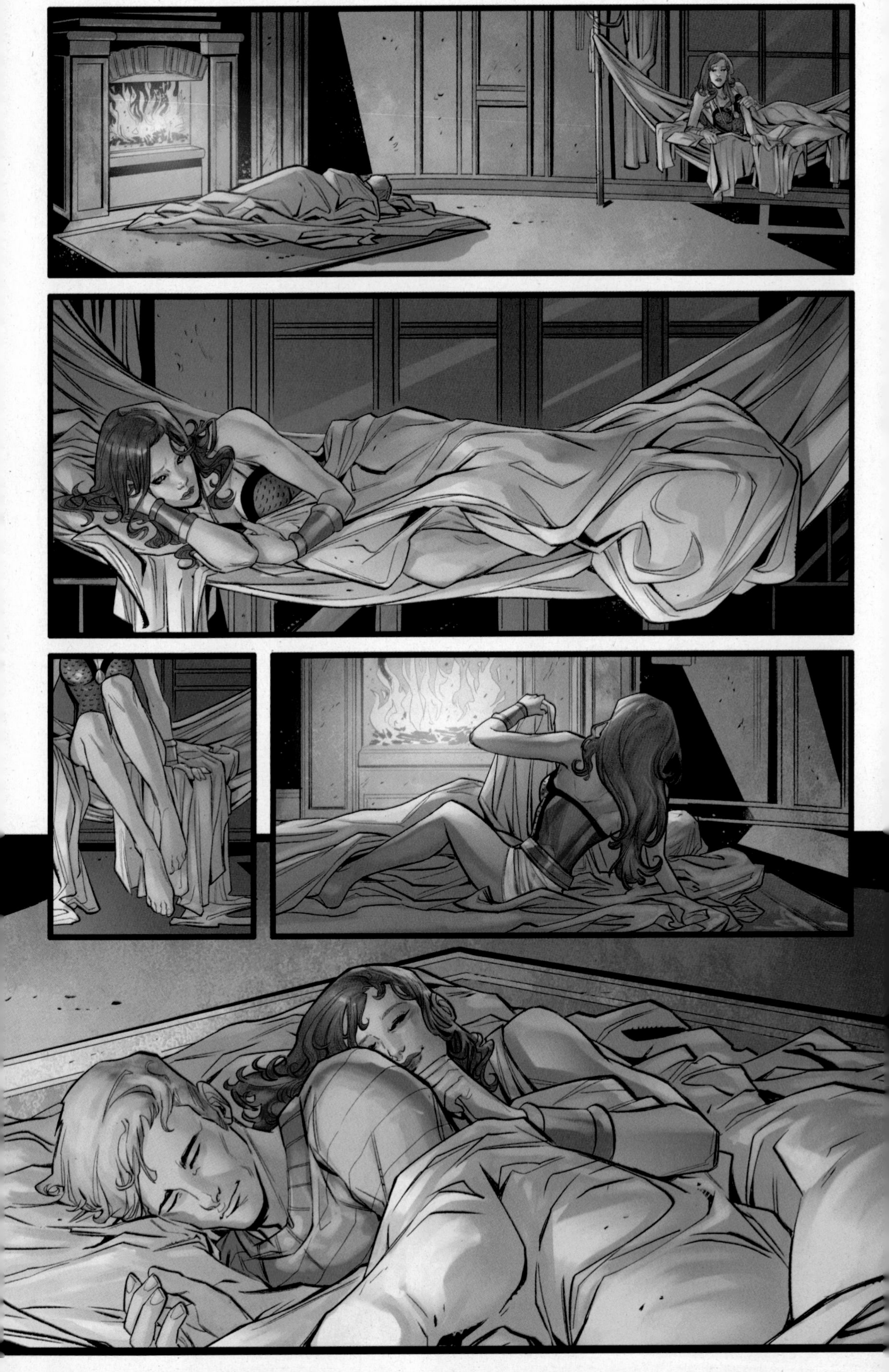

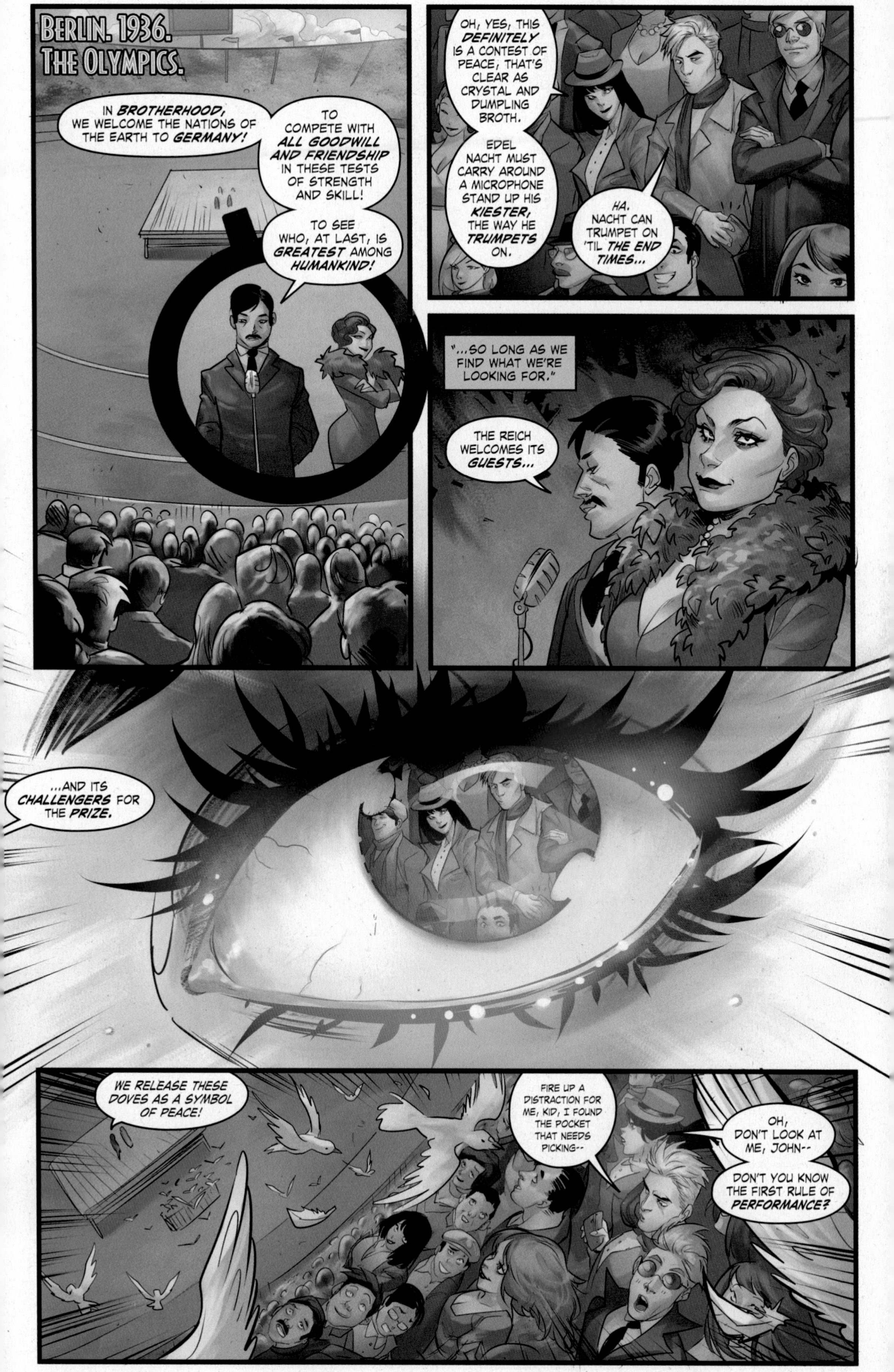
BERLIN. 1936. THE OLYMPICS.
IN BROTHERHOOD, WE WELCOME THE NATIONS OF THE EARTH TO GERMANY!
TO COMPETE WITH ALL GOODWILL AND FRIENDSHIP IN THESE TESTS OF STRENGTH AND SKILL!
TO SEE WHO, AT LAST, IS GREATEST AMONG HUMANKIND!
OH, YES, THIS DEFINITELY IS A CONTEST OF PEACE; THAT'S CLEAR AS CRYSTAL AND DUMPLING BROTH.
EDEL NACHT MUST CARRY AROUND A MICROPHONE STAND UP HIS KIESTER, THE WAY HE TRUMPETS ON.
HA. NACHT CAN TRUMPET ON 'TIL THE END TIMES...
"...SO LONG AS WE FIND WHAT WE'RE LOOKING FOR."
THE REICH WELCOMES ITS GUESTS...
...AND ITS CHALLENGERS FOR THE PRIZE.
WE RELEASE THESE DOVES AS A SYMBOL OF PEACE!
FIRE UP A DISTRACTION FOR ME, KID, I FOUND THE POCKET THAT NEEDS PICKING--
OH, DON'T LOOK AT ME, JOHN--
DON'T YOU KNOW THE FIRST RULE OF PERFORMANCE?

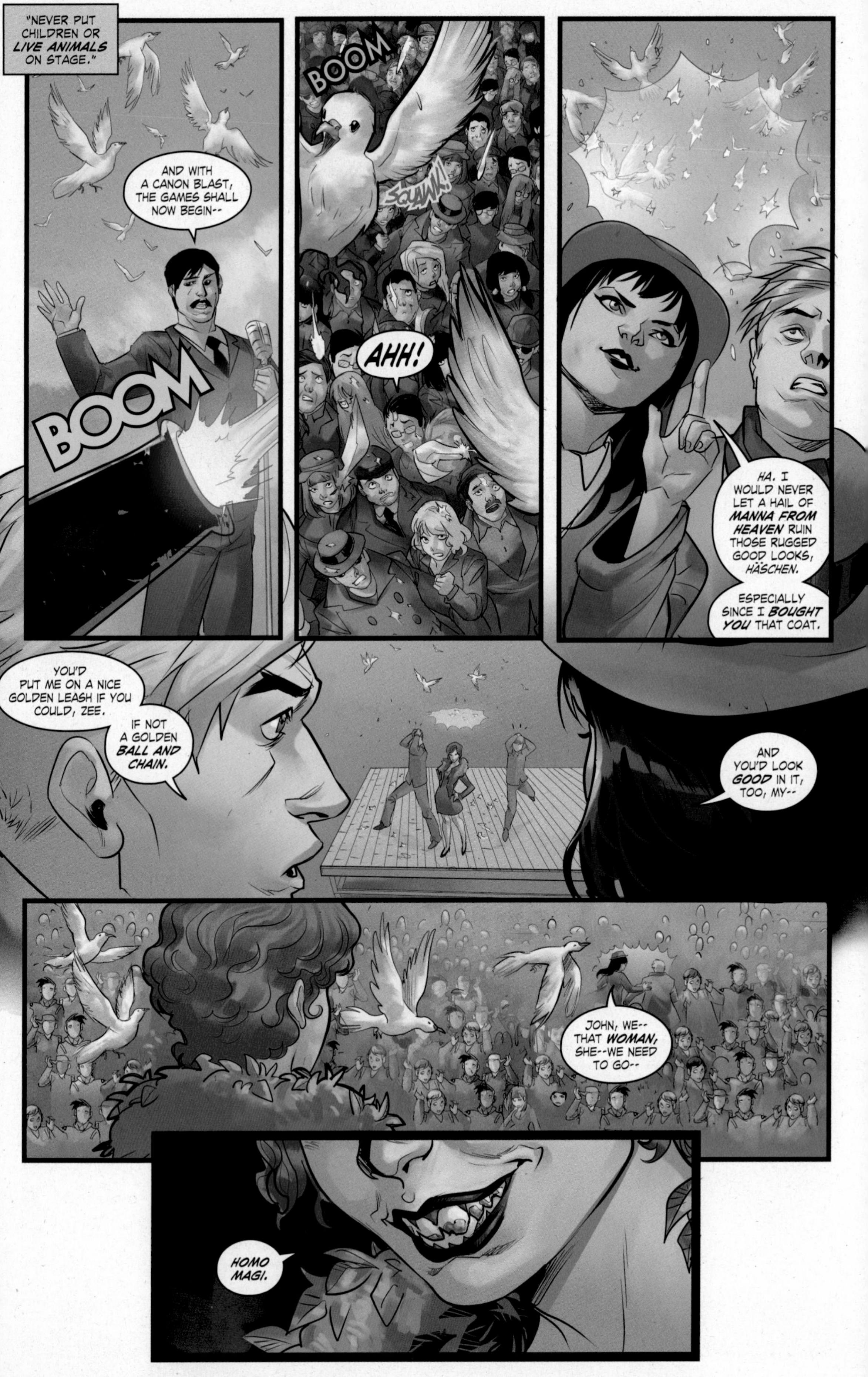
"NEVER PUT CHILDREN OR LIVE ANIMALS ON STAGE."
AND WITH A CANON BLAST, THE GAMES SHALL NOW BEGIN--
BOOM
BOOM
SQUAWK!
AHH!
HA. I WOULD NEVER LET A HAIL OF MANNA FROM HEAVEN RUIN THOSE RUGGED GOOD LOOKS, HÄSCHEN.
ESPECIALLY SINCE I BOUGHT YOU THAT COAT.
YOU'D PUT ME ON A NICE GOLDEN LEASH IF YOU COULD, ZEE.
IF NOT A GOLDEN BALL AND CHAIN.
AND YOU'D LOOK GOOD IN IT, TOO, MY--
JOHN, WE-- THAT WOMAN, SHE--WE NEED TO GO--
HOMO MAGI.

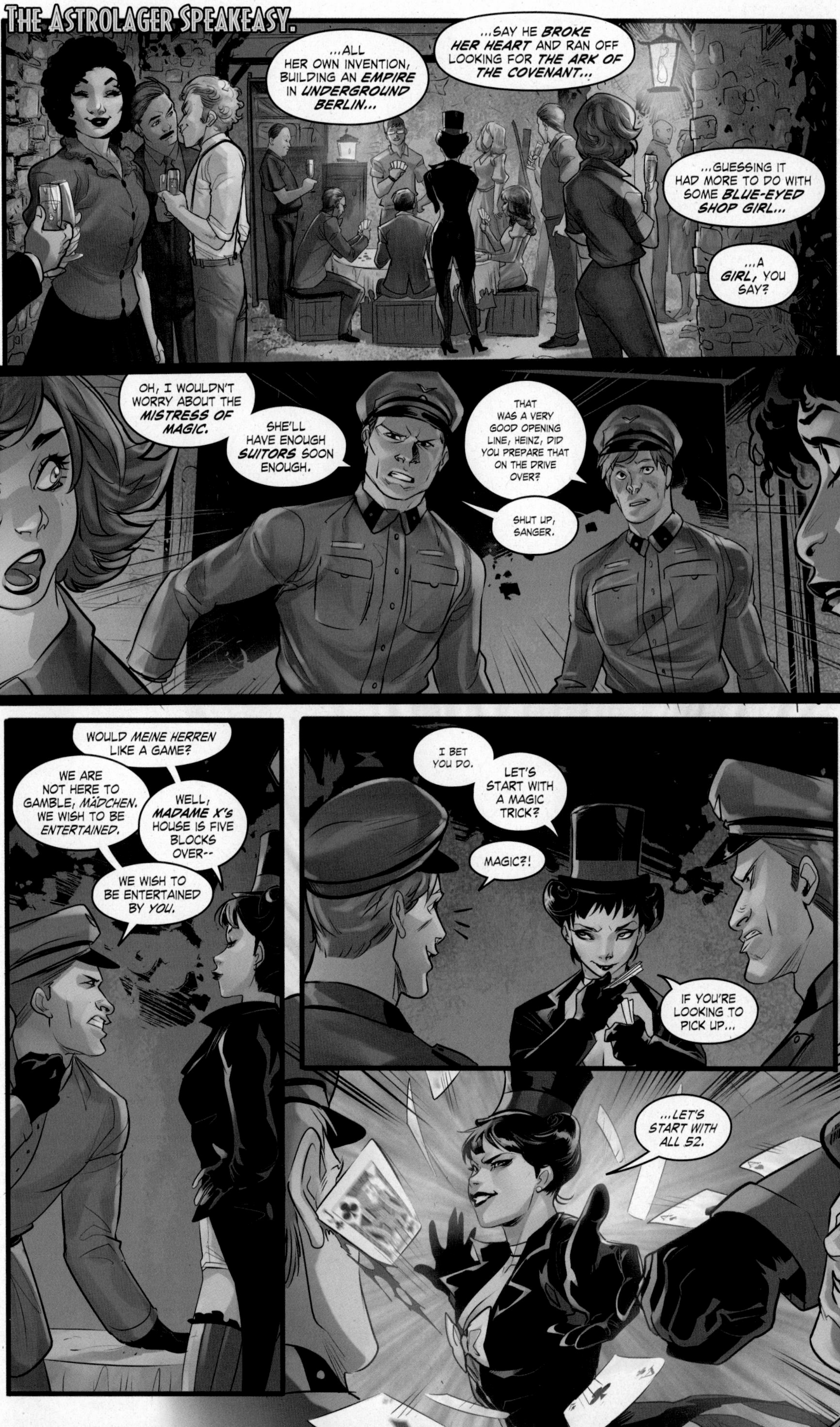
THE ASTROLAGER SPEAKEASY.
...ALL HER OWN INVENTION, BUILDING AN EMPIRE IN UNDERGROUND BERLIN...
...SAY HE BROKE HER HEART AND RAN OFF LOOKING FOR THE ARK OF THE COVENANT...
...GUESSING IT HAD MORE TO DO WITH SOME BLUE-EYED SHOP GIRL...
...A GIRL, YOU SAY?
OH, I WOULDN'T WORRY ABOUT THE MISTRESS OF MAGIC.
SHE'LL HAVE ENOUGH SUITORS SOON ENOUGH.
THAT WAS A VERY GOOD OPENING LINE, HEINZ, DID YOU PREPARE THAT ON THE DRIVE OVER?
SHUT UP, SANGER.
WOULD MEINE HERREN LIKE A GAME?
WE ARE NOT HERE TO GAMBLE, MÄDCHEN. WE WISH TO BE ENTERTAINED.
WELL, MADAME X's HOUSE IS FIVE BLOCKS OVER--
WE WISH TO BE ENTERTAINED BY YOU.
I BET YOU DO.
LET'S START WITH A MAGIC TRICK?
MAGIC?!
IF YOU'RE LOOKING TO PICK UP...
...LET'S START WITH ALL 52.

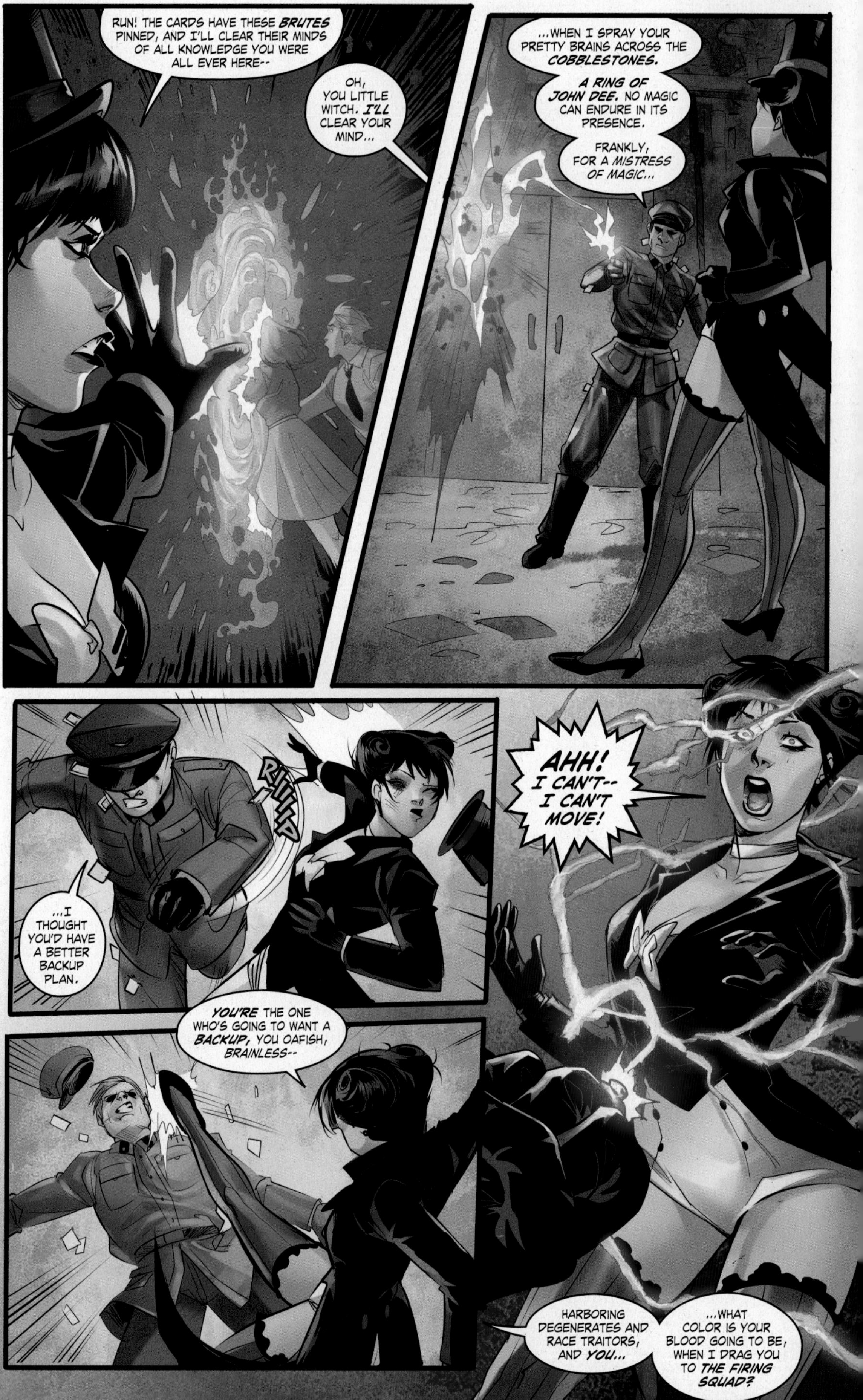
RUN! THE CARDS HAVE THESE BRUTES PINNED, AND I'LL CLEAR THEIR MINDS OF ALL KNOWLEDGE YOU WERE ALL EVER HERE--
OH, YOU LITTLE WITCH. I'LL CLEAR YOUR MIND...
...WHEN I SPRAY YOUR PRETTY BRAINS ACROSS THE COBBLESTONES.
A RING OF JOHN DEE. NO MAGIC CAN ENDURE IN ITS PRESENCE.
FRANKLY, FOR A MISTRESS OF MAGIC...
RIIIP
...I THOUGHT YOU'D HAVE A BETTER BACKUP PLAN.
YOU'RE THE ONE WHO'S GOING TO WANT A BACKUP, YOU OAFISH, BRAINLESS--
AHH! I CAN'T-- I CAN'T MOVE!
HARBORING DEGENERATES AND RACE TRAITORS, AND YOU...
...WHAT COLOR IS YOUR BLOOD GOING TO BE, WHEN I DRAG YOU TO THE FIRING SQUAD?

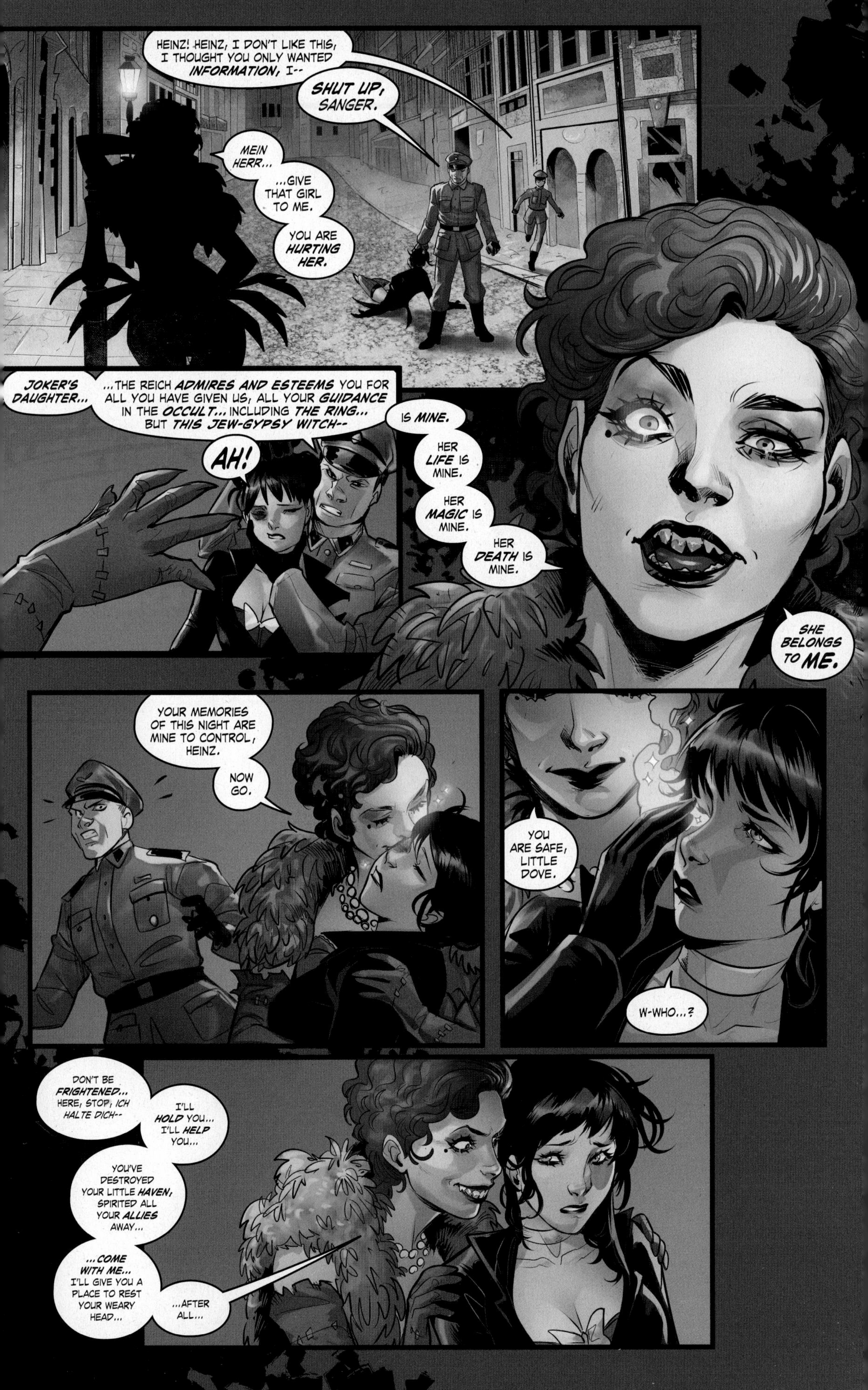
HEINZ! HEINZ, I DON'T LIKE THIS, I THOUGHT YOU ONLY WANTED INFORMATION, I--
SHUT UP, SANGER.
MEIN HERR...
...GIVE THAT GIRL TO ME.
YOU ARE HURTING HER.
JOKER'S DAUGHTER...
...THE REICH ADMIRES AND ESTEEMS YOU FOR ALL YOU HAVE GIVEN US, ALL YOUR GUIDANCE IN THE OCCULT... INCLUDING THE RING... BUT THIS JEW-GYPSY WITCH--
AH!
IS MINE.
HER LIFE IS MINE.
HER MAGIC IS MINE.
HER DEATH IS MINE.
SHE BELONGS TO ME.
YOUR MEMORIES OF THIS NIGHT ARE MINE TO CONTROL, HEINZ.
NOW GO.
YOU ARE SAFE, LITTLE DOVE.
W-WHO...?
DON'T BE FRIGHTENED... HERE, STOP, ICH HALTE DICH--
I'LL HOLD YOU... I'LL HELP YOU...
YOU'VE DESTROYED YOUR LITTLE HAVEN, SPIRITED ALL YOUR ALLIES AWAY...
...COME WITH ME... I'LL GIVE YOU A PLACE TO REST YOUR WEARY HEAD...
...AFTER ALL...

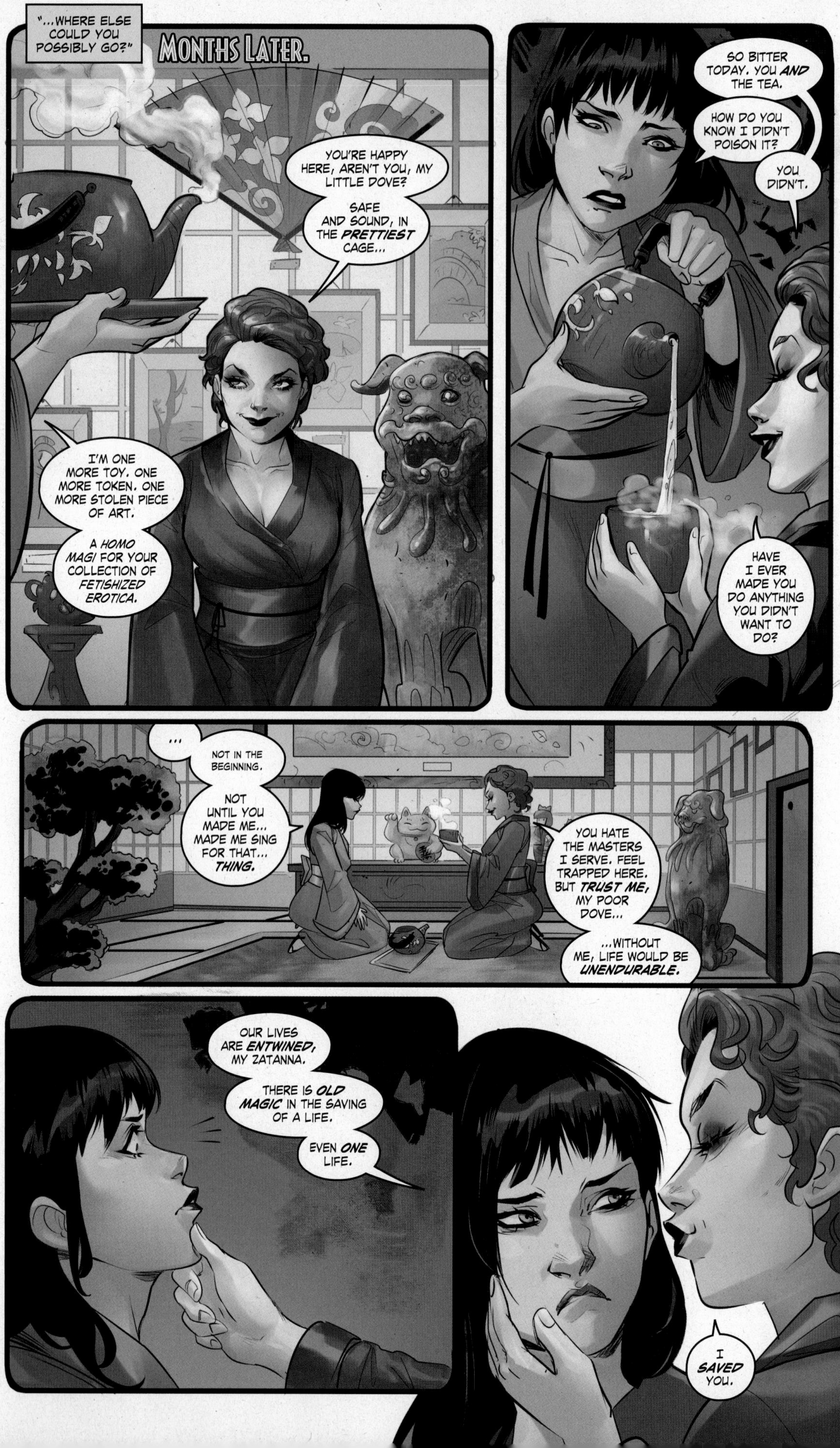

"...WHERE ELSE COULD YOU POSSIBLY GO?"
MONTHS LATER.
YOU'RE HAPPY HERE, AREN'T YOU, MY LITTLE DOVE?
SAFE AND SOUND, IN THE PRETTIEST CAGE...
I'M ONE MORE TOY. ONE MORE TOKEN. ONE MORE STOLEN PIECE OF ART.
A HOMO MAGI FOR YOUR COLLECTION OF FETISHIZED EROTICA.
SO BITTER TODAY. YOU AND THE TEA.
HOW DO YOU KNOW I DIDN'T POISON IT?
YOU DIDN'T.
HAVE I EVER MADE YOU DO ANYTHING YOU DIDN'T WANT TO DO?
...
NOT IN THE BEGINNING.
NOT UNTIL YOU MADE ME... MADE ME SING FOR THAT... THING.
YOU HATE THE MASTERS I SERVE. FEEL TRAPPED HERE. BUT TRUST ME, MY POOR DOVE...
...WITHOUT ME, LIFE WOULD BE UNENDURABLE.
OUR LIVES ARE ENTWINED, MY ZATANNA.
THERE IS OLD MAGIC IN THE SAVING OF A LIFE.
EVEN ONE LIFE.
I SAVED YOU.

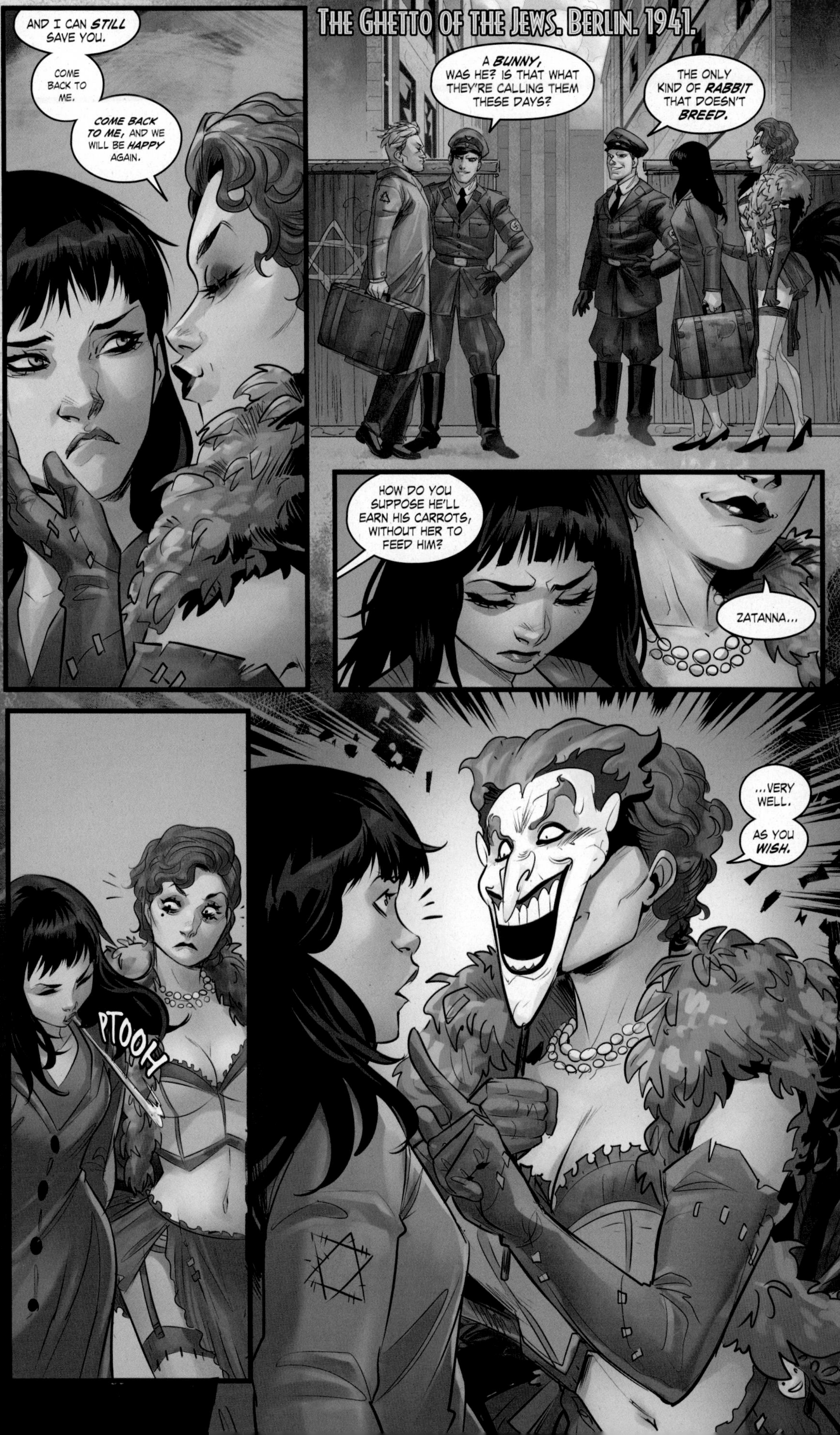

AND I CAN STILL SAVE YOU.
COME BACK TO ME.
COME BACK TO ME, AND WE WILL BE HAPPY AGAIN.
THE GHETTO OF THE JEWS. BERLIN. 1941.
A BUNNY, WAS HE? IS THAT WHAT THEY'RE CALLING THEM THESE DAYS?
THE ONLY KIND OF RABBIT THAT DOESN'T BREED.
HOW DO YOU SUPPOSE HE'LL EARN HIS CARROTS, WITHOUT HER TO FEED HIM?
ZATANNA...
PTOOH
...VERY WELL.
AS YOU WISH.

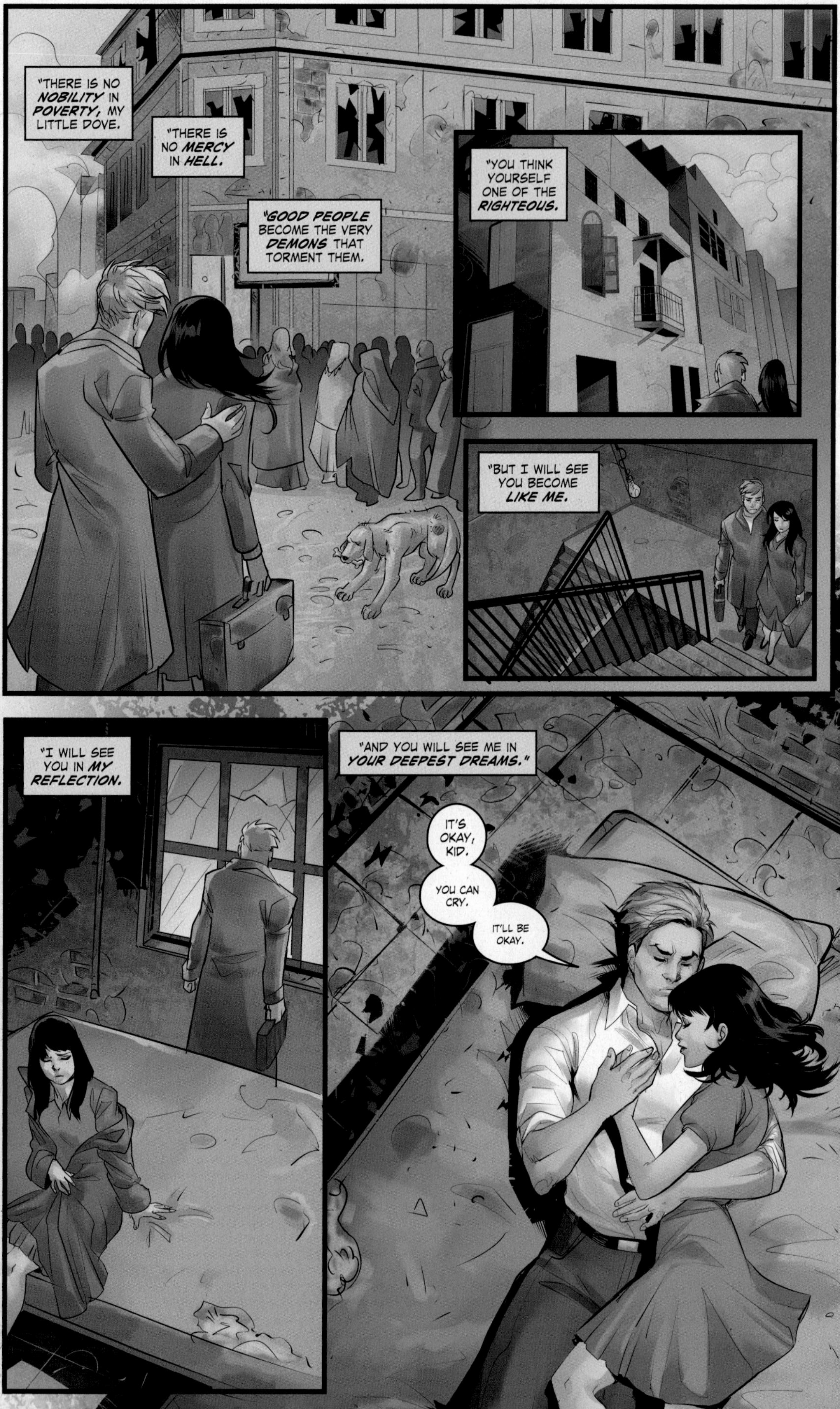
"THERE IS NO NOBILITY IN POVERTY, MY LITTLE DOVE.
"THERE IS NO MERCY IN HELL.
"GOOD PEOPLE BECOME THE VERY DEMONS THAT TORMENT THEM.
"YOU THINK YOURSELF ONE OF THE RIGHTEOUS.
"BUT I WILL SEE YOU BECOME LIKE ME.
"I WILL SEE YOU IN MY REFLECTION.
"AND YOU WILL SEE ME IN YOUR DEEPEST DREAMS."
IT'S OKAY, KID.
YOU CAN CRY.
IT'LL BE OKAY.

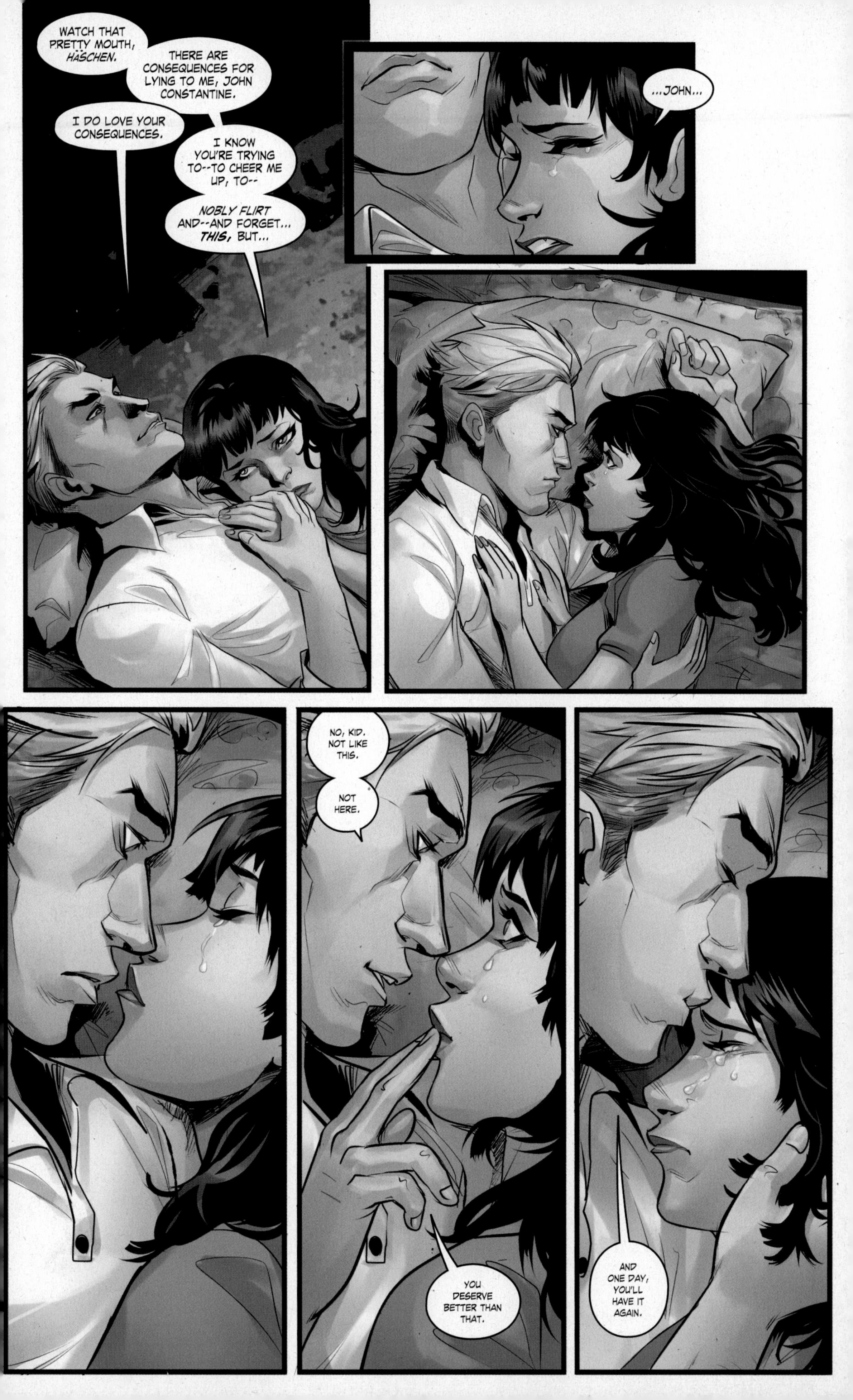
WATCH THAT PRETTY MOUTH, HÄSCHEN.
THERE ARE CONSEQUENCES FOR LYING TO ME, JOHN CONSTANTINE.
I DO LOVE YOUR CONSEQUENCES.
I KNOW YOU'RE TRYING TO--TO CHEER ME UP, TO--
NOBLY FLIRT AND--AND FORGET... THIS, BUT...
...JOHN...
NO, KID. NOT LIKE THIS.
NOT HERE.
YOU DESERVE BETTER THAN THAT.
AND ONE DAY, YOU'LL HAVE IT AGAIN.

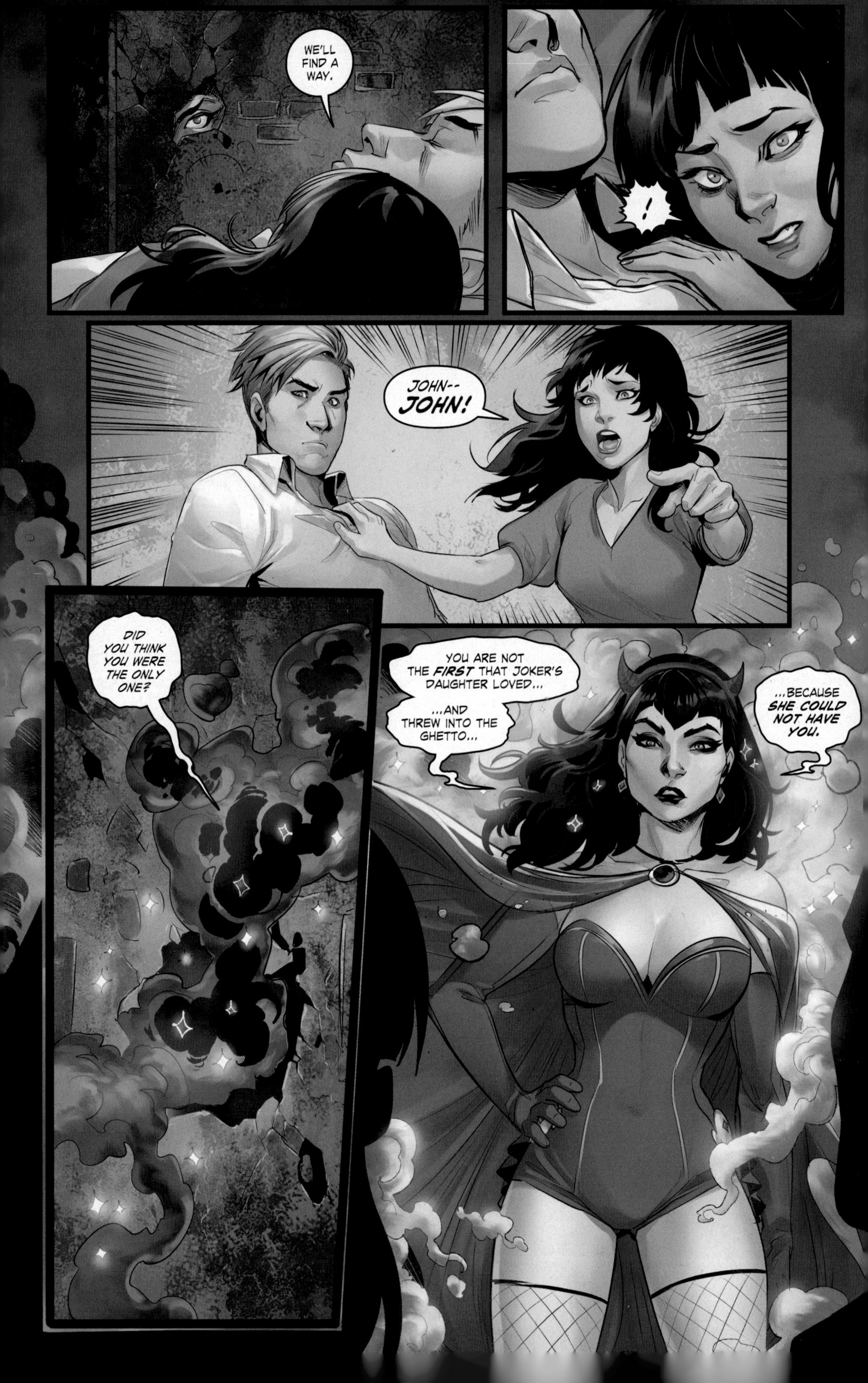
WE'LL FIND A WAY.
!
JOHN-- JOHN!
DID YOU THINK YOU WERE THE ONLY ONE?
YOU ARE NOT THE FIRST THAT JOKER'S DAUGHTER LOVED...
...AND THREW INTO THE GHETTO...
...BECAUSE SHE COULD NOT HAVE YOU.

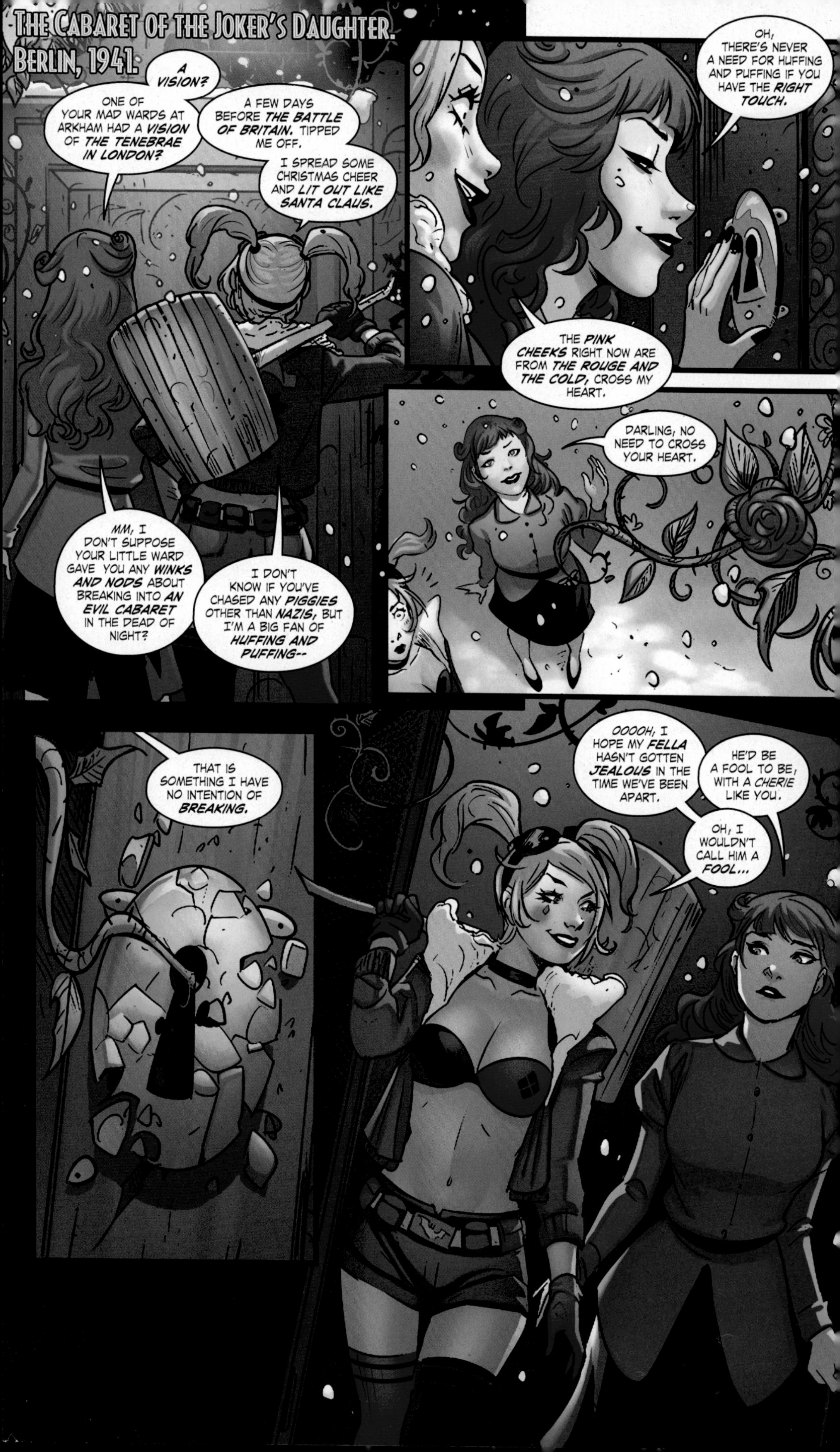

THE CABARET OF THE JOKER'S DAUGHTER. BERLIN, 1941.
A VISION?
ONE OF YOUR MAD WARDS AT ARKHAM HAD A VISION OF THE TENEBRAE IN LONDON?
A FEW DAYS BEFORE THE BATTLE OF BRITAIN. TIPPED ME OFF.
I SPREAD SOME CHRISTMAS CHEER AND LIT OUT LIKE SANTA CLAUS.
MM, I DON'T SUPPOSE YOUR LITTLE WARD GAVE YOU ANY WINKS AND NODS ABOUT BREAKING INTO AN EVIL CABARET IN THE DEAD OF NIGHT?
I DON'T KNOW IF YOU'VE CHASED ANY PIGGIES OTHER THAN NAZIS, BUT I'M A BIG FAN OF HUFFING AND PUFFING--
OH, THERE'S NEVER A NEED FOR HUFFING AND PUFFING IF YOU HAVE THE RIGHT TOUCH.
THE PINK CHEEKS RIGHT NOW ARE FROM THE ROUGE AND THE COLD, CROSS MY HEART.
DARLING, NO NEED TO CROSS YOUR HEART.
THAT IS SOMETHING I HAVE NO INTENTION OF BREAKING.
OOOOH, I HOPE MY FELLA HASN'T GOTTEN JEALOUS IN THE TIME WE'VE BEEN APART.
HE'D BE A FOOL TO BE, WITH A CHERIE LIKE YOU.
OH, I WOULDN'T CALL HIM A FOOL...

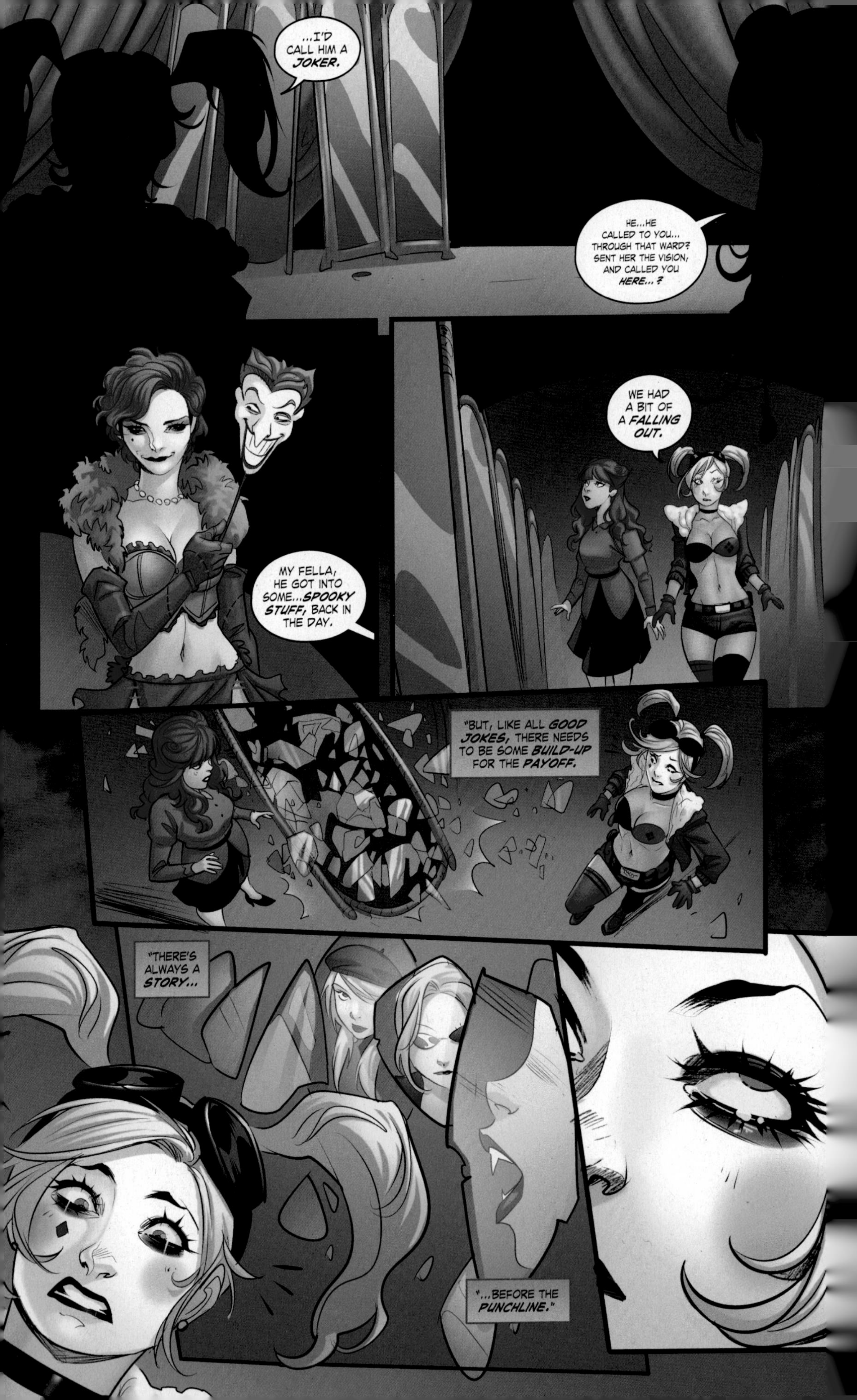
...I'D CALL HIM A JOKER.
HE...HE CALLED TO YOU... THROUGH THAT WARD? SENT HER THE VISION, AND CALLED YOU HERE...?
MY FELLA, HE GOT INTO SOME...SPOOKY STUFF, BACK IN THE DAY.
WE HAD A BIT OF A FALLING OUT.
"BUT, LIKE ALL GOOD JOKES, THERE NEEDS TO BE SOME BUILD-UP FOR THE PAYOFF.
"THERE'S ALWAYS A STORY...
"...BEFORE THE PUNCHLINE."

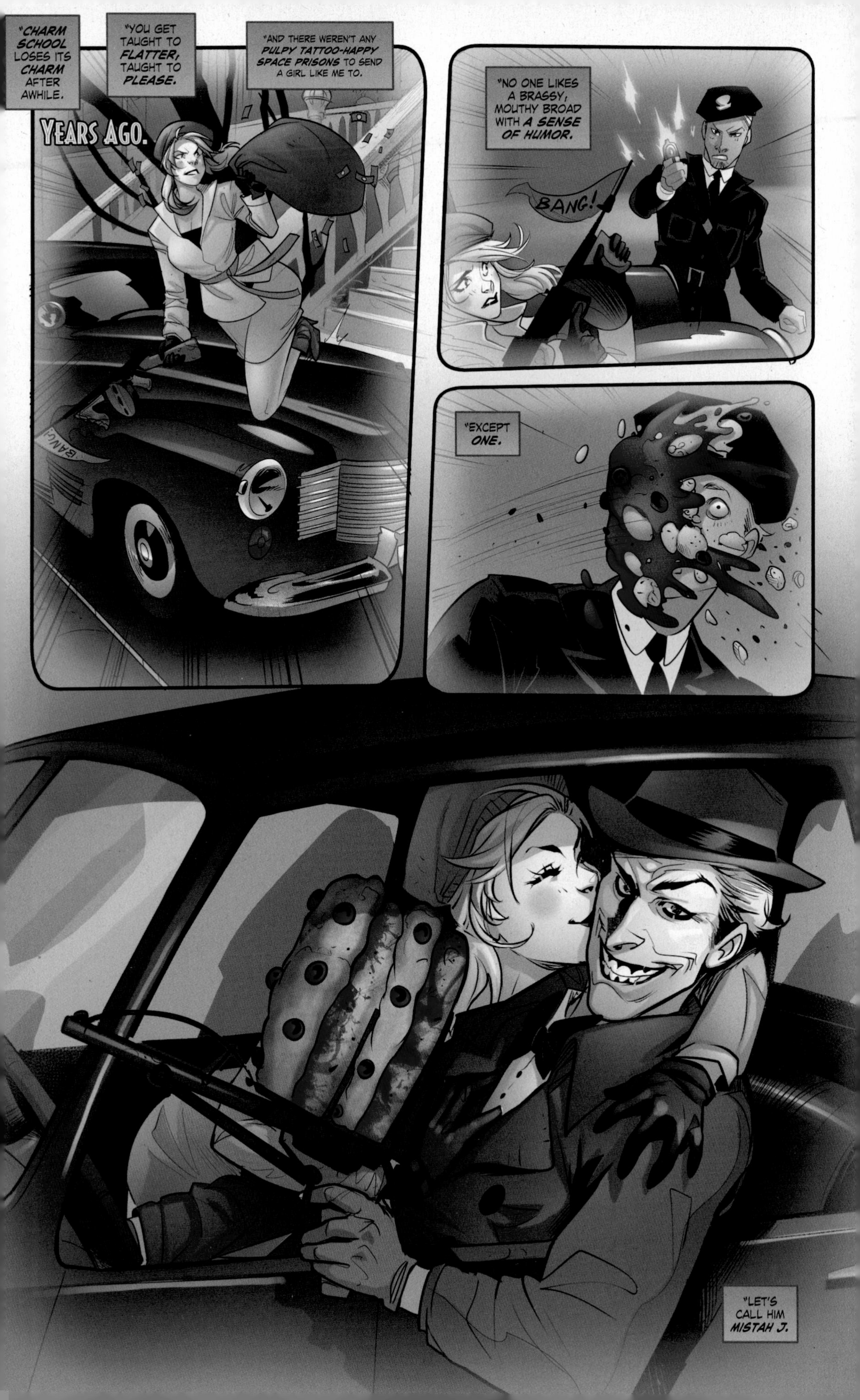
"CHARM SCHOOL LOSES ITS CHARM AFTER AWHILE.
"YOU GET TAUGHT TO FLATTER, TAUGHT TO PLEASE.
"AND THERE WEREN'T ANY PULPY TATTOO-HAPPY SPACE PRISONS TO SEND A GIRL LIKE ME TO.
YEARS AGO.
BANG!
"NO ONE LIKES A BRASSY, MOUTHY BROAD WITH A SENSE OF HUMOR.
BANG!
"EXCEPT ONE.
"LET'S CALL HIM MISTAH J.

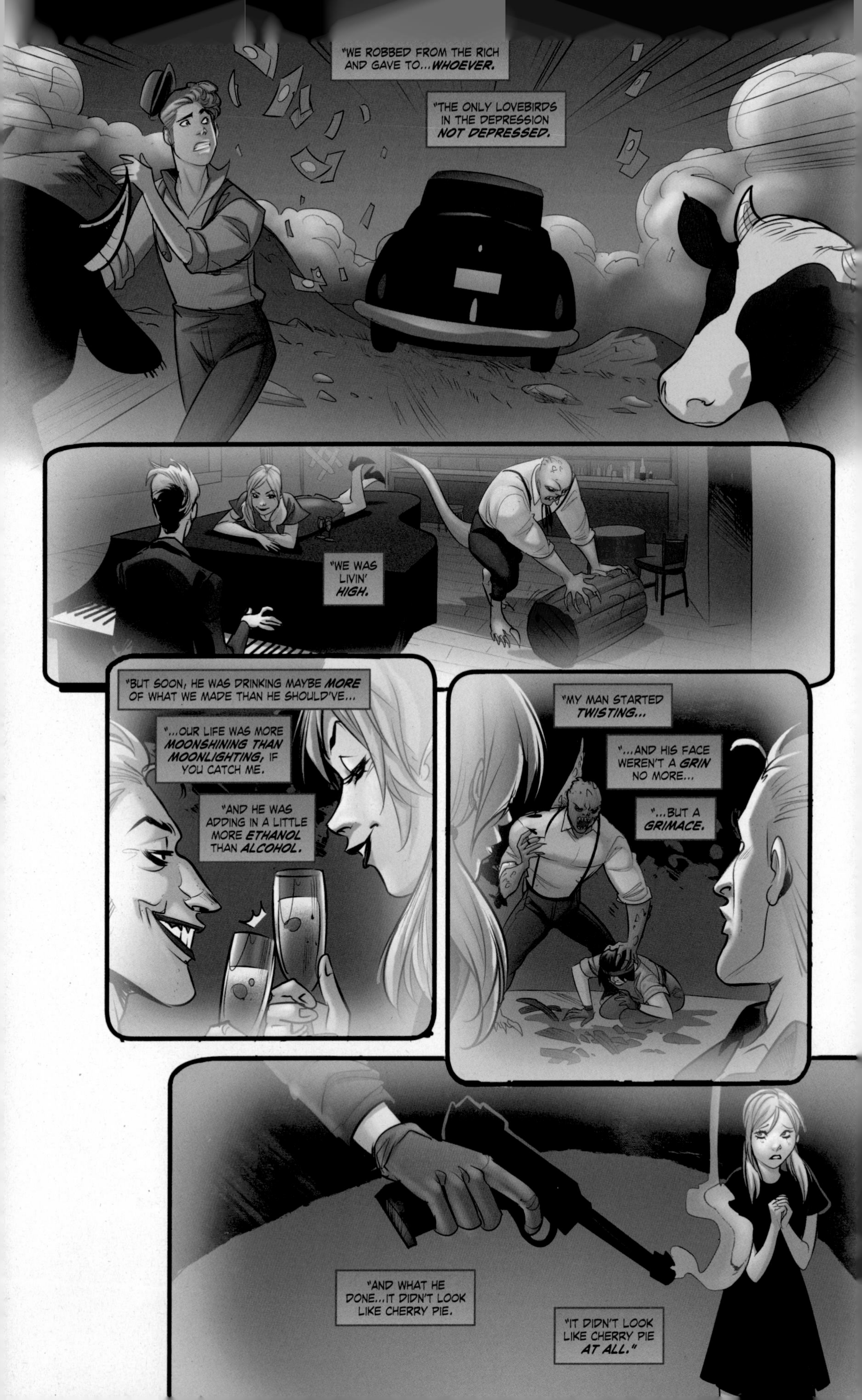
"WE ROBBED FROM THE RICH AND GAVE TO...WHOEVER.
"THE ONLY LOVEBIRDS IN THE DEPRESSION NOT DEPRESSED.
"WE WAS LIVIN' HIGH.
"BUT SOON, HE WAS DRINKING MAYBE MORE OF WHAT WE MADE THAN HE SHOULD'VE...
"...OUR LIFE WAS MORE MOONSHINING THAN MOONLIGHTING, IF YOU CATCH ME.
"AND HE WAS ADDING IN A LITTLE MORE ETHANOL THAN ALCOHOL.
"MY MAN STARTED TWISTING...
"...AND HIS FACE WEREN'T A GRIN NO MORE...
"...BUT A GRIMACE.
"AND WHAT HE DONE...IT DIDN'T LOOK LIKE CHERRY PIE.
"IT DIDN'T LOOK LIKE CHERRY PIE AT ALL."

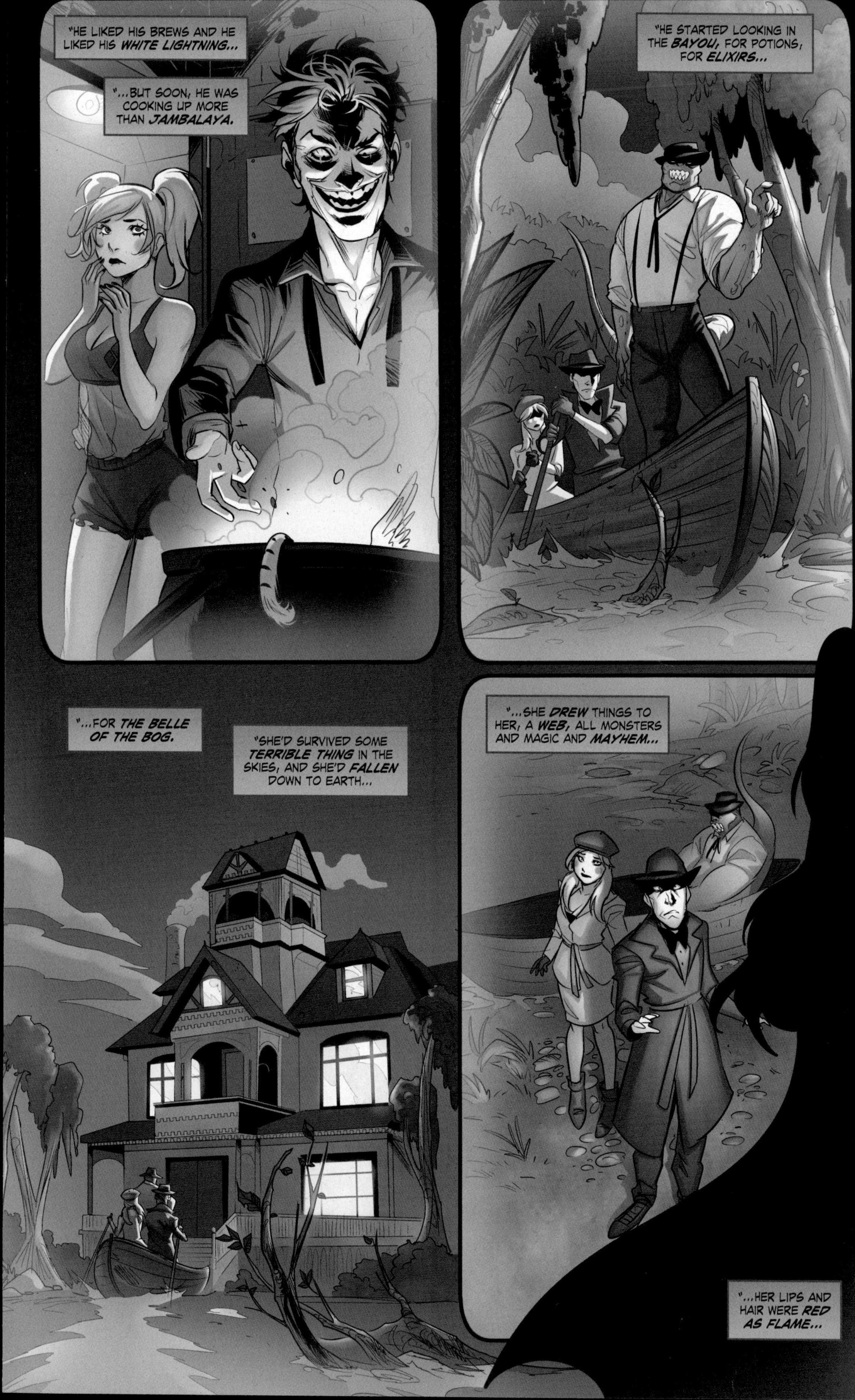
"HE LIKED HIS BREWS AND HE LIKED HIS WHITE LIGHTNING...
"...BUT SOON, HE WAS COOKING UP MORE THAN JAMBALAYA.
"HE STARTED LOOKING IN THE BAYOU, FOR POTIONS, FOR ELIXIRS...
"...FOR THE BELLE OF THE BOG.
"SHE'D SURVIVED SOME TERRIBLE THING IN THE SKIES, AND SHE'D FALLEN DOWN TO EARTH...
"...SHE DREW THINGS TO HER, A WEB, ALL MONSTERS AND MAGIC AND MAYHEM...
"...HER LIPS AND HAIR WERE RED AS FLAME...

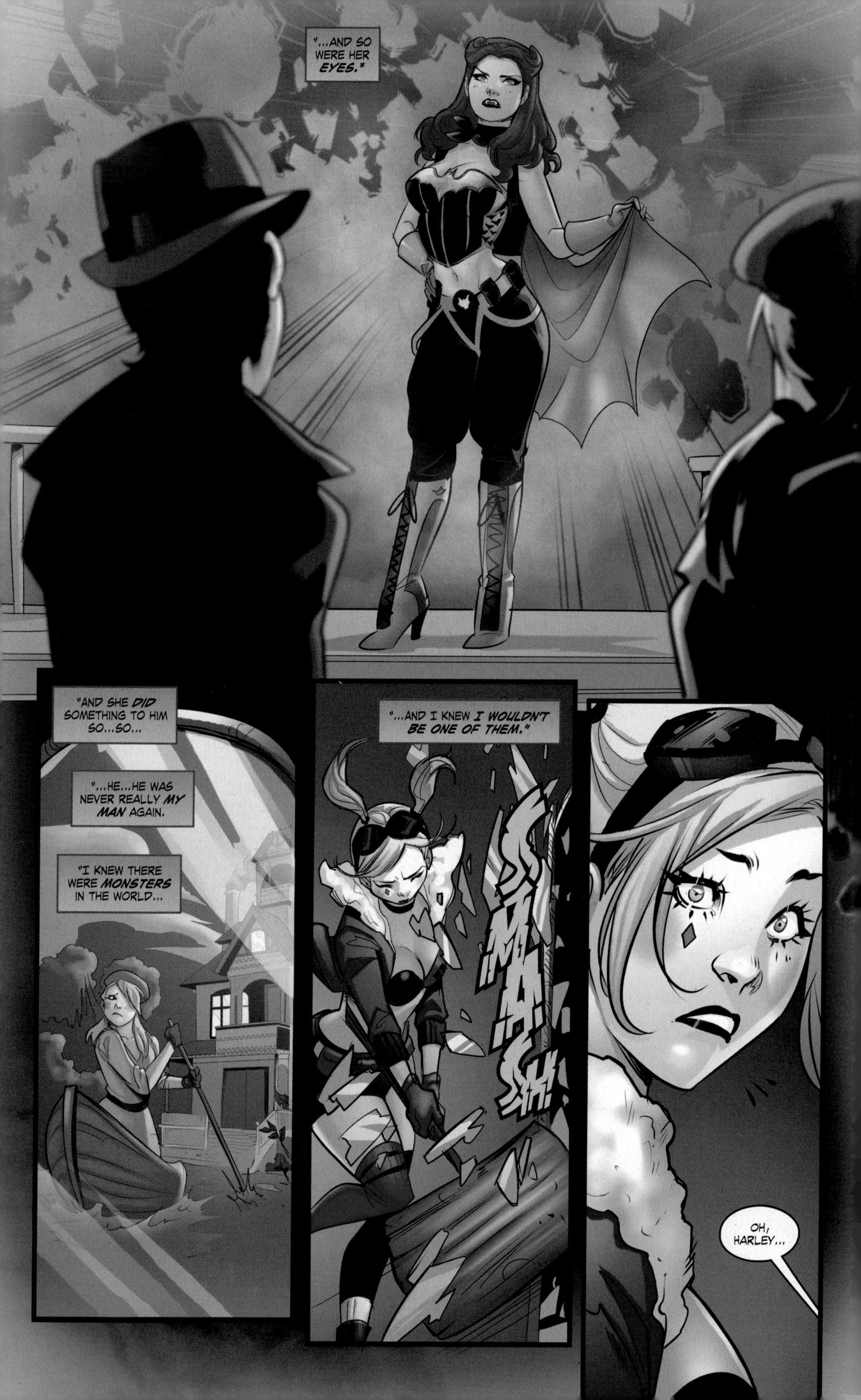
"...AND SO WERE HER *EYES*.*
"AND SHE *DID* SOMETHING TO HIM SO...SO...
"...HE...HE WAS NEVER REALLY *MY MAN* AGAIN.
"I KNEW THERE WERE *MONSTERS* IN THE WORLD...
"...AND I KNEW *I WOULDN'T BE ONE OF THEM*."
SMASH!
OH, HARLEY...

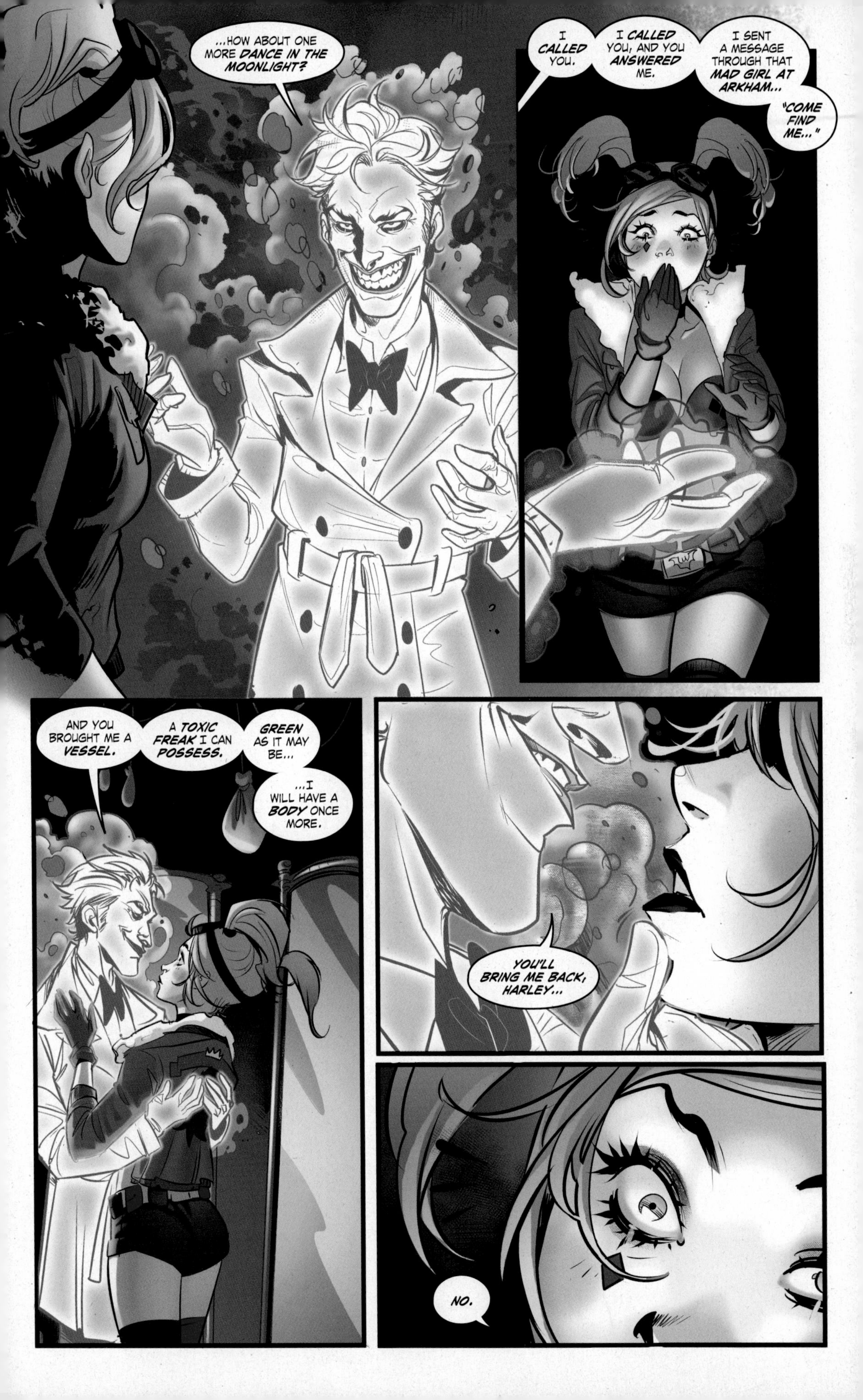
...HOW ABOUT ONE MORE DANCE IN THE MOONLIGHT?
I CALLED YOU.
I CALLED YOU, AND YOU ANSWERED ME.
I SENT A MESSAGE THROUGH THAT MAD GIRL AT ARKHAM...
"COME FIND ME..."
AND YOU BROUGHT ME A VESSEL.
A TOXIC FREAK I CAN POSSESS.
GREEN AS IT MAY BE...
...I WILL HAVE A BODY ONCE MORE.
YOU'LL BRING ME BACK, HARLEY...
NO.

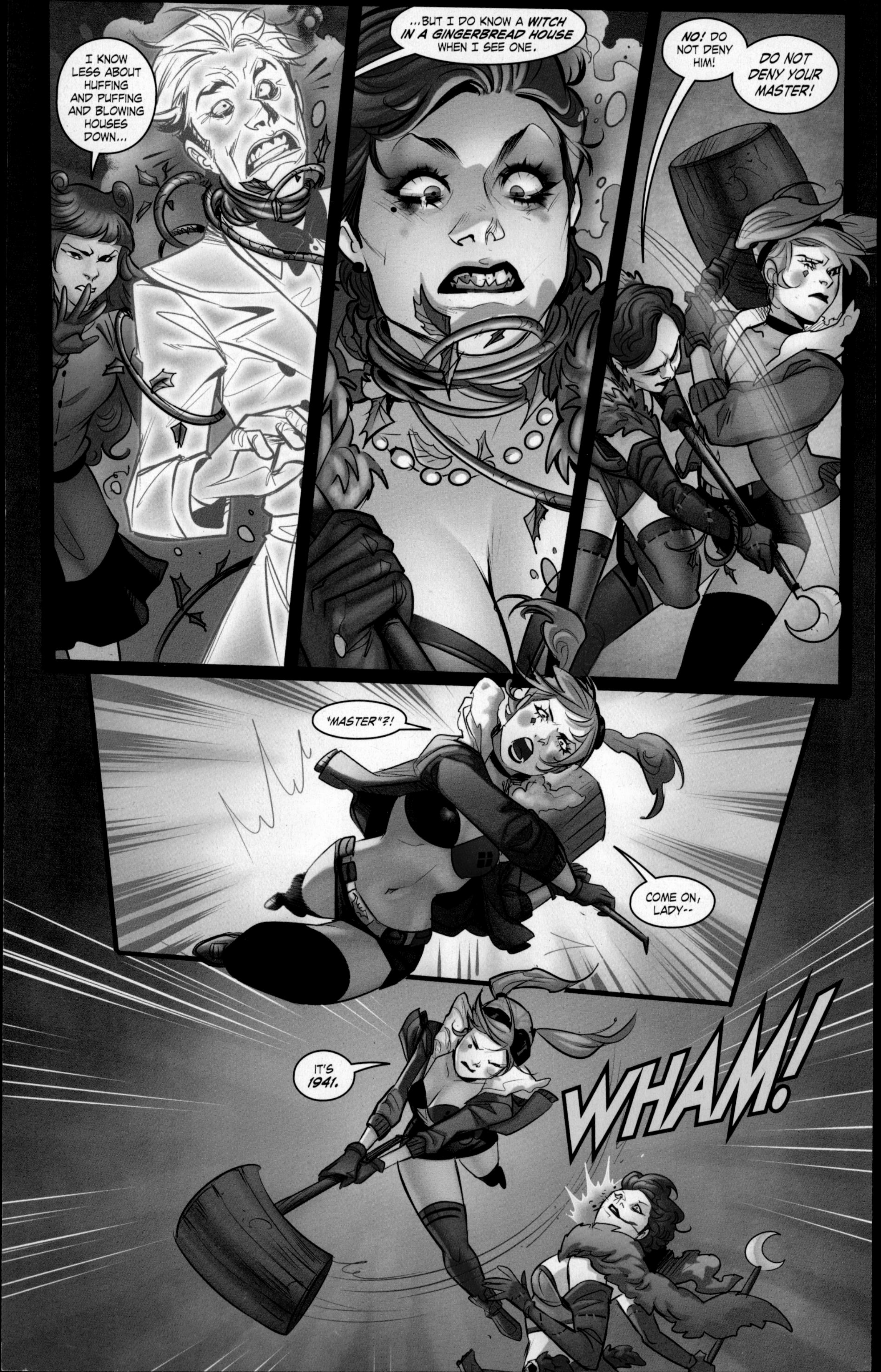

I KNOW LESS ABOUT HUFFING AND PUFFING AND BLOWING HOUSES DOWN...
...BUT I DO KNOW A WITCH IN A GINGERBREAD HOUSE WHEN I SEE ONE.
NO! DO NOT DENY HIM!
DO NOT DENY YOUR MASTER!
"MASTER"?!
COME ON, LADY--
IT'S 1941.
WHAM!

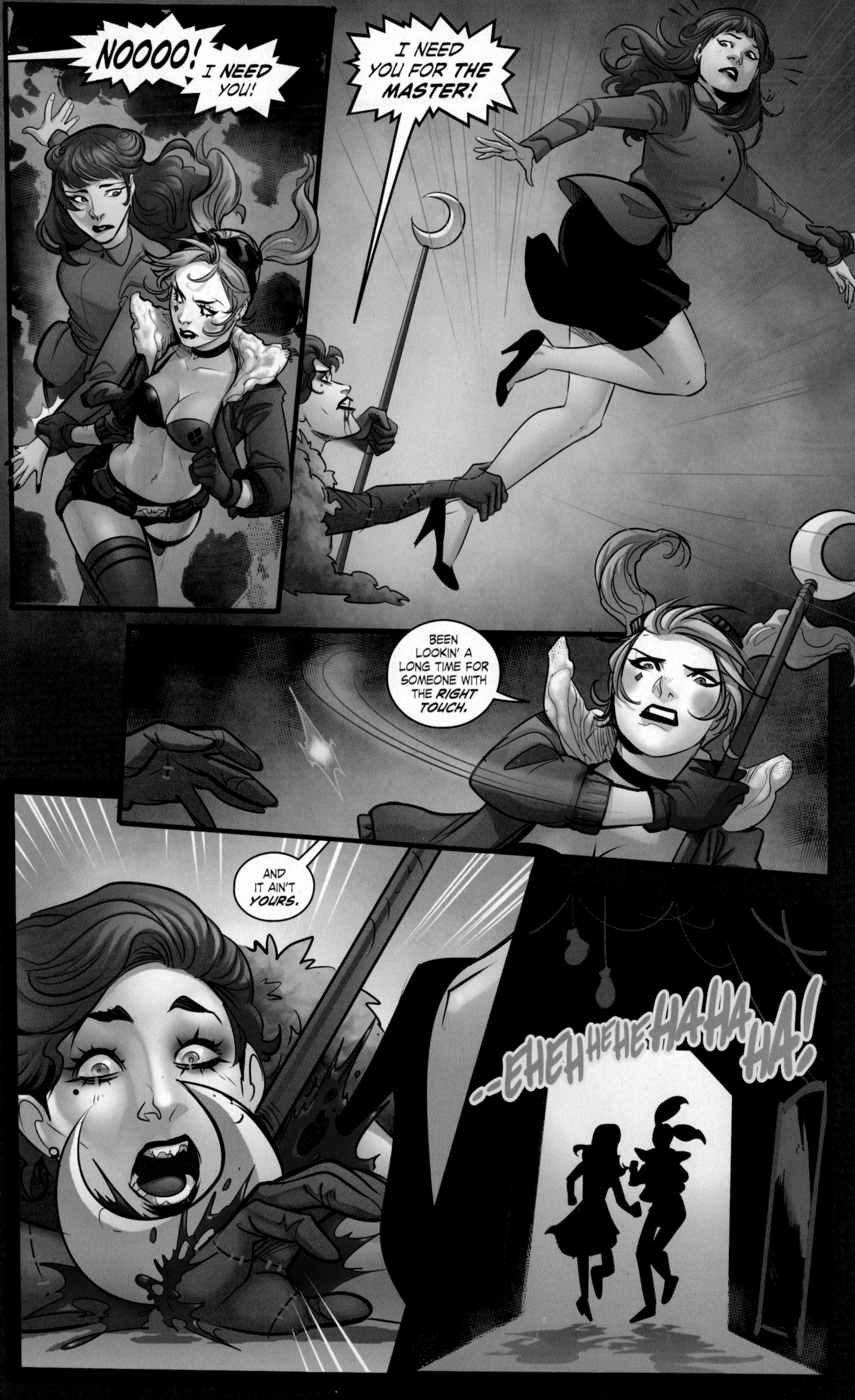
NOOOO! I NEED YOU!
I NEED YOU FOR THE MASTER!
BEEN LOOKIN' A LONG TIME FOR SOMEONE WITH THE RIGHT TOUCH.
AND IT AIN'T YOURS.
--EHEH HEHE HAHA HA!

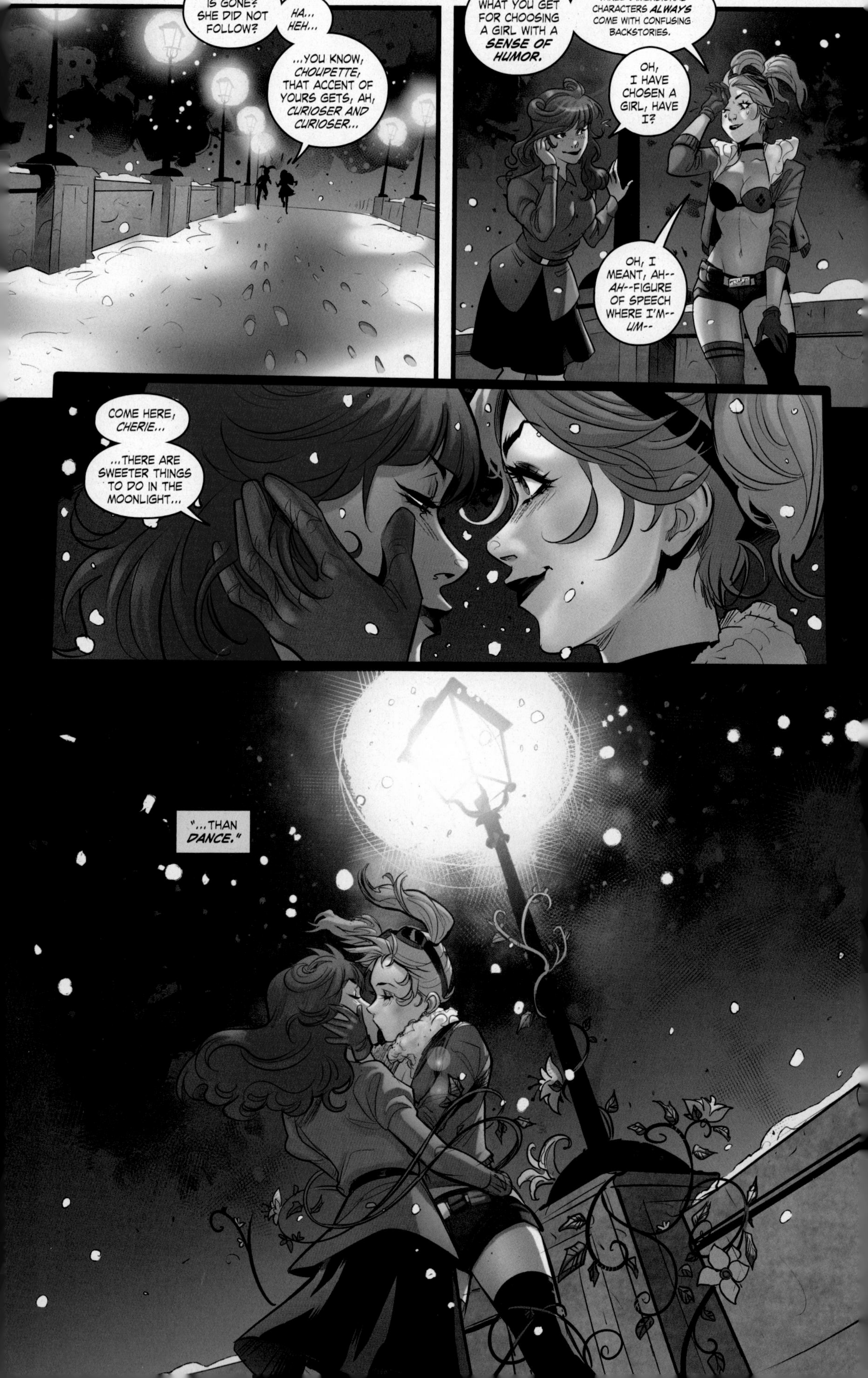
SHE IS GONE? SHE DID NOT FOLLOW?
HA... HEH...
...YOU KNOW, CHOUPETTE, THAT ACCENT OF YOURS GETS, AH, CURIOSER AND CURIOSER...
THAT'S WHAT YOU GET FOR CHOOSING A GIRL WITH A SENSE OF HUMOR.
THREE-DIMENSIONAL CHARACTERS ALWAYS COME WITH CONFUSING BACKSTORIES.
OH, I HAVE CHOSEN A GIRL, HAVE I?
OH, I MEANT, AH--AH--FIGURE OF SPEECH WHERE I'M--UM--
COME HERE, CHERIE...
...THERE ARE SWEETER THINGS TO DO IN THE MOONLIGHT...
"...THAN DANCE."

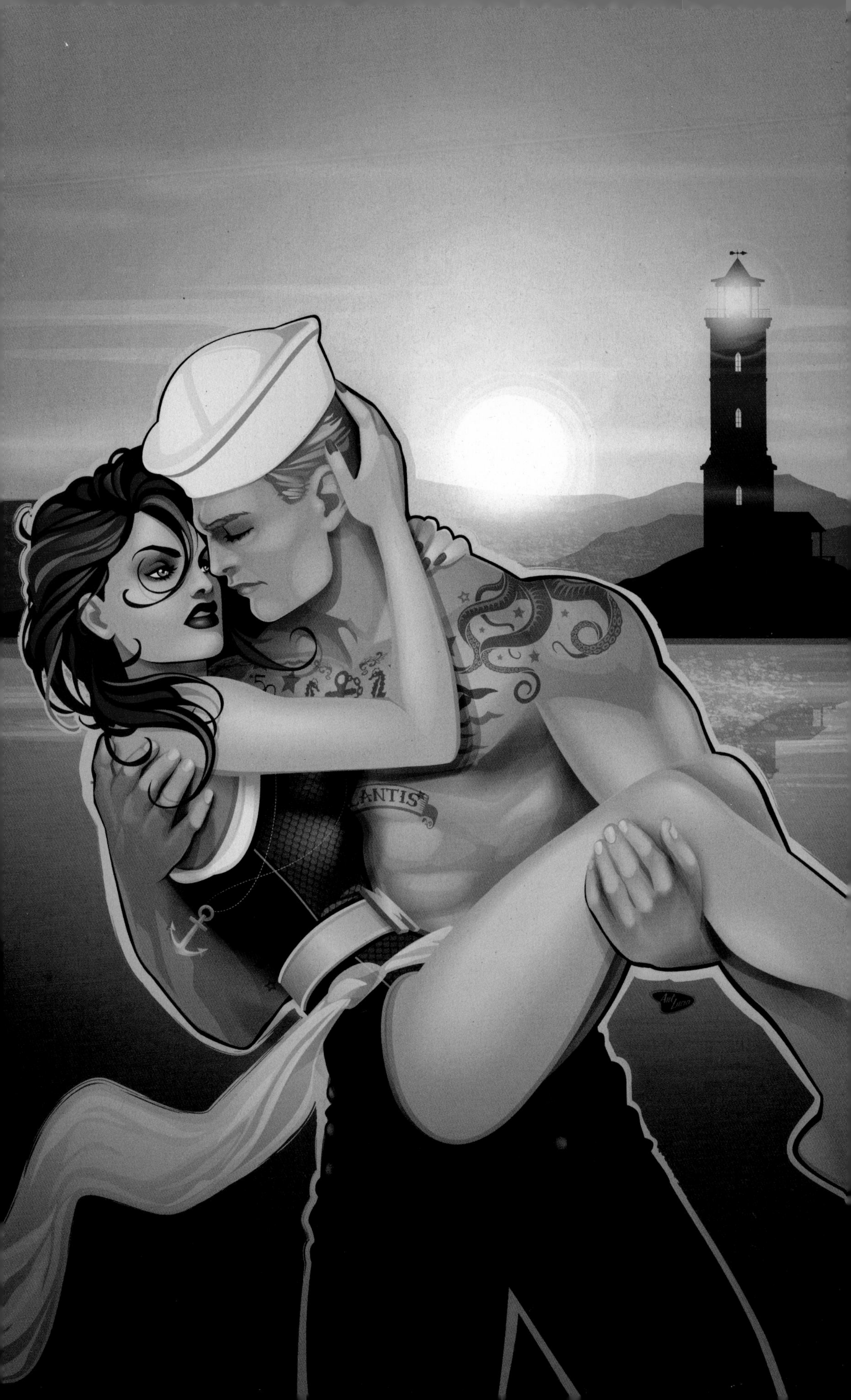

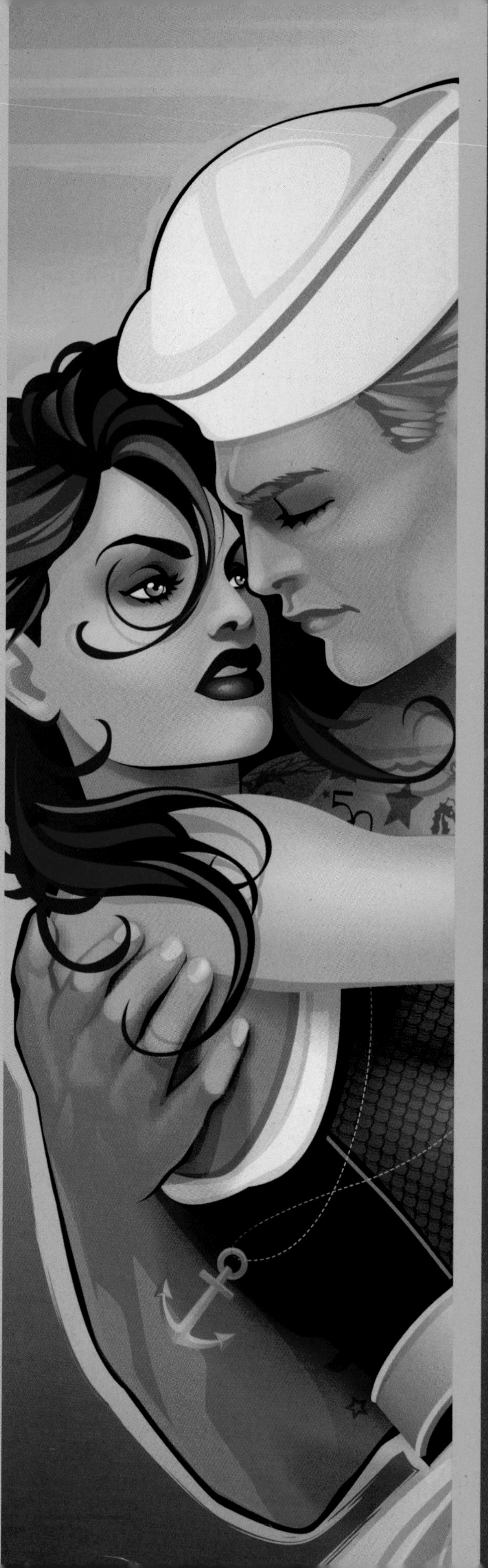

GHOST STORIES

MARGUERITE BENNETT
Writer

LAURA BRAGA
MIRKA ANDOLFO
SANDY JARRELL
Artists

J. NANJAN
WENDY BROOME
KELLY FITZPATRICK
Colorists

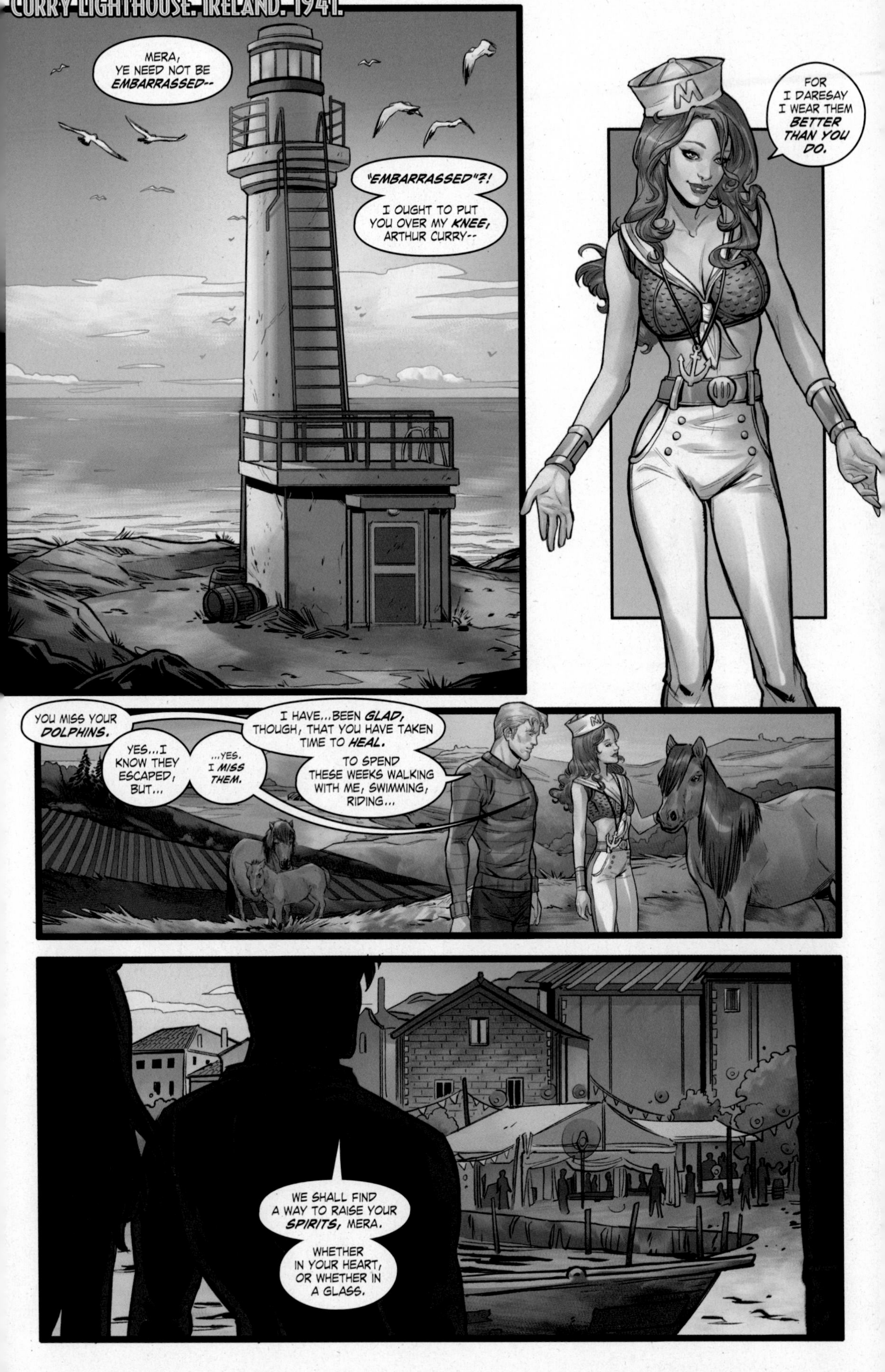
CURRY LIGHTHOUSE. IRELAND. 1941.
MERA, YE NEED NOT BE EMBARRASSED--
"EMBARRASSED"?!
I OUGHT TO PUT YOU OVER MY KNEE, ARTHUR CURRY--
FOR I DARESAY I WEAR THEM BETTER THAN YOU DO.
YOU MISS YOUR DOLPHINS.
YES...I KNOW THEY ESCAPED, BUT...
...YES. I MISS THEM.
I HAVE...BEEN GLAD, THOUGH, THAT YOU HAVE TAKEN TIME TO HEAL.
TO SPEND THESE WEEKS WALKING WITH ME, SWIMMING, RIDING...
WE SHALL FIND A WAY TO RAISE YOUR SPIRITS, MERA.
WHETHER IN YOUR HEART, OR WHETHER IN A GLASS.

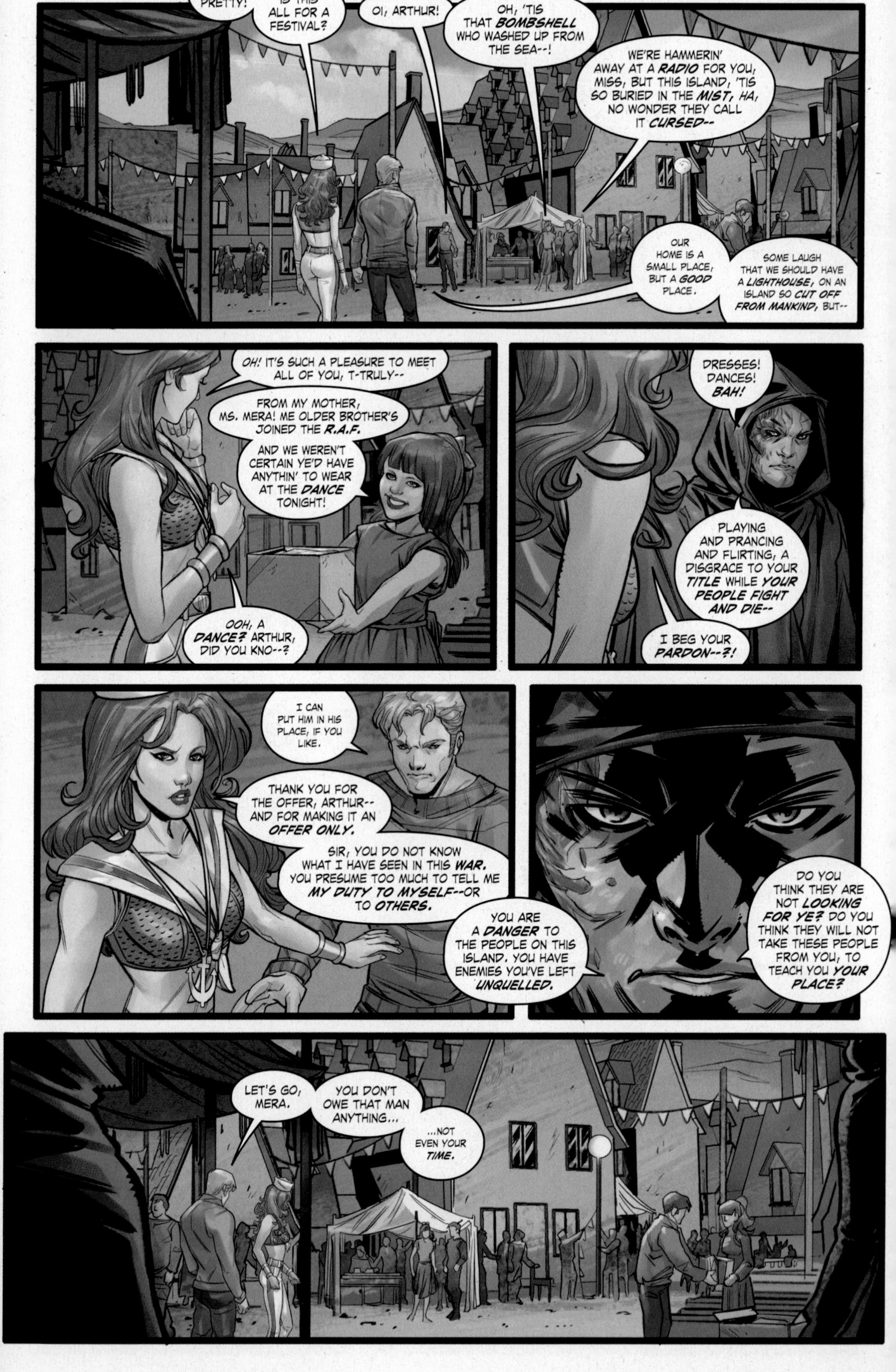
OH, IT'S SO PRETTY!
IS THIS ALL FOR A FESTIVAL?
OI, ARTHUR!
OH, 'TIS THAT BOMBSHELL WHO WASHED UP FROM THE SEA--!
WE'RE HAMMERIN' AWAY AT A RADIO FOR YOU, MISS, BUT THIS ISLAND, 'TIS SO BURIED IN THE MIST, HA, NO WONDER THEY CALL IT CURSED--
OUR HOME IS A SMALL PLACE, BUT A GOOD PLACE.
SOME LAUGH THAT WE SHOULD HAVE A LIGHTHOUSE, ON AN ISLAND SO CUT OFF FROM MANKIND, BUT--
OH! IT'S SUCH A PLEASURE TO MEET ALL OF YOU, T-TRULY--
FROM MY MOTHER, MS. MERA! ME OLDER BROTHER'S JOINED THE R.A.F.
AND WE WEREN'T CERTAIN YE'D HAVE ANYTHIN' TO WEAR AT THE DANCE TONIGHT!
OOH, A DANCE? ARTHUR, DID YOU KNO--?
DRESSES! DANCES! BAH!
PLAYING AND PRANCING AND FLIRTING, A DISGRACE TO YOUR TITLE WHILE YOUR PEOPLE FIGHT AND DIE--
I BEG YOUR PARDON--?!
I CAN PUT HIM IN HIS PLACE, IF YOU LIKE.
THANK YOU FOR THE OFFER, ARTHUR-- AND FOR MAKING IT AN OFFER ONLY.
SIR, YOU DO NOT KNOW WHAT I HAVE SEEN IN THIS WAR. YOU PRESUME TOO MUCH TO TELL ME MY DUTY TO MYSELF--OR TO OTHERS.
YOU ARE A DANGER TO THE PEOPLE ON THIS ISLAND. YOU HAVE ENEMIES YOU'VE LEFT UNQUELLED.
DO YOU THINK THEY ARE NOT LOOKING FOR YE? DO YOU THINK THEY WILL NOT TAKE THESE PEOPLE FROM YOU, TO TEACH YOU YOUR PLACE?
LET'S GO, MERA.
YOU DON'T OWE THAT MAN ANYTHING...
...NOT EVEN YOUR TIME.

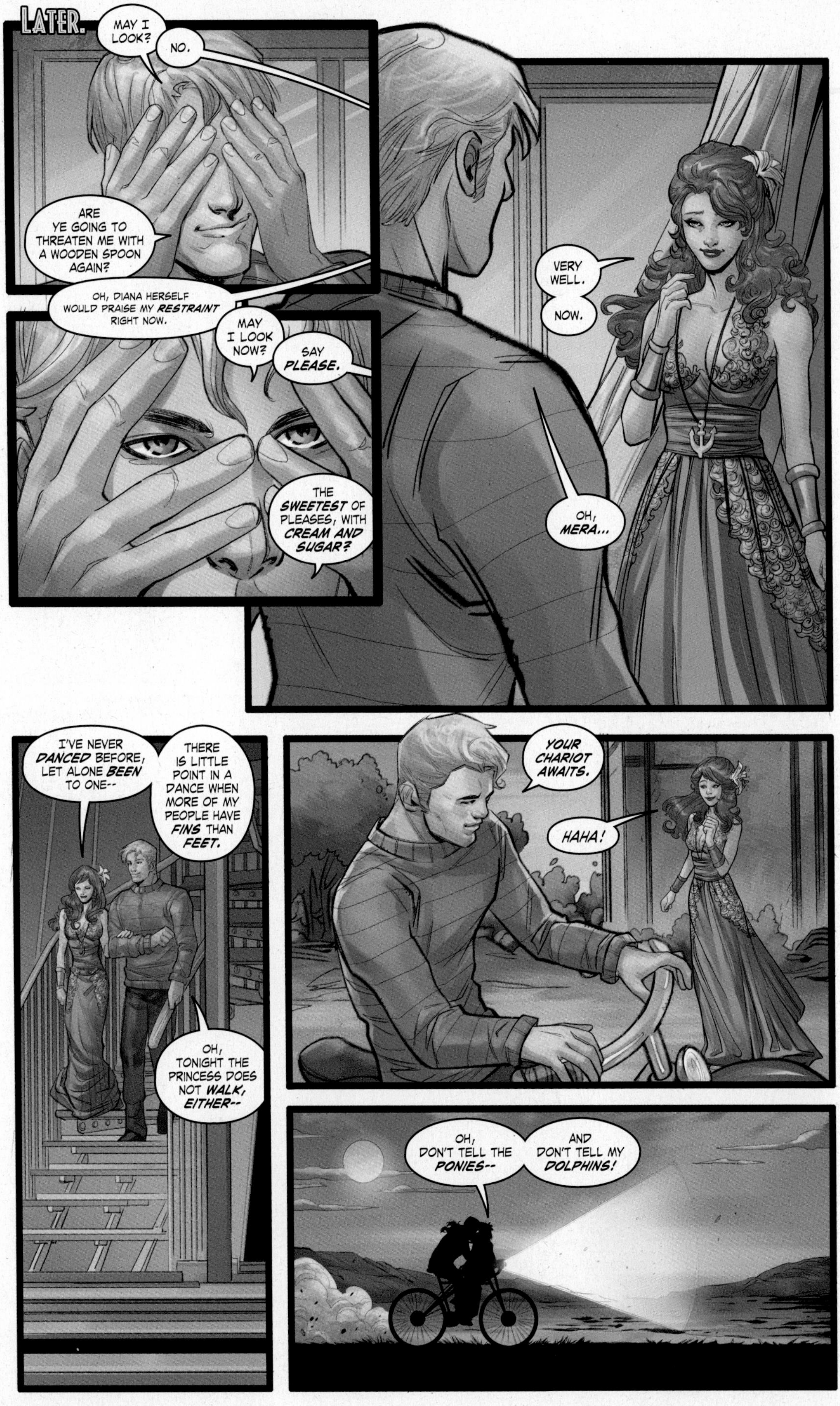
LATER.
MAY I LOOK?
NO.
ARE YE GOING TO THREATEN ME WITH A WOODEN SPOON AGAIN?
OH, DIANA HERSELF WOULD PRAISE MY RESTRAINT RIGHT NOW.
MAY I LOOK NOW?
SAY PLEASE.
THE SWEETEST OF PLEASES, WITH CREAM AND SUGAR?
VERY WELL.
NOW.
OH, MERA...
I'VE NEVER DANCED BEFORE, LET ALONE BEEN TO ONE--
THERE IS LITTLE POINT IN A DANCE WHEN MORE OF MY PEOPLE HAVE FINS THAN FEET.
OH, TONIGHT THE PRINCESS DOES NOT WALK, EITHER--
YOUR CHARIOT AWAITS.
HAHA!
OH, DON'T TELL THE PONIES--
AND DON'T TELL MY DOLPHINS!

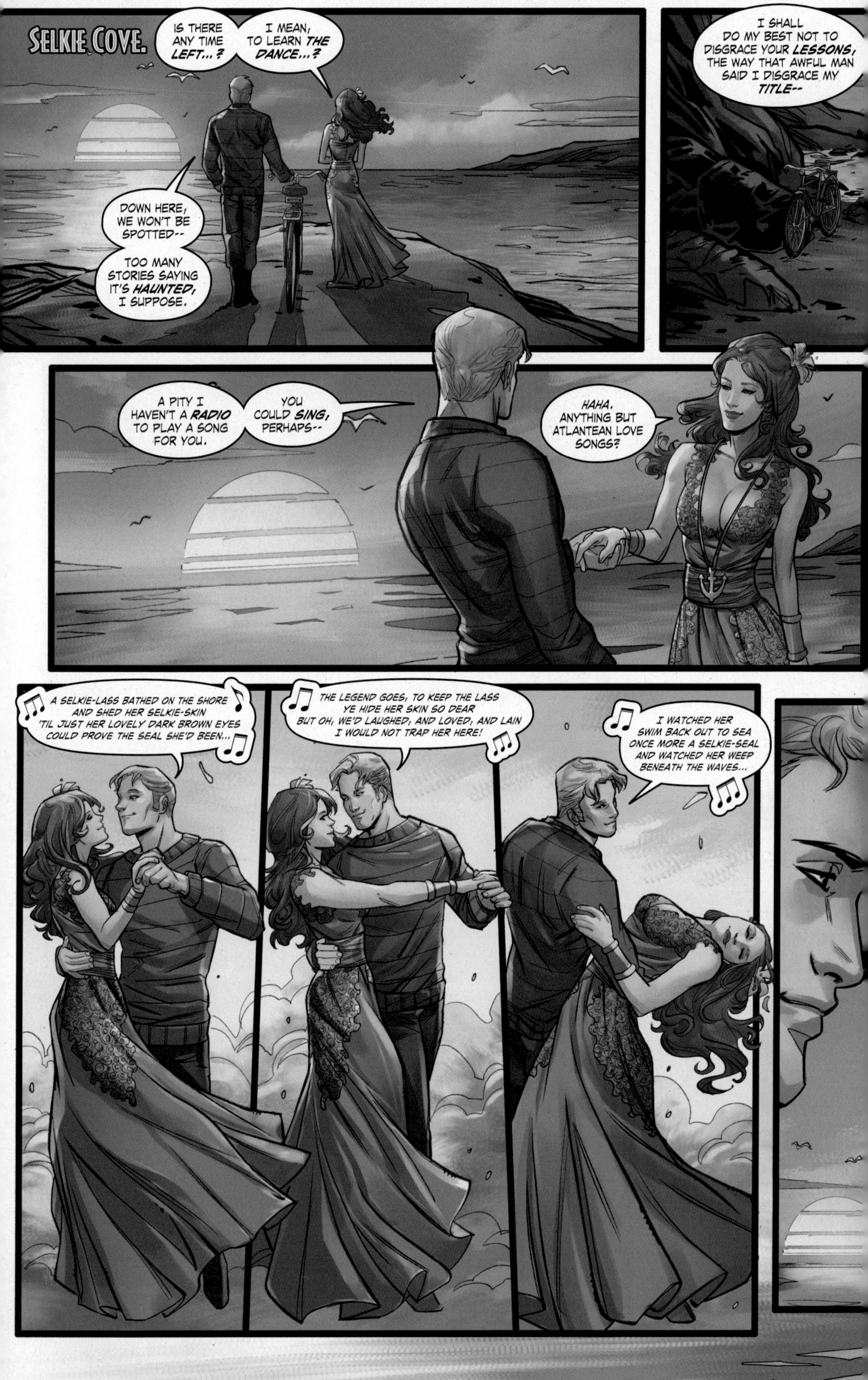
SELKIE COVE.
IS THERE ANY TIME LEFT...?
I MEAN, TO LEARN THE DANCE...?
DOWN HERE, WE WON'T BE SPOTTED--
TOO MANY STORIES SAYING IT'S HAUNTED, I SUPPOSE.
I SHALL DO MY BEST NOT TO DISGRACE YOUR LESSONS, THE WAY THAT AWFUL MAN SAID I DISGRACE MY TITLE--
A PITY I HAVEN'T A RADIO TO PLAY A SONG FOR YOU.
YOU COULD SING, PERHAPS--
HAHA. ANYTHING BUT ATLANTEAN LOVE SONGS?
A SELKIE-LASS BATHED ON THE SHORE AND SHED HER SELKIE-SKIN 'TIL JUST HER LOVELY DARK BROWN EYES COULD PROVE THE SEAL SHE'D BEEN...
THE LEGEND GOES, TO KEEP THE LASS YE HIDE HER SKIN SO DEAR BUT OH, WE'D LAUGHED, AND LOVED, AND LAIN I WOULD NOT TRAP HER HERE!
I WATCHED HER SWIM BACK OUT TO SEA ONCE MORE A SELKIE-SEAL AND WATCHED HER WEEP BENEATH THE WAVES...

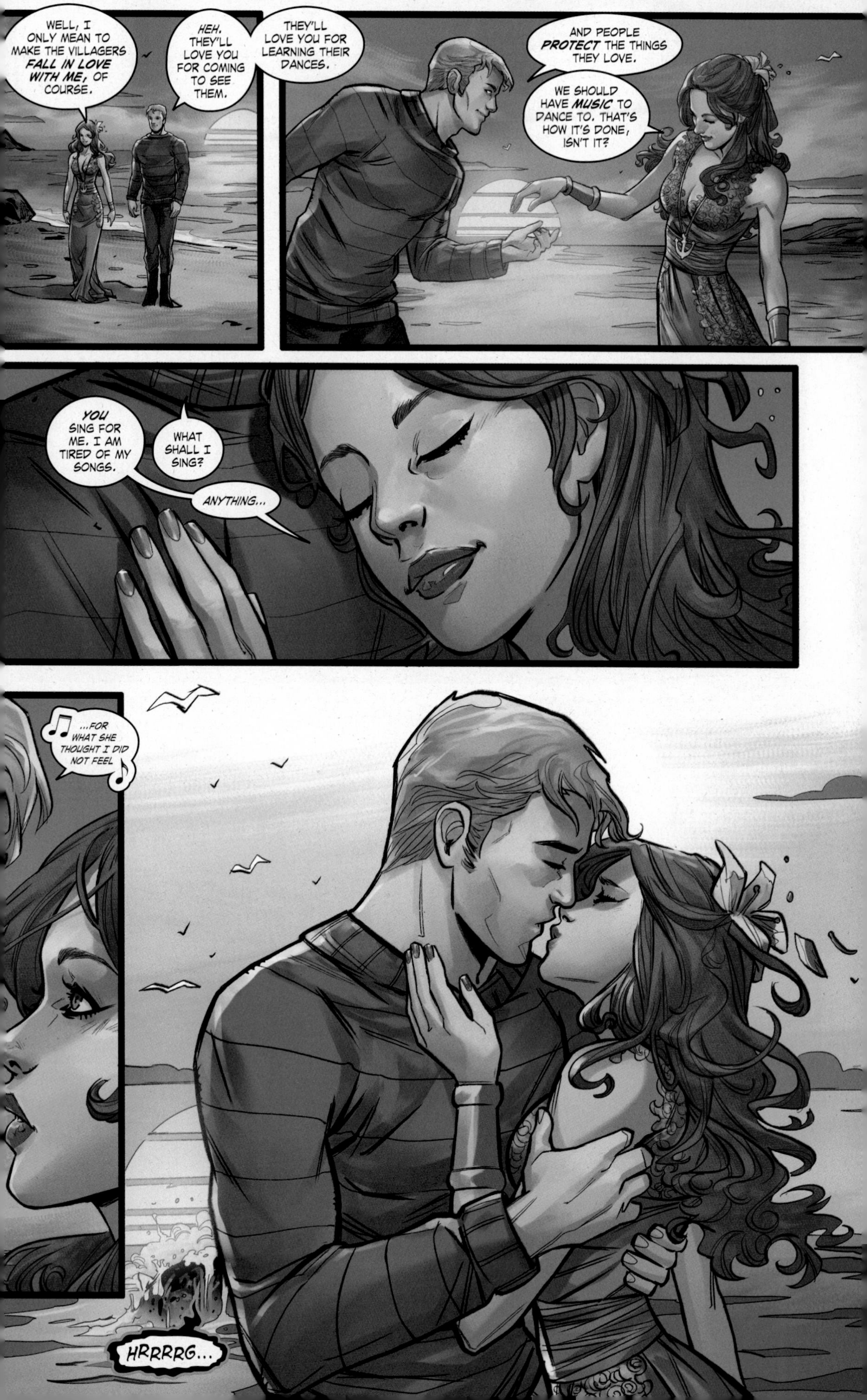
WELL, I ONLY MEAN TO MAKE THE VILLAGERS FALL IN LOVE WITH ME, OF COURSE.
HEH. THEY'LL LOVE YOU FOR COMING TO SEE THEM.
THEY'LL LOVE YOU FOR LEARNING THEIR DANCES.
AND PEOPLE PROTECT THE THINGS THEY LOVE.
WE SHOULD HAVE MUSIC TO DANCE TO. THAT'S HOW IT'S DONE, ISN'T IT?
YOU SING FOR ME. I AM TIRED OF MY SONGS.
WHAT SHALL I SING?
ANYTHING...
...FOR WHAT SHE THOUGHT I DID NOT FEEL
HRRRRG...

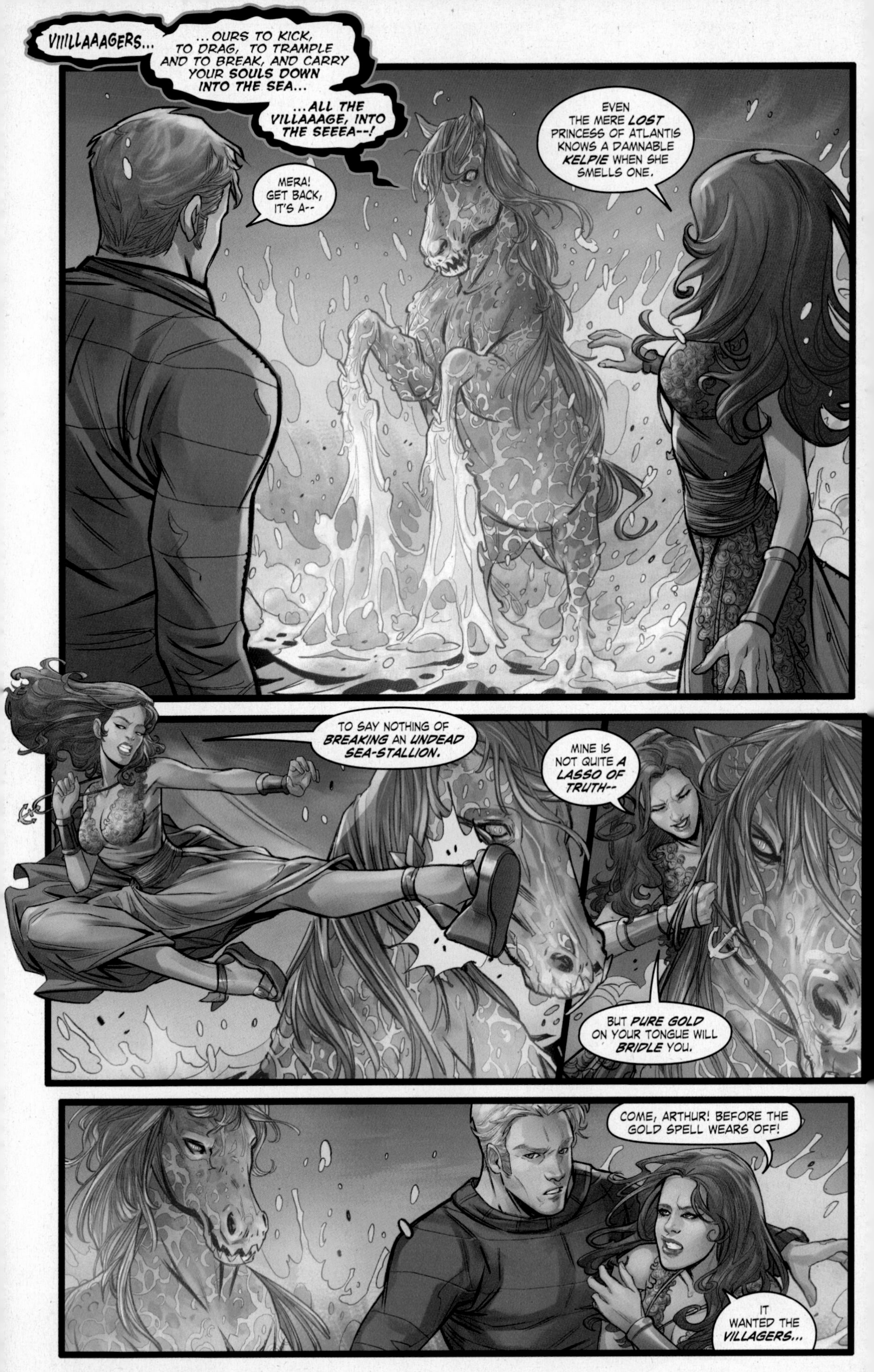
VIIILLAAAGERS...
...OURS TO KICK, TO DRAG, TO TRAMPLE AND TO BREAK, AND CARRY YOUR SOULS DOWN INTO THE SEA...
...ALL THE VILLAAAGE, INTO THE SEEEA--!
MERA! GET BACK, IT'S A--
EVEN THE MERE LOST PRINCESS OF ATLANTIS KNOWS A DAMNABLE KELPIE WHEN SHE SMELLS ONE.
TO SAY NOTHING OF BREAKING AN UNDEAD SEA-STALLION.
MINE IS NOT QUITE A LASSO OF TRUTH--
BUT PURE GOLD ON YOUR TONGUE WILL BRIDLE YOU.
COME, ARTHUR! BEFORE THE GOLD SPELL WEARS OFF!
IT WANTED THE VILLAGERS...

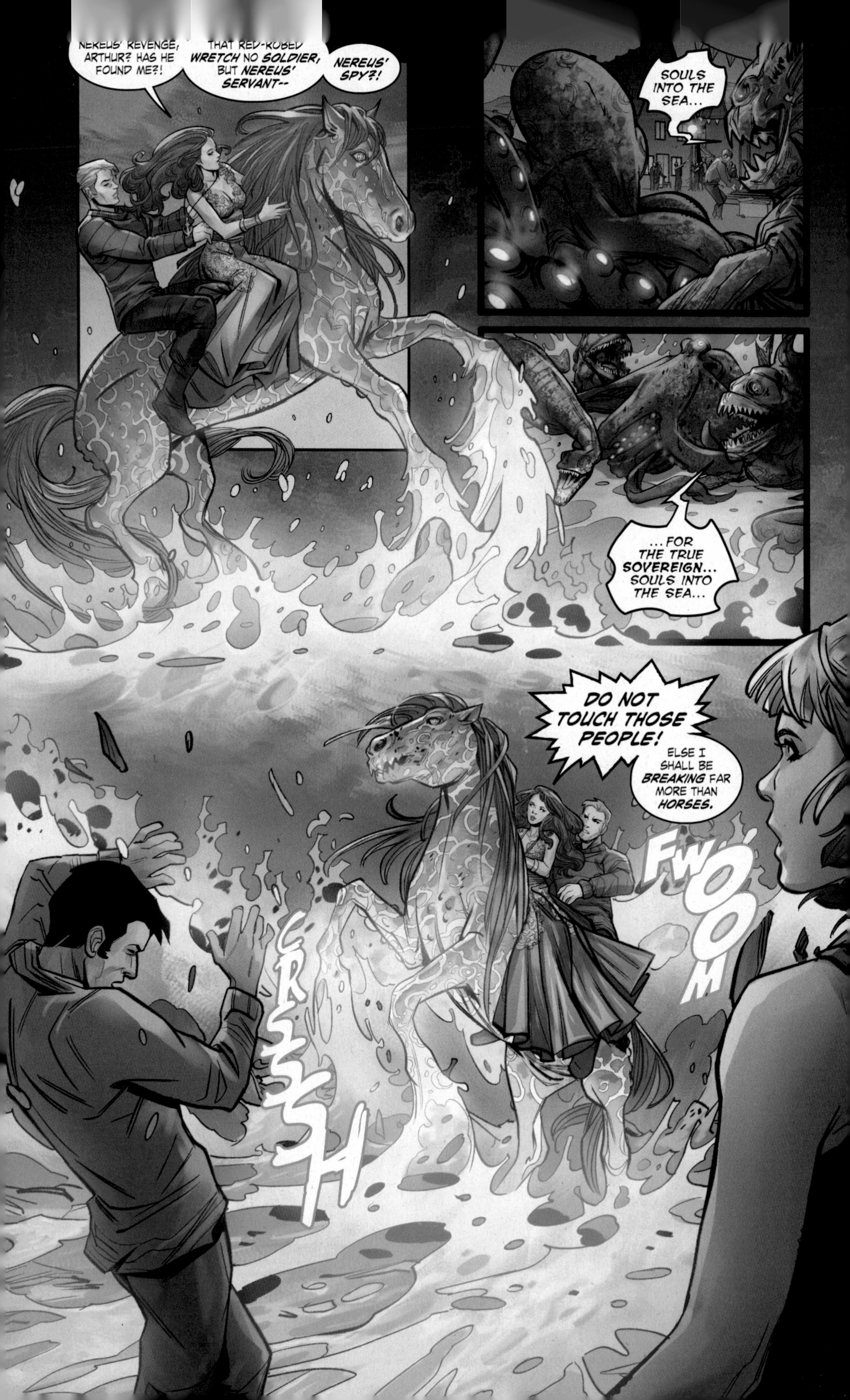
NEREUS' REVENGE, ARTHUR? HAS HE FOUND ME?!
THAT RED-ROBED WRETCH NO SOLDIER, BUT NEREUS' SERVANT--
NEREUS' SPY?!
SOULS INTO THE SEA...
...FOR THE TRUE SOVEREIGN... SOULS INTO THE SEA...
DO NOT TOUCH THOSE PEOPLE!
ELSE I SHALL BE BREAKING FAR MORE THAN HORSES.
CRSSSH
FWOOOM

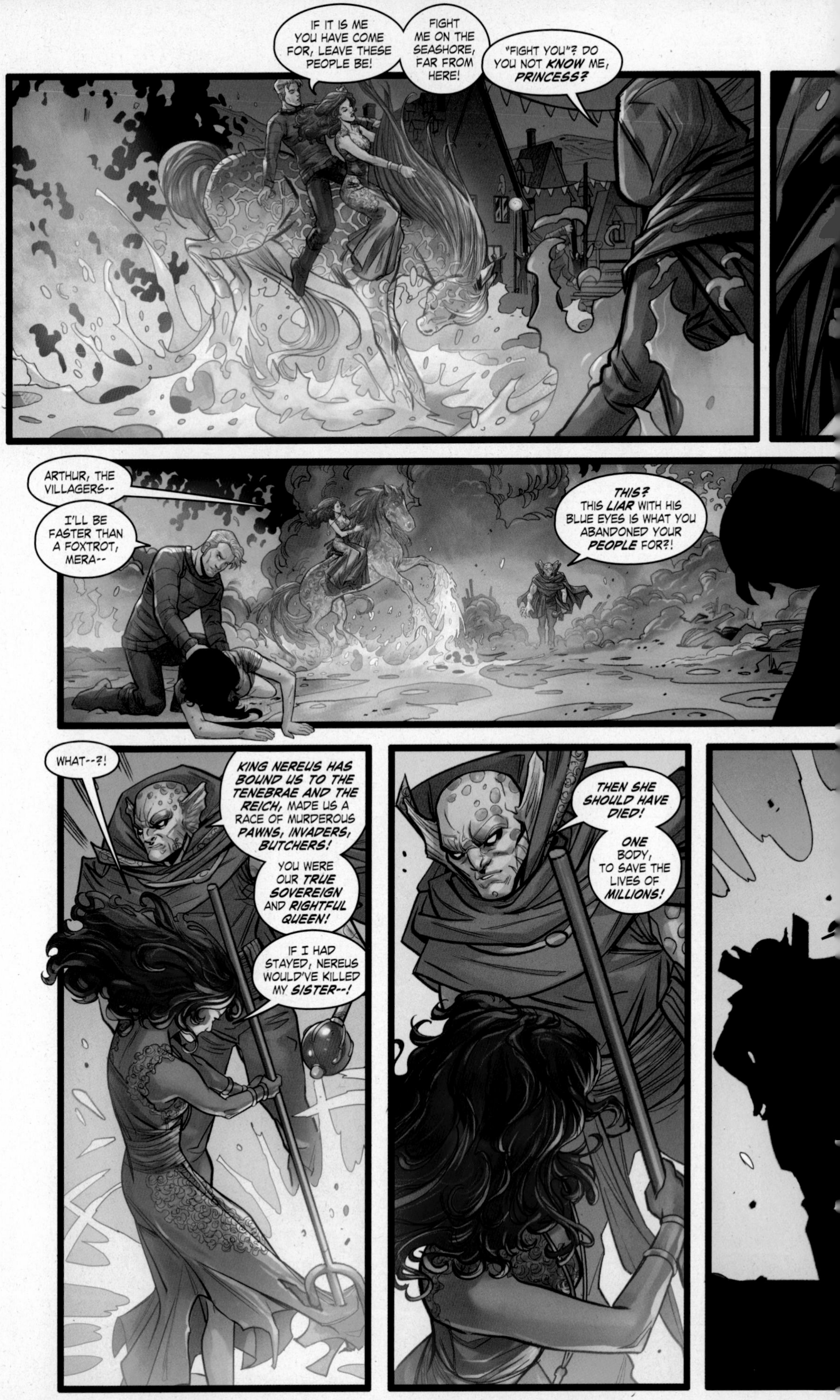
IF IT IS ME YOU HAVE COME FOR, LEAVE THESE PEOPLE BE!
FIGHT ME ON THE SEASHORE, FAR FROM HERE!
"FIGHT YOU"? DO YOU NOT KNOW ME, PRINCESS?
ARTHUR, THE VILLAGERS--
I'LL BE FASTER THAN A FOXTROT, MERA--
THIS? THIS LIAR WITH HIS BLUE EYES IS WHAT YOU ABANDONED YOUR PEOPLE FOR?!
WHAT--?!
KING NEREUS HAS BOUND US TO THE TENEBRAE AND THE REICH, MADE US A RACE OF MURDEROUS PAWNS, INVADERS, BUTCHERS!
YOU WERE OUR TRUE SOVEREIGN AND RIGHTFUL QUEEN!
IF I HAD STAYED, NEREUS WOULD'VE KILLED MY SISTER--!
THEN SHE SHOULD HAVE DIED!
ONE BODY, TO SAVE THE LIVES OF MILLIONS!

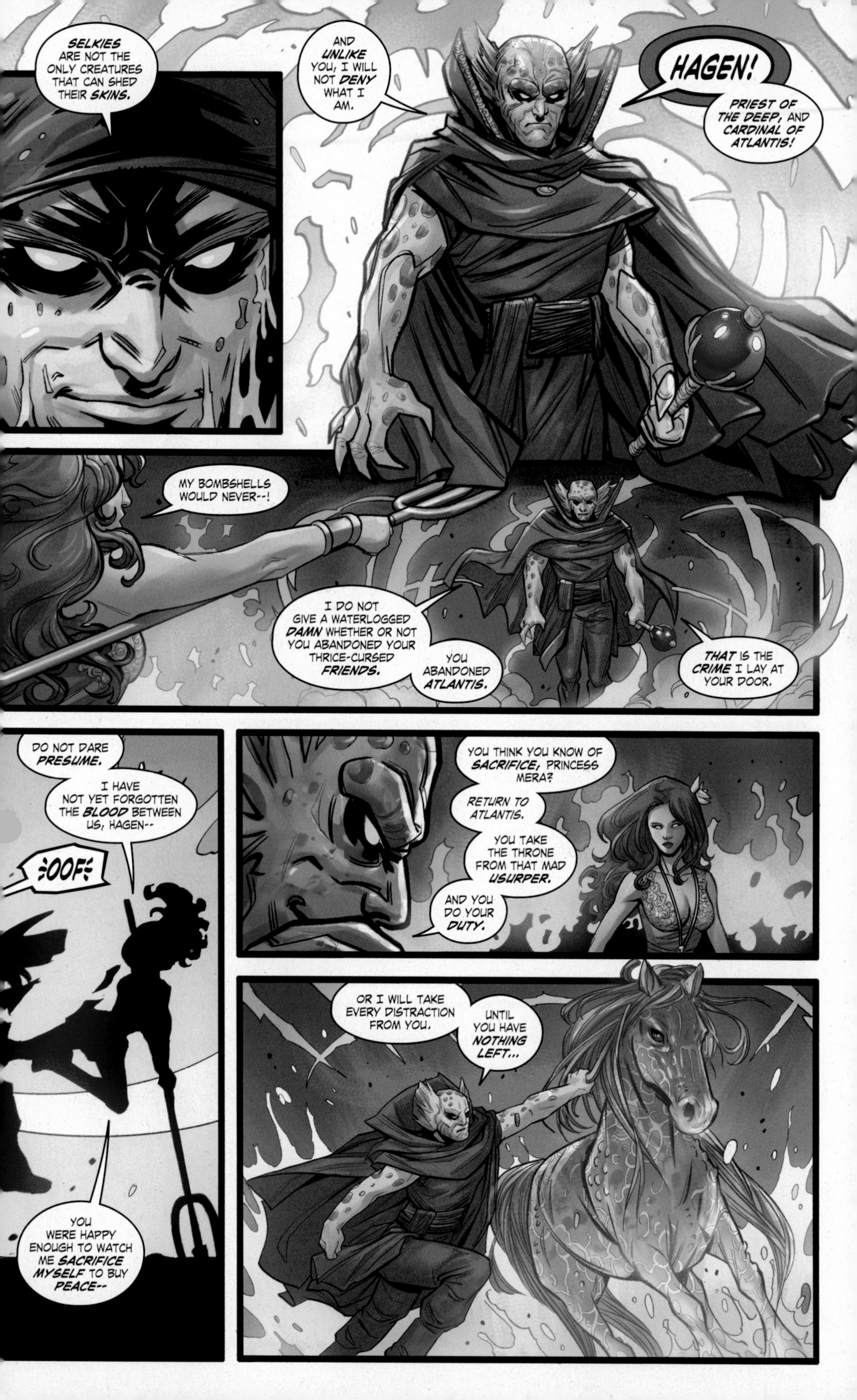
SELKIES ARE NOT THE ONLY CREATURES THAT CAN SHED THEIR SKINS.
AND UNLIKE YOU, I WILL NOT DENY WHAT I AM.
HAGEN!
PRIEST OF THE DEEP, AND CARDINAL OF ATLANTIS!
MY BOMBSHELLS WOULD NEVER--!
I DO NOT GIVE A WATERLOGGED DAMN WHETHER OR NOT YOU ABANDONED YOUR THRICE-CURSED FRIENDS.
YOU ABANDONED ATLANTIS.
THAT IS THE CRIME I LAY AT YOUR DOOR.
DO NOT DARE PRESUME.
I HAVE NOT YET FORGOTTEN THE BLOOD BETWEEN US, HAGEN--
OOF!
YOU WERE HAPPY ENOUGH TO WATCH ME SACRIFICE MYSELF TO BUY PEACE--
YOU THINK YOU KNOW OF SACRIFICE, PRINCESS MERA?
RETURN TO ATLANTIS.
YOU TAKE THE THRONE FROM THAT MAD USURPER.
AND YOU DO YOUR DUTY.
OR I WILL TAKE EVERY DISTRACTION FROM YOU.
UNTIL YOU HAVE NOTHING LEFT...

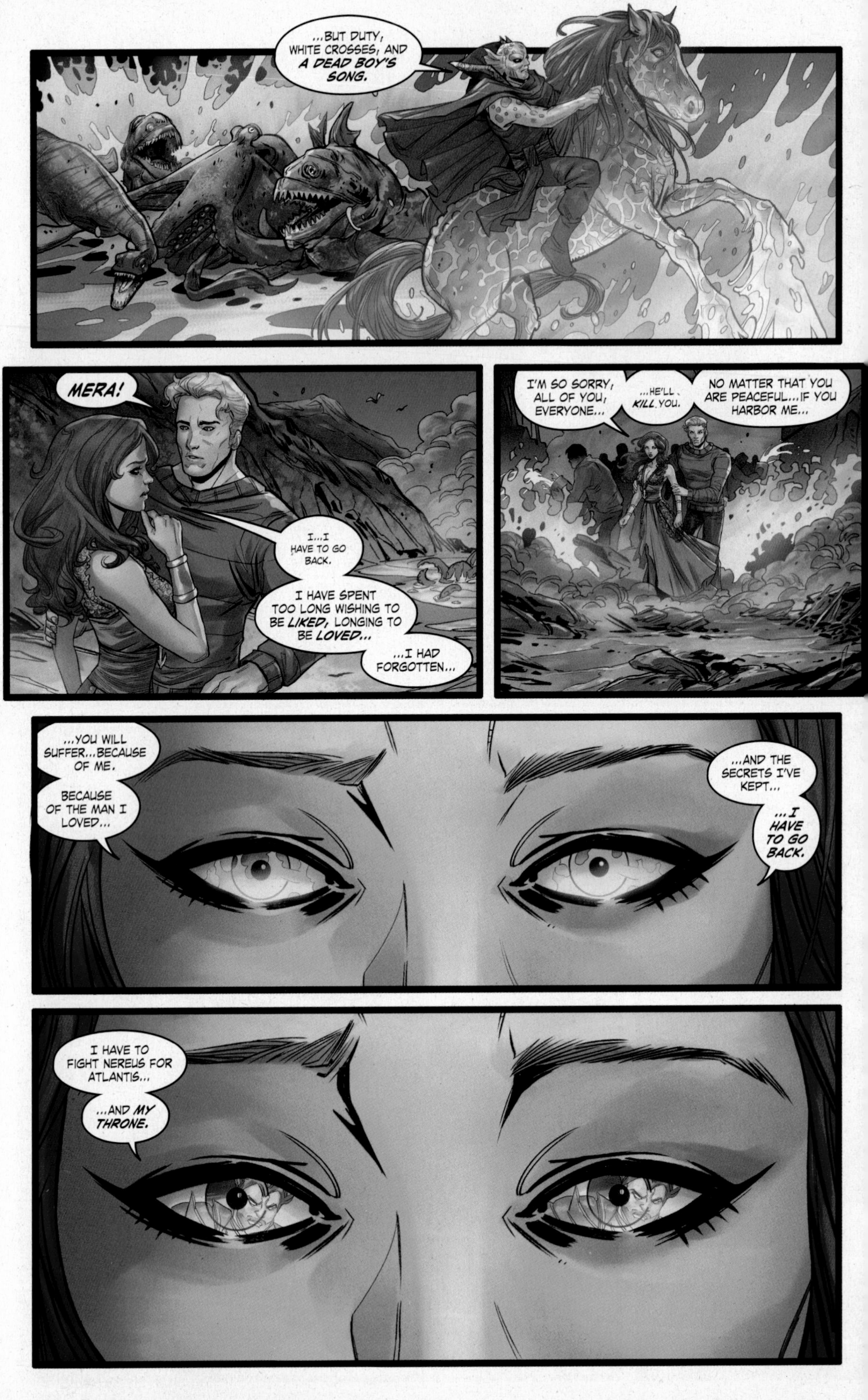
...BUT DUTY, WHITE CROSSES, AND A DEAD BOY'S SONG.
MERA!
I...I HAVE TO GO BACK.
I HAVE SPENT TOO LONG WISHING TO BE LIKED, LONGING TO BE LOVED...
...I HAD FORGOTTEN...
I'M SO SORRY, ALL OF YOU, EVERYONE...
NO MATTER THAT YOU ARE PEACEFUL...IF YOU HARBOR ME...
...HE'LL KILL YOU.
...YOU WILL SUFFER...BECAUSE OF ME.
BECAUSE OF THE MAN I LOVED...
...AND THE SECRETS I'VE KEPT...
...I HAVE TO GO BACK.
I HAVE TO FIGHT NEREUS FOR ATLANTIS...
...AND MY THRONE.

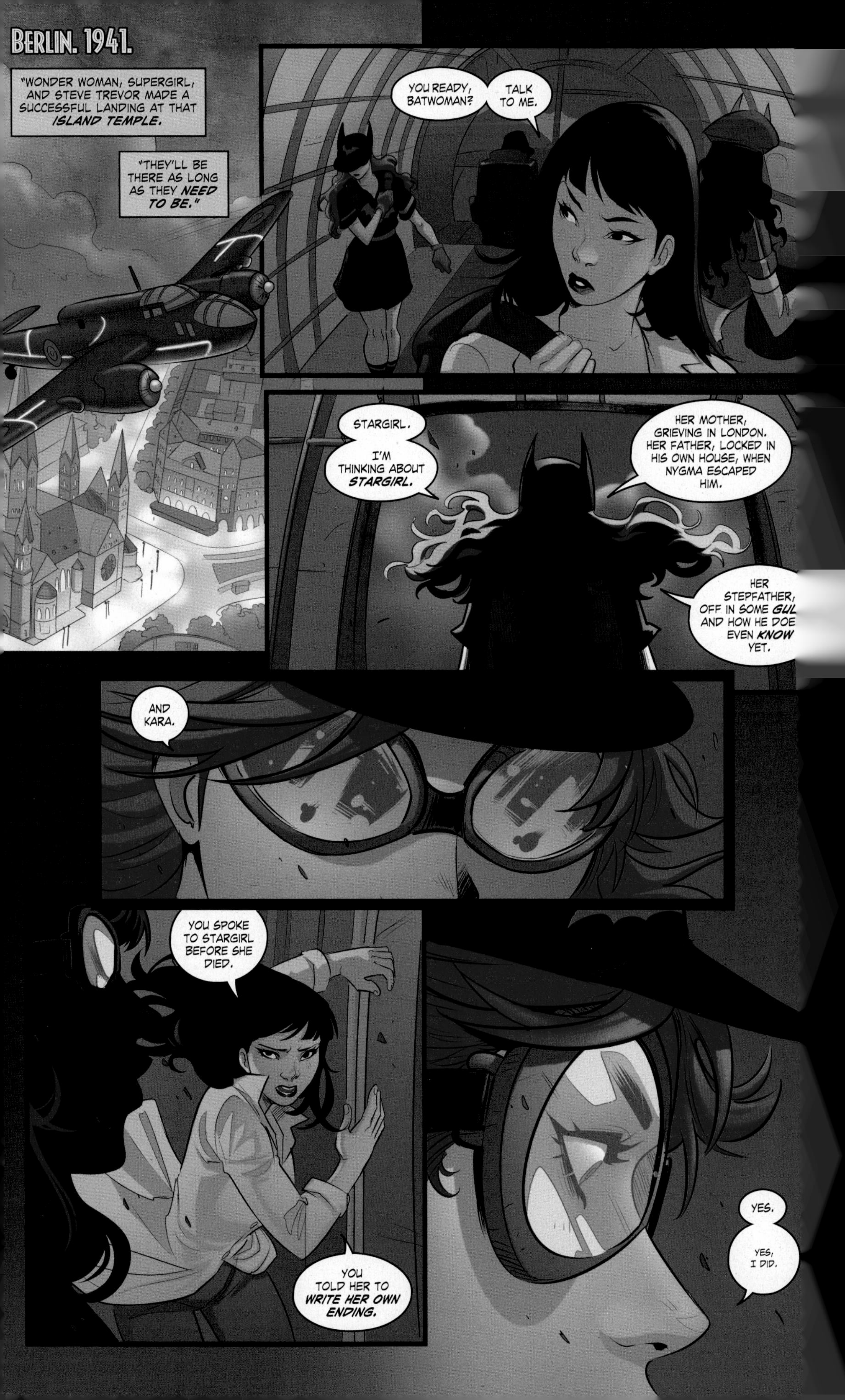
BERLIN. 1941.
"WONDER WOMAN, SUPERGIRL, AND STEVE TREVOR MADE A SUCCESSFUL LANDING AT THAT ISLAND TEMPLE.
"THEY'LL BE THERE AS LONG AS THEY NEED TO BE."
YOU READY, BATWOMAN?
TALK TO ME.
STARGIRL.
I'M THINKING ABOUT STARGIRL.
HER MOTHER, GRIEVING IN LONDON. HER FATHER, LOCKED IN HIS OWN HOUSE, WHEN NYGMA ESCAPED HIM.
HER STEPFATHER, OFF IN SOME GUL
AND HOW HE DOE
EVEN KNOW YET.
AND KARA.
YOU SPOKE TO STARGIRL BEFORE SHE DIED.
YOU TOLD HER TO WRITE HER OWN ENDING.
YES.
YES, I DID.

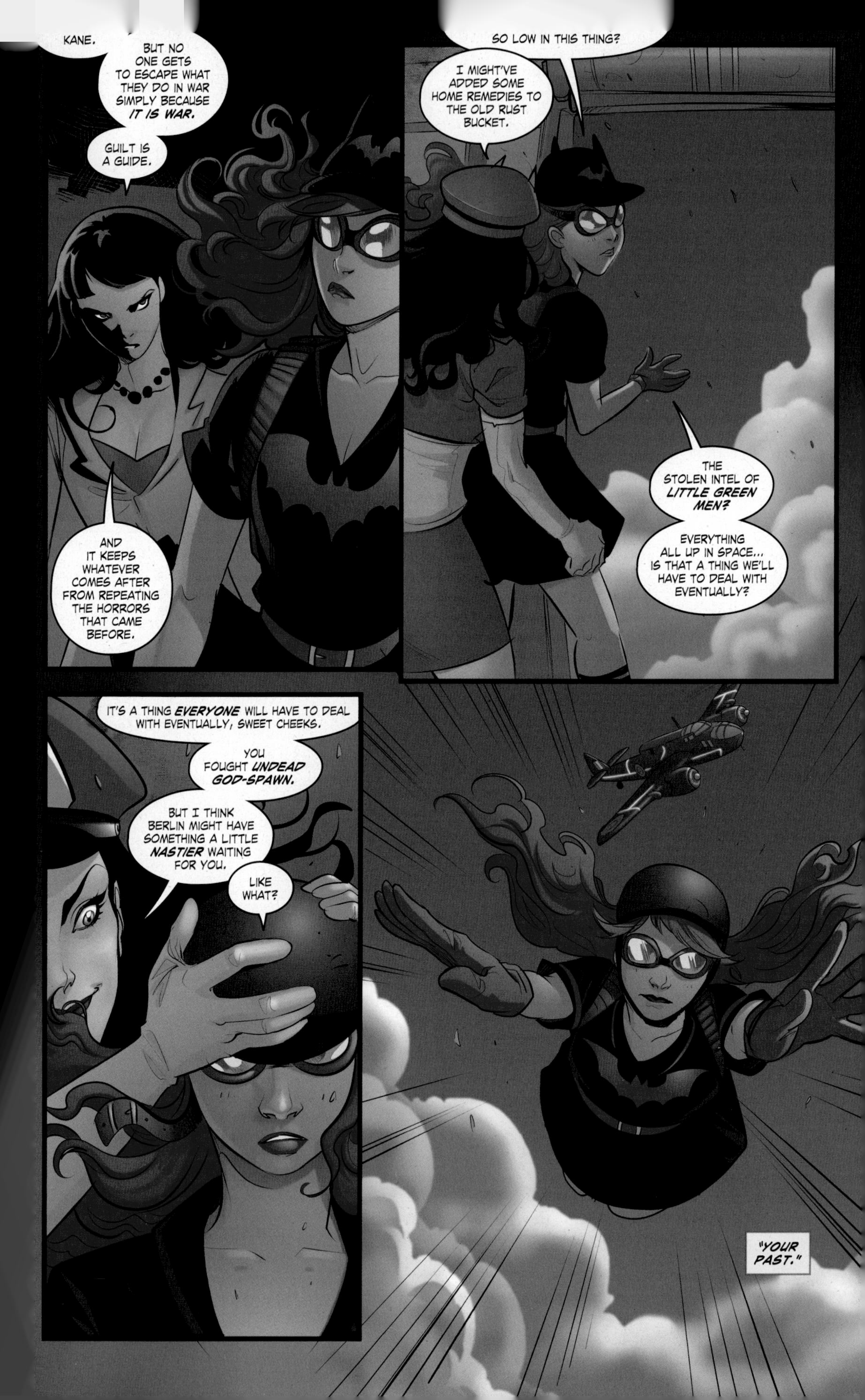
KANE.
BUT NO ONE GETS TO ESCAPE WHAT THEY DO IN WAR SIMPLY BECAUSE *IT IS WAR.*
GUILT IS A GUIDE.
AND IT KEEPS WHATEVER COMES AFTER FROM REPEATING THE HORRORS THAT CAME BEFORE.
SO LOW IN THIS THING?
I MIGHT'VE ADDED SOME HOME REMEDIES TO THE OLD RUST BUCKET.
THE STOLEN INTEL OF *LITTLE GREEN MEN?*
EVERYTHING ALL UP IN SPACE... IS THAT A THING WE'LL HAVE TO DEAL WITH EVENTUALLY?
IT'S A THING *EVERYONE* WILL HAVE TO DEAL WITH EVENTUALLY, SWEET CHEEKS.
YOU FOUGHT *UNDEAD GOD-SPAWN.*
BUT I THINK BERLIN MIGHT HAVE SOMETHING A LITTLE *NASTIER* WAITING FOR YOU.
LIKE WHAT?
"YOUR PAST."

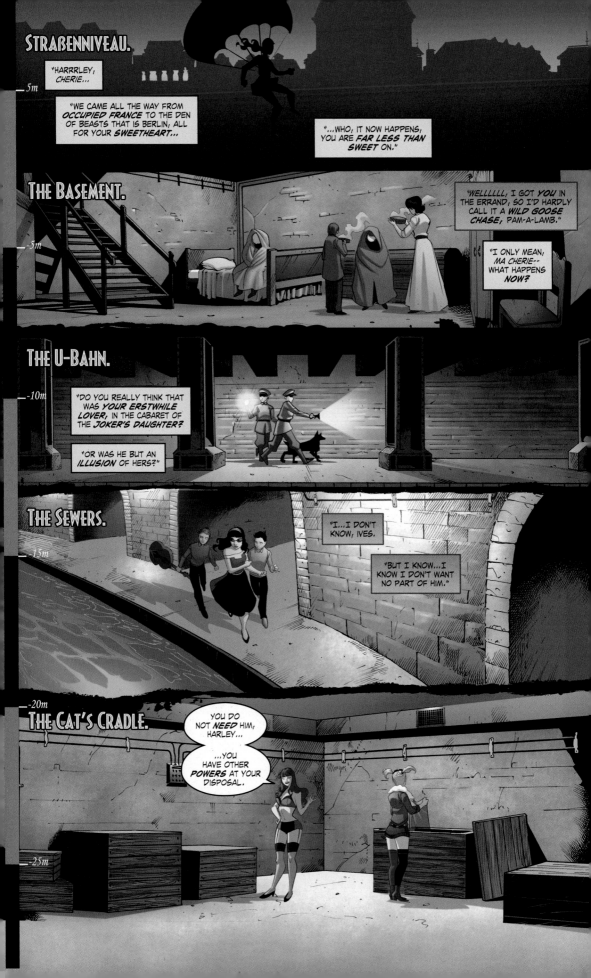

STRAßENNIVEAU.

—5m

"HARRRLEY, CHERIE...

"WE CAME ALL THE WAY FROM *OCCUPIED FRANCE* TO THE DEN OF BEASTS THAT IS BERLIN, ALL FOR YOUR *SWEETHEART*...

"...WHO, IT NOW HAPPENS, YOU ARE *FAR LESS THAN SWEET* ON."

THE BASEMENT.

—5m

"WELLLLLL, I GOT *YOU* IN THE ERRAND, SO I'D HARDLY CALL IT A *WILD GOOSE CHASE*, PAM-A-LAMB."

"I ONLY MEAN, MA CHERIE-- WHAT HAPPENS *NOW?*

THE U-BAHN.

—10m

"DO YOU REALLY THINK THAT WAS *YOUR ERSTWHILE LOVER,* IN THE CABARET OF THE *JOKER'S DAUGHTER?*

"OR WAS HE BUT AN *ILLUSION* OF HERS?"

THE SEWERS.

—15m

"I...I DON'T KNOW, IVES.

"BUT I KNOW...I KNOW I DON'T WANT NO PART OF HIM."

THE CAT'S CRADLE.

—20m

YOU DO NOT *NEED* HIM, HARLEY...

...YOU HAVE OTHER *POWERS* AT YOUR DISPOSAL.

—25m

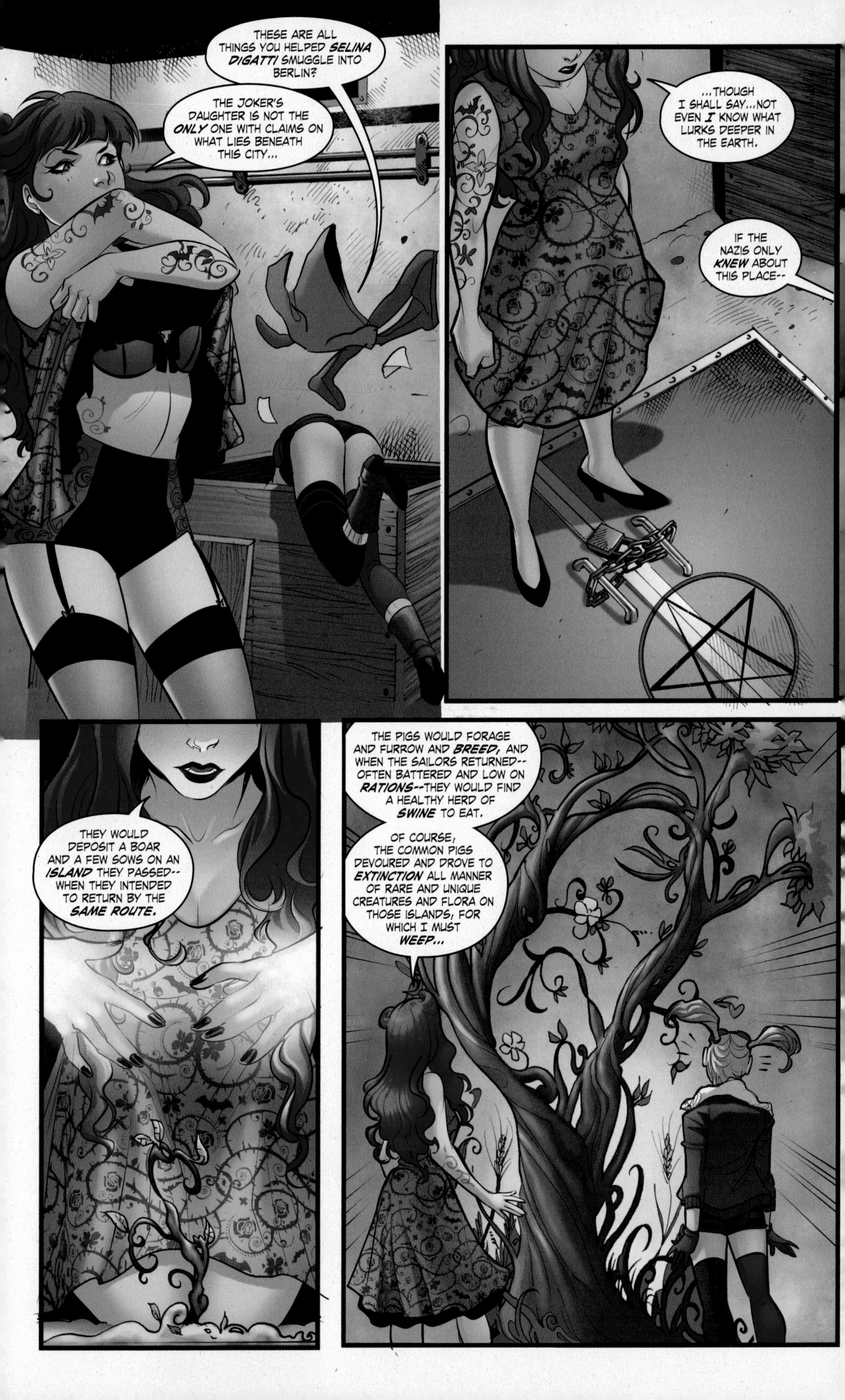
THESE ARE ALL THINGS YOU HELPED SELINA DIGATTI SMUGGLE INTO BERLIN?
THE JOKER'S DAUGHTER IS NOT THE ONLY ONE WITH CLAIMS ON WHAT LIES BENEATH THIS CITY...
...THOUGH I SHALL SAY...NOT EVEN I KNOW WHAT LURKS DEEPER IN THE EARTH.
IF THE NAZIS ONLY KNEW ABOUT THIS PLACE--
THEY WOULD DEPOSIT A BOAR AND A FEW SOWS ON AN ISLAND THEY PASSED-- WHEN THEY INTENDED TO RETURN BY THE SAME ROUTE.
THE PIGS WOULD FORAGE AND FURROW AND BREED, AND WHEN THE SAILORS RETURNED-- OFTEN BATTERED AND LOW ON RATIONS--THEY WOULD FIND A HEALTHY HERD OF SWINE TO EAT.
OF COURSE, THE COMMON PIGS DEVOURED AND DROVE TO EXTINCTION ALL MANNER OF RARE AND UNIQUE CREATURES AND FLORA ON THOSE ISLANDS, FOR WHICH I MUST WEEP...
...

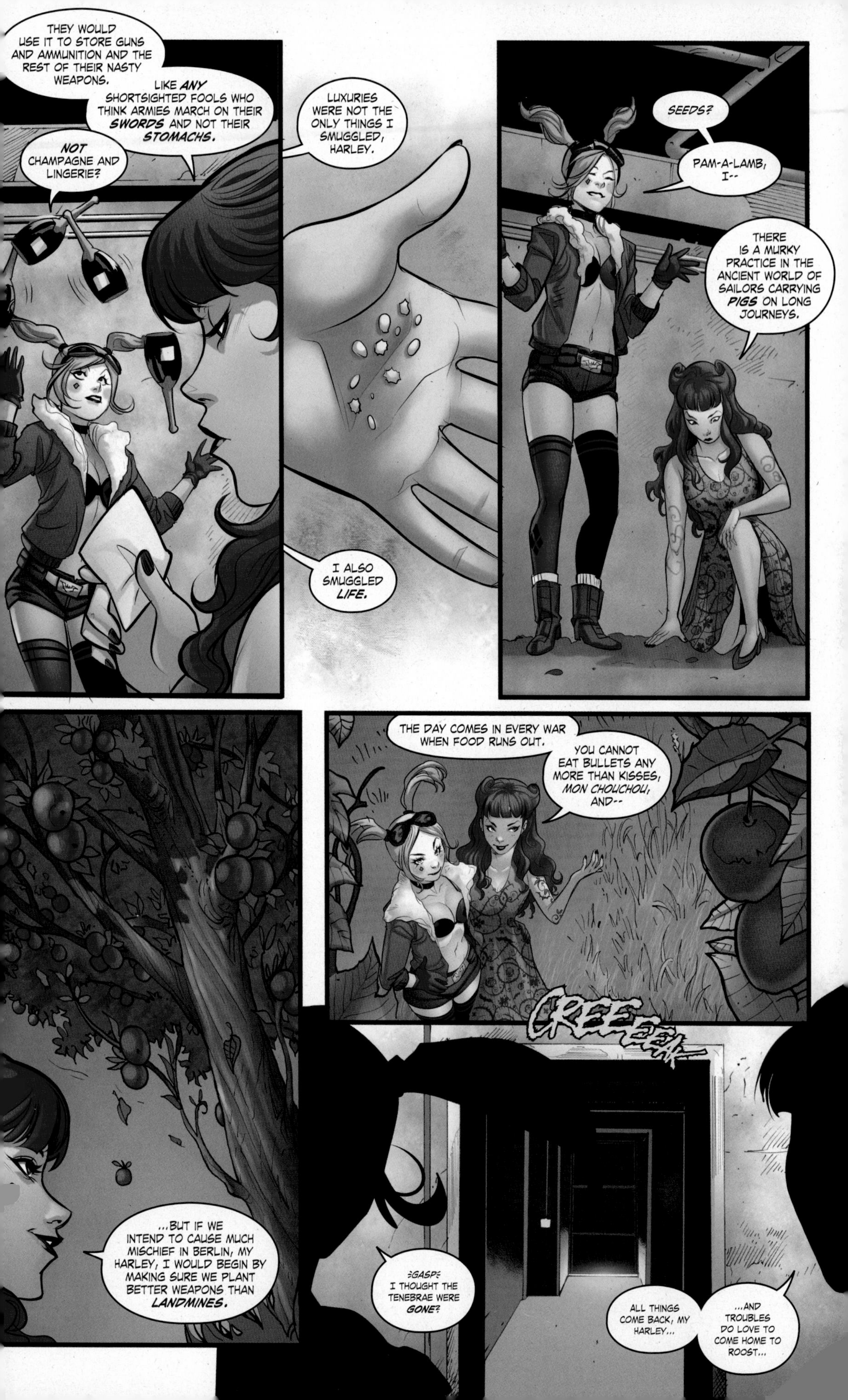

THEY WOULD USE IT TO STORE GUNS AND AMMUNITION AND THE REST OF THEIR NASTY WEAPONS.
LIKE ANY SHORTSIGHTED FOOLS WHO THINK ARMIES MARCH ON THEIR SWORDS AND NOT THEIR STOMACHS.
NOT CHAMPAGNE AND LINGERIE?
LUXURIES WERE NOT THE ONLY THINGS I SMUGGLED, HARLEY.
I ALSO SMUGGLED LIFE.
SEEDS?
PAM-A-LAMB, I--
THERE IS A MURKY PRACTICE IN THE ANCIENT WORLD OF SAILORS CARRYING PIGS ON LONG JOURNEYS.
...BUT IF WE INTEND TO CAUSE MUCH MISCHIEF IN BERLIN, MY HARLEY, I WOULD BEGIN BY MAKING SURE WE PLANT BETTER WEAPONS THAN LANDMINES.
THE DAY COMES IN EVERY WAR WHEN FOOD RUNS OUT.
YOU CANNOT EAT BULLETS ANY MORE THAN KISSES, MON CHOUCHOU, AND--
CREEEEEAK
GASP I THOUGHT THE TENEBRAE WERE GONE?
ALL THINGS COME BACK, MY HARLEY...
...AND TROUBLES DO LOVE TO COME HOME TO ROOST...

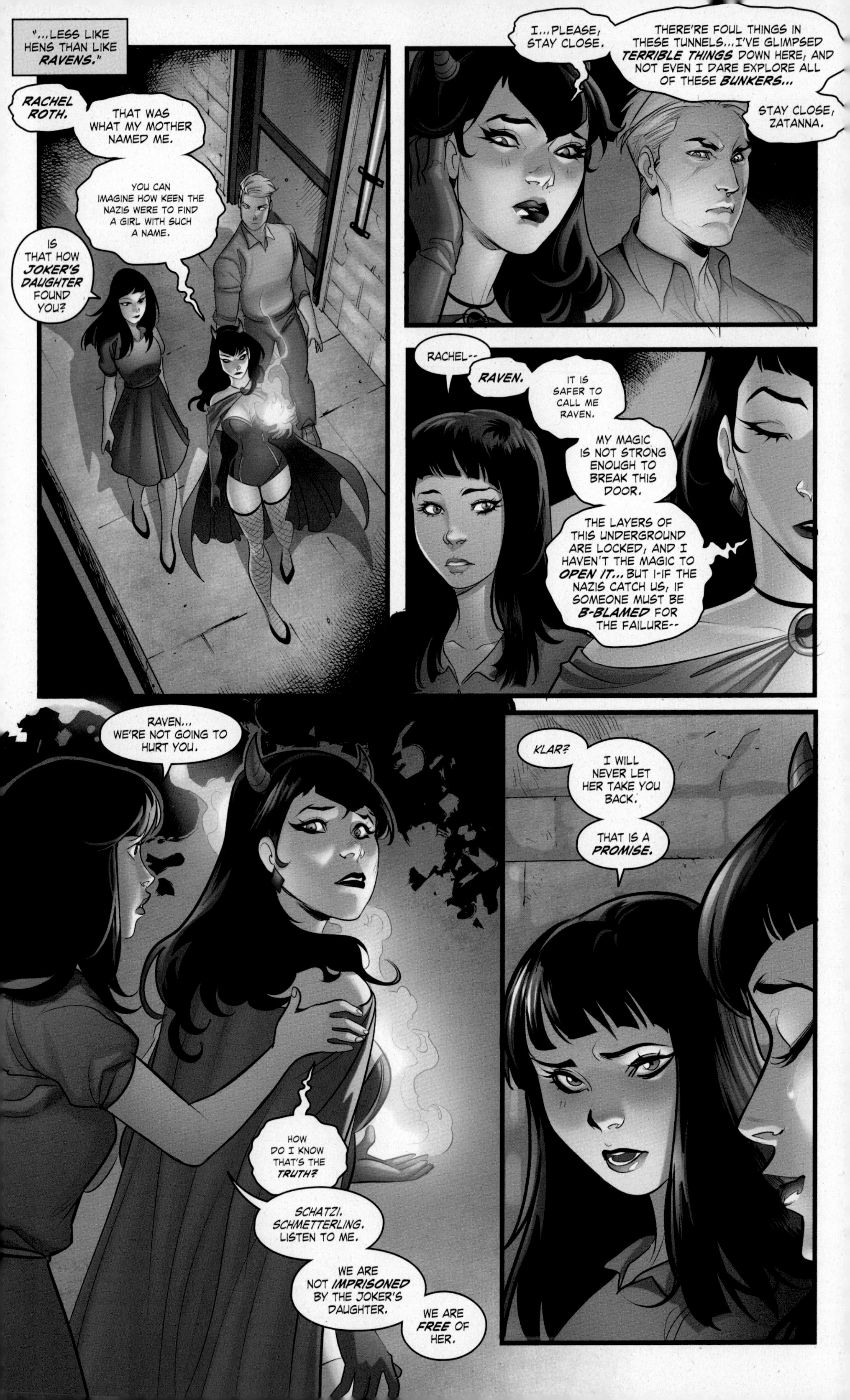
"...LESS LIKE HENS THAN LIKE *RAVENS.*"
RACHEL ROTH.
THAT WAS WHAT MY MOTHER NAMED ME.
YOU CAN IMAGINE HOW KEEN THE NAZIS WERE TO FIND A GIRL WITH SUCH A NAME.
IS THAT HOW *JOKER'S DAUGHTER* FOUND YOU?
I...PLEASE, STAY CLOSE.
THERE'RE FOUL THINGS IN THESE TUNNELS...I'VE GLIMPSED *TERRIBLE THINGS* DOWN HERE, AND NOT EVEN I DARE EXPLORE ALL OF THESE *BUNKERS...*
STAY CLOSE, ZATANNA.
RACHEL--
RAVEN.
IT IS SAFER TO CALL ME RAVEN.
MY MAGIC IS NOT STRONG ENOUGH TO BREAK THIS DOOR.
THE LAYERS OF THIS UNDERGROUND ARE LOCKED, AND I HAVEN'T THE MAGIC TO *OPEN IT...* BUT I-IF THE NAZIS CATCH US, IF SOMEONE MUST BE *B-BLAMED* FOR THE FAILURE--
RAVEN... WE'RE NOT GOING TO HURT YOU.
HOW DO I KNOW THAT'S THE *TRUTH?*
SCHATZI. SCHMETTERLING. LISTEN TO ME.
WE ARE NOT *IMPRISONED* BY THE JOKER'S DAUGHTER.
WE ARE *FREE* OF HER.
KLAR?
I WILL NEVER LET HER TAKE YOU BACK.
THAT IS A *PROMISE.*

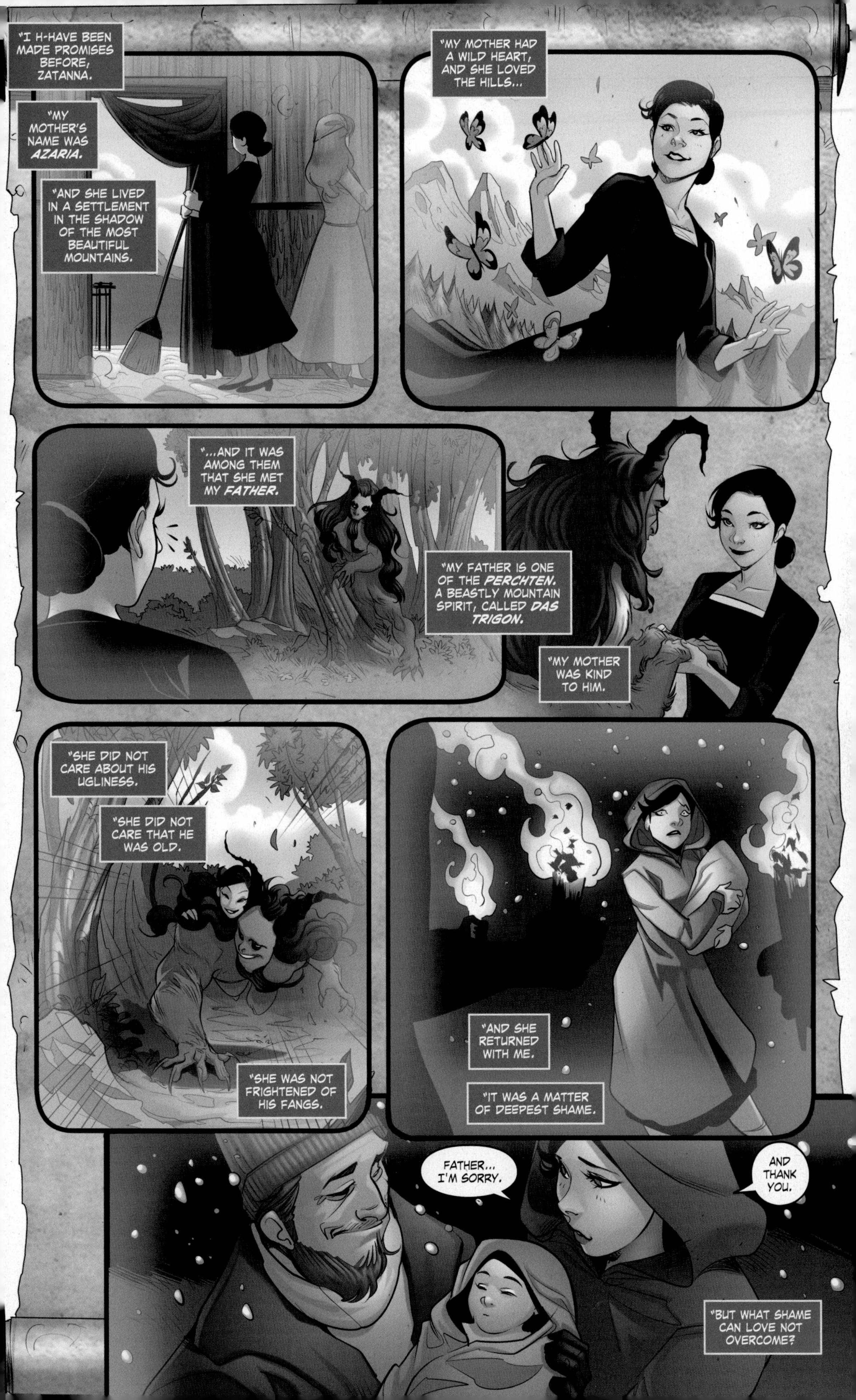
"I H-HAVE BEEN MADE PROMISES BEFORE, ZATANNA.
"MY MOTHER'S NAME WAS *AZARIA.*
"AND SHE LIVED IN A SETTLEMENT IN THE SHADOW OF THE MOST BEAUTIFUL MOUNTAINS.
"MY MOTHER HAD A WILD HEART, AND SHE LOVED THE HILLS...
"...AND IT WAS AMONG THEM THAT SHE MET MY *FATHER.*
"MY FATHER IS ONE OF THE *PERCHTEN.* A BEASTLY MOUNTAIN SPIRIT, CALLED *DAS TRIGON.*
"MY MOTHER WAS KIND TO HIM.
"SHE DID NOT CARE ABOUT HIS UGLINESS.
"SHE DID NOT CARE THAT HE WAS OLD.
"SHE WAS NOT FRIGHTENED OF HIS FANGS.
"AND SHE RETURNED WITH ME.
"IT WAS A MATTER OF DEEPEST SHAME.
FATHER... I'M SORRY.
AND THANK YOU.
"BUT WHAT SHAME CAN LOVE NOT OVERCOME?

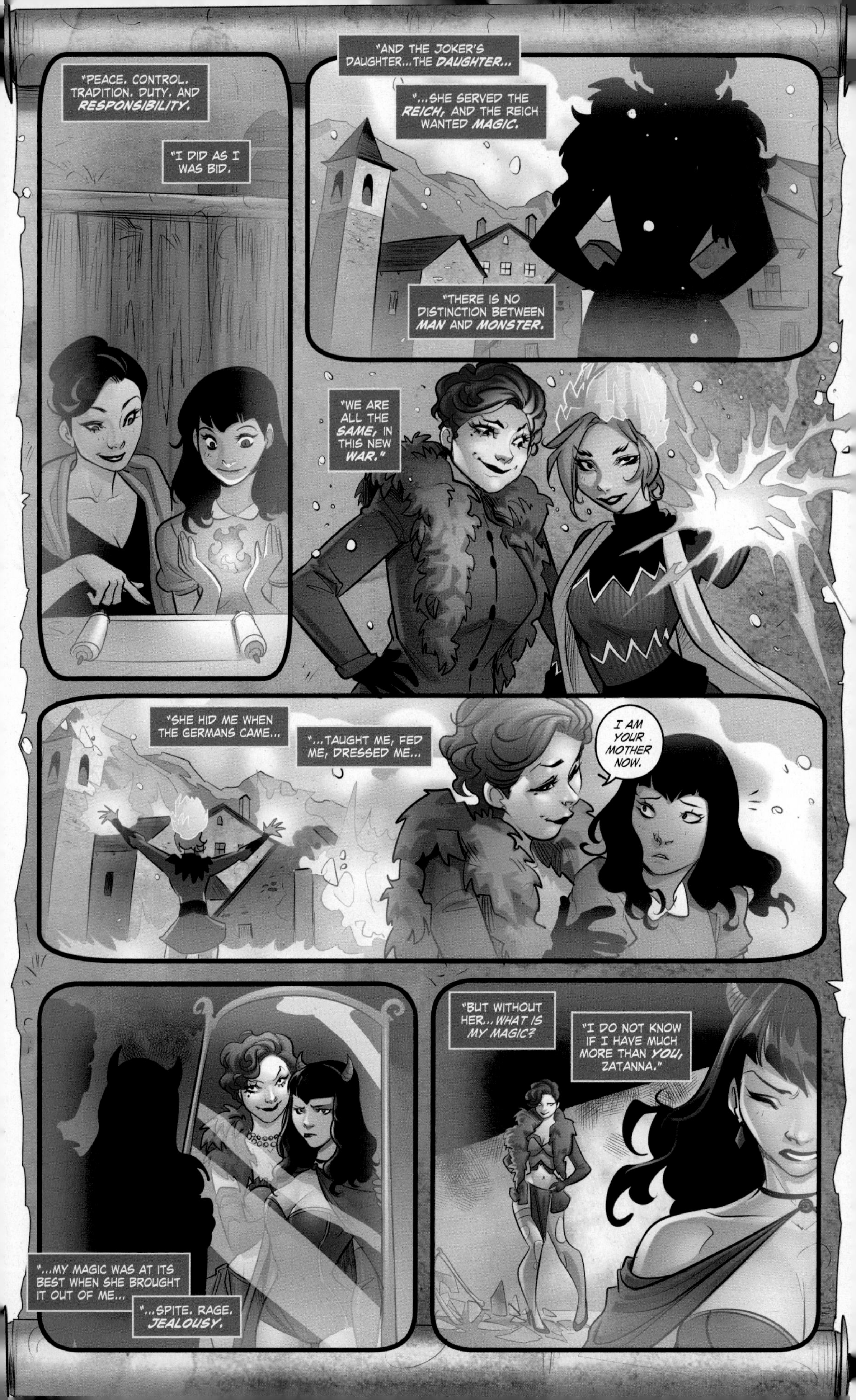
"PEACE. CONTROL. TRADITION. DUTY. AND RESPONSIBILITY.
"I DID AS I WAS BID.
"AND THE JOKER'S DAUGHTER...THE DAUGHTER...
"...SHE SERVED THE REICH, AND THE REICH WANTED MAGIC.
"THERE IS NO DISTINCTION BETWEEN MAN AND MONSTER.
"WE ARE ALL THE SAME, IN THIS NEW WAR."
"SHE HID ME WHEN THE GERMANS CAME...
"...TAUGHT ME, FED ME, DRESSED ME...
I AM YOUR MOTHER NOW.
"...MY MAGIC WAS AT ITS BEST WHEN SHE BROUGHT IT OUT OF ME...
"...SPITE. RAGE. JEALOUSY.
"BUT WITHOUT HER...WHAT IS MY MAGIC?
"I DO NOT KNOW IF I HAVE MUCH MORE THAN YOU, ZATANNA."

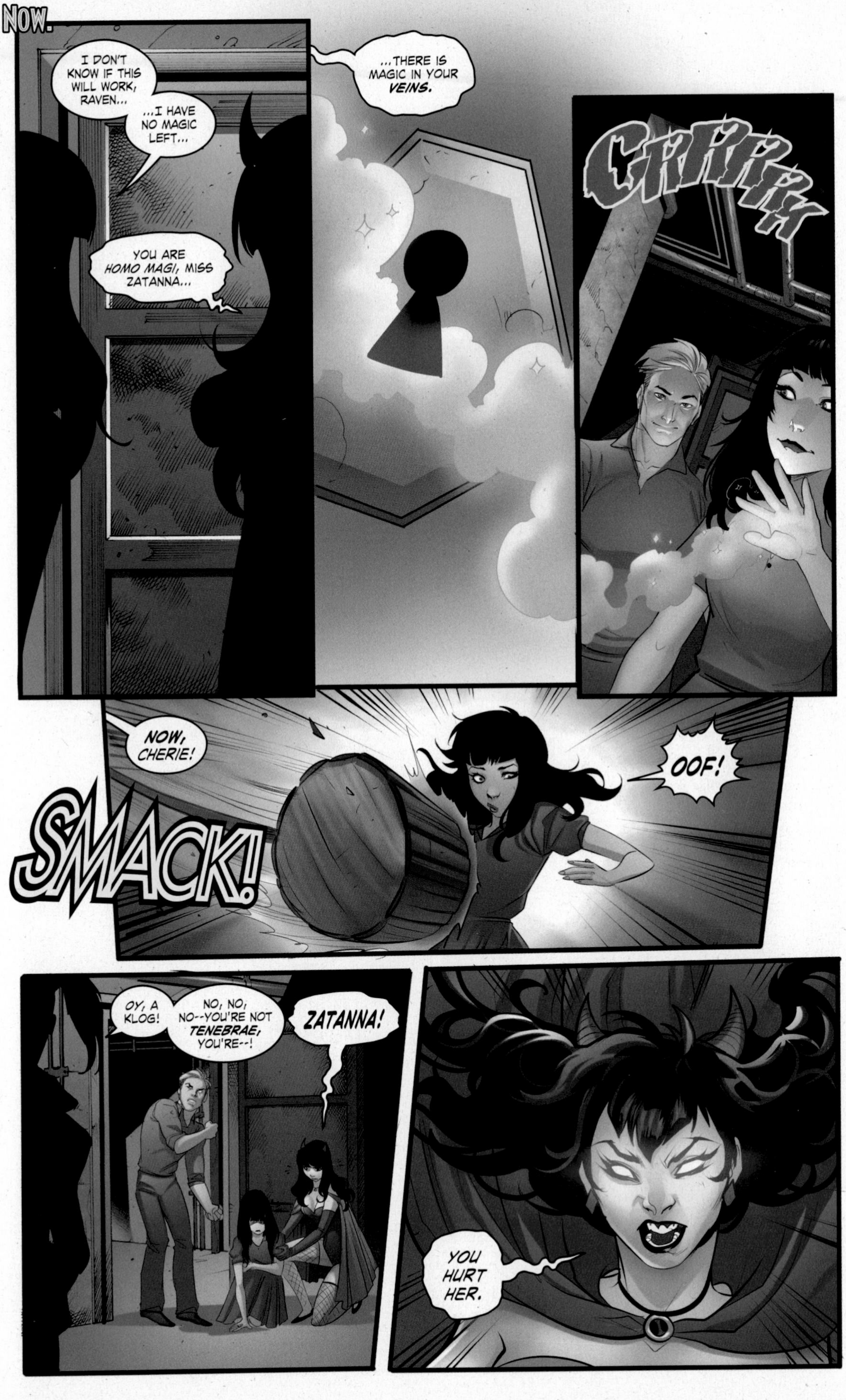
NOW.
I DON'T KNOW IF THIS WILL WORK, RAVEN...
...I HAVE NO MAGIC LEFT...
YOU ARE HOMO MAGI, MISS ZATANNA...
...THERE IS MAGIC IN YOUR VEINS.
GRRRKK
NOW, CHERIE!
SMACK!
OOF!
OY, A KLOG!
NO, NO, NO--YOU'RE NOT TENEBRAE, YOU'RE--!
ZATANNA!
YOU HURT HER.

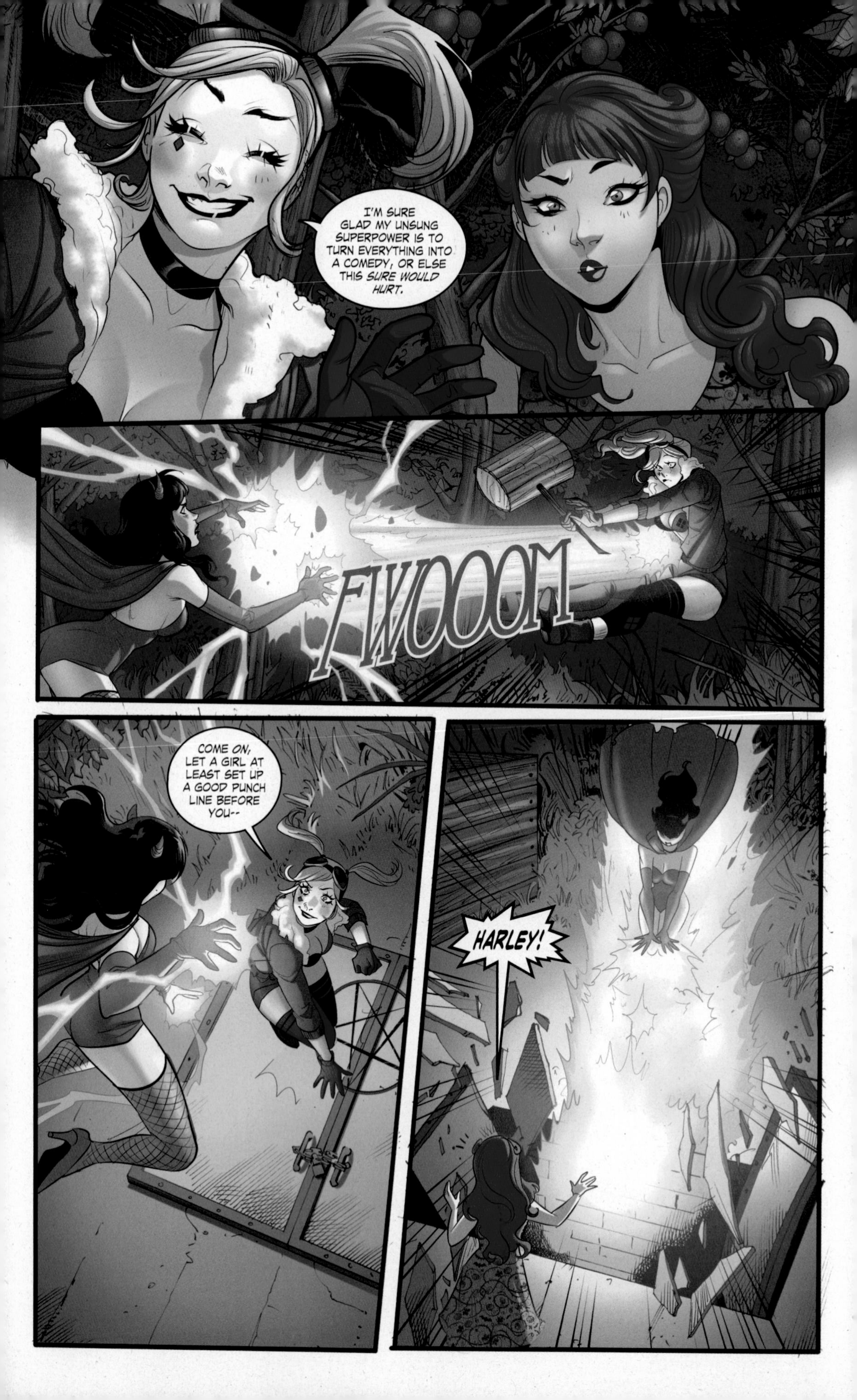
I'M SURE GLAD MY UNSUNG SUPERPOWER IS TO TURN EVERYTHING INTO A COMEDY, OR ELSE THIS SURE WOULD HURT.
FWOOOM
COME ON, LET A GIRL AT LEAST SET UP A GOOD PUNCH LINE BEFORE YOU--
HARLEY!

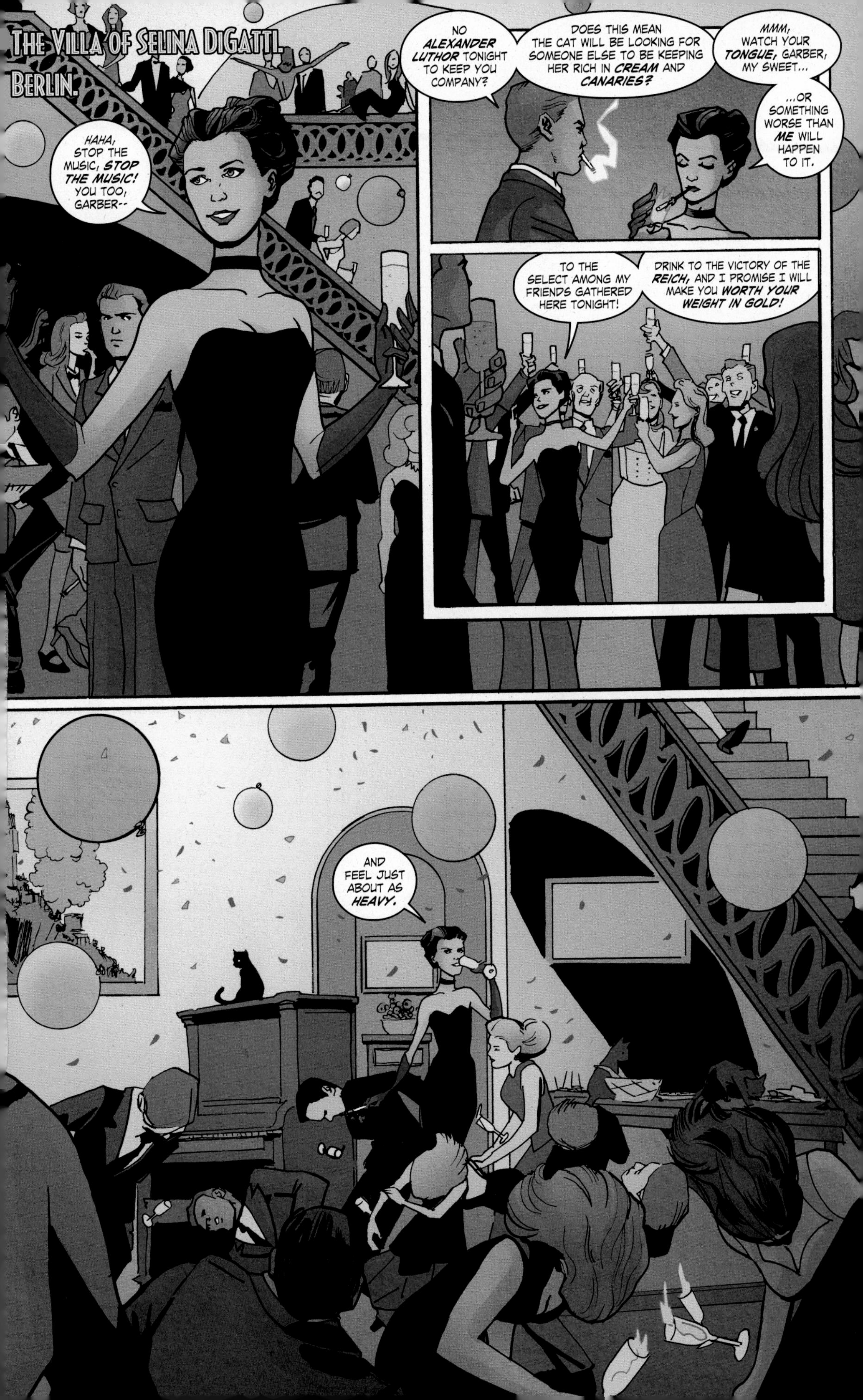
THE VILLA OF SELINA DIGATTI.
BERLIN.
HAHA, STOP THE MUSIC, STOP THE MUSIC! YOU TOO, GARBER--
NO ALEXANDER LUTHOR TONIGHT TO KEEP YOU COMPANY?
DOES THIS MEAN THE CAT WILL BE LOOKING FOR SOMEONE ELSE TO BE KEEPING HER RICH IN CREAM AND CANARIES?
MMM, WATCH YOUR TONGUE, GARBER, MY SWEET...
...OR SOMETHING WORSE THAN ME WILL HAPPEN TO IT.
TO THE SELECT AMONG MY FRIENDS GATHERED HERE TONIGHT!
DRINK TO THE VICTORY OF THE REICH, AND I PROMISE I WILL MAKE YOU WORTH YOUR WEIGHT IN GOLD!
AND FEEL JUST ABOUT AS HEAVY.

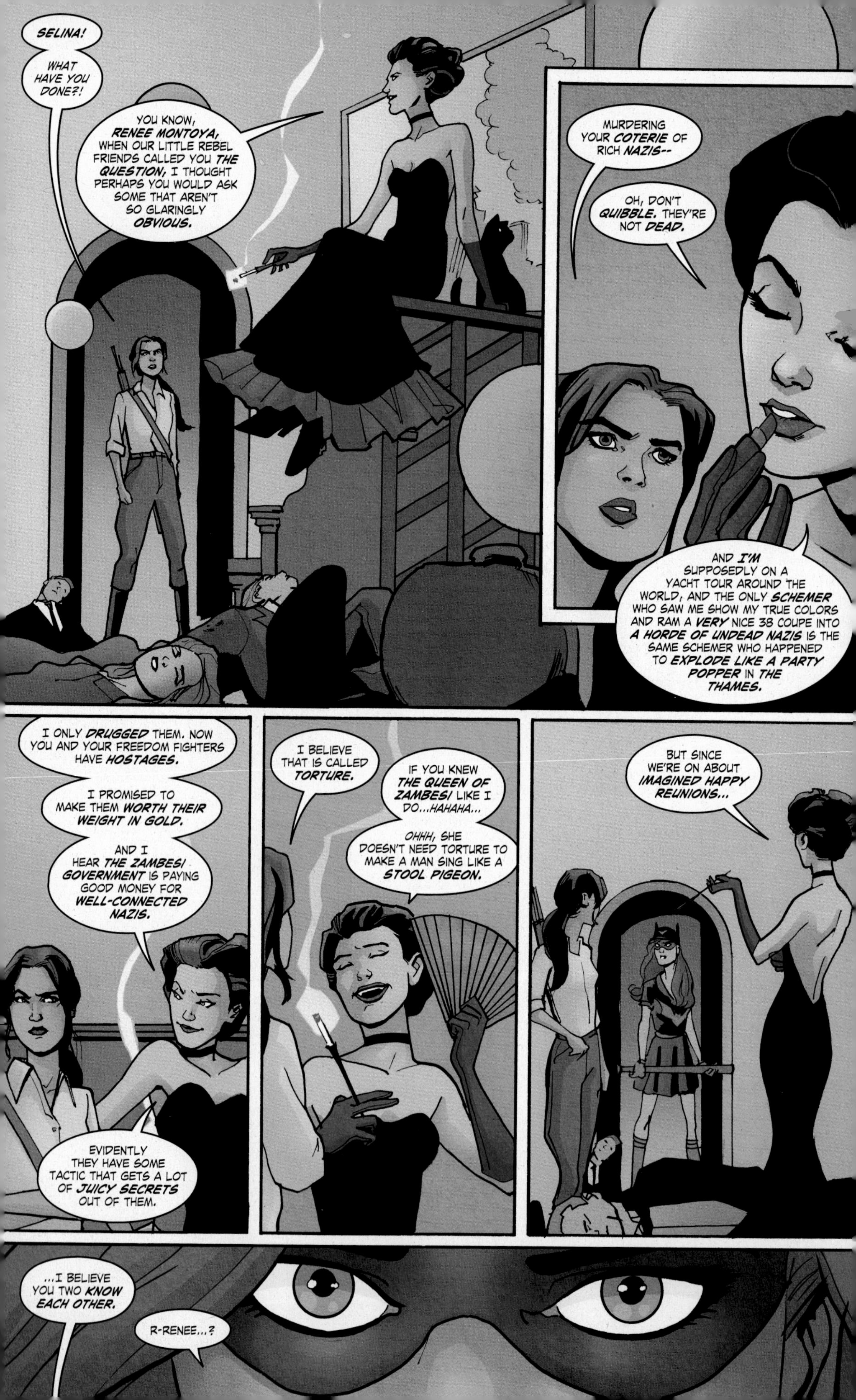
SELINA!
WHAT HAVE YOU DONE?!
YOU KNOW, RENEE MONTOYA, WHEN OUR LITTLE REBEL FRIENDS CALLED YOU THE QUESTION, I THOUGHT PERHAPS YOU WOULD ASK SOME THAT AREN'T SO GLARINGLY OBVIOUS.
MURDERING YOUR COTERIE OF RICH NAZIS--
OH, DON'T QUIBBLE. THEY'RE NOT DEAD.
AND I'M SUPPOSEDLY ON A YACHT TOUR AROUND THE WORLD, AND THE ONLY SCHEMER WHO SAW ME SHOW MY TRUE COLORS AND RAM A VERY NICE 38 COUPE INTO A HORDE OF UNDEAD NAZIS IS THE SAME SCHEMER WHO HAPPENED TO EXPLODE LIKE A PARTY POPPER IN THE THAMES.
I ONLY DRUGGED THEM. NOW YOU AND YOUR FREEDOM FIGHTERS HAVE HOSTAGES.
I PROMISED TO MAKE THEM WORTH THEIR WEIGHT IN GOLD.
AND I HEAR THE ZAMBESI GOVERNMENT IS PAYING GOOD MONEY FOR WELL-CONNECTED NAZIS.
EVIDENTLY THEY HAVE SOME TACTIC THAT GETS A LOT OF JUICY SECRETS OUT OF THEM.
I BELIEVE THAT IS CALLED TORTURE.
IF YOU KNEW THE QUEEN OF ZAMBESI LIKE I DO...HAHAHA...
OHHH, SHE DOESN'T NEED TORTURE TO MAKE A MAN SING LIKE A STOOL PIGEON.
BUT SINCE WE'RE ON ABOUT IMAGINED HAPPY REUNIONS...
...I BELIEVE YOU TWO KNOW EACH OTHER.
R-RENEE...?

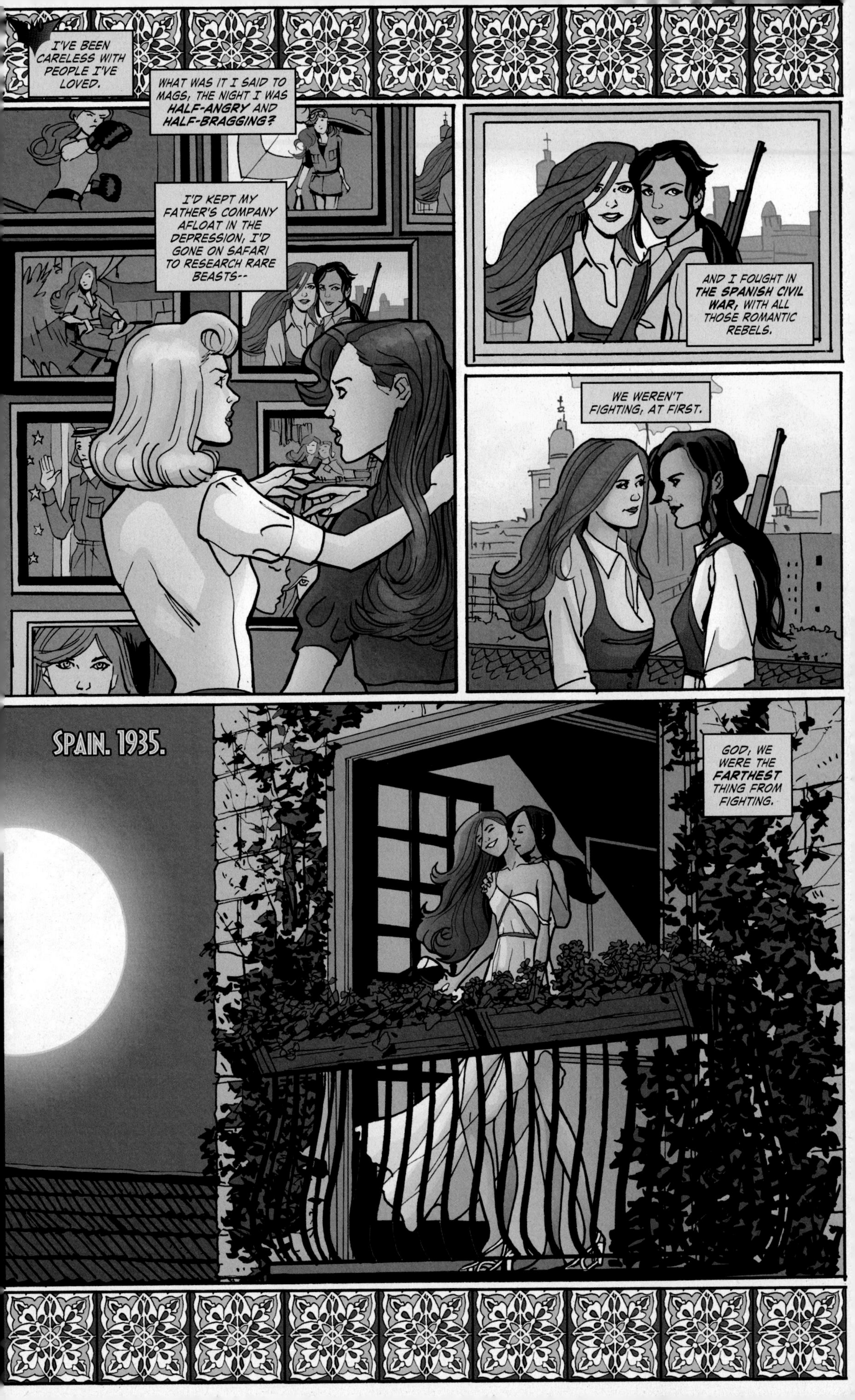

I'VE BEEN CARELESS WITH PEOPLE I'VE LOVED.
WHAT WAS IT I SAID TO MAGS, THE NIGHT I WAS HALF-ANGRY AND HALF-BRAGGING?
I'D KEPT MY FATHER'S COMPANY AFLOAT IN THE DEPRESSION, I'D GONE ON SAFARI TO RESEARCH RARE BEASTS--
AND I FOUGHT IN THE SPANISH CIVIL WAR, WITH ALL THOSE ROMANTIC REBELS.
WE WEREN'T FIGHTING, AT FIRST.
SPAIN. 1935.
GOD, WE WERE THE FARTHEST THING FROM FIGHTING.

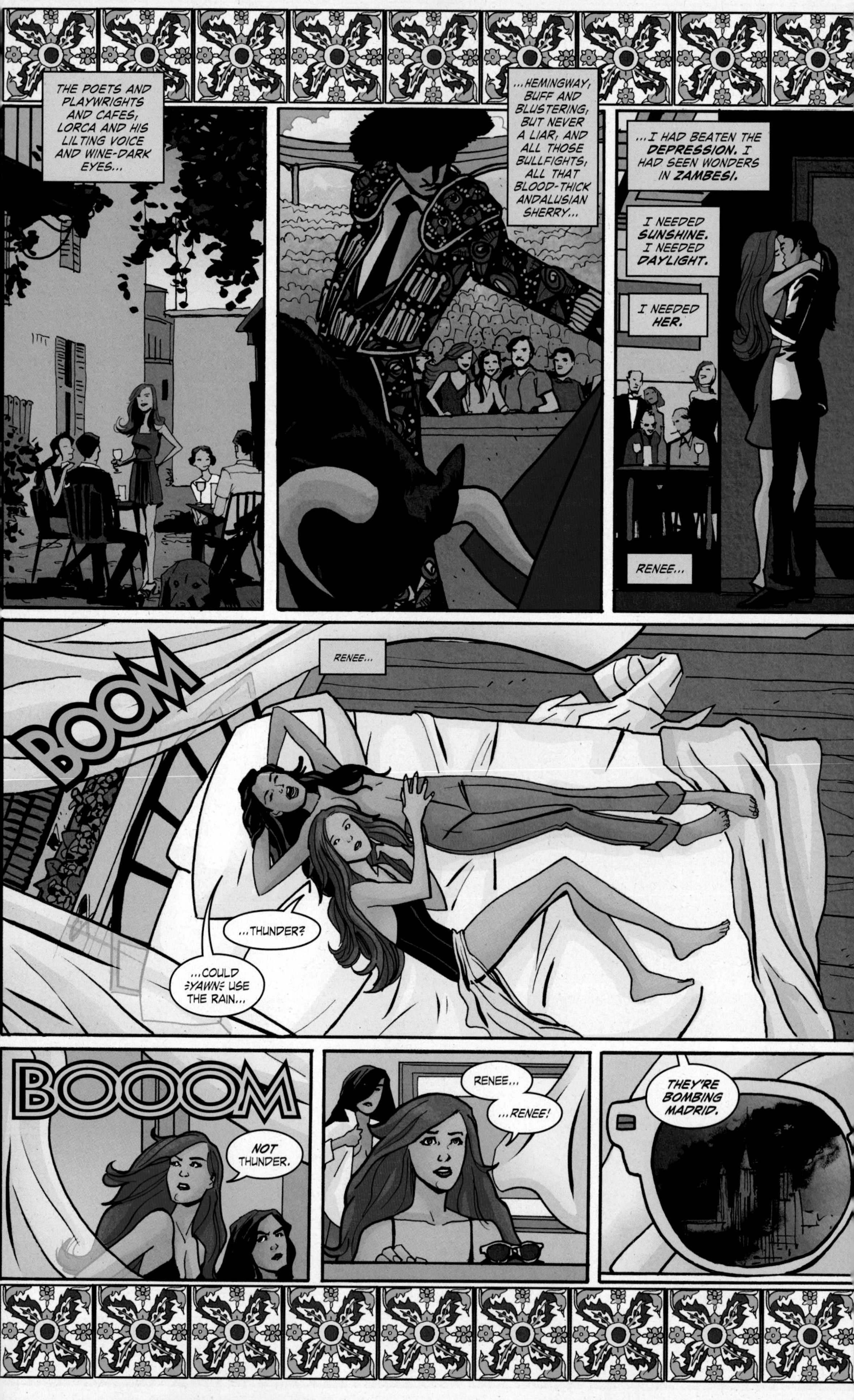
THE POETS AND PLAYWRIGHTS AND CAFES, LORCA AND HIS LILTING VOICE AND WINE-DARK EYES...
...HEMINGWAY, BUFF AND BLUSTERING, BUT NEVER A LIAR, AND ALL THOSE BULLFIGHTS, ALL THAT BLOOD-THICK ANDALUSIAN SHERRY...
...I HAD BEATEN THE DEPRESSION. I HAD SEEN WONDERS IN ZAMBESI.
I NEEDED SUNSHINE. I NEEDED DAYLIGHT.
I NEEDED HER.
RENEE...
RENEE...
BOOM
...THUNDER?
...COULD =YAWN= USE THE RAIN...
BOOOM
NOT THUNDER.
RENEE...
...RENEE!
THEY'RE BOMBING MADRID.

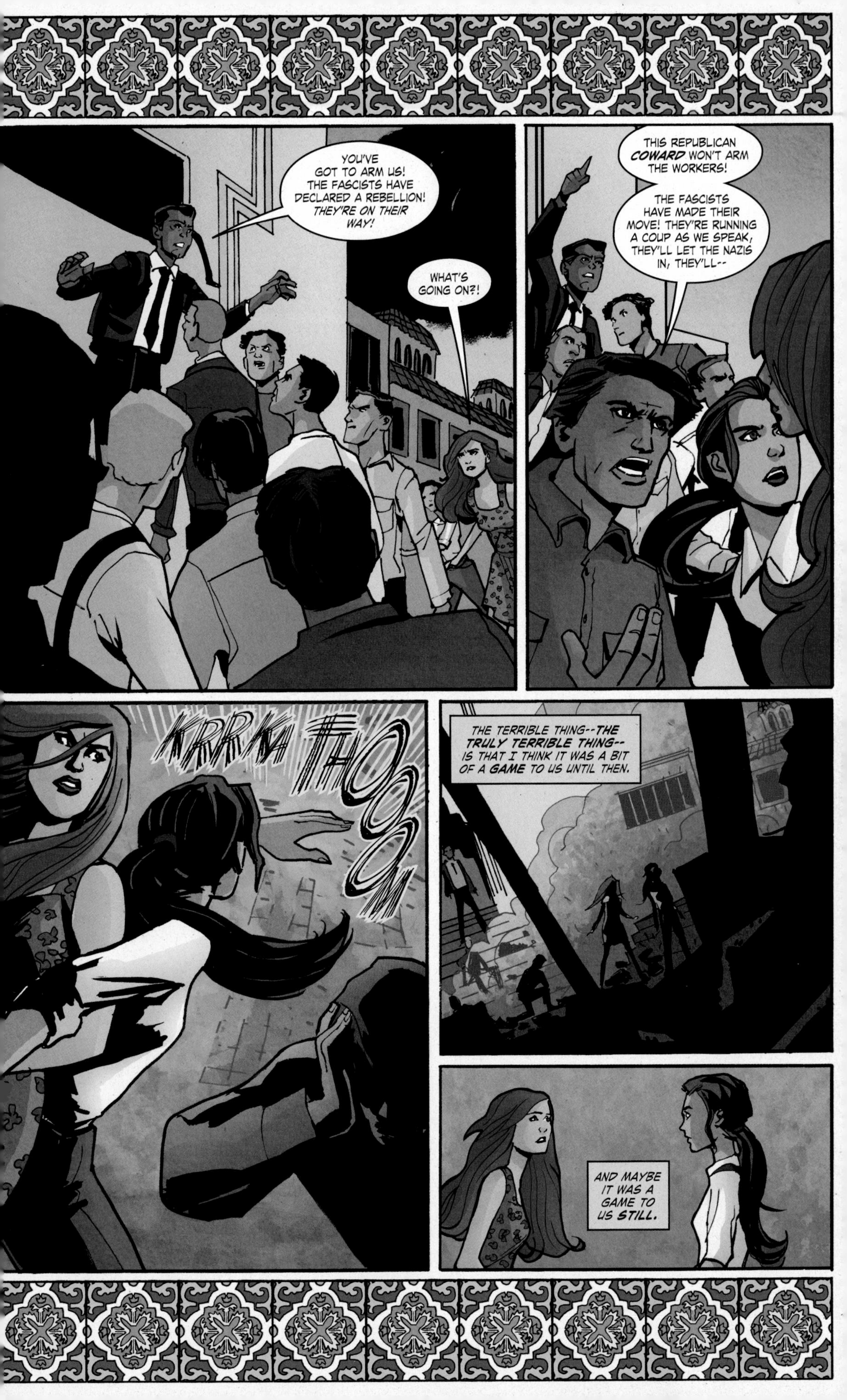
YOU'VE GOT TO ARM US! THE FASCISTS HAVE DECLARED A REBELLION! THEY'RE ON THEIR WAY!
WHAT'S GOING ON?!
THIS REPUBLICAN COWARD WON'T ARM THE WORKERS!
THE FASCISTS HAVE MADE THEIR MOVE! THEY'RE RUNNING A COUP AS WE SPEAK, THEY'LL LET THE NAZIS IN, THEY'LL--
KRRKA THOOOOM
THE TERRIBLE THING--THE TRULY TERRIBLE THING--IS THAT I THINK IT WAS A BIT OF A GAME TO US UNTIL THEN.
AND MAYBE IT WAS A GAME TO US STILL.

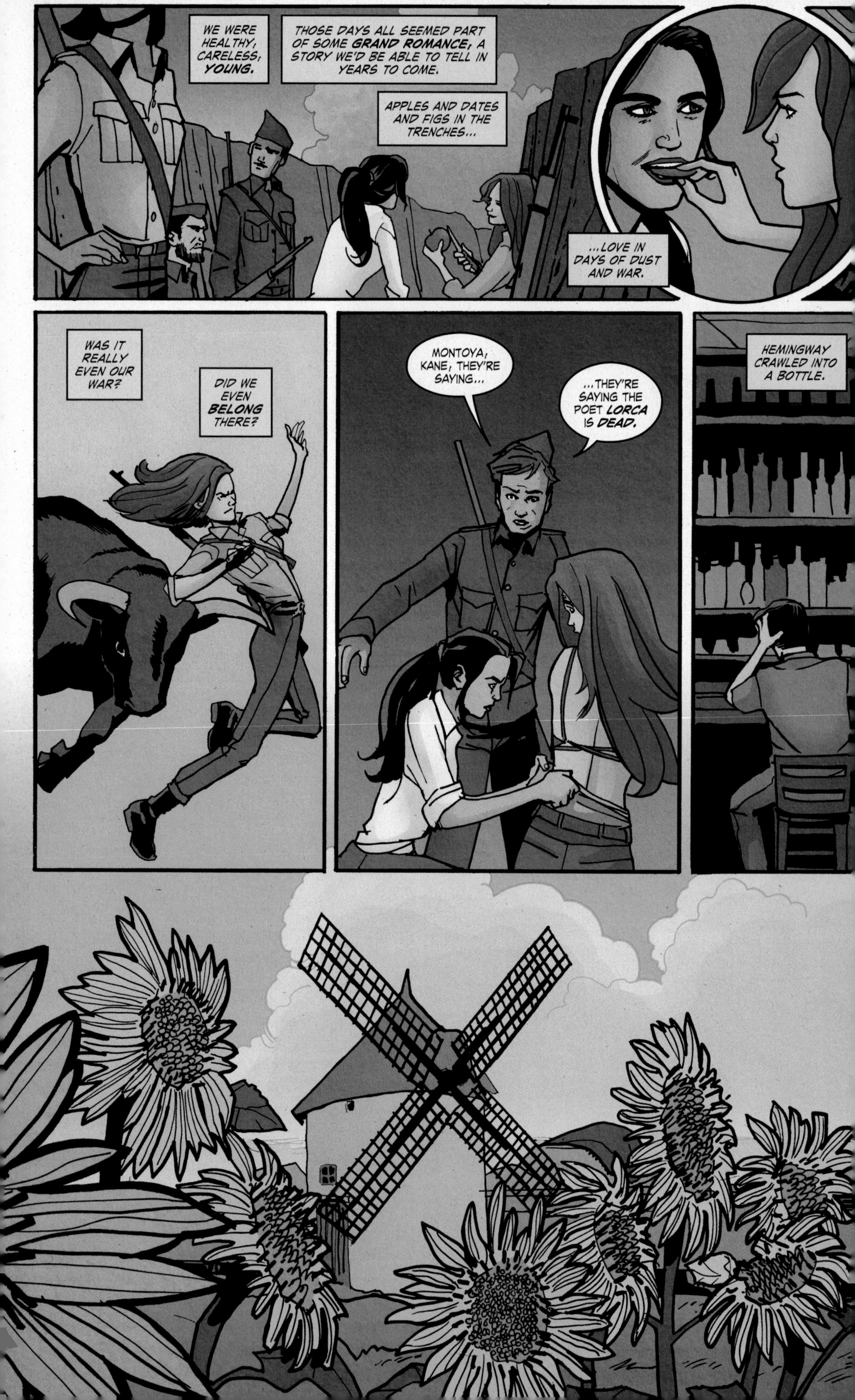
WE WERE HEALTHY, CARELESS, YOUNG.
THOSE DAYS ALL SEEMED PART OF SOME GRAND ROMANCE, A STORY WE'D BE ABLE TO TELL IN YEARS TO COME.
APPLES AND DATES AND FIGS IN THE TRENCHES...
...LOVE IN DAYS OF DUST AND WAR.
WAS IT REALLY EVEN OUR WAR?
DID WE EVEN BELONG THERE?
MONTOYA, KANE, THEY'RE SAYING...
...THEY'RE SAYING THE POET LORCA IS DEAD.
HEMINGWAY CRAWLED INTO A BOTTLE.

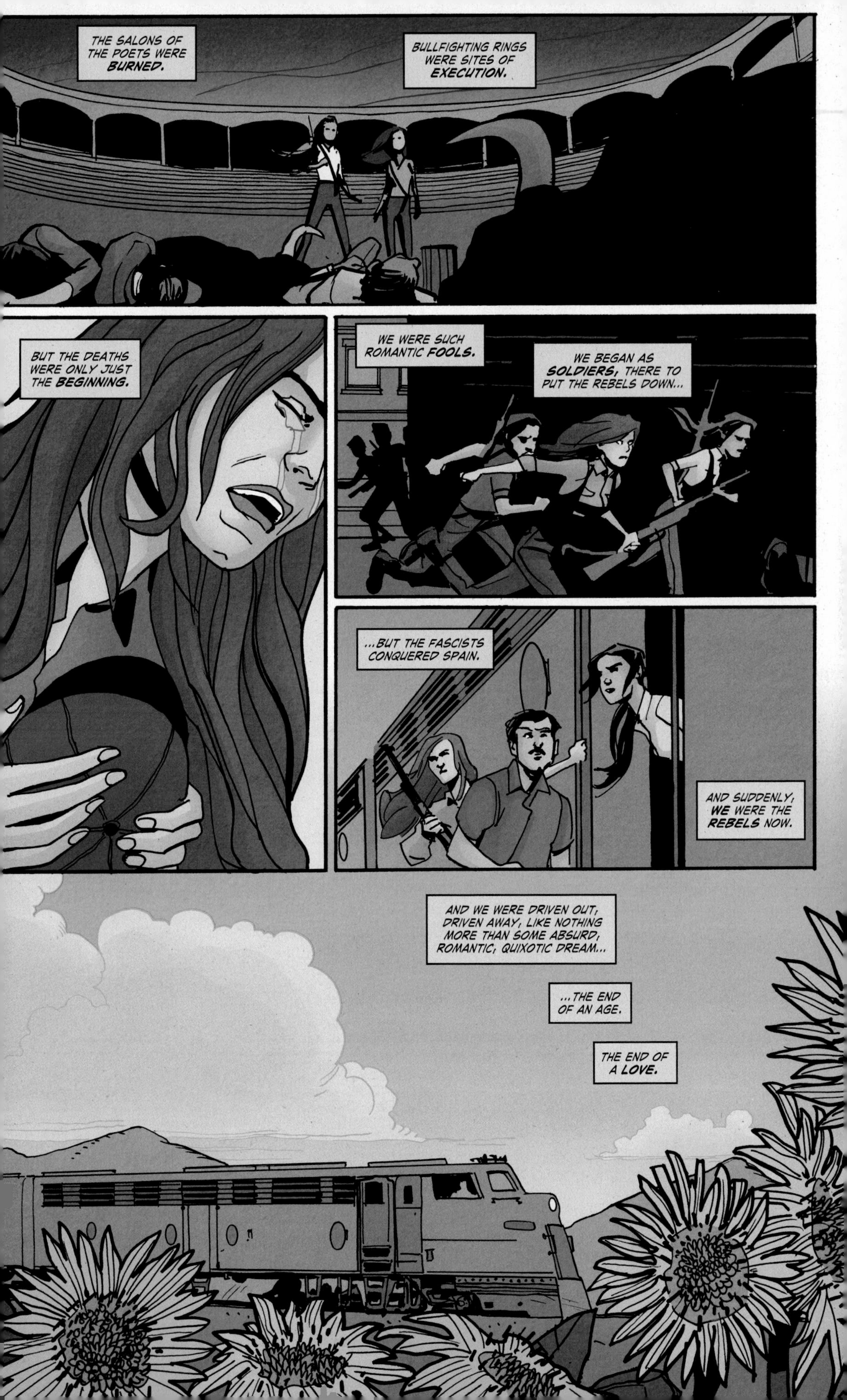
THE SALONS OF THE POETS WERE BURNED.
BULLFIGHTING RINGS WERE SITES OF EXECUTION.
BUT THE DEATHS WERE ONLY JUST THE BEGINNING.
WE WERE SUCH ROMANTIC FOOLS.
WE BEGAN AS SOLDIERS, THERE TO PUT THE REBELS DOWN...
...BUT THE FASCISTS CONQUERED SPAIN.
AND SUDDENLY, WE WERE THE REBELS NOW.
AND WE WERE DRIVEN OUT, DRIVEN AWAY, LIKE NOTHING MORE THAN SOME ABSURD, ROMANTIC, QUIXOTIC DREAM...
...THE END OF AN AGE.
THE END OF A LOVE.

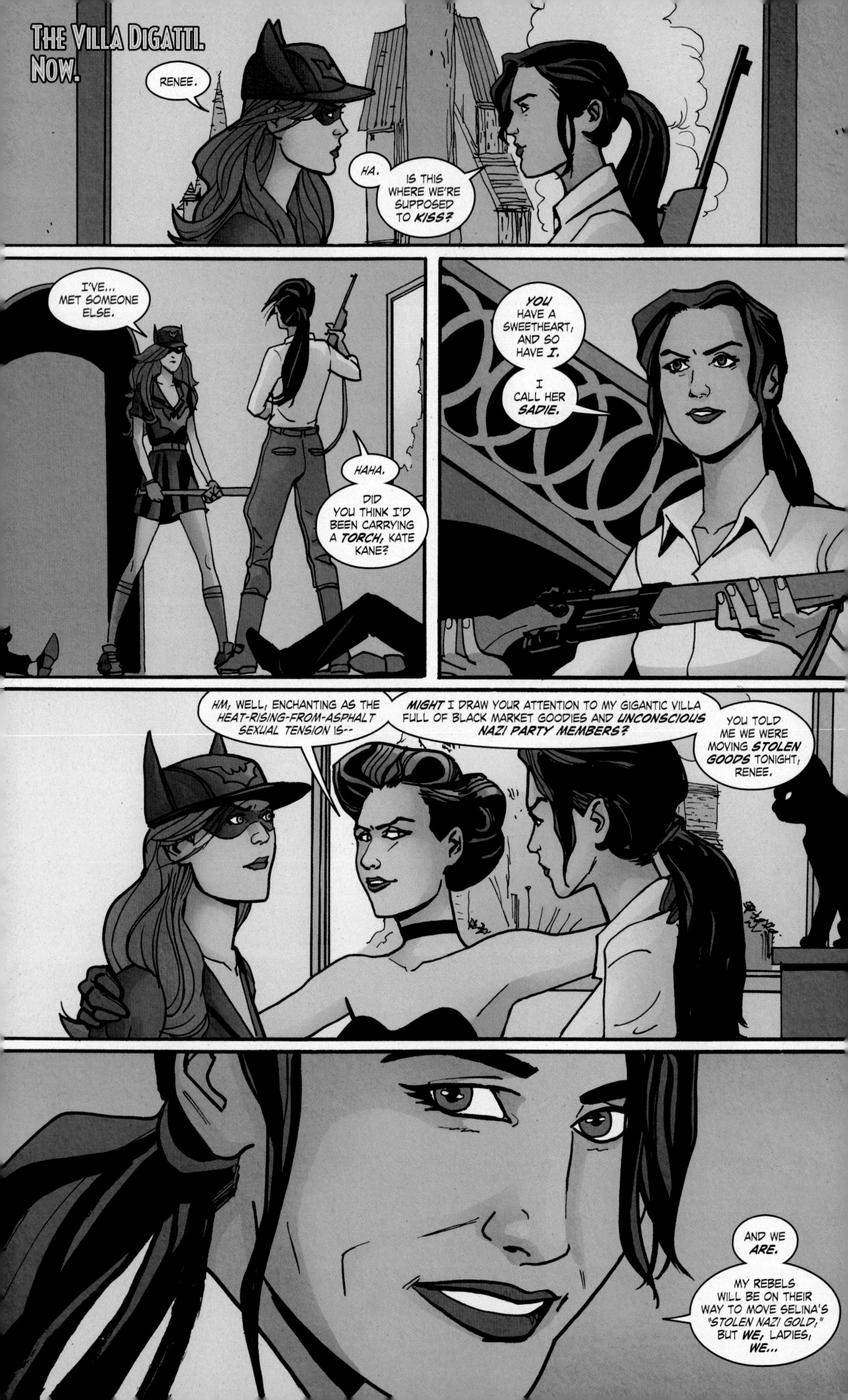
THE VILLA DIGATTI. NOW.
RENEE.
HA.
IS THIS WHERE WE'RE SUPPOSED TO KISS?
I'VE... MET SOMEONE ELSE.
HAHA.
DID YOU THINK I'D BEEN CARRYING A TORCH, KATE KANE?
YOU HAVE A SWEETHEART, AND SO HAVE I.
I CALL HER SADIE.
HM, WELL, ENCHANTING AS THE HEAT-RISING-FROM-ASPHALT SEXUAL TENSION IS--
MIGHT I DRAW YOUR ATTENTION TO MY GIGANTIC VILLA FULL OF BLACK MARKET GOODIES AND UNCONSCIOUS NAZI PARTY MEMBERS?
YOU TOLD ME WE WERE MOVING STOLEN GOODS TONIGHT, RENEE.
AND WE ARE.
MY REBELS WILL BE ON THEIR WAY TO MOVE SELINA'S "STOLEN NAZI GOLD," BUT WE, LADIES, WE...

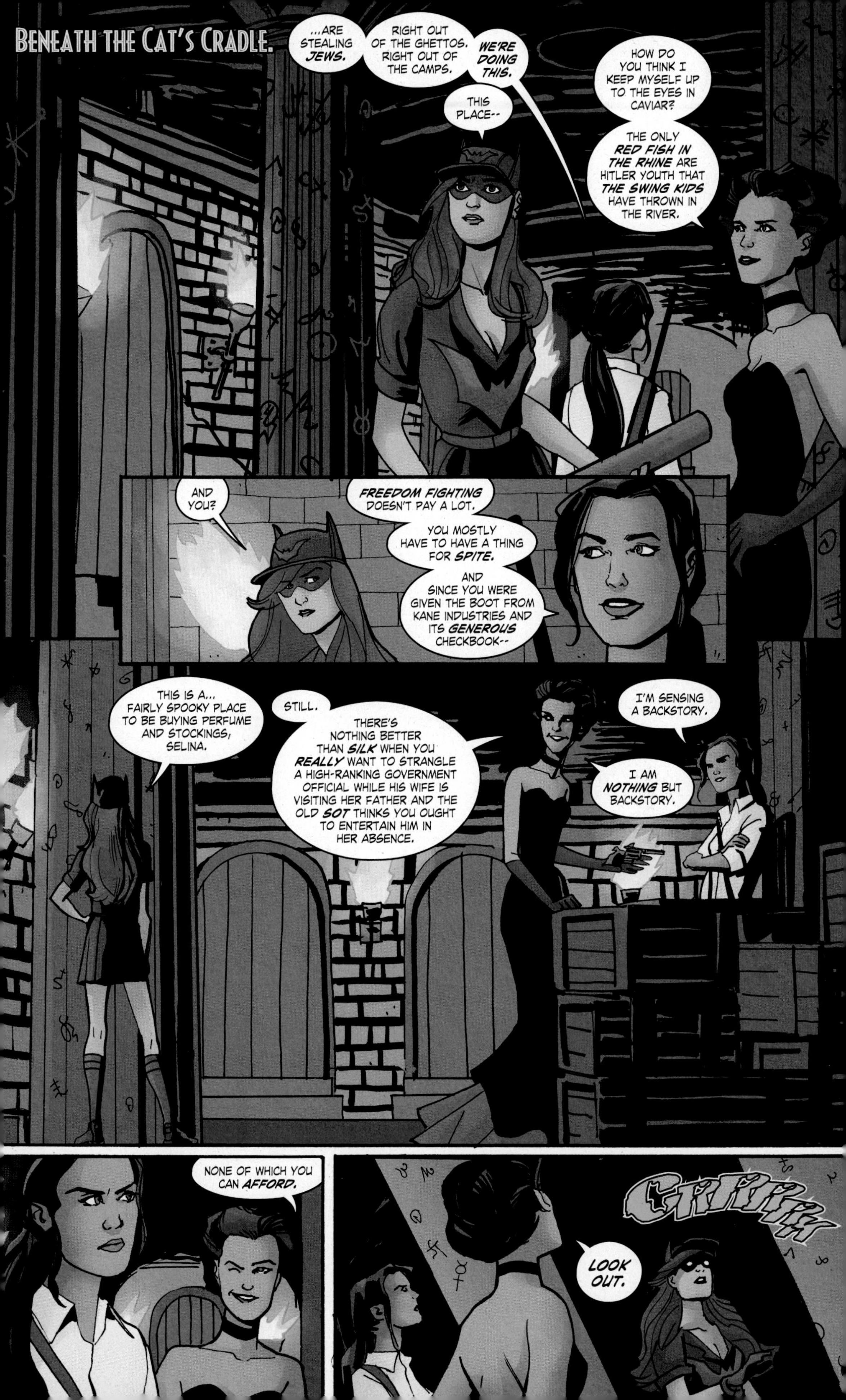
BENEATH THE CAT'S CRADLE.
...ARE STEALING JEWS.
RIGHT OUT OF THE GHETTOS. RIGHT OUT OF THE CAMPS.
WE'RE DOING THIS.
THIS PLACE--
HOW DO YOU THINK I KEEP MYSELF UP TO THE EYES IN CAVIAR?
THE ONLY RED FISH IN THE RHINE ARE HITLER YOUTH THAT THE SWING KIDS HAVE THROWN IN THE RIVER.
AND YOU?
FREEDOM FIGHTING DOESN'T PAY A LOT.
YOU MOSTLY HAVE TO HAVE A THING FOR SPITE.
AND SINCE YOU WERE GIVEN THE BOOT FROM KANE INDUSTRIES AND ITS GENEROUS CHECKBOOK--
THIS IS A... FAIRLY SPOOKY PLACE TO BE BUYING PERFUME AND STOCKINGS, SELINA.
STILL.
THERE'S NOTHING BETTER THAN SILK WHEN YOU REALLY WANT TO STRANGLE A HIGH-RANKING GOVERNMENT OFFICIAL WHILE HIS WIFE IS VISITING HER FATHER AND THE OLD SOT THINKS YOU OUGHT TO ENTERTAIN HIM IN HER ABSENCE.
I'M SENSING A BACKSTORY.
I AM NOTHING BUT BACKSTORY.
NONE OF WHICH YOU CAN AFFORD.
CRRRK
LOOK OUT.

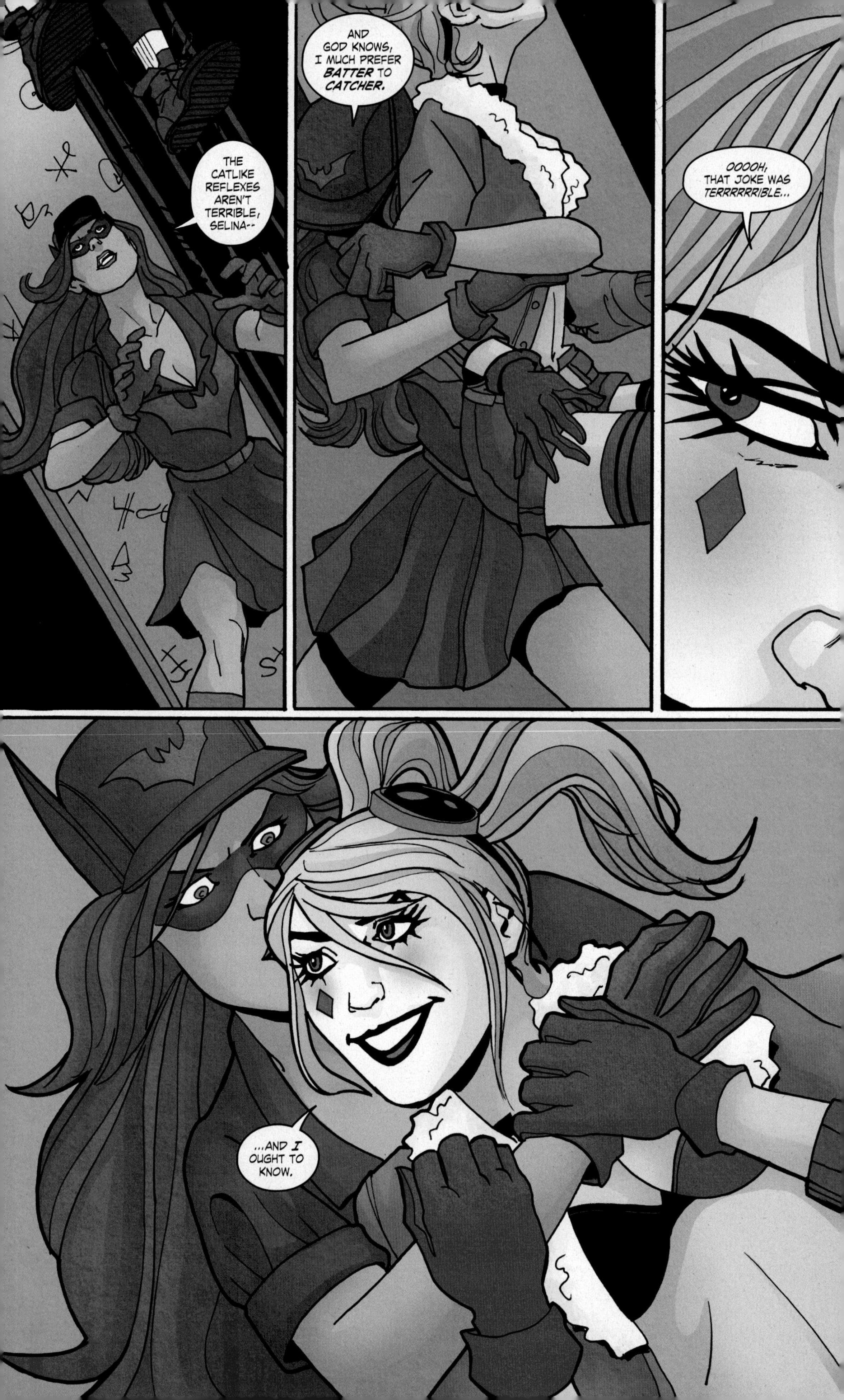
THE CATLIKE REFLEXES AREN'T TERRIBLE, SELINA--
AND GOD KNOWS, I MUCH PREFER **BATTER** TO **CATCHER**.
OOOOH, THAT JOKE WAS *TERRRRRRIBLE*...
...AND *I* OUGHT TO KNOW.

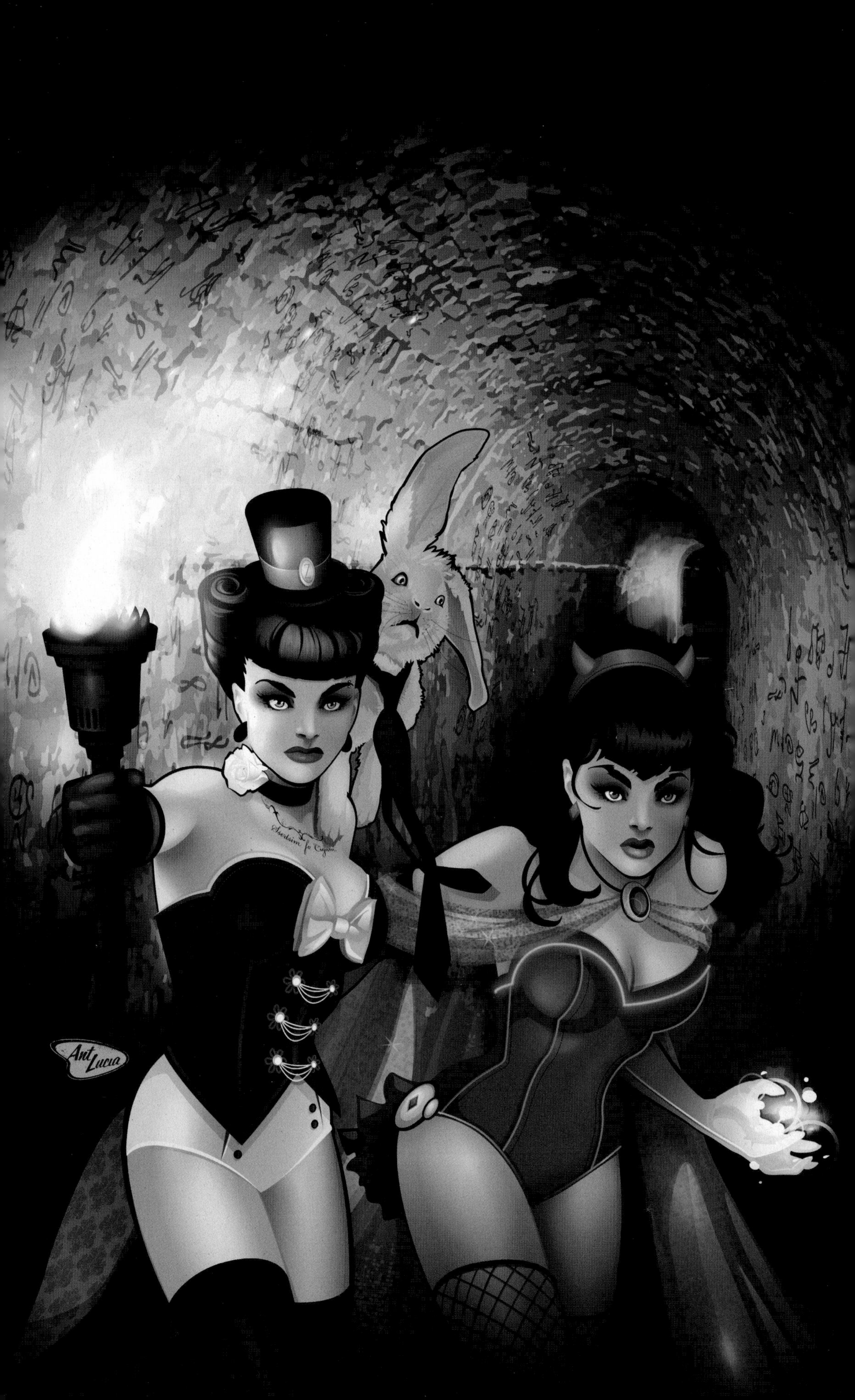
Ant Lucia

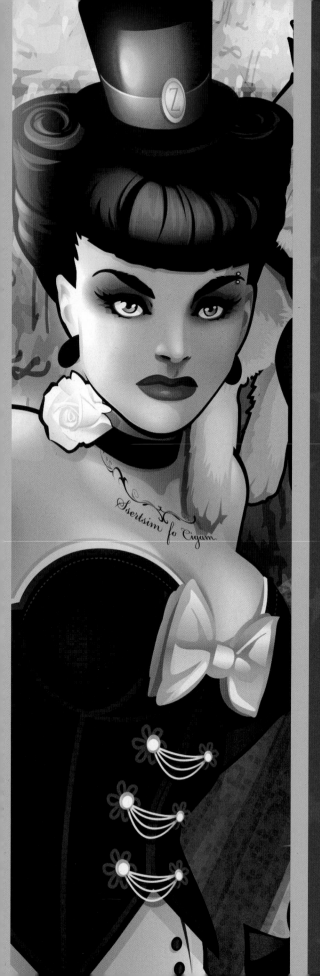

WAR STORIES

MARGUERITE BENNETT
Writer

MIRKA ANDOLFO
LAURA BRAGA
Artists

J. NANJAN
Colorist

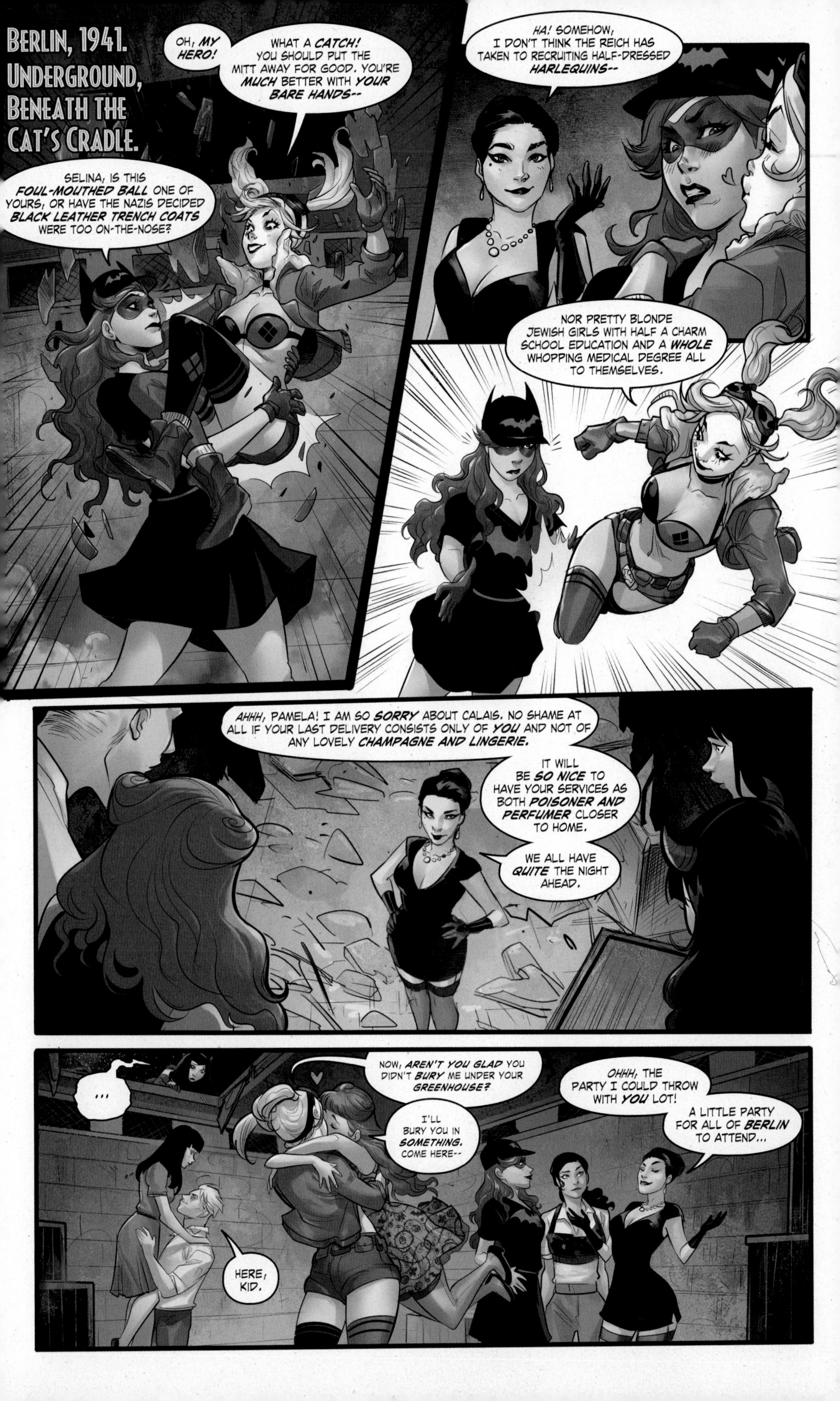
BERLIN, 1941. UNDERGROUND, BENEATH THE CAT'S CRADLE.
OH, MY HERO!
WHAT A CATCH! YOU SHOULD PUT THE MITT AWAY FOR GOOD. YOU'RE MUCH BETTER WITH YOUR BARE HANDS--
SELINA, IS THIS FOUL-MOUTHED BALL ONE OF YOURS, OR HAVE THE NAZIS DECIDED BLACK LEATHER TRENCH COATS WERE TOO ON-THE-NOSE?
HA! SOMEHOW, I DON'T THINK THE REICH HAS TAKEN TO RECRUITING HALF-DRESSED HARLEQUINS--
NOR PRETTY BLONDE JEWISH GIRLS WITH HALF A CHARM SCHOOL EDUCATION AND A WHOLE WHOPPING MEDICAL DEGREE ALL TO THEMSELVES.
AHHH, PAMELA! I AM SO SORRY ABOUT CALAIS. NO SHAME AT ALL IF YOUR LAST DELIVERY CONSISTS ONLY OF YOU AND NOT OF ANY LOVELY CHAMPAGNE AND LINGERIE.
IT WILL BE SO NICE TO HAVE YOUR SERVICES AS BOTH POISONER AND PERFUMER CLOSER TO HOME.
WE ALL HAVE QUITE THE NIGHT AHEAD.
...
NOW, AREN'T YOU GLAD YOU DIDN'T BURY ME UNDER YOUR GREENHOUSE?
I'LL BURY YOU IN SOMETHING. COME HERE--
OHHH, THE PARTY I COULD THROW WITH YOU LOT!
A LITTLE PARTY FOR ALL OF BERLIN TO ATTEND...
HERE, KID.

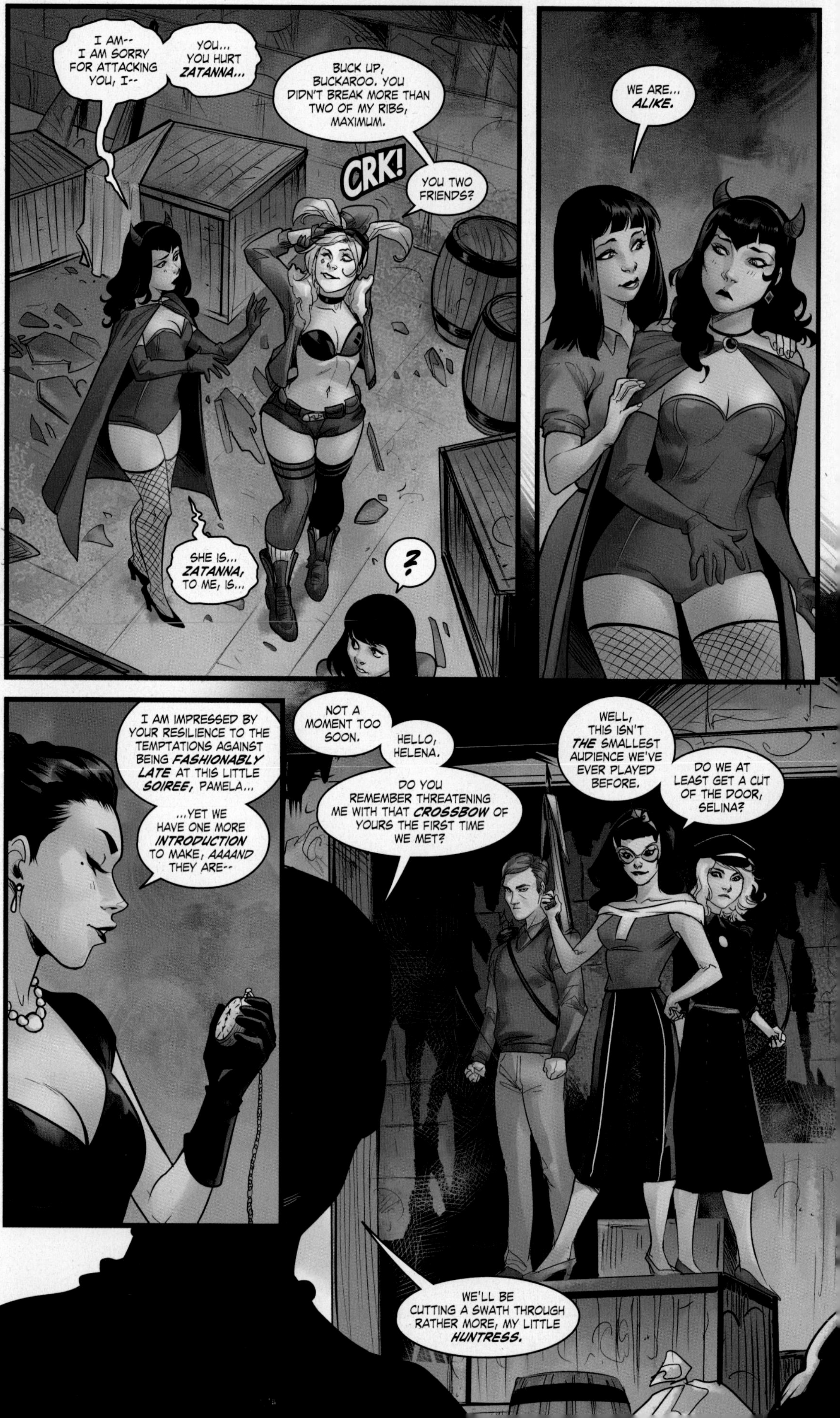
I AM-- I AM SORRY FOR ATTACKING YOU, I--
YOU... YOU HURT ZATANNA...
BUCK UP, BUCKAROO. YOU DIDN'T BREAK MORE THAN TWO OF MY RIBS, MAXIMUM.
CRK!
YOU TWO FRIENDS?
SHE IS... ZATANNA, TO ME, IS...
?
WE ARE... ALIKE.
I AM IMPRESSED BY YOUR RESILIENCE TO THE TEMPTATIONS AGAINST BEING FASHIONABLY LATE AT THIS LITTLE SOIREE, PAMELA...
...YET WE HAVE ONE MORE INTRODUCTION TO MAKE, AAAAND THEY ARE--
NOT A MOMENT TOO SOON.
HELLO, HELENA.
DO YOU REMEMBER THREATENING ME WITH THAT CROSSBOW OF YOURS THE FIRST TIME WE MET?
WELL, THIS ISN'T THE SMALLEST AUDIENCE WE'VE EVER PLAYED BEFORE.
DO WE AT LEAST GET A CUT OF THE DOOR, SELINA?
WE'LL BE CUTTING A SWATH THROUGH RATHER MORE, MY LITTLE HUNTRESS.

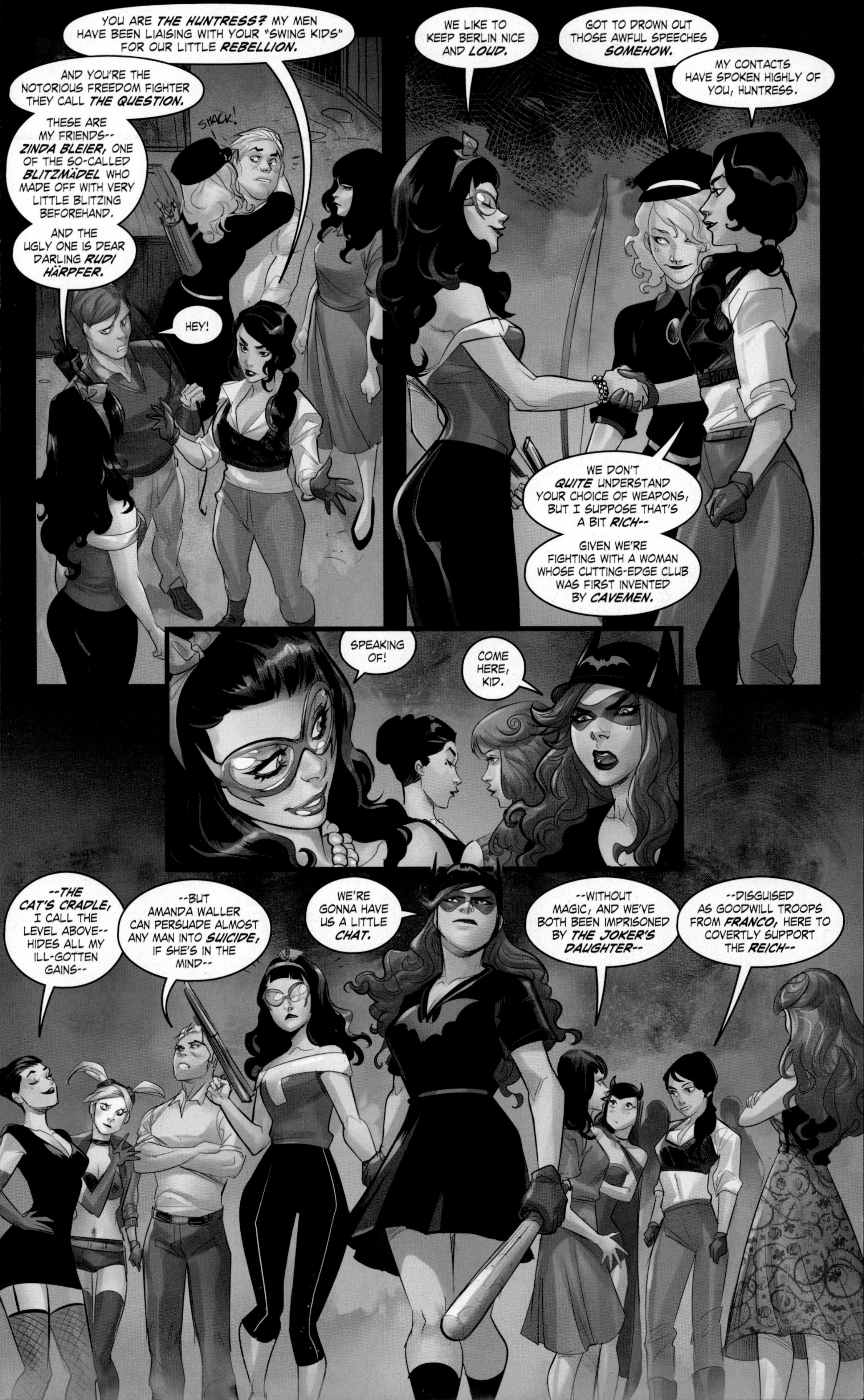
YOU ARE THE HUNTRESS? MY MEN HAVE BEEN LIAISING WITH YOUR "SWING KIDS" FOR OUR LITTLE REBELLION.
AND YOU'RE THE NOTORIOUS FREEDOM FIGHTER THEY CALL THE QUESTION.
THESE ARE MY FRIENDS-- ZINDA BLEIER, ONE OF THE SO-CALLED BLITZMÄDEL WHO MADE OFF WITH VERY LITTLE BLITZING BEFOREHAND.
AND THE UGLY ONE IS DEAR DARLING RUDI HÄRPFER.
SMACK!
HEY!
WE LIKE TO KEEP BERLIN NICE AND LOUD.
GOT TO DROWN OUT THOSE AWFUL SPEECHES SOMEHOW.
MY CONTACTS HAVE SPOKEN HIGHLY OF YOU, HUNTRESS.
WE DON'T QUITE UNDERSTAND YOUR CHOICE OF WEAPONS, BUT I SUPPOSE THAT'S A BIT RICH--
GIVEN WE'RE FIGHTING WITH A WOMAN WHOSE CUTTING-EDGE CLUB WAS FIRST INVENTED BY CAVEMEN.
SPEAKING OF!
COME HERE, KID.
--THE CAT'S CRADLE, I CALL THE LEVEL ABOVE-- HIDES ALL MY ILL-GOTTEN GAINS--
--BUT AMANDA WALLER CAN PERSUADE ALMOST ANY MAN INTO SUICIDE, IF SHE'S IN THE MIND--
WE'RE GONNA HAVE US A LITTLE CHAT.
--WITHOUT MAGIC, AND WE'VE BOTH BEEN IMPRISONED BY THE JOKER'S DAUGHTER--
--DISGUISED AS GOODWILL TROOPS FROM FRANCO, HERE TO COVERTLY SUPPORT THE REICH--

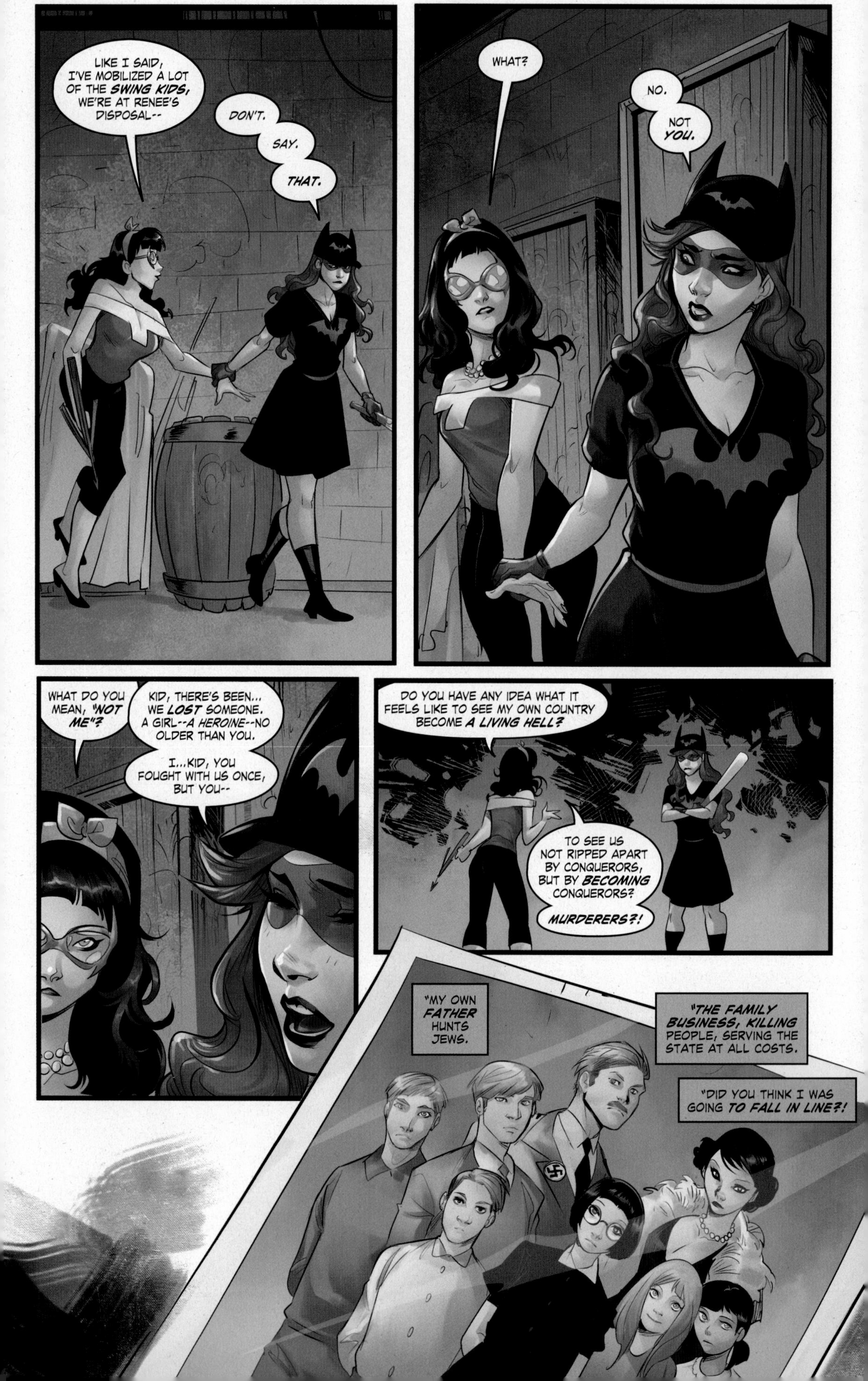

LIKE I SAID, I'VE MOBILIZED A LOT OF THE SWING KIDS, WE'RE AT RENEE'S DISPOSAL--
DON'T.
SAY.
THAT.
WHAT?
NO.
NOT YOU.
WHAT DO YOU MEAN, "NOT ME"?
KID, THERE'S BEEN... WE LOST SOMEONE. A GIRL--A HEROINE--NO OLDER THAN YOU.
I...KID, YOU FOUGHT WITH US ONCE, BUT YOU--
DO YOU HAVE ANY IDEA WHAT IT FEELS LIKE TO SEE MY OWN COUNTRY BECOME A LIVING HELL?
TO SEE US NOT RIPPED APART BY CONQUERORS, BUT BY BECOMING CONQUERORS?
MURDERERS?!
"MY OWN FATHER HUNTS JEWS.
"THE FAMILY BUSINESS, KILLING PEOPLE, SERVING THE STATE AT ALL COSTS.
"DID YOU THINK I WAS GOING TO FALL IN LINE?!

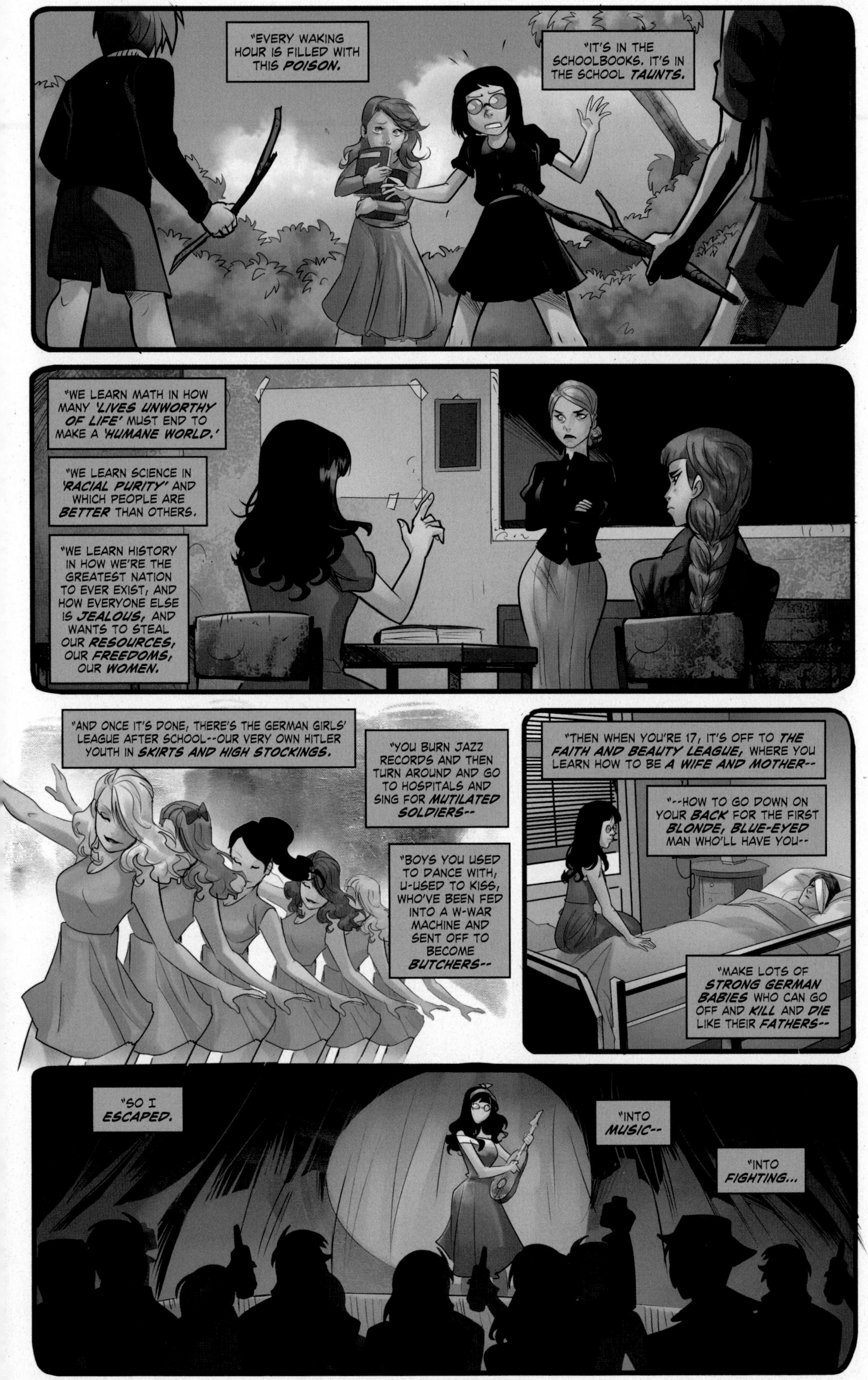
"EVERY WAKING HOUR IS FILLED WITH THIS POISON.
"IT'S IN THE SCHOOLBOOKS. IT'S IN THE SCHOOL TAUNTS.
"WE LEARN MATH IN HOW MANY 'LIVES UNWORTHY OF LIFE' MUST END TO MAKE A 'HUMANE WORLD.'
"WE LEARN SCIENCE IN 'RACIAL PURITY' AND WHICH PEOPLE ARE BETTER THAN OTHERS.
"WE LEARN HISTORY IN HOW WE'RE THE GREATEST NATION TO EVER EXIST, AND HOW EVERYONE ELSE IS JEALOUS, AND WANTS TO STEAL OUR RESOURCES, OUR FREEDOMS, OUR WOMEN.
"AND ONCE IT'S DONE, THERE'S THE GERMAN GIRLS' LEAGUE AFTER SCHOOL--OUR VERY OWN HITLER YOUTH IN SKIRTS AND HIGH STOCKINGS.
"YOU BURN JAZZ RECORDS AND THEN TURN AROUND AND GO TO HOSPITALS AND SING FOR MUTILATED SOLDIERS--
"BOYS YOU USED TO DANCE WITH, U-USED TO KISS, WHO'VE BEEN FED INTO A W-WAR MACHINE AND SENT OFF TO BECOME BUTCHERS--
"THEN WHEN YOU'RE 17, IT'S OFF TO THE FAITH AND BEAUTY LEAGUE, WHERE YOU LEARN HOW TO BE A WIFE AND MOTHER--
"--HOW TO GO DOWN ON YOUR BACK FOR THE FIRST BLONDE, BLUE-EYED MAN WHO'LL HAVE YOU--
"MAKE LOTS OF STRONG GERMAN BABIES WHO CAN GO OFF AND KILL AND DIE LIKE THEIR FATHERS--
"SO I ESCAPED.
"INTO MUSIC--
"INTO FIGHTING...

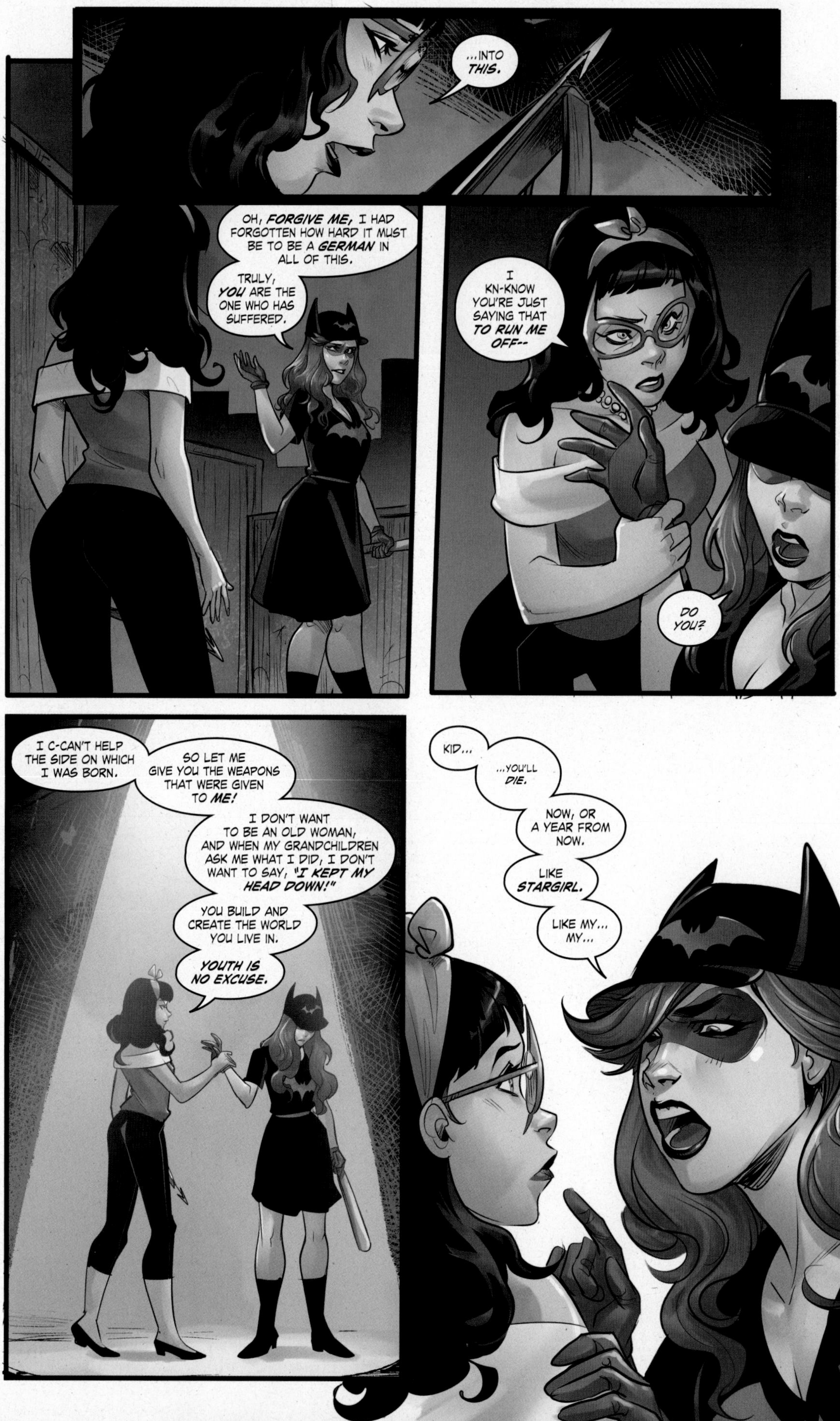

...INTO THIS.
OH, FORGIVE ME, I HAD FORGOTTEN HOW HARD IT MUST BE TO BE A GERMAN IN ALL OF THIS.
TRULY, YOU ARE THE ONE WHO HAS SUFFERED.
I KN-KNOW YOU'RE JUST SAYING THAT TO RUN ME OFF--
DO YOU?
I C-CAN'T HELP THE SIDE ON WHICH I WAS BORN.
SO LET ME GIVE YOU THE WEAPONS THAT WERE GIVEN TO ME!
I DON'T WANT TO BE AN OLD WOMAN, AND WHEN MY GRANDCHILDREN ASK ME WHAT I DID, I DON'T WANT TO SAY, "I KEPT MY HEAD DOWN!"
YOU BUILD AND CREATE THE WORLD YOU LIVE IN.
YOUTH IS NO EXCUSE.
KID...
...YOU'LL DIE.
NOW, OR A YEAR FROM NOW.
LIKE STARGIRL.
LIKE MY... MY...

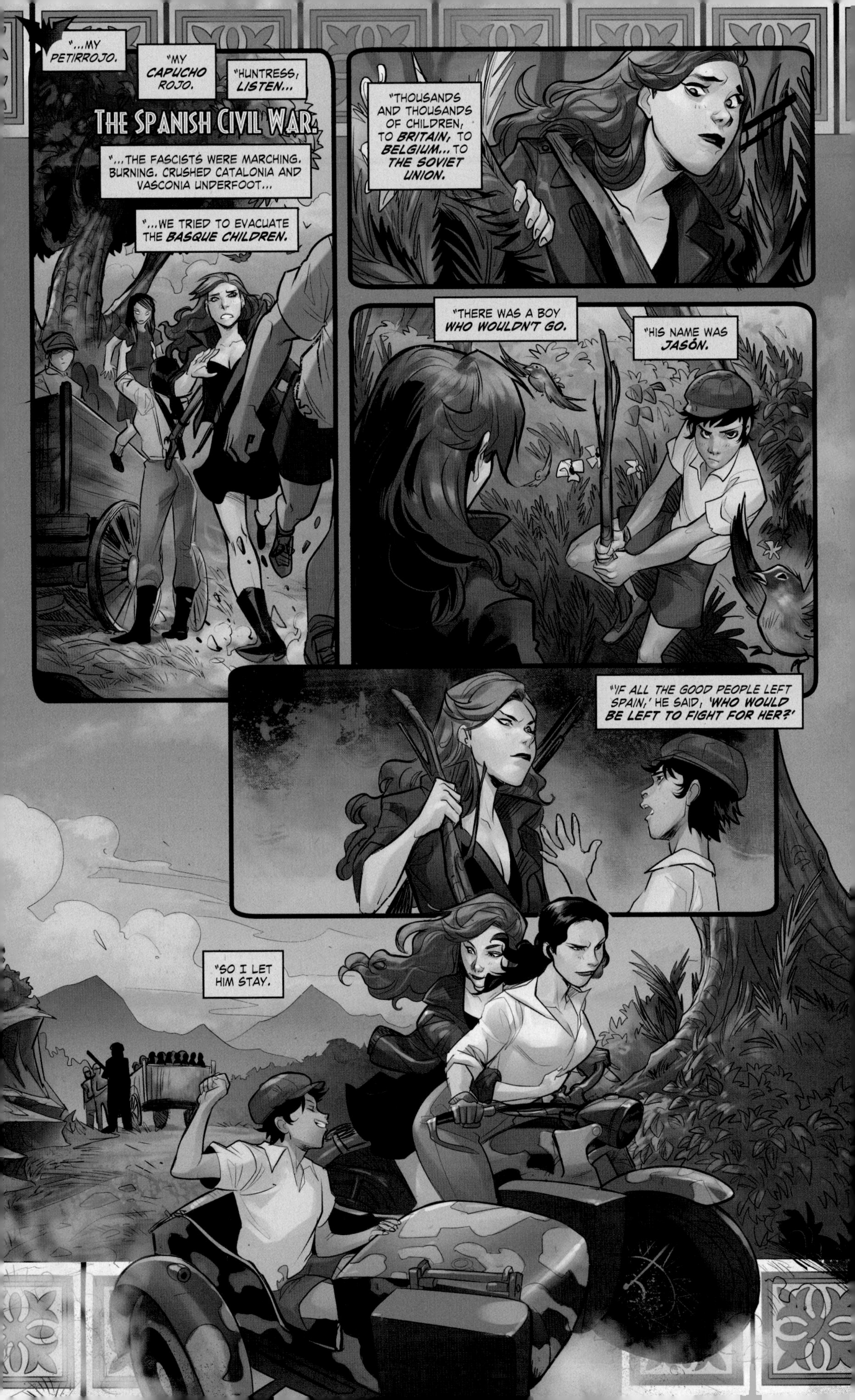
"...MY PETIRROJO.
"MY CAPUCHO ROJO.
"HUNTRESS, LISTEN...
THE SPANISH CIVIL WAR.
"...THE FASCISTS WERE MARCHING. BURNING. CRUSHED CATALONIA AND VASCONIA UNDERFOOT...
"...WE TRIED TO EVACUATE THE BASQUE CHILDREN.
"THOUSANDS AND THOUSANDS OF CHILDREN, TO BRITAIN, TO BELGIUM... TO THE SOVIET UNION.
"THERE WAS A BOY WHO WOULDN'T GO.
"HIS NAME WAS JASÓN.
"'IF ALL THE GOOD PEOPLE LEFT SPAIN,' HE SAID, 'WHO WOULD BE LEFT TO FIGHT FOR HER?'
"SO I LET HIM STAY.

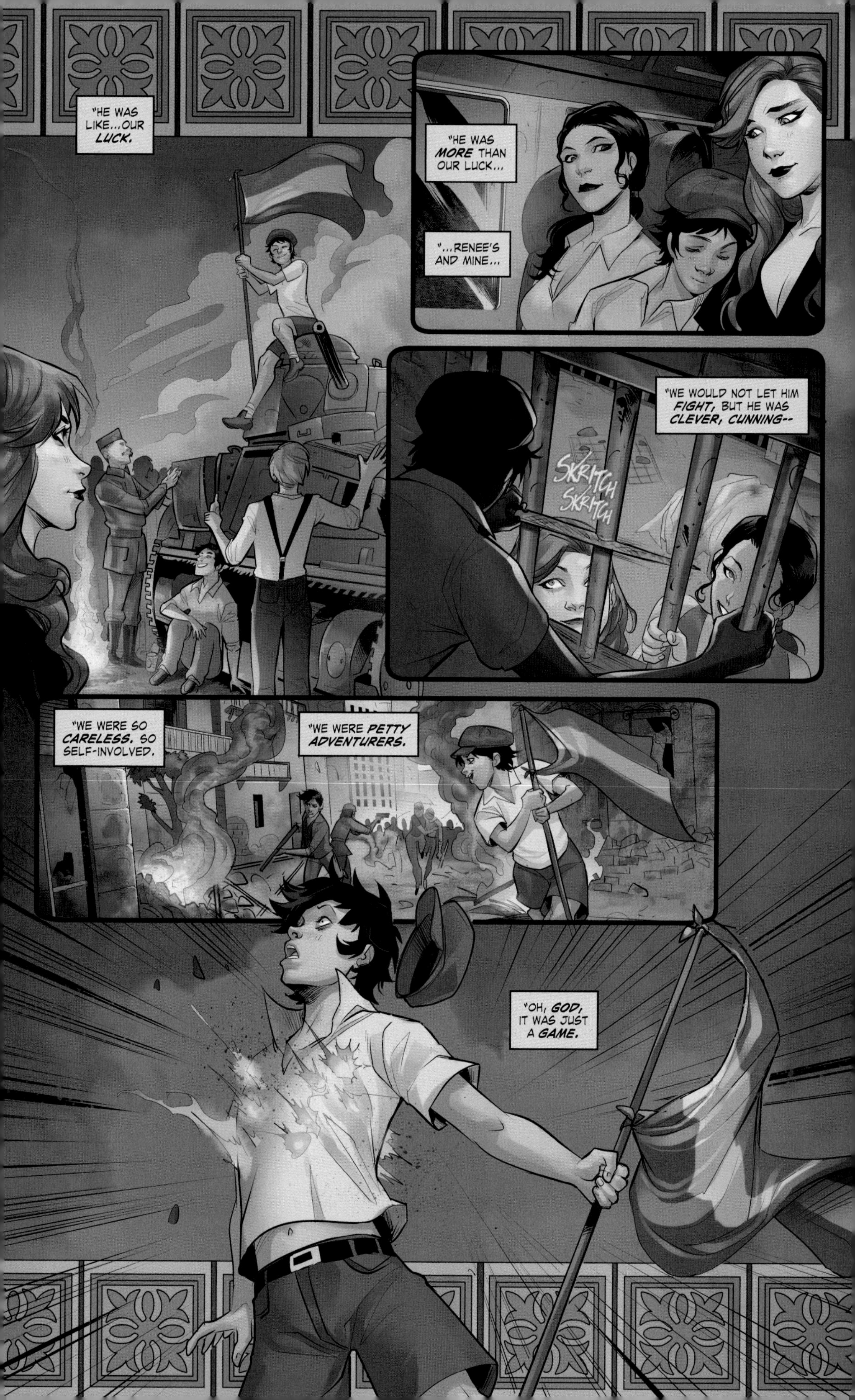
"HE WAS LIKE...OUR LUCK.
"HE WAS MORE THAN OUR LUCK...
"...RENEE'S AND MINE...
"WE WOULD NOT LET HIM FIGHT, BUT HE WAS CLEVER, CUNNING--
SKRITCH SKRITCH
"WE WERE SO CARELESS. SO SELF-INVOLVED.
"WE WERE PETTY ADVENTURERS.
"OH, GOD, IT WAS JUST A GAME.

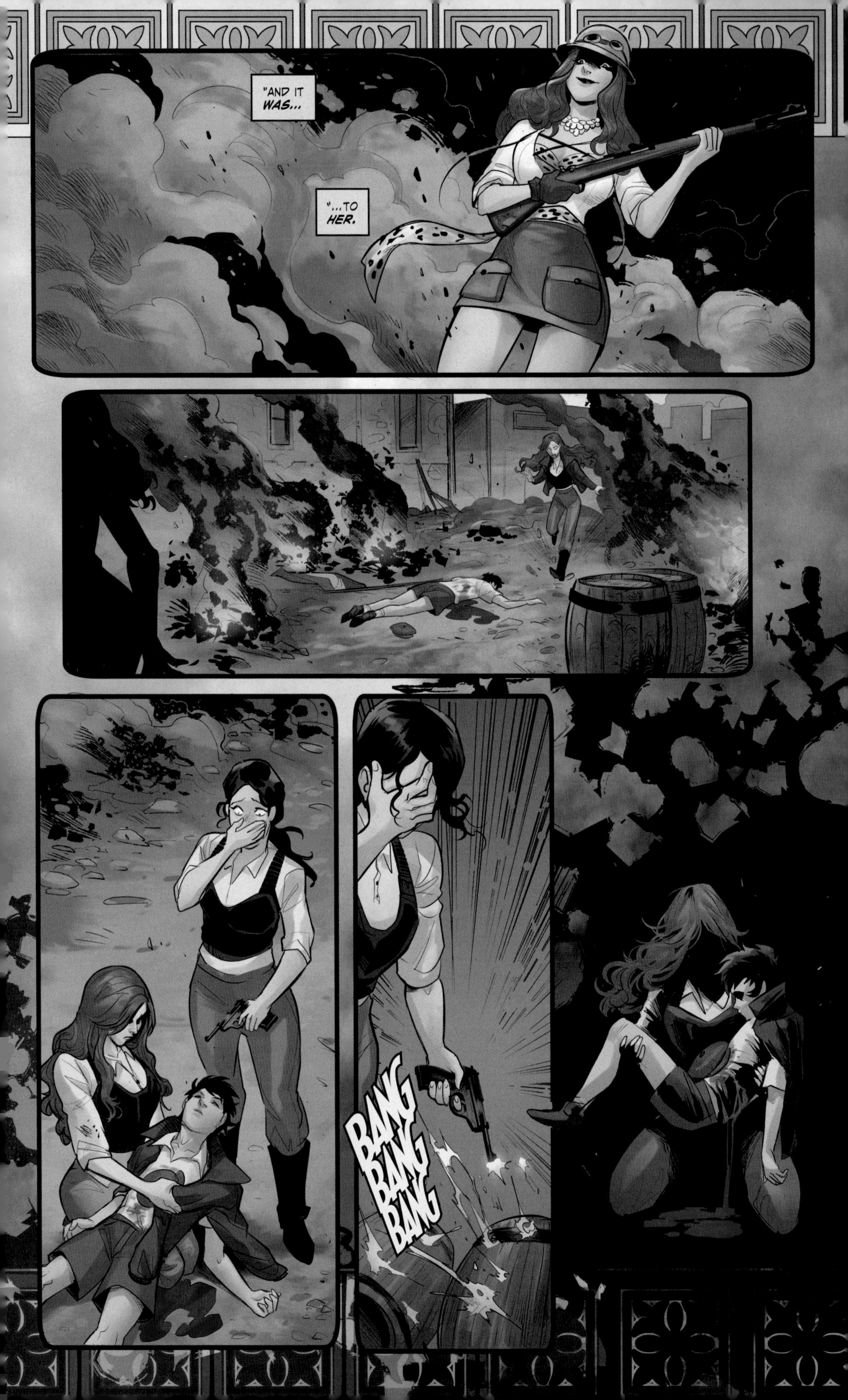
"AND IT WAS...
"...TO HER.
BANG BANG BANG

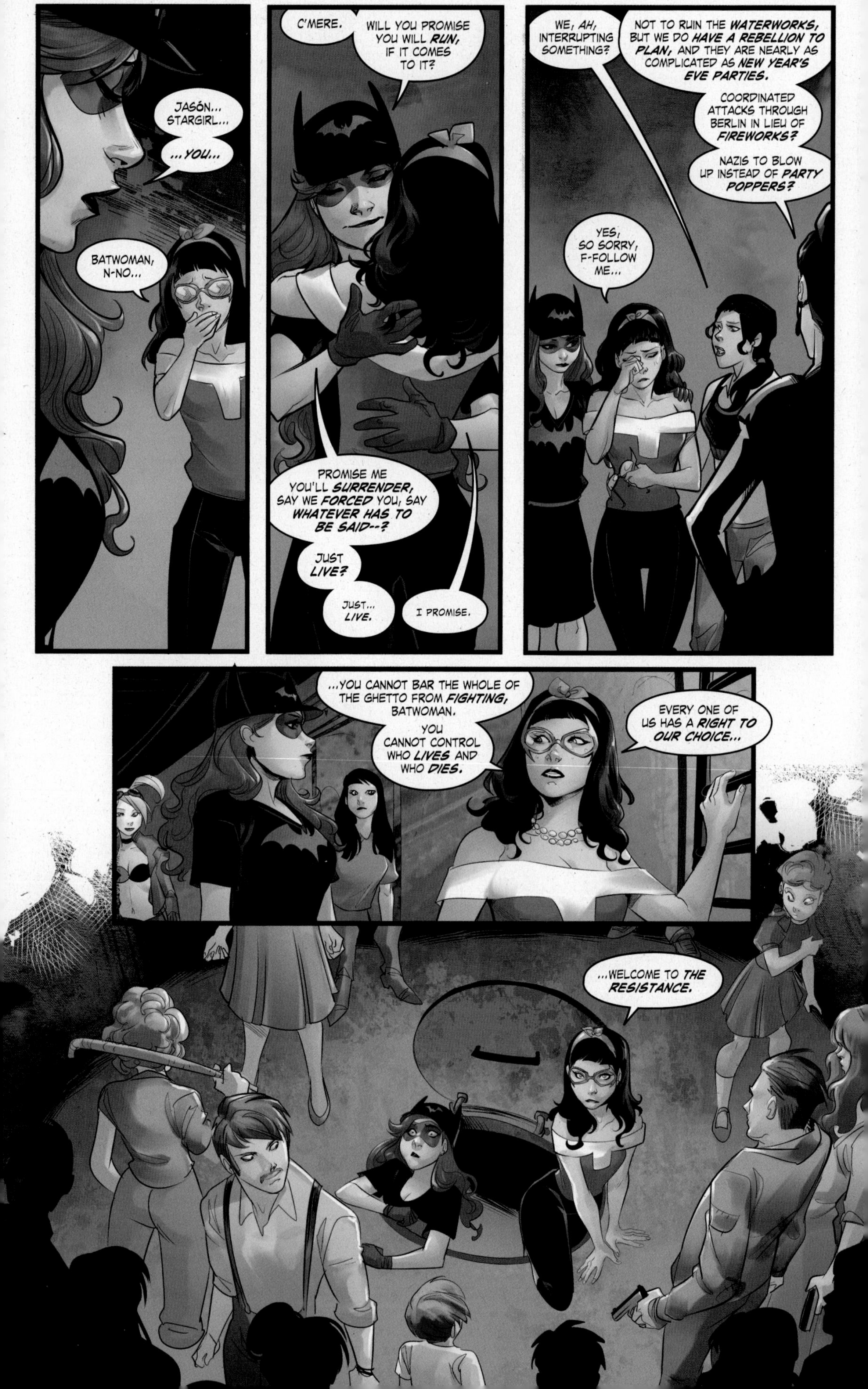
JASÓN... STARGIRL...
...YOU...
BATWOMAN, N-NO...
C'MERE.
WILL YOU PROMISE YOU WILL RUN, IF IT COMES TO IT?
PROMISE ME YOU'LL SURRENDER, SAY WE FORCED YOU, SAY WHATEVER HAS TO BE SAID--?
JUST LIVE?
JUST... LIVE.
I PROMISE.
WE, AH, INTERRUPTING SOMETHING?
NOT TO RUIN THE WATERWORKS, BUT WE DO HAVE A REBELLION TO PLAN, AND THEY ARE NEARLY AS COMPLICATED AS NEW YEAR'S EVE PARTIES.
COORDINATED ATTACKS THROUGH BERLIN IN LIEU OF FIREWORKS?
NAZIS TO BLOW UP INSTEAD OF PARTY POPPERS?
YES, SO SORRY, F-FOLLOW ME...
...YOU CANNOT BAR THE WHOLE OF THE GHETTO FROM FIGHTING, BATWOMAN.
YOU CANNOT CONTROL WHO LIVES AND WHO DIES.
EVERY ONE OF US HAS A RIGHT TO OUR CHOICE...
...WELCOME TO THE RESISTANCE.

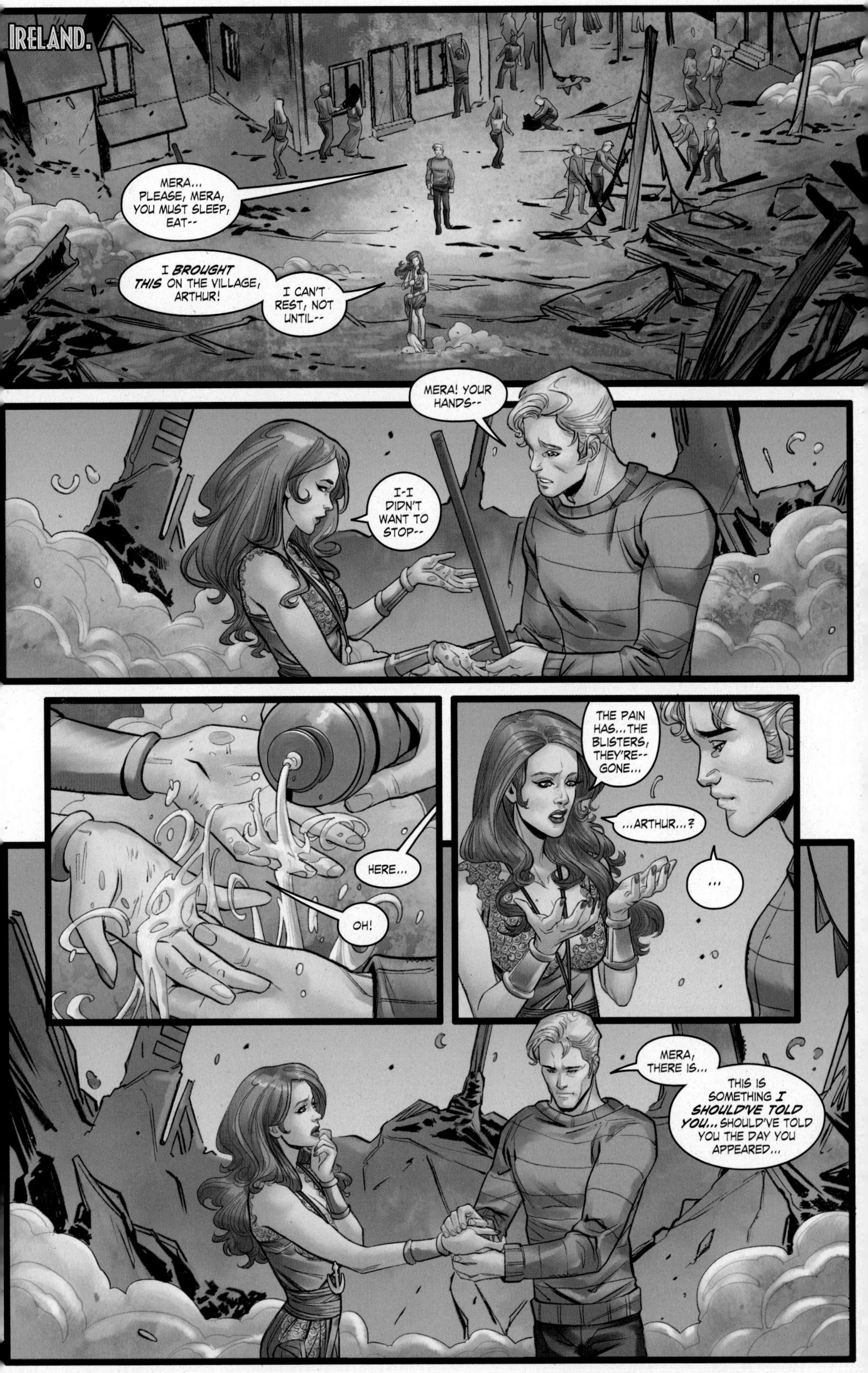
IRELAND.
MERA... PLEASE, MERA, YOU MUST SLEEP, EAT--
I BROUGHT THIS ON THE VILLAGE, ARTHUR!
I CAN'T REST, NOT UNTIL--
MERA! YOUR HANDS--
I-I DIDN'T WANT TO STOP--
HERE...
OH!
THE PAIN HAS...THE BLISTERS, THEY'RE--GONE...
...ARTHUR...?
...
MERA, THERE IS...
THIS IS SOMETHING I SHOULD'VE TOLD YOU... SHOULD'VE TOLD YOU THE DAY YOU APPEARED...

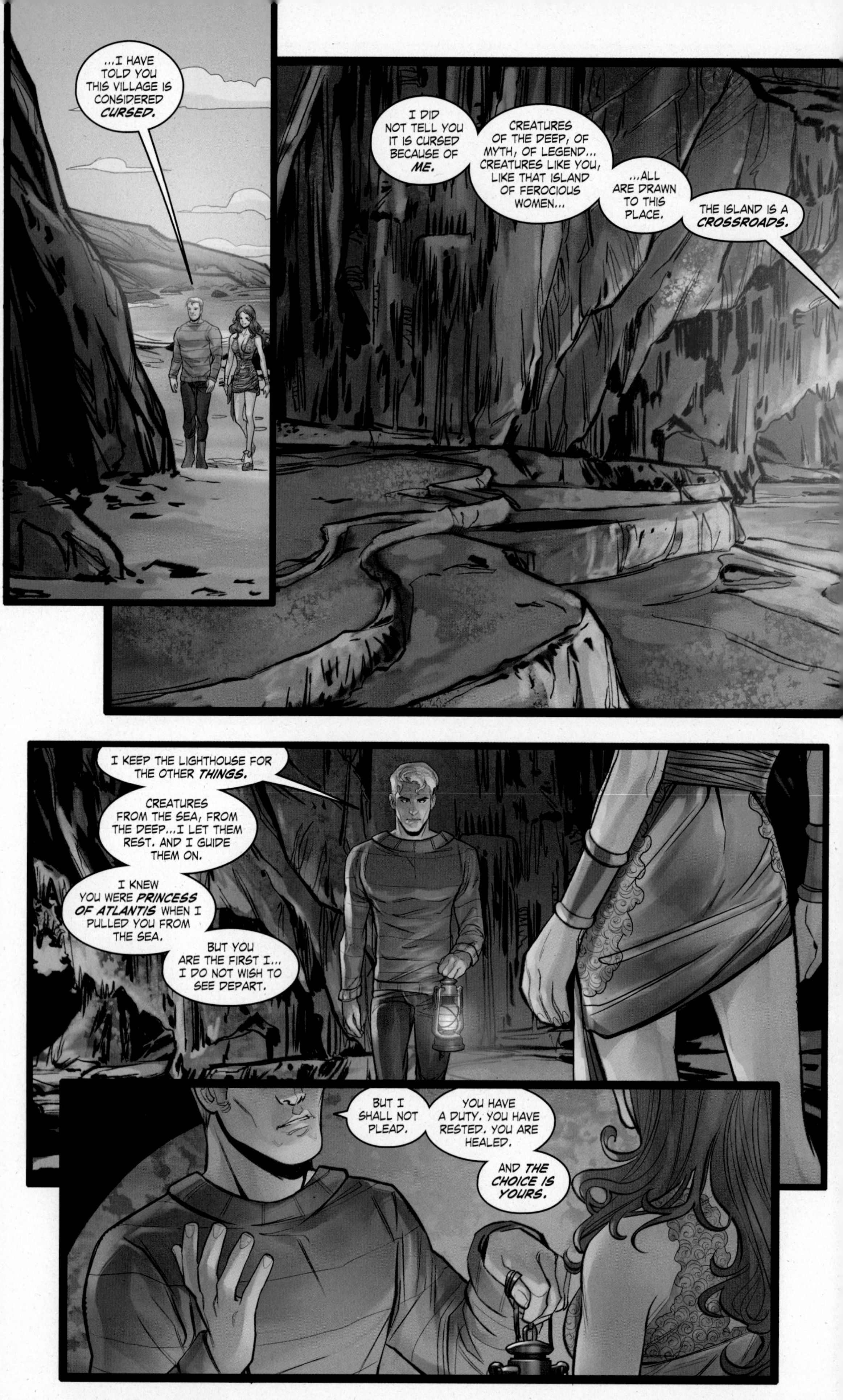
...I HAVE TOLD YOU THIS VILLAGE IS CONSIDERED *CURSED.*
I DID NOT TELL YOU IT IS CURSED BECAUSE OF *ME.*
CREATURES OF THE DEEP, OF MYTH, OF LEGEND... CREATURES LIKE YOU, LIKE THAT ISLAND OF FEROCIOUS WOMEN...
...ALL ARE DRAWN TO THIS PLACE.
THE ISLAND IS A *CROSSROADS.*
I KEEP THE LIGHTHOUSE FOR THE OTHER *THINGS.*
CREATURES FROM THE SEA, FROM THE DEEP...I LET THEM REST. AND I GUIDE THEM ON.
I KNEW YOU WERE *PRINCESS OF ATLANTIS* WHEN I PULLED YOU FROM THE SEA.
BUT YOU ARE THE FIRST I... I DO NOT WISH TO SEE DEPART.
BUT I SHALL NOT PLEAD.
YOU HAVE A DUTY. YOU HAVE RESTED. YOU ARE HEALED.
AND *THE CHOICE IS YOURS.*

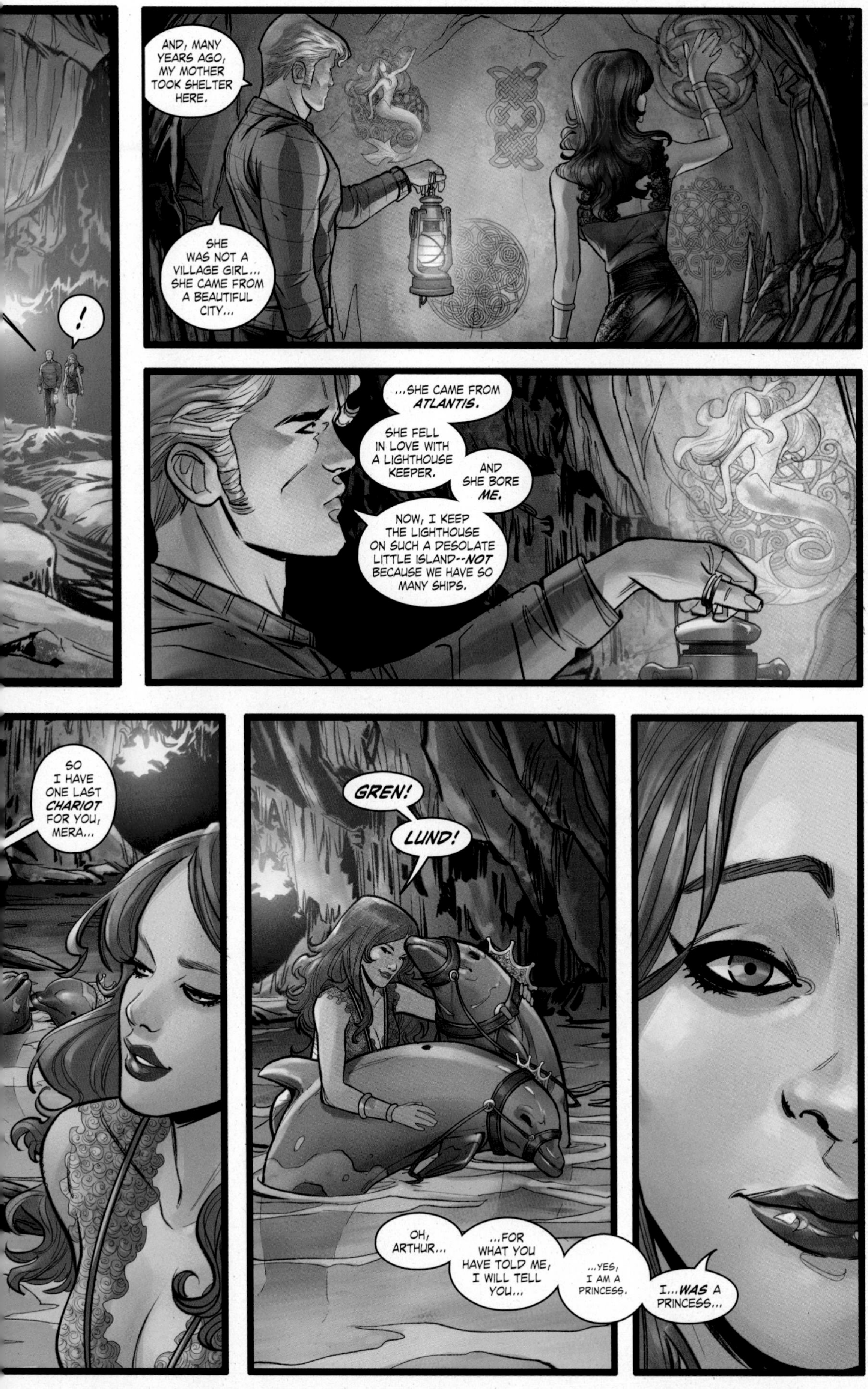
!
AND, MANY YEARS AGO, MY MOTHER TOOK SHELTER HERE.
SHE WAS NOT A VILLAGE GIRL... SHE CAME FROM A BEAUTIFUL CITY...
...SHE CAME FROM ATLANTIS.
SHE FELL IN LOVE WITH A LIGHTHOUSE KEEPER.
AND SHE BORE ME.
NOW, I KEEP THE LIGHTHOUSE ON SUCH A DESOLATE LITTLE ISLAND--NOT BECAUSE WE HAVE SO MANY SHIPS.
SO I HAVE ONE LAST CHARIOT FOR YOU, MERA...
GREN!
LUND!
OH, ARTHUR...
...FOR WHAT YOU HAVE TOLD ME, I WILL TELL YOU...
...YES, I AM A PRINCESS.
I...WAS A PRINCESS...

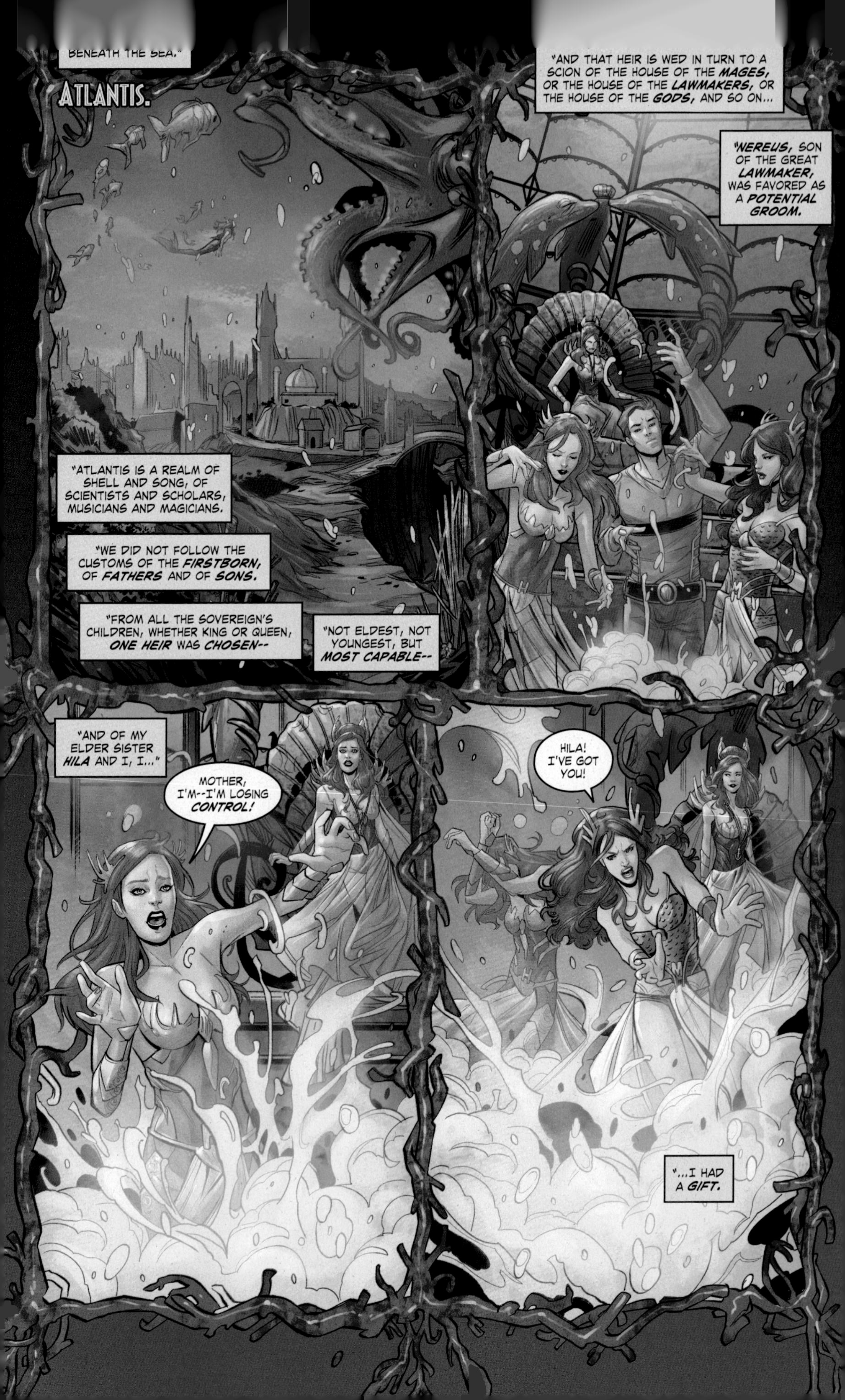
BENEATH THE SEA."
ATLANTIS.
"ATLANTIS IS A REALM OF SHELL AND SONG, OF SCIENTISTS AND SCHOLARS, MUSICIANS AND MAGICIANS.
"WE DID NOT FOLLOW THE CUSTOMS OF THE FIRSTBORN, OF FATHERS AND OF SONS.
"FROM ALL THE SOVEREIGN'S CHILDREN, WHETHER KING OR QUEEN, ONE HEIR WAS CHOSEN--
"NOT ELDEST, NOT YOUNGEST, BUT MOST CAPABLE--
"AND THAT HEIR IS WED IN TURN TO A SCION OF THE HOUSE OF THE MAGES, OR THE HOUSE OF THE LAWMAKERS, OR THE HOUSE OF THE GODS, AND SO ON...
"NEREUS, SON OF THE GREAT LAWMAKER, WAS FAVORED AS A POTENTIAL GROOM.
"AND OF MY ELDER SISTER HILA AND I, I..."
MOTHER, I'M--I'M LOSING CONTROL!
HILA! I'VE GOT YOU!
"...I HAD A GIFT.

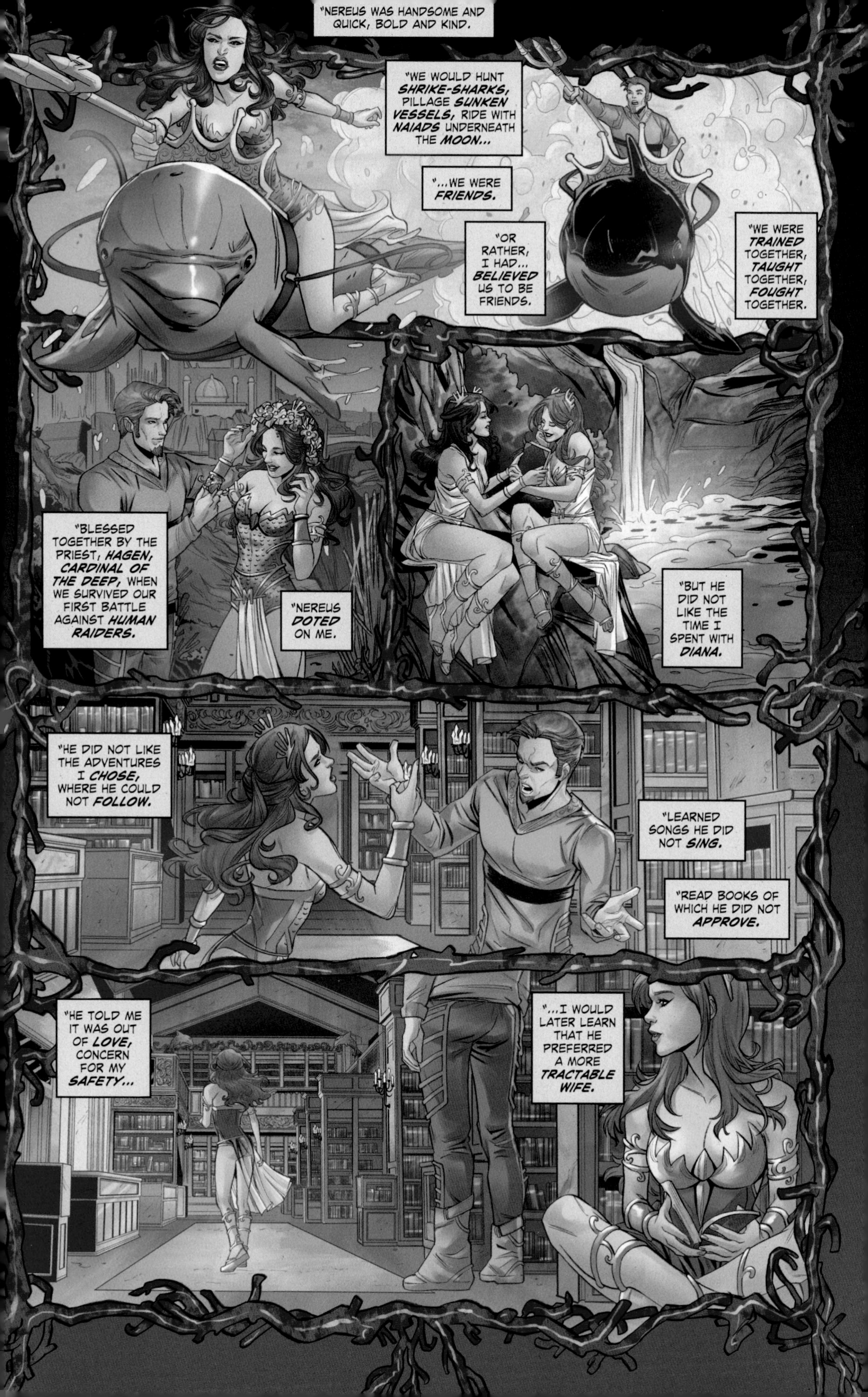
"NEREUS WAS HANDSOME AND QUICK, BOLD AND KIND.
"WE WOULD HUNT SHRIKE-SHARKS, PILLAGE SUNKEN VESSELS, RIDE WITH NAIADS UNDERNEATH THE MOON...
"...WE WERE FRIENDS.
"OR RATHER, I HAD... BELIEVED US TO BE FRIENDS.
"WE WERE TRAINED TOGETHER, TAUGHT TOGETHER, FOUGHT TOGETHER.
"BLESSED TOGETHER BY THE PRIEST, HAGEN, CARDINAL OF THE DEEP, WHEN WE SURVIVED OUR FIRST BATTLE AGAINST HUMAN RAIDERS.
"NEREUS DOTED ON ME.
"BUT HE DID NOT LIKE THE TIME I SPENT WITH DIANA.
"HE DID NOT LIKE THE ADVENTURES I CHOSE, WHERE HE COULD NOT FOLLOW.
"LEARNED SONGS HE DID NOT SING.
"READ BOOKS OF WHICH HE DID NOT APPROVE.
"HE TOLD ME IT WAS OUT OF LOVE, CONCERN FOR MY SAFETY...
"...I WOULD LATER LEARN THAT HE PREFERRED A MORE TRACTABLE WIFE.

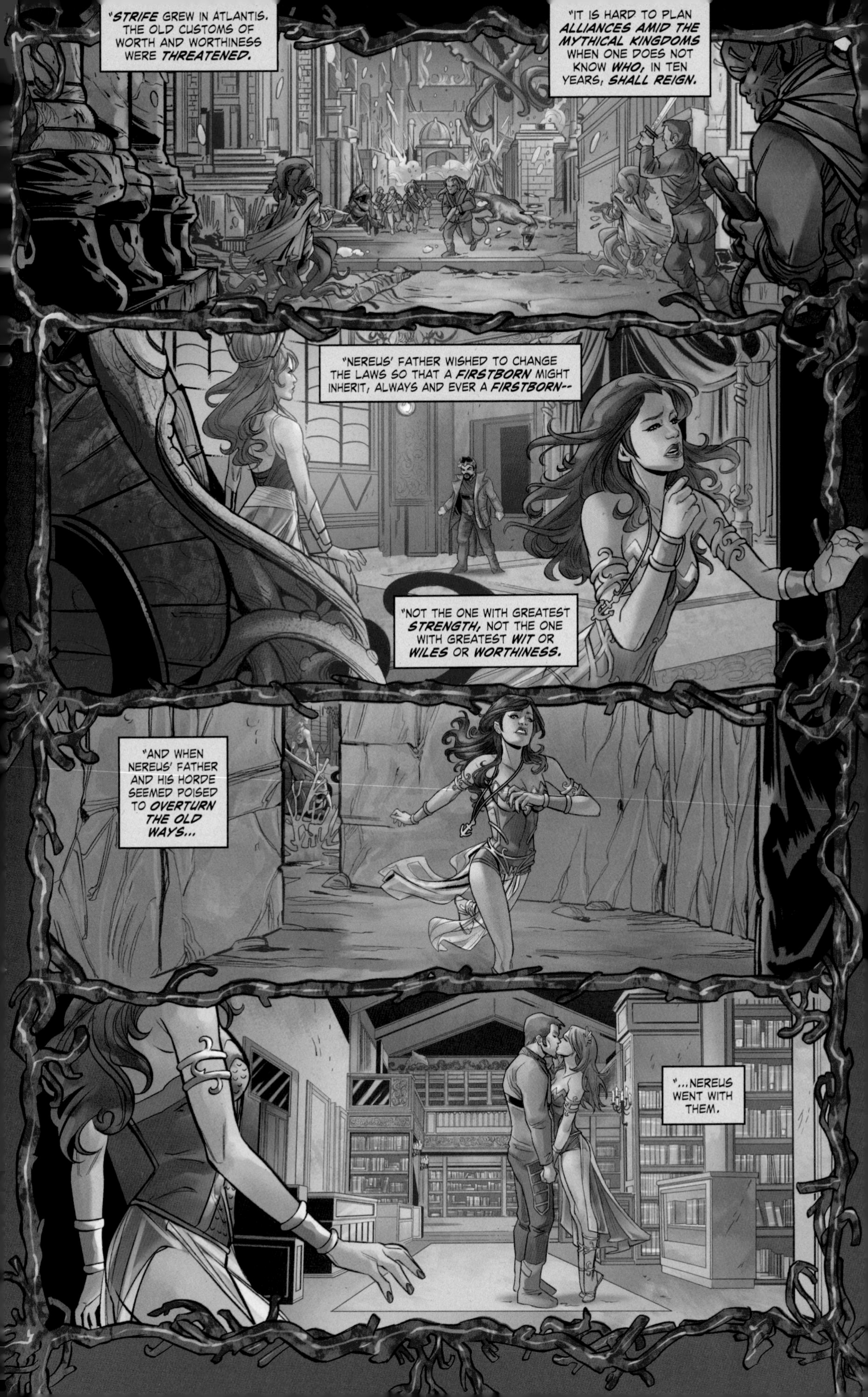
"STRIFE GREW IN ATLANTIS. THE OLD CUSTOMS OF WORTH AND WORTHINESS WERE THREATENED.
"IT IS HARD TO PLAN ALLIANCES AMID THE MYTHICAL KINGDOMS WHEN ONE DOES NOT KNOW WHO, IN TEN YEARS, SHALL REIGN.
"NEREUS' FATHER WISHED TO CHANGE THE LAWS SO THAT A FIRSTBORN MIGHT INHERIT, ALWAYS AND EVER A FIRSTBORN--
"NOT THE ONE WITH GREATEST STRENGTH, NOT THE ONE WITH GREATEST WIT OR WILES OR WORTHINESS.
"AND WHEN NEREUS' FATHER AND HIS HORDE SEEMED POISED TO OVERTURN THE OLD WAYS...
"...NEREUS WENT WITH THEM.

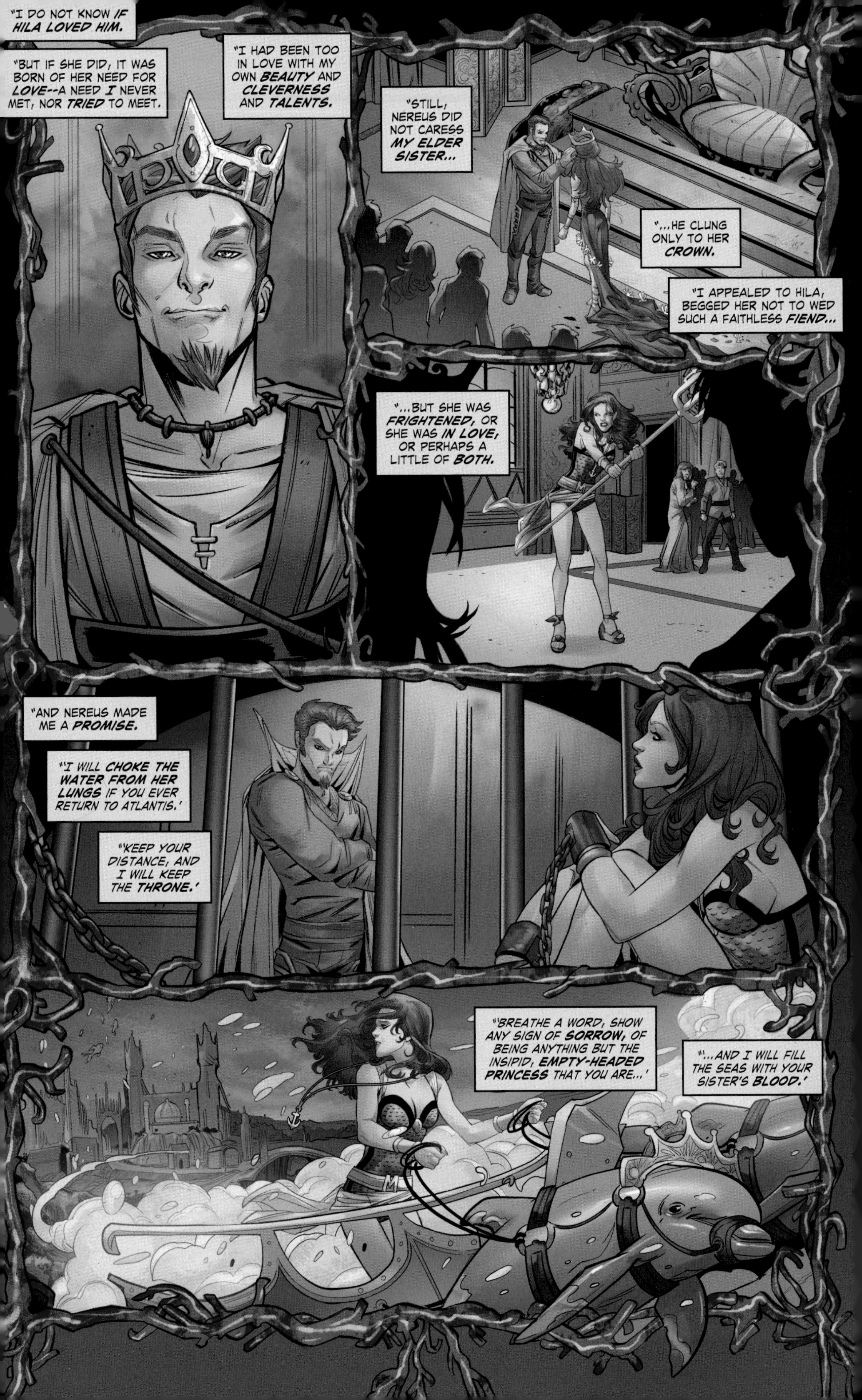
"I DO NOT KNOW IF HILA LOVED HIM.
"BUT IF SHE DID, IT WAS BORN OF HER NEED FOR LOVE--A NEED I NEVER MET, NOR TRIED TO MEET.
"I HAD BEEN TOO IN LOVE WITH MY OWN BEAUTY AND CLEVERNESS AND TALENTS.
"STILL, NEREUS DID NOT CARESS MY ELDER SISTER...
"...HE CLUNG ONLY TO HER CROWN.
"I APPEALED TO HILA, BEGGED HER NOT TO WED SUCH A FAITHLESS FIEND...
"...BUT SHE WAS FRIGHTENED, OR SHE WAS IN LOVE, OR PERHAPS A LITTLE OF BOTH.
"AND NEREUS MADE ME A PROMISE.
"'I WILL CHOKE THE WATER FROM HER LUNGS IF YOU EVER RETURN TO ATLANTIS.'
"'KEEP YOUR DISTANCE, AND I WILL KEEP THE THRONE.'
"'BREATHE A WORD, SHOW ANY SIGN OF SORROW, OF BEING ANYTHING BUT THE INSIPID, EMPTY-HEADED PRINCESS THAT YOU ARE...'
"'...AND I WILL FILL THE SEAS WITH YOUR SISTER'S BLOOD.'

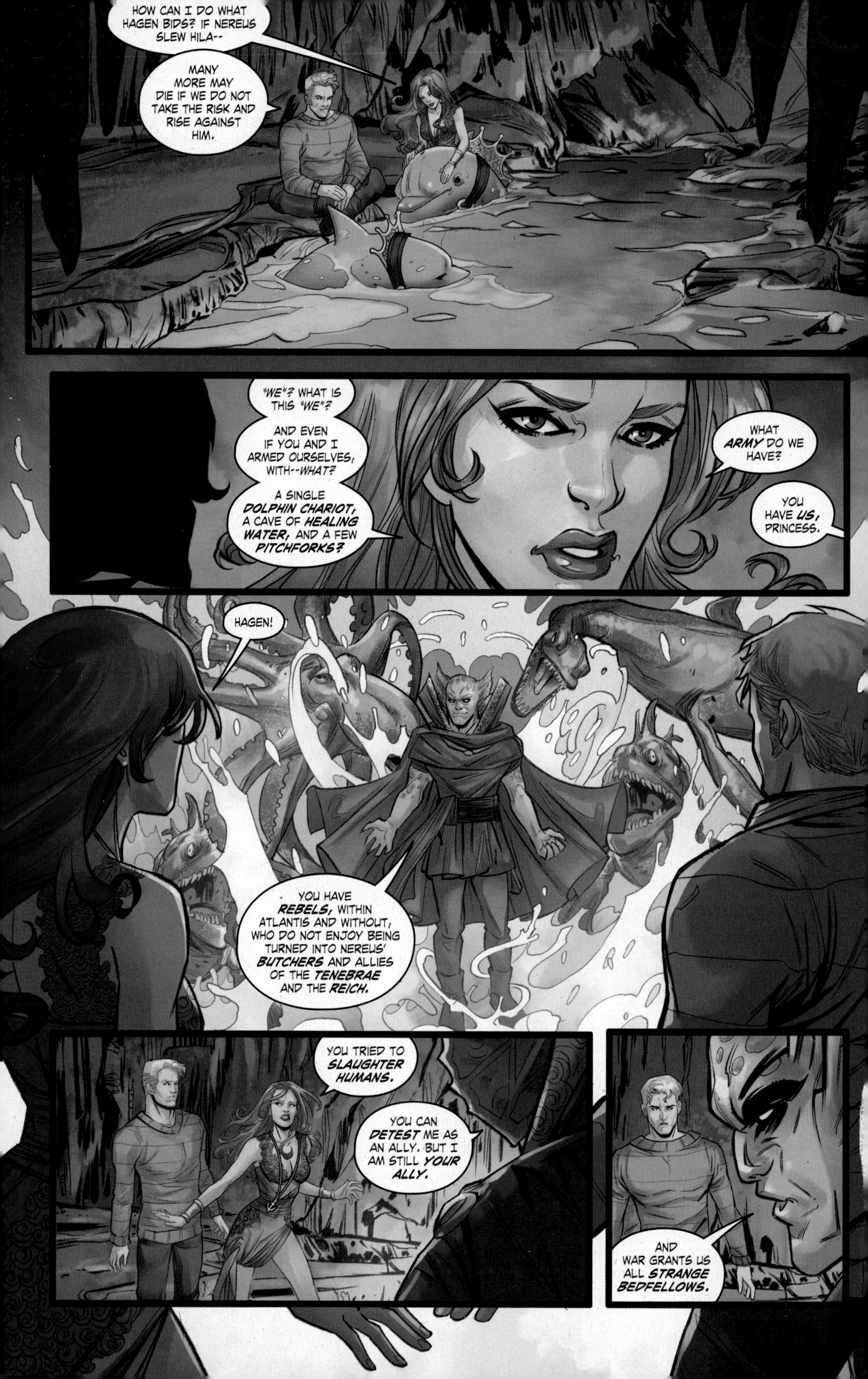
HOW CAN I DO WHAT HAGEN BIDS? IF NEREUS SLEW HILA--
MANY MORE MAY DIE IF WE DO NOT TAKE THE RISK AND RISE AGAINST HIM.
"WE"? WHAT IS THIS "WE"?
AND EVEN IF YOU AND I ARMED OURSELVES, WITH--WHAT?
A SINGLE DOLPHIN CHARIOT, A CAVE OF HEALING WATER, AND A FEW PITCHFORKS?
WHAT ARMY DO WE HAVE?
YOU HAVE US, PRINCESS.
HAGEN!
YOU HAVE REBELS, WITHIN ATLANTIS AND WITHOUT, WHO DO NOT ENJOY BEING TURNED INTO NEREUS' BUTCHERS AND ALLIES OF THE TENEBRAE AND THE REICH.
YOU TRIED TO SLAUGHTER HUMANS.
YOU CAN DETEST ME AS AN ALLY. BUT I AM STILL YOUR ALLY.
AND WAR GRANTS US ALL STRANGE BEDFELLOWS.

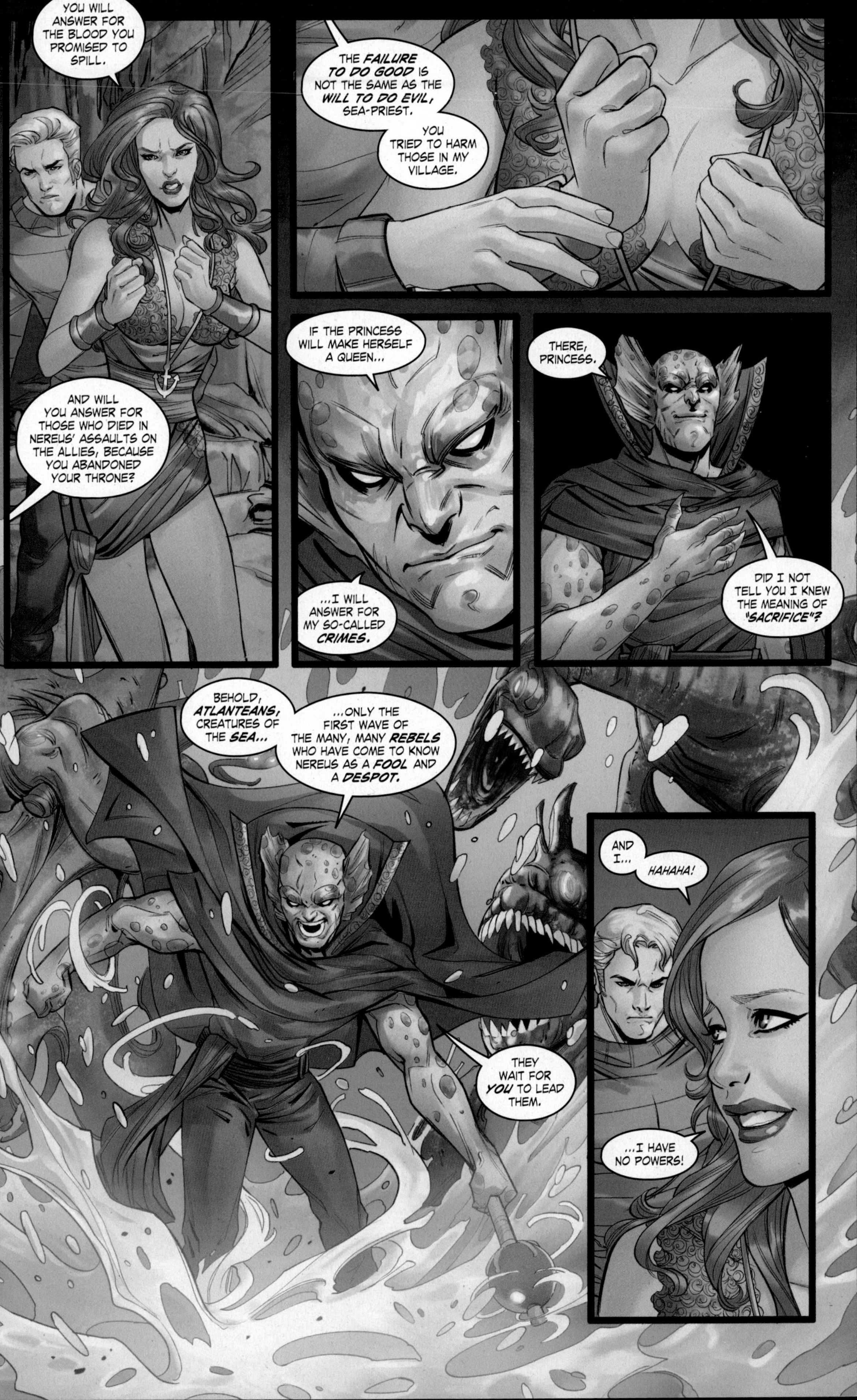
YOU WILL ANSWER FOR THE BLOOD YOU PROMISED TO SPILL.
AND WILL YOU ANSWER FOR THOSE WHO DIED IN NEREUS' ASSAULTS ON THE ALLIES, BECAUSE YOU ABANDONED YOUR THRONE?
THE FAILURE TO DO GOOD IS NOT THE SAME AS THE WILL TO DO EVIL, SEA-PRIEST.
YOU TRIED TO HARM THOSE IN MY VILLAGE.
IF THE PRINCESS WILL MAKE HERSELF A QUEEN...
...I WILL ANSWER FOR MY SO-CALLED CRIMES.
THERE, PRINCESS.
DID I NOT TELL YOU I KNEW THE MEANING OF "SACRIFICE"?
BEHOLD, ATLANTEANS, CREATURES OF THE SEA...
...ONLY THE FIRST WAVE OF THE MANY, MANY REBELS WHO HAVE COME TO KNOW NEREUS AS A FOOL AND A DESPOT.
THEY WAIT FOR YOU TO LEAD THEM.
AND I...
HAHAHA!
...I HAVE NO POWERS!

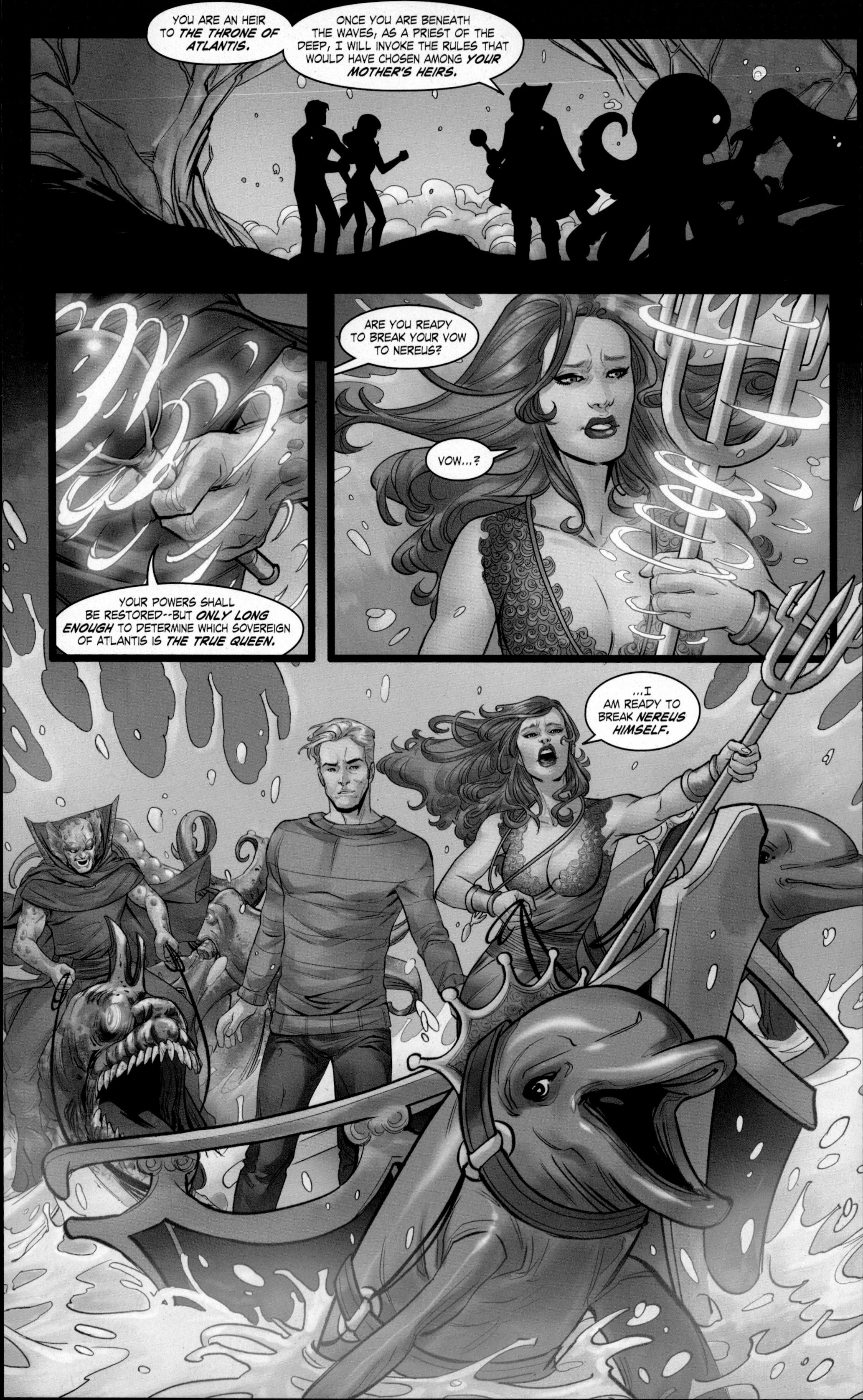
YOU ARE AN HEIR TO THE THRONE OF ATLANTIS.
ONCE YOU ARE BENEATH THE WAVES, AS A PRIEST OF THE DEEP, I WILL INVOKE THE RULES THAT WOULD HAVE CHOSEN AMONG YOUR MOTHER'S HEIRS.
YOUR POWERS SHALL BE RESTORED--BUT ONLY LONG ENOUGH TO DETERMINE WHICH SOVEREIGN OF ATLANTIS IS THE TRUE QUEEN.
ARE YOU READY TO BREAK YOUR VOW TO NEREUS?
VOW...?
...I AM READY TO BREAK NEREUS HIMSELF.

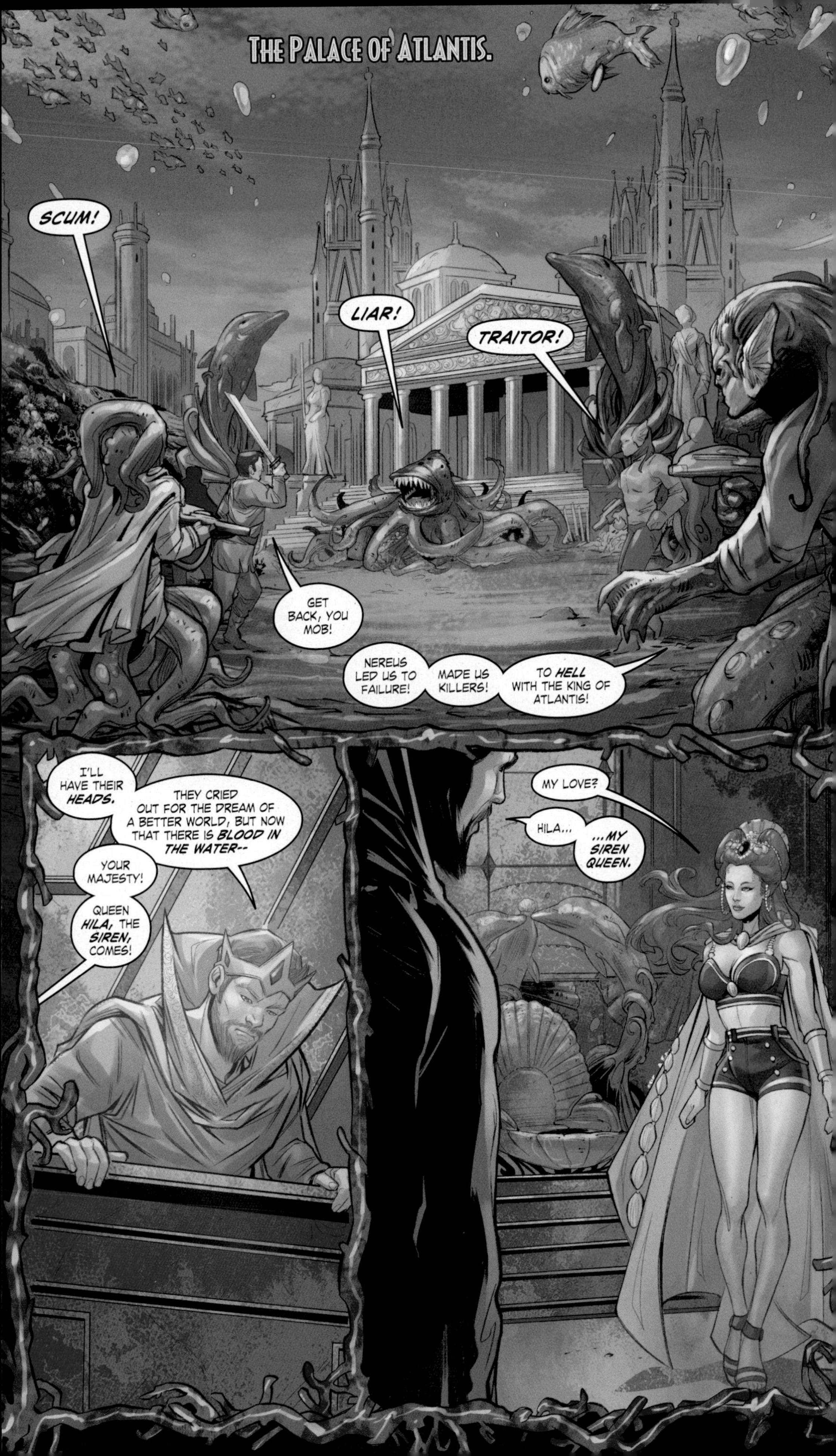
THE PALACE OF ATLANTIS.
SCUM!
LIAR!
TRAITOR!
GET BACK, YOU MOB!
NEREUS LED US TO FAILURE!
MADE US KILLERS!
TO HELL WITH THE KING OF ATLANTIS!
I'LL HAVE THEIR HEADS.
THEY CRIED OUT FOR THE DREAM OF A BETTER WORLD, BUT NOW THAT THERE IS BLOOD IN THE WATER--
YOUR MAJESTY!
QUEEN HILA, THE SIREN, COMES!
MY LOVE?
HILA...
...MY SIREN QUEEN.

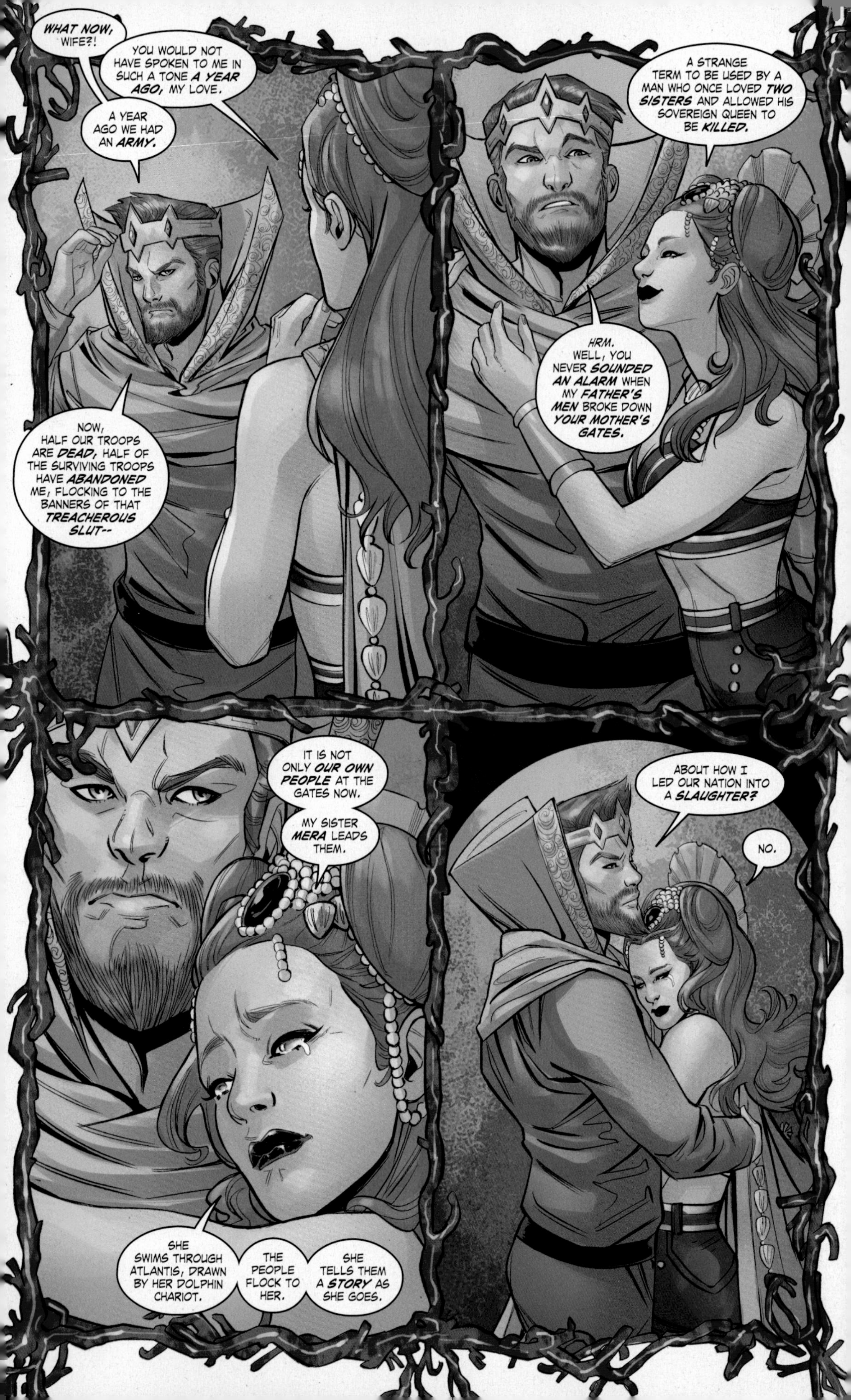
WHAT NOW, WIFE?!
YOU WOULD NOT HAVE SPOKEN TO ME IN SUCH A TONE A YEAR AGO, MY LOVE.
A YEAR AGO WE HAD AN ARMY.
NOW, HALF OUR TROOPS ARE DEAD, HALF OF THE SURVIVING TROOPS HAVE ABANDONED ME, FLOCKING TO THE BANNERS OF THAT TREACHEROUS SLUT--
A STRANGE TERM TO BE USED BY A MAN WHO ONCE LOVED TWO SISTERS AND ALLOWED HIS SOVEREIGN QUEEN TO BE KILLED.
HRM. WELL, YOU NEVER SOUNDED AN ALARM WHEN MY FATHER'S MEN BROKE DOWN YOUR MOTHER'S GATES.
IT IS NOT ONLY OUR OWN PEOPLE AT THE GATES NOW.
MY SISTER MERA LEADS THEM.
SHE SWIMS THROUGH ATLANTIS, DRAWN BY HER DOLPHIN CHARIOT.
THE PEOPLE FLOCK TO HER.
SHE TELLS THEM A STORY AS SHE GOES.
ABOUT HOW I LED OUR NATION INTO A SLAUGHTER?
NO.

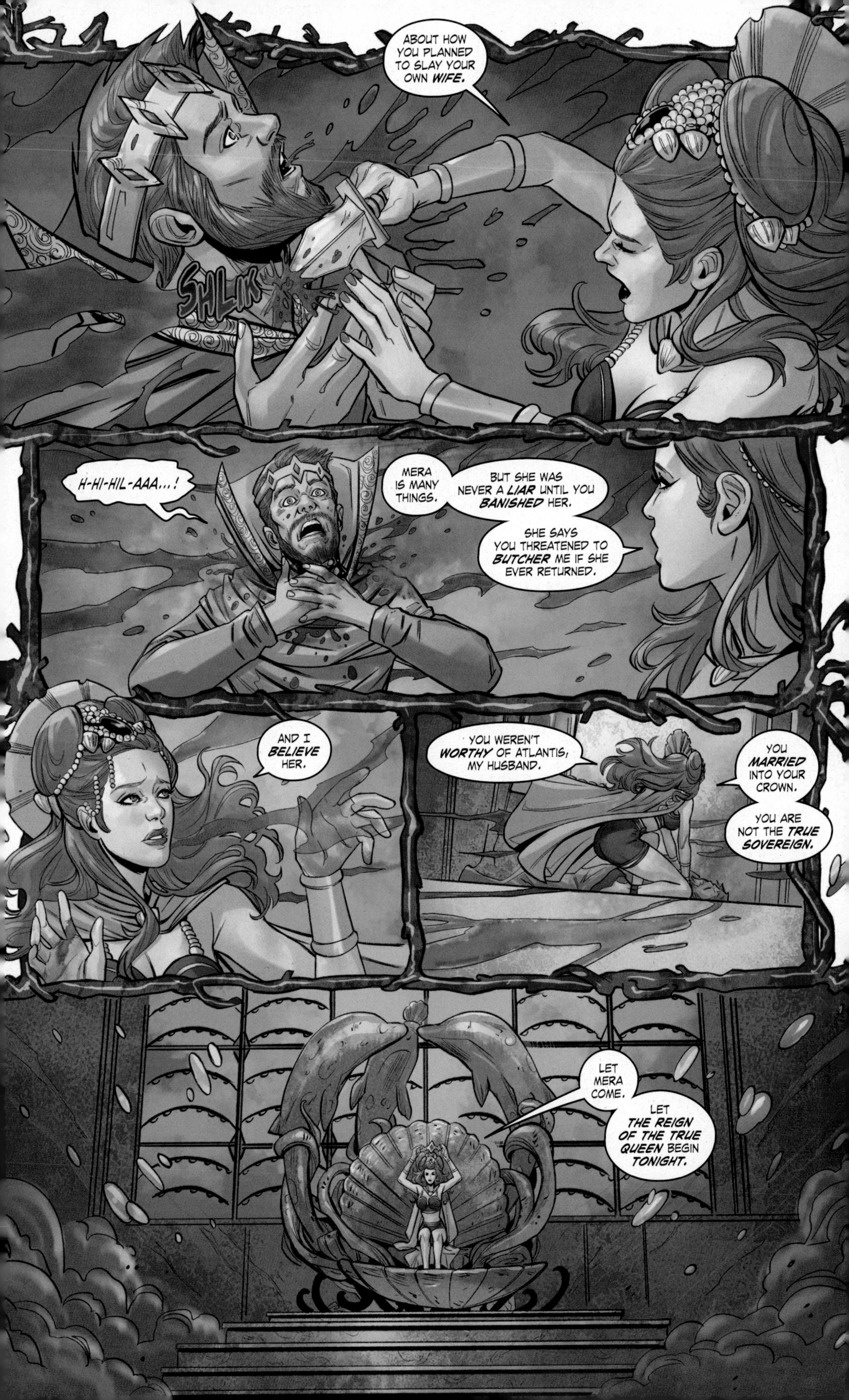
ABOUT HOW YOU PLANNED TO SLAY YOUR OWN WIFE.
SHLIK
H-HI-HIL-AAA...!
MERA IS MANY THINGS.
BUT SHE WAS NEVER A LIAR UNTIL YOU BANISHED HER.
SHE SAYS YOU THREATENED TO BUTCHER ME IF SHE EVER RETURNED.
AND I BELIEVE HER.
YOU WEREN'T WORTHY OF ATLANTIS, MY HUSBAND.
YOU MARRIED INTO YOUR CROWN.
YOU ARE NOT THE TRUE SOVEREIGN.
LET MERA COME.
LET THE REIGN OF THE TRUE QUEEN BEGIN TONIGHT.

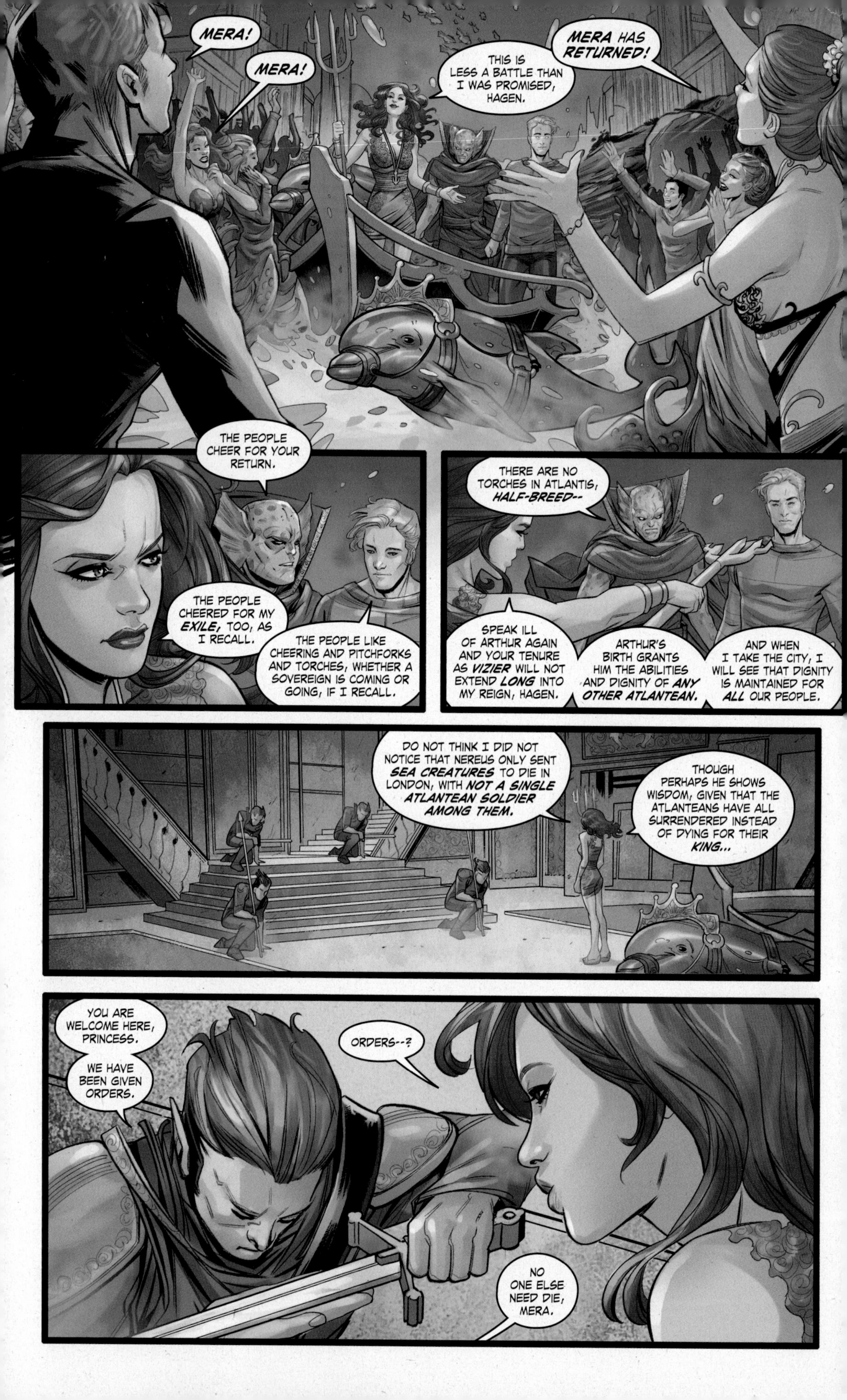
MERA!
MERA!
THIS IS LESS A BATTLE THAN I WAS PROMISED, HAGEN.
MERA HAS RETURNED!
THE PEOPLE CHEER FOR YOUR RETURN.
THE PEOPLE CHEERED FOR MY EXILE, TOO, AS I RECALL.
THE PEOPLE LIKE CHEERING AND PITCHFORKS AND TORCHES, WHETHER A SOVEREIGN IS COMING OR GOING, IF I RECALL.
THERE ARE NO TORCHES IN ATLANTIS, HALF-BREED--
SPEAK ILL OF ARTHUR AGAIN AND YOUR TENURE AS VIZIER WILL NOT EXTEND LONG INTO MY REIGN, HAGEN.
ARTHUR'S BIRTH GRANTS HIM THE ABILITIES AND DIGNITY OF ANY OTHER ATLANTEAN.
AND WHEN I TAKE THE CITY, I WILL SEE THAT DIGNITY IS MAINTAINED FOR ALL OUR PEOPLE.
DO NOT THINK I DID NOT NOTICE THAT NEREUS ONLY SENT SEA CREATURES TO DIE IN LONDON, WITH NOT A SINGLE ATLANTEAN SOLDIER AMONG THEM.
THOUGH PERHAPS HE SHOWS WISDOM, GIVEN THAT THE ATLANTEANS HAVE ALL SURRENDERED INSTEAD OF DYING FOR THEIR KING...
YOU ARE WELCOME HERE, PRINCESS.
WE HAVE BEEN GIVEN ORDERS.
ORDERS--?
NO ONE ELSE NEED DIE, MERA.

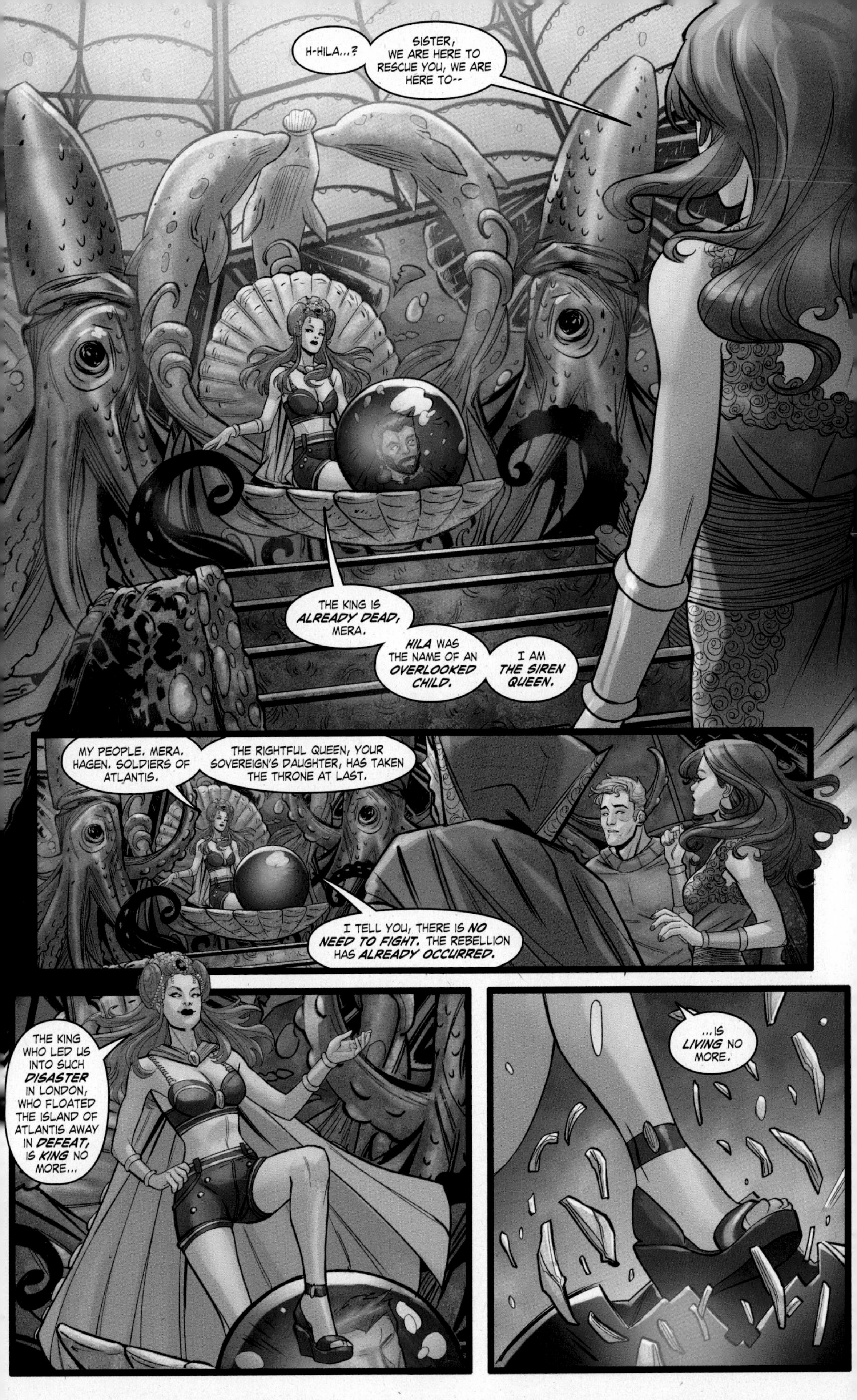
H-HILA...?
SISTER, WE ARE HERE TO RESCUE YOU, WE ARE HERE TO--
THE KING IS *ALREADY DEAD*, MERA.
HILA WAS THE NAME OF AN *OVERLOOKED CHILD.*
I AM *THE SIREN QUEEN.*
MY PEOPLE. MERA. HAGEN. SOLDIERS OF ATLANTIS.
THE RIGHTFUL QUEEN, YOUR SOVEREIGN'S DAUGHTER, HAS TAKEN THE THRONE AT LAST.
I TELL YOU, THERE IS *NO NEED TO FIGHT.* THE REBELLION HAS *ALREADY OCCURRED.*
THE KING WHO LED US INTO SUCH *DISASTER* IN LONDON, WHO FLOATED THE ISLAND OF ATLANTIS AWAY IN *DEFEAT*, IS *KING* NO MORE...
...IS *LIVING* NO MORE.

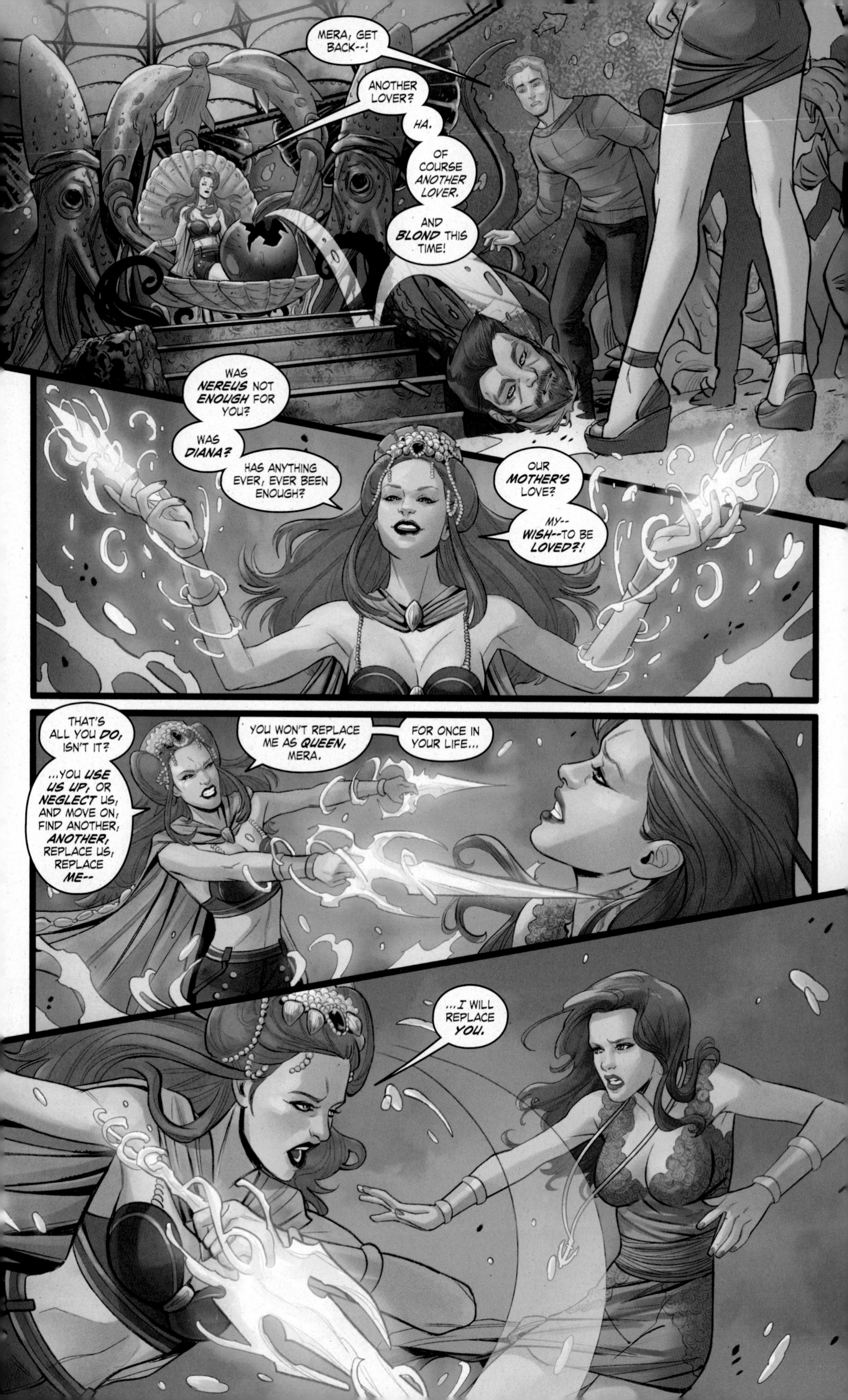
MERA, GET BACK--!
ANOTHER LOVER?
HA.
OF COURSE ANOTHER LOVER.
AND BLOND THIS TIME!
WAS NEREUS NOT ENOUGH FOR YOU?
WAS DIANA?
HAS ANYTHING EVER, EVER BEEN ENOUGH?
OUR MOTHER'S LOVE?
MY-- WISH--TO BE LOVED?!
THAT'S ALL YOU DO, ISN'T IT?
...YOU USE US UP, OR NEGLECT US, AND MOVE ON, FIND ANOTHER, ANOTHER, REPLACE US, REPLACE ME--
YOU WON'T REPLACE ME AS QUEEN, MERA.
FOR ONCE IN YOUR LIFE...
...I WILL REPLACE YOU.

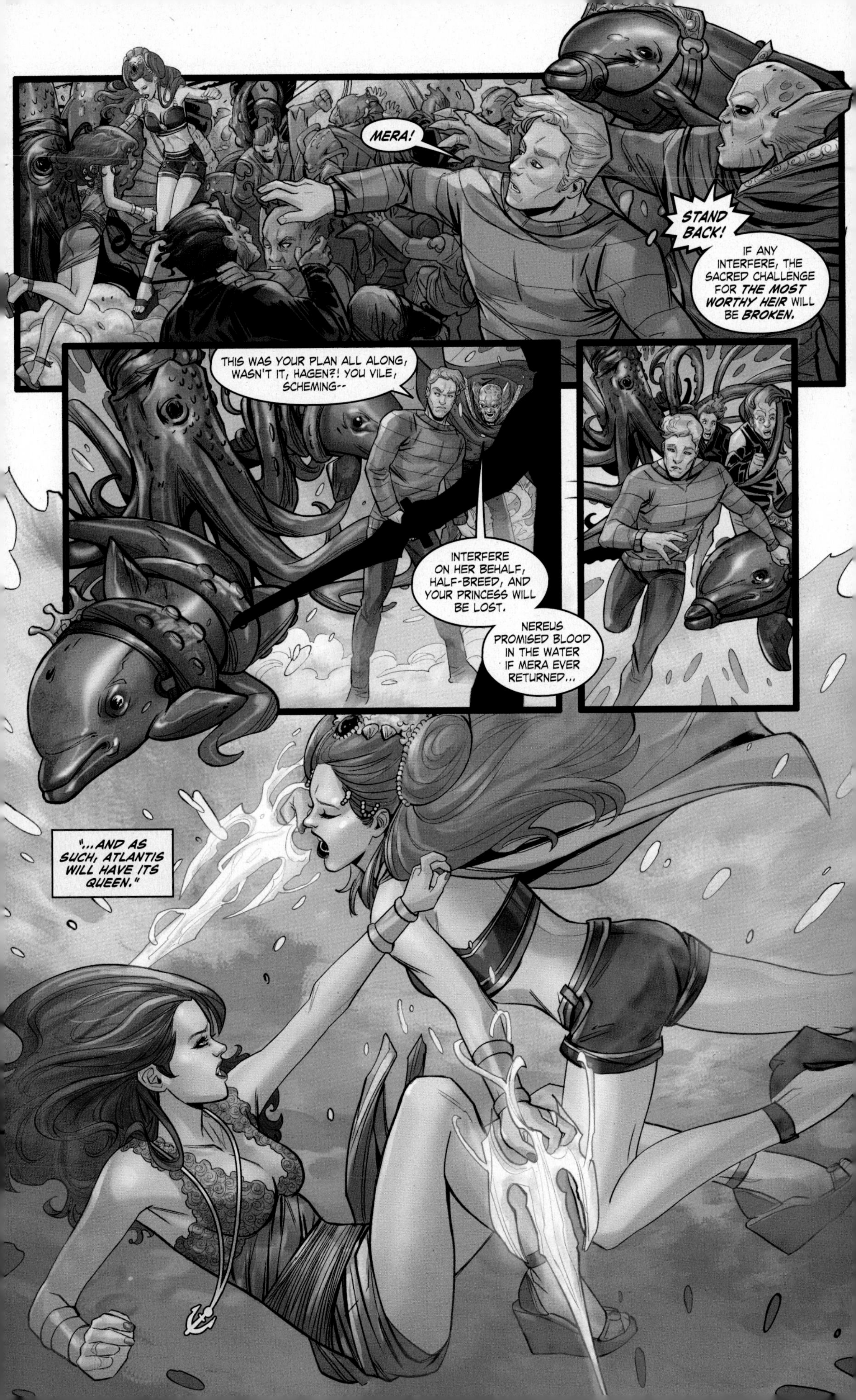
MERA!
STAND BACK!
IF ANY INTERFERE, THE SACRED CHALLENGE FOR THE MOST WORTHY HEIR WILL BE BROKEN.
THIS WAS YOUR PLAN ALL ALONG, WASN'T IT, HAGEN?! YOU VILE, SCHEMING--
INTERFERE ON HER BEHALF, HALF-BREED, AND YOUR PRINCESS WILL BE LOST.
NEREUS PROMISED BLOOD IN THE WATER IF MERA EVER RETURNED...
"...AND AS SUCH, ATLANTIS WILL HAVE ITS QUEEN."

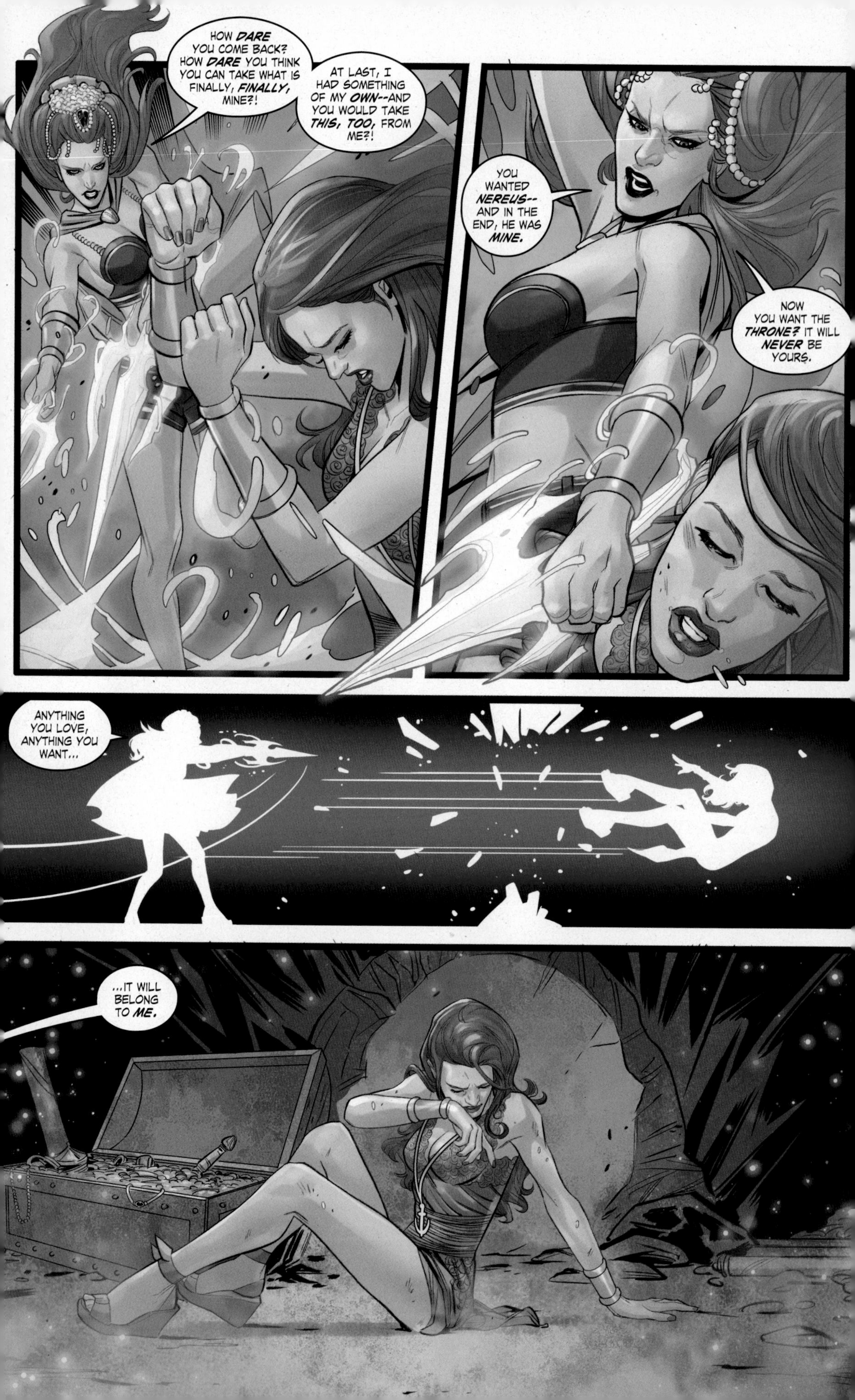
HOW DARE YOU COME BACK? HOW DARE YOU THINK YOU CAN TAKE WHAT IS FINALLY, FINALLY, MINE?!
AT LAST, I HAD SOMETHING OF MY OWN--AND YOU WOULD TAKE THIS, TOO, FROM ME?!
YOU WANTED NEREUS--AND IN THE END, HE WAS MINE.
NOW YOU WANT THE THRONE? IT WILL NEVER BE YOURS.
ANYTHING YOU LOVE, ANYTHING YOU WANT...
...IT WILL BELONG TO ME.

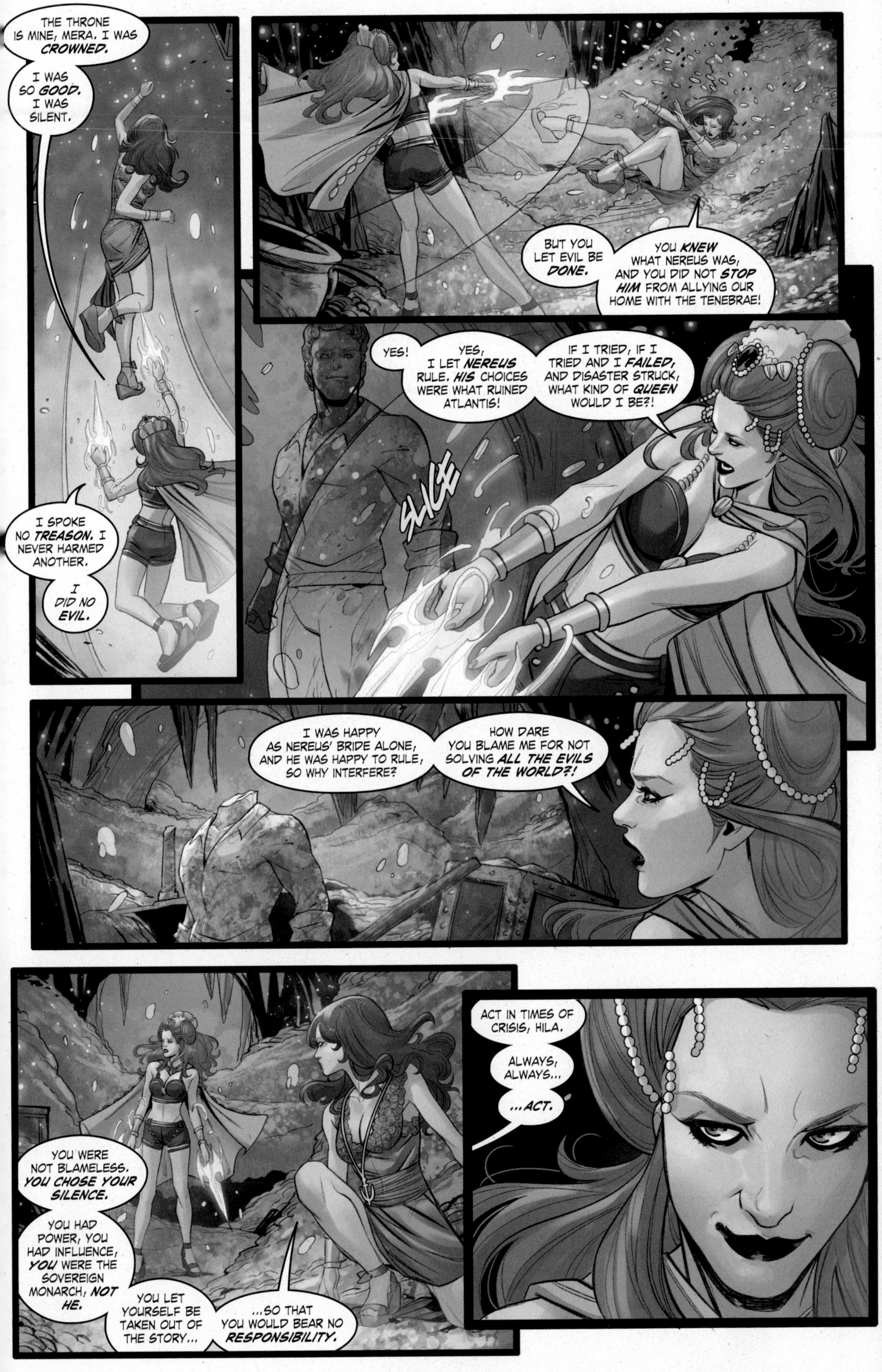
THE THRONE IS MINE, MERA. I WAS CROWNED.
I WAS SO GOOD. I WAS SILENT.
I SPOKE NO TREASON. I NEVER HARMED ANOTHER.
I DID NO EVIL.
BUT YOU LET EVIL BE DONE.
YOU KNEW WHAT NEREUS WAS, AND YOU DID NOT STOP HIM FROM ALLYING OUR HOME WITH THE TENEBRAE!
YES!
YES, I LET NEREUS RULE. HIS CHOICES WERE WHAT RUINED ATLANTIS!
IF I TRIED, IF I TRIED AND I FAILED, AND DISASTER STRUCK, WHAT KIND OF QUEEN WOULD I BE?!
SLICE
I WAS HAPPY AS NEREUS' BRIDE ALONE, AND HE WAS HAPPY TO RULE, SO WHY INTERFERE?
HOW DARE YOU BLAME ME FOR NOT SOLVING ALL THE EVILS OF THE WORLD?!
YOU WERE NOT BLAMELESS. YOU CHOSE YOUR SILENCE.
YOU HAD POWER, YOU HAD INFLUENCE, YOU WERE THE SOVEREIGN MONARCH, NOT HE.
YOU LET YOURSELF BE TAKEN OUT OF THE STORY...
...SO THAT YOU WOULD BEAR NO RESPONSIBILITY.
ACT IN TIMES OF CRISIS, HILA.
ALWAYS, ALWAYS...
...ACT.

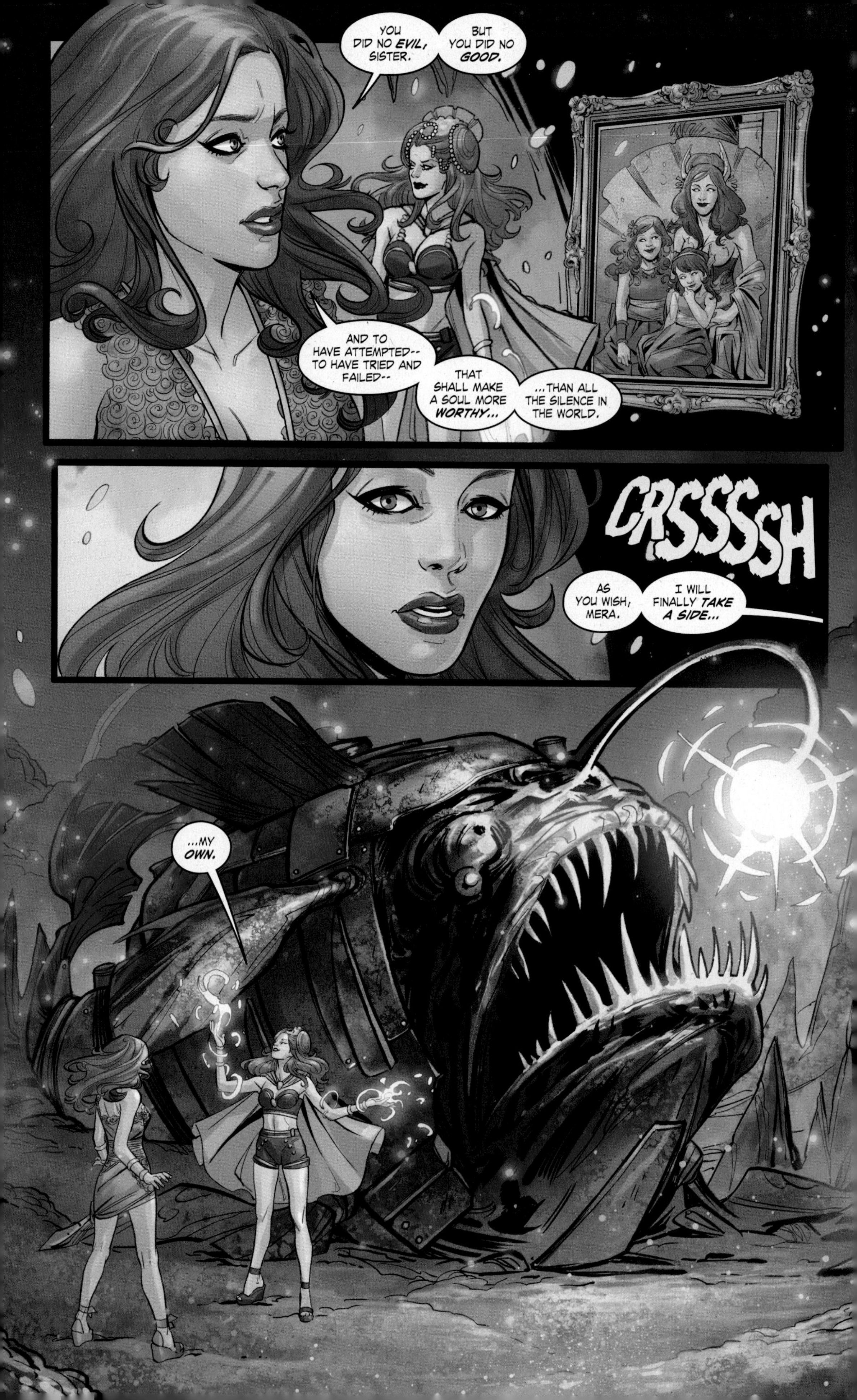
YOU DID NO EVIL, SISTER.
BUT YOU DID NO GOOD.
AND TO HAVE ATTEMPTED-- TO HAVE TRIED AND FAILED--
THAT SHALL MAKE A SOUL MORE WORTHY...
...THAN ALL THE SILENCE IN THE WORLD.
CRSSSSH
AS YOU WISH, MERA.
I WILL FINALLY TAKE A SIDE...
...MY OWN.

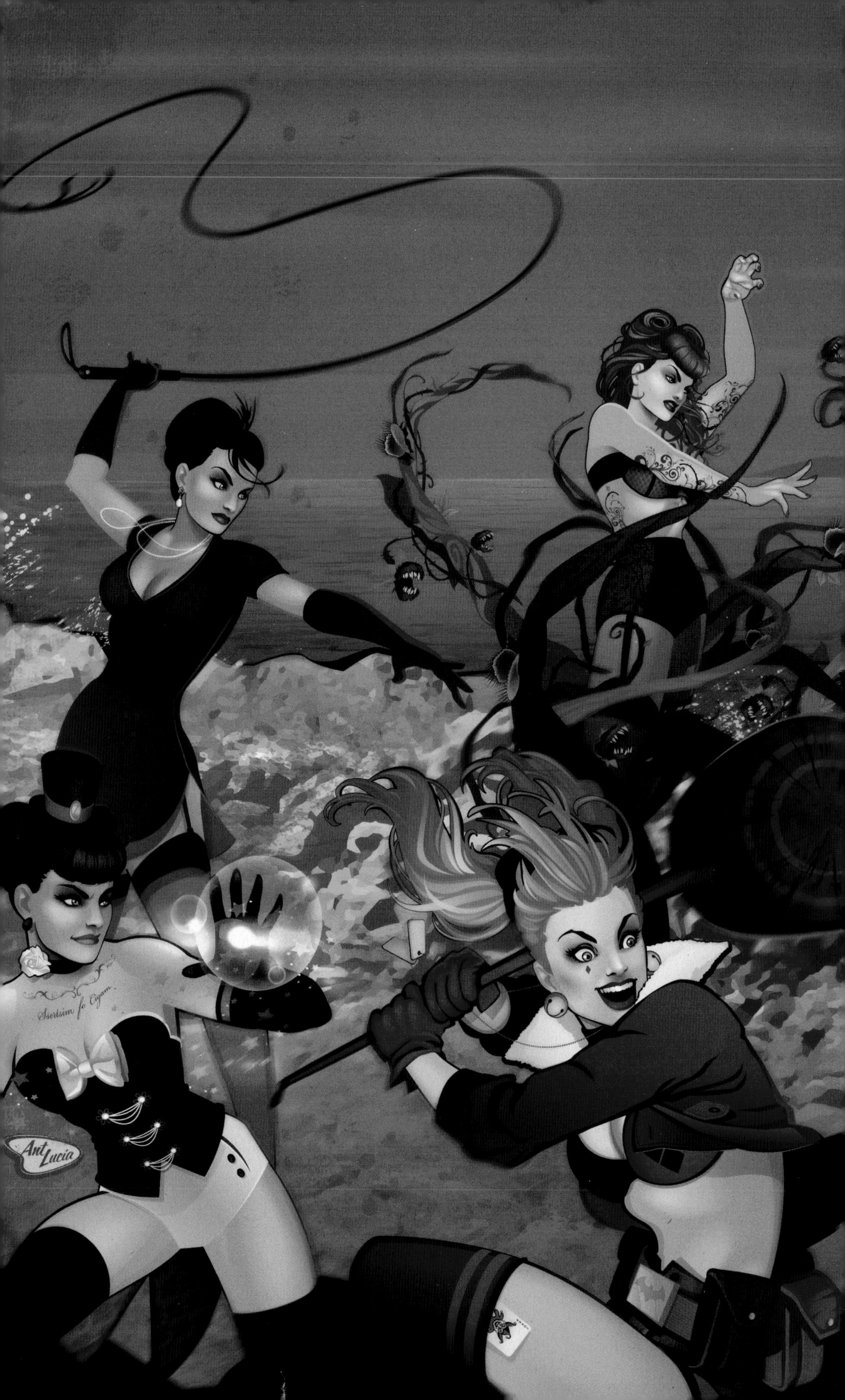
Ssertsim fo Cigam
Ant Lucia

UPRISING
PART ONE

MARGUERITE BENNETT
Writer

SANDY JARRELL
MIRKA ANDOLFO
Artists

KELLY FITZPATRICK
WENDY BROOME
Colorists

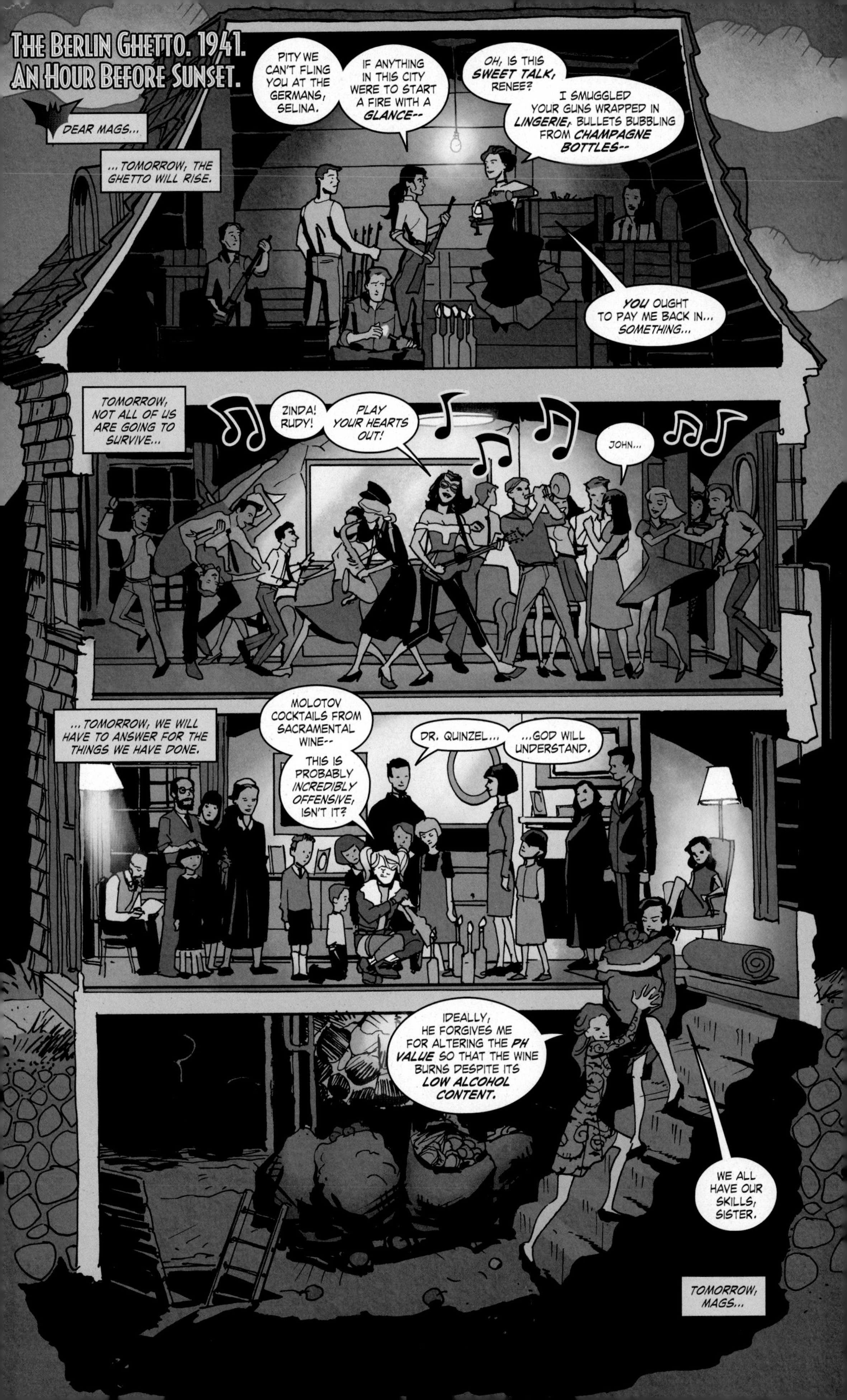

THE BERLIN GHETTO. 1941. AN HOUR BEFORE SUNSET.
DEAR MAGS...
...TOMORROW, THE GHETTO WILL RISE.
PITY WE CAN'T FLING YOU AT THE GERMANS, SELINA.
IF ANYTHING IN THIS CITY WERE TO START A FIRE WITH A GLANCE--
OH, IS THIS SWEET TALK, RENEE?
I SMUGGLED YOUR GUNS WRAPPED IN LINGERIE, BULLETS BUBBLING FROM CHAMPAGNE BOTTLES--
YOU OUGHT TO PAY ME BACK IN... SOMETHING...
TOMORROW, NOT ALL OF US ARE GOING TO SURVIVE...
ZINDA! RUDY!
PLAY YOUR HEARTS OUT!
JOHN...
...TOMORROW, WE WILL HAVE TO ANSWER FOR THE THINGS WE HAVE DONE.
MOLOTOV COCKTAILS FROM SACRAMENTAL WINE--
THIS IS PROBABLY INCREDIBLY OFFENSIVE, ISN'T IT?
DR. QUINZEL...
...GOD WILL UNDERSTAND.
IDEALLY, HE FORGIVES ME FOR ALTERING THE PH VALUE SO THAT THE WINE BURNS DESPITE ITS LOW ALCOHOL CONTENT.
WE ALL HAVE OUR SKILLS, SISTER.
TOMORROW, MAGS...

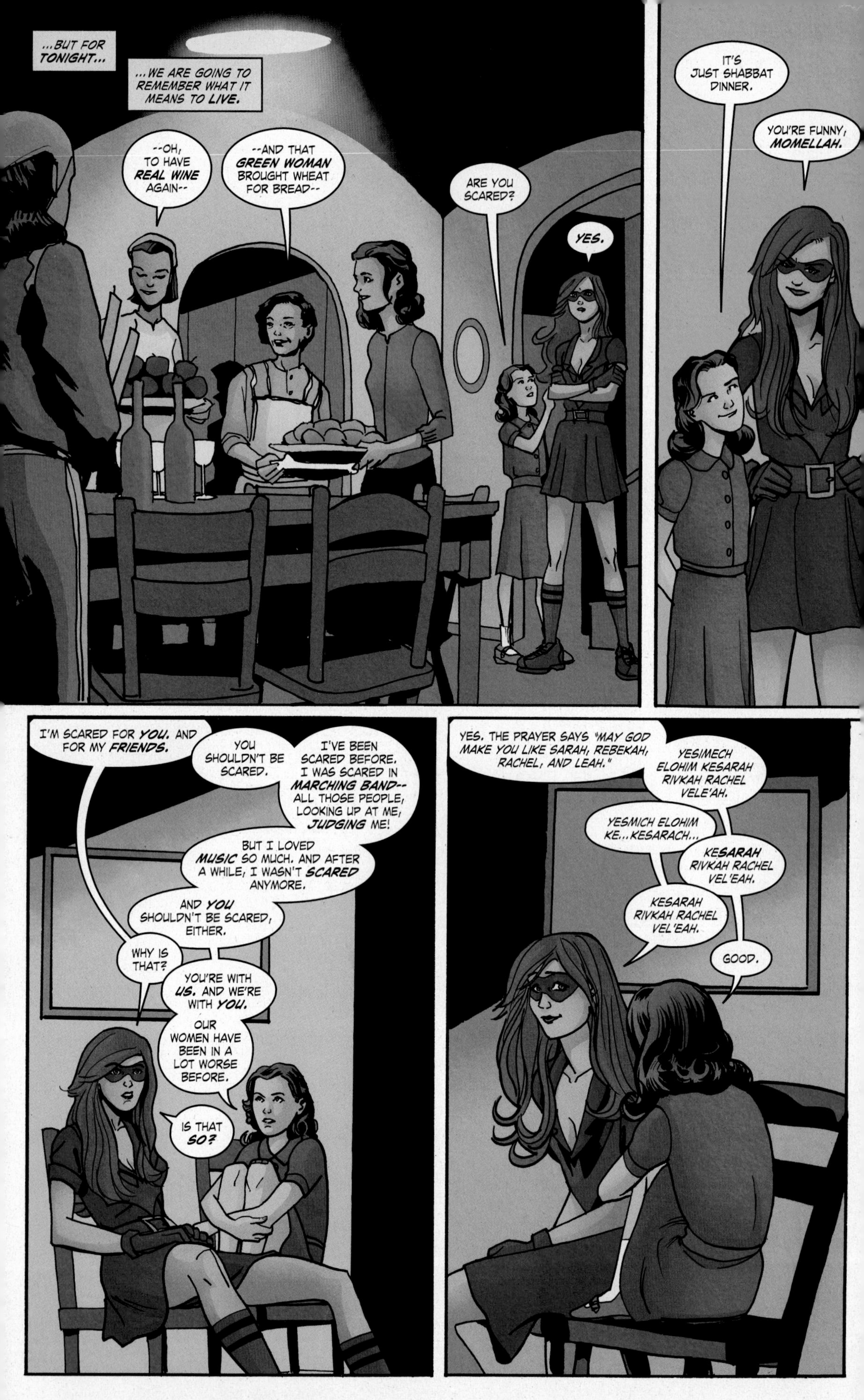
...BUT FOR TONIGHT...
...WE ARE GOING TO REMEMBER WHAT IT MEANS TO LIVE.
--OH, TO HAVE REAL WINE AGAIN--
--AND THAT GREEN WOMAN BROUGHT WHEAT FOR BREAD--
ARE YOU SCARED?
YES.
IT'S JUST SHABBAT DINNER.
YOU'RE FUNNY, MOMELLAH.
I'M SCARED FOR YOU. AND FOR MY FRIENDS.
YOU SHOULDN'T BE SCARED.
I'VE BEEN SCARED BEFORE. I WAS SCARED IN MARCHING BAND-- ALL THOSE PEOPLE, LOOKING UP AT ME, JUDGING ME!
BUT I LOVED MUSIC SO MUCH. AND AFTER A WHILE, I WASN'T SCARED ANYMORE.
AND YOU SHOULDN'T BE SCARED, EITHER.
WHY IS THAT?
YOU'RE WITH US. AND WE'RE WITH YOU.
OUR WOMEN HAVE BEEN IN A LOT WORSE BEFORE.
IS THAT SO?
YES. THE PRAYER SAYS "MAY GOD MAKE YOU LIKE SARAH, REBEKAH, RACHEL, AND LEAH."
YESIMECH ELOHIM KESARAH RIVKAH RACHEL VELE'AH.
YESMICH ELOHIM KE...KESARACH...
KESARAH RIVKAH RACHEL VEL'EAH.
KESARAH RIVKAH RACHEL VEL'EAH.
GOOD.

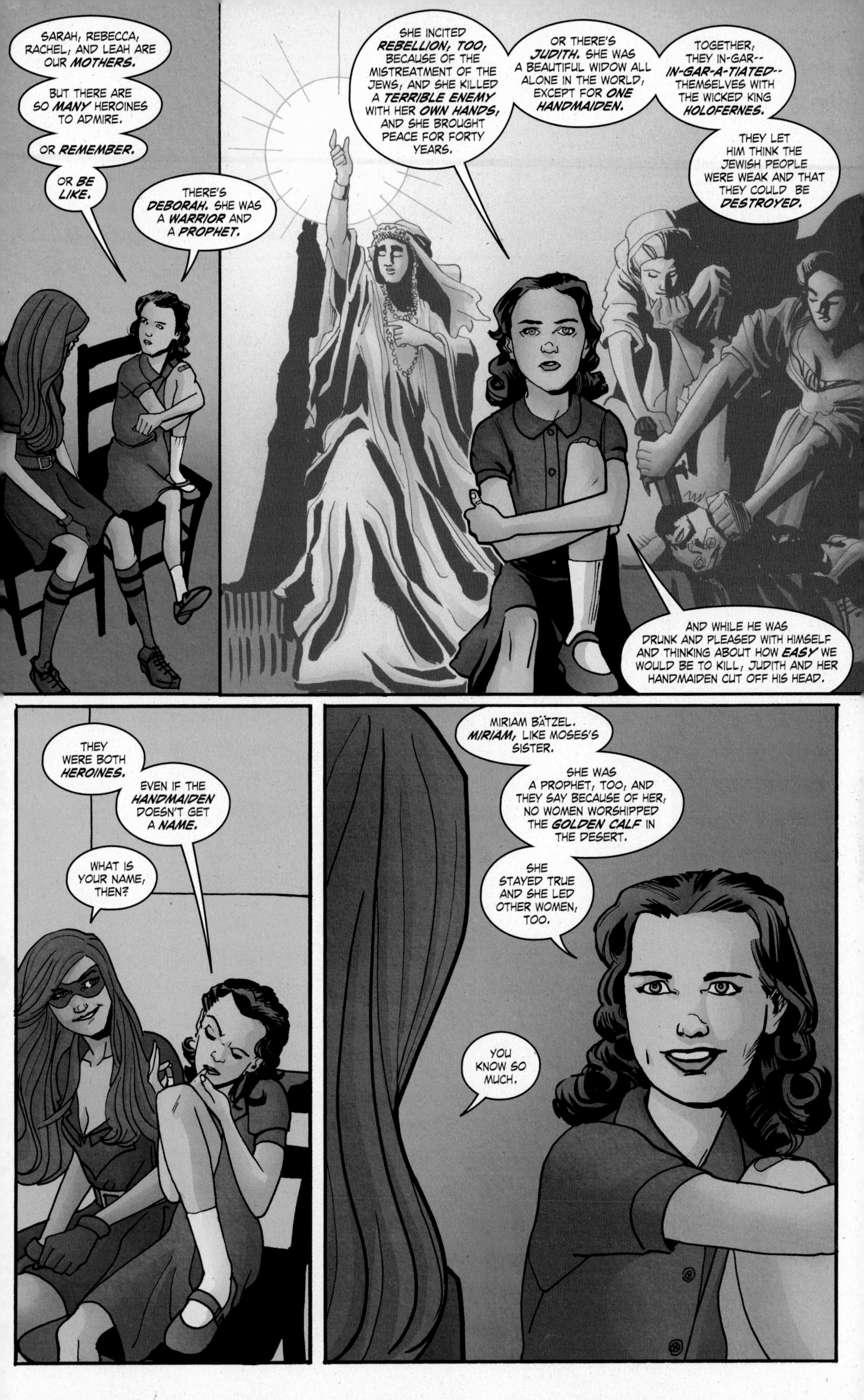
SARAH, REBECCA, RACHEL, AND LEAH ARE OUR MOTHERS.
BUT THERE ARE SO MANY HEROINES TO ADMIRE.
OR REMEMBER.
OR BE LIKE.
THERE'S DEBORAH. SHE WAS A WARRIOR AND A PROPHET.
SHE INCITED REBELLION, TOO, BECAUSE OF THE MISTREATMENT OF THE JEWS, AND SHE KILLED A TERRIBLE ENEMY WITH HER OWN HANDS, AND SHE BROUGHT PEACE FOR FORTY YEARS.
OR THERE'S JUDITH. SHE WAS A BEAUTIFUL WIDOW ALL ALONE IN THE WORLD, EXCEPT FOR ONE HANDMAIDEN.
TOGETHER, THEY IN-GAR-- IN-GAR-A-TIATED-- THEMSELVES WITH THE WICKED KING HOLOFERNES.
THEY LET HIM THINK THE JEWISH PEOPLE WERE WEAK AND THAT THEY COULD BE DESTROYED.
AND WHILE HE WAS DRUNK AND PLEASED WITH HIMSELF AND THINKING ABOUT HOW EASY WE WOULD BE TO KILL, JUDITH AND HER HANDMAIDEN CUT OFF HIS HEAD.
THEY WERE BOTH HEROINES.
EVEN IF THE HANDMAIDEN DOESN'T GET A NAME.
WHAT IS YOUR NAME, THEN?
MIRIAM BÄTZEL. MIRIAM, LIKE MOSES'S SISTER.
SHE WAS A PROPHET, TOO, AND THEY SAY BECAUSE OF HER, NO WOMEN WORSHIPPED THE GOLDEN CALF IN THE DESERT.
SHE STAYED TRUE AND SHE LED OTHER WOMEN, TOO.
YOU KNOW SO MUCH.

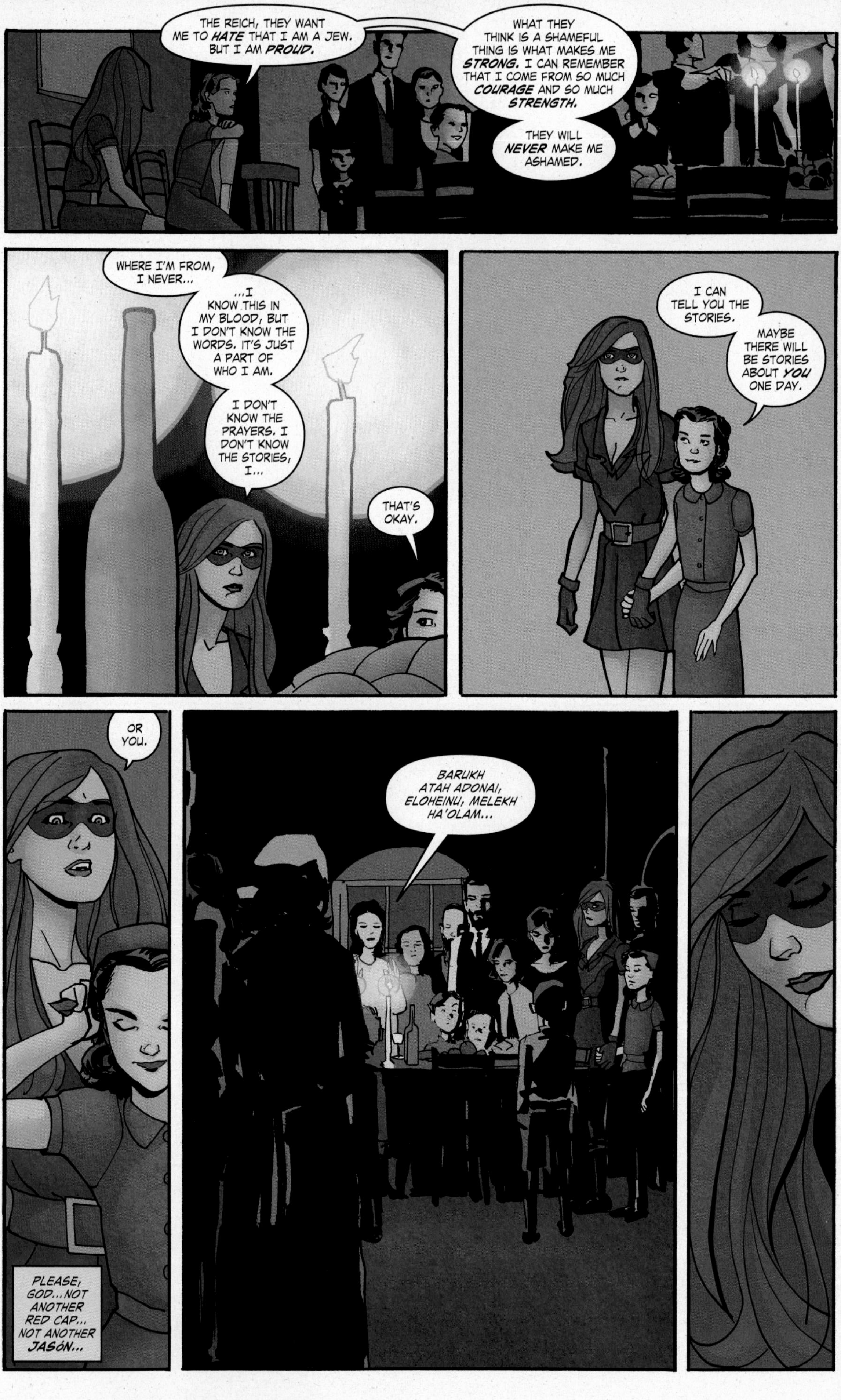
THE REICH, THEY WANT ME TO HATE THAT I AM A JEW. BUT I AM PROUD.
WHAT THEY THINK IS A SHAMEFUL THING IS WHAT MAKES ME STRONG. I CAN REMEMBER THAT I COME FROM SO MUCH COURAGE AND SO MUCH STRENGTH.
THEY WILL NEVER MAKE ME ASHAMED.
WHERE I'M FROM, I NEVER...
...I KNOW THIS IN MY BLOOD, BUT I DON'T KNOW THE WORDS. IT'S JUST A PART OF WHO I AM.
I DON'T KNOW THE PRAYERS. I DON'T KNOW THE STORIES, I...
THAT'S OKAY.
I CAN TELL YOU THE STORIES.
MAYBE THERE WILL BE STORIES ABOUT YOU ONE DAY.
OR YOU.
PLEASE, GOD...NOT ANOTHER RED CAP... NOT ANOTHER JASÓN...
BARUKH ATAH ADONAI, ELOHEINU, MELEKH HA'OLAM...

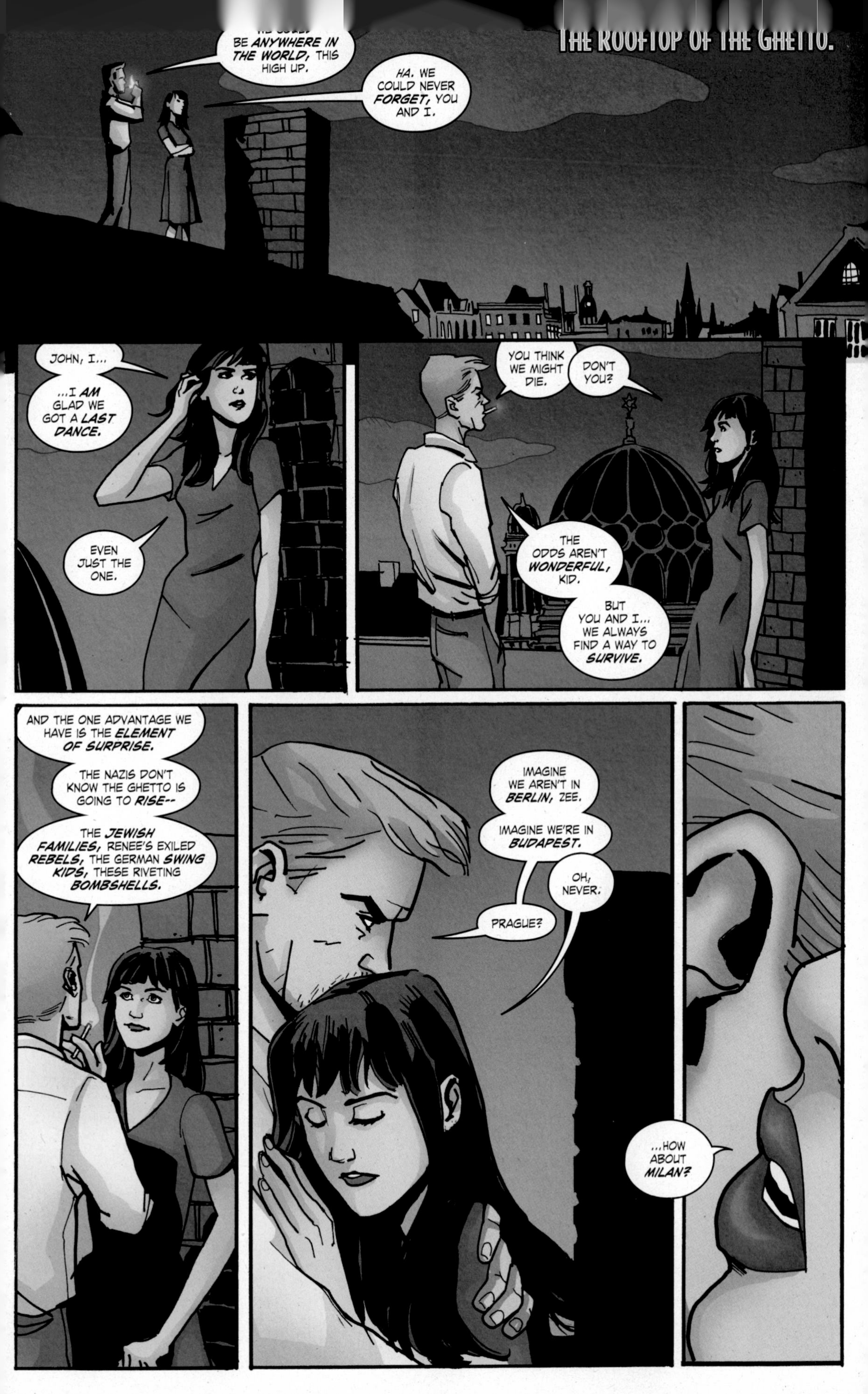
THE ROOFTOP OF THE GHETTO.
BE ANYWHERE IN THE WORLD, THIS HIGH UP.
HA. WE COULD NEVER FORGET, YOU AND I.
JOHN, I...
...I AM GLAD WE GOT A LAST DANCE.
EVEN JUST THE ONE.
YOU THINK WE MIGHT DIE.
DON'T YOU?
THE ODDS AREN'T WONDERFUL, KID.
BUT YOU AND I... WE ALWAYS FIND A WAY TO SURVIVE.
AND THE ONE ADVANTAGE WE HAVE IS THE ELEMENT OF SURPRISE.
THE NAZIS DON'T KNOW THE GHETTO IS GOING TO RISE--
THE JEWISH FAMILIES, RENEE'S EXILED REBELS, THE GERMAN SWING KIDS, THESE RIVETING BOMBSHELLS.
IMAGINE WE AREN'T IN BERLIN, ZEE.
IMAGINE WE'RE IN BUDAPEST.
OH, NEVER.
PRAGUE?
...HOW ABOUT MILAN?

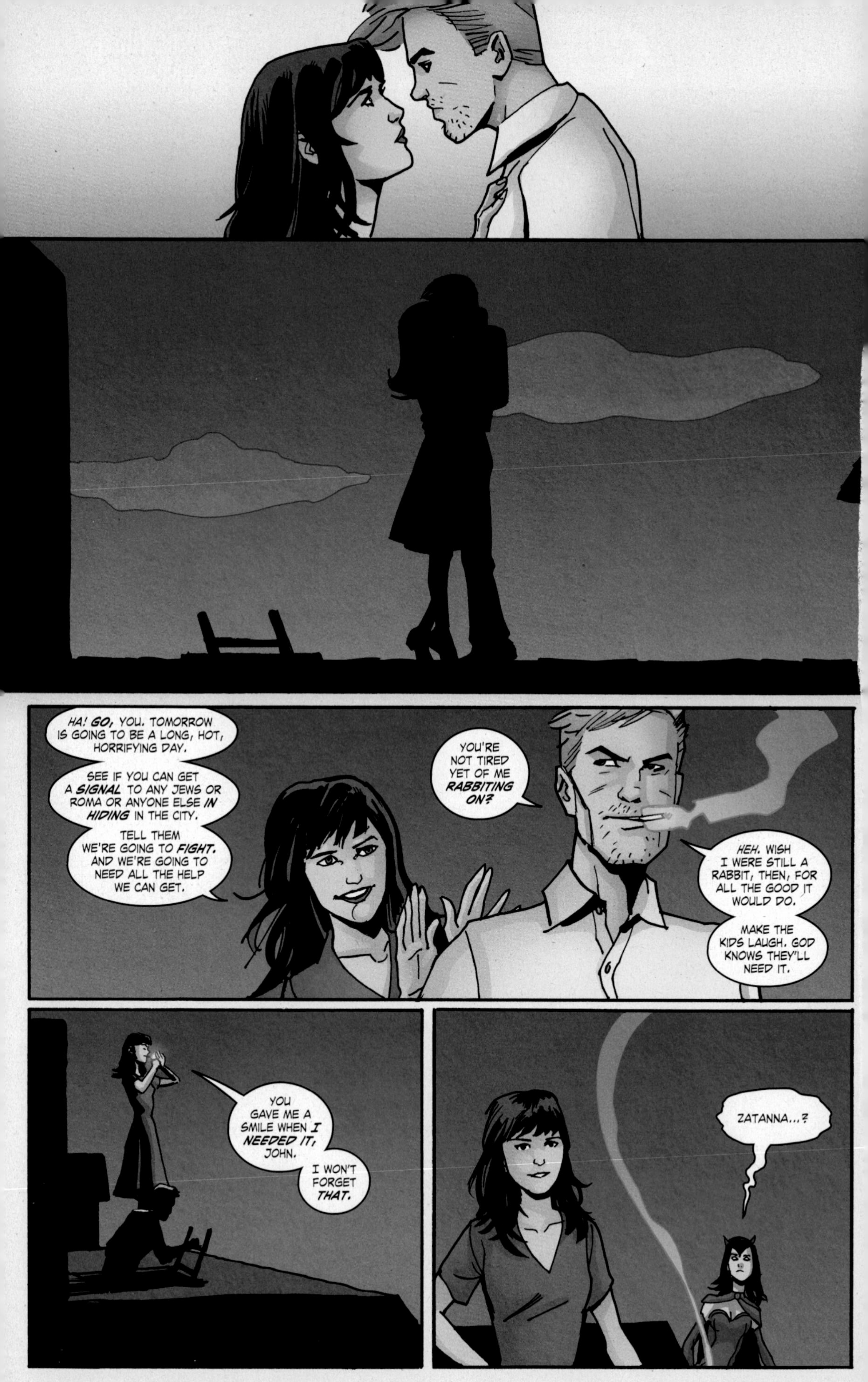
HA! GO, YOU. TOMORROW IS GOING TO BE A LONG, HOT, HORRIFYING DAY.
SEE IF YOU CAN GET A SIGNAL TO ANY JEWS OR ROMA OR ANYONE ELSE IN HIDING IN THE CITY.
TELL THEM WE'RE GOING TO FIGHT. AND WE'RE GOING TO NEED ALL THE HELP WE CAN GET.
YOU'RE NOT TIRED YET OF ME RABBITING ON?
HEH. WISH I WERE STILL A RABBIT, THEN, FOR ALL THE GOOD IT WOULD DO.
MAKE THE KIDS LAUGH. GOD KNOWS THEY'LL NEED IT.
YOU GAVE ME A SMILE WHEN I NEEDED IT, JOHN.
I WON'T FORGET THAT.
ZATANNA...?

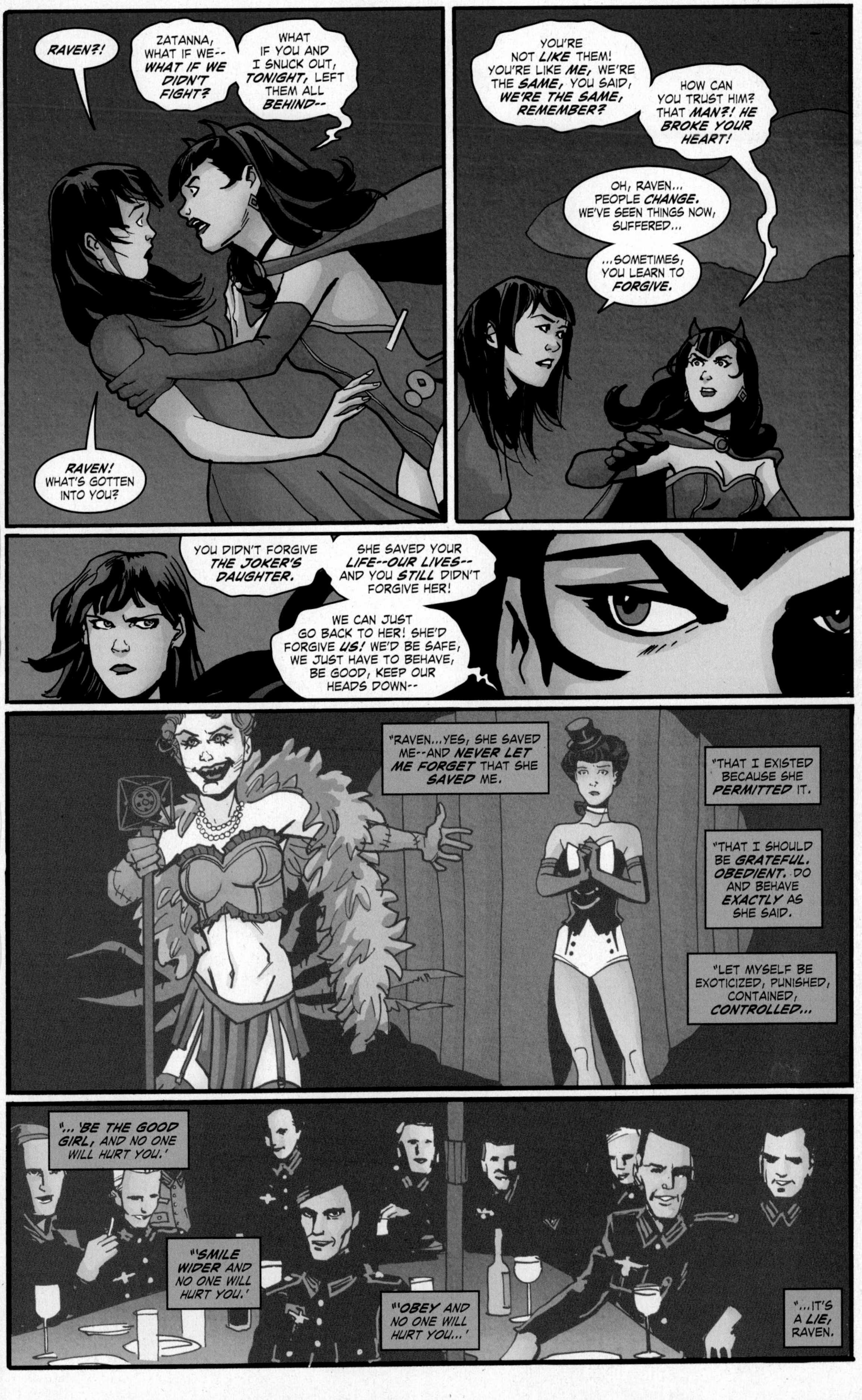
RAVEN?!
ZATANNA, WHAT IF WE-- WHAT IF WE DIDN'T FIGHT?
WHAT IF YOU AND I SNUCK OUT, TONIGHT, LEFT THEM ALL BEHIND--
RAVEN! WHAT'S GOTTEN INTO YOU?
YOU'RE NOT LIKE THEM! YOU'RE LIKE ME, WE'RE THE SAME, YOU SAID, WE'RE THE SAME, REMEMBER?
HOW CAN YOU TRUST HIM? THAT MAN?! HE BROKE YOUR HEART!
OH, RAVEN... PEOPLE CHANGE. WE'VE SEEN THINGS NOW, SUFFERED...
...SOMETIMES, YOU LEARN TO FORGIVE.
YOU DIDN'T FORGIVE THE JOKER'S DAUGHTER.
SHE SAVED YOUR LIFE--OUR LIVES-- AND YOU STILL DIDN'T FORGIVE HER!
WE CAN JUST GO BACK TO HER! SHE'D FORGIVE US! WE'D BE SAFE, WE JUST HAVE TO BEHAVE, BE GOOD, KEEP OUR HEADS DOWN--
"RAVEN...YES, SHE SAVED ME--AND NEVER LET ME FORGET THAT SHE SAVED ME.
"THAT I EXISTED BECAUSE SHE PERMITTED IT.
"THAT I SHOULD BE GRATEFUL. OBEDIENT. DO AND BEHAVE EXACTLY AS SHE SAID.
"LET MYSELF BE EXOTICIZED, PUNISHED, CONTAINED, CONTROLLED...
"...'BE THE GOOD GIRL, AND NO ONE WILL HURT YOU.'
"'SMILE WIDER AND NO ONE WILL HURT YOU.'
"'OBEY AND NO ONE WILL HURT YOU...'
"...IT'S A LIE, RAVEN.

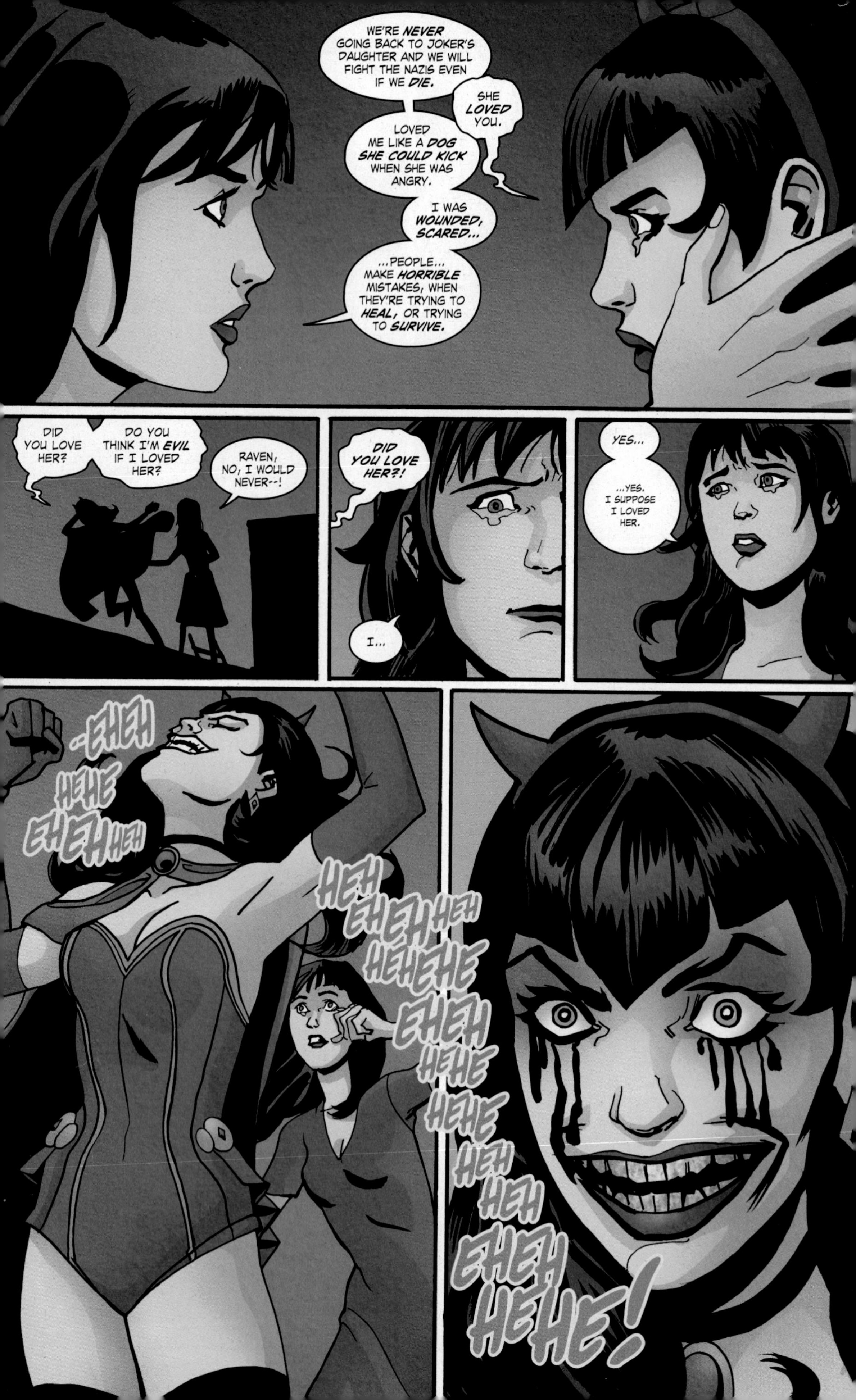
WE'RE NEVER GOING BACK TO JOKER'S DAUGHTER AND WE WILL FIGHT THE NAZIS EVEN IF WE DIE.
SHE LOVED YOU.
LOVED ME LIKE A DOG SHE COULD KICK WHEN SHE WAS ANGRY.
I WAS WOUNDED, SCARED...
...PEOPLE... MAKE HORRIBLE MISTAKES, WHEN THEY'RE TRYING TO HEAL, OR TRYING TO SURVIVE.
DID YOU LOVE HER?
DO YOU THINK I'M EVIL IF I LOVED HER?
RAVEN, NO, I WOULD NEVER--!
DID YOU LOVE HER?!
I...
YES...
...YES. I SUPPOSE I LOVED HER.
-EHEH HEHE EHEH HEH
HEH EHEH HEH HEHEHE EHEH HEHE HEHE HEH HEH EHEH HEHE!

YES, YOU DID! YOU SAID IT! YOU SAID THE WORDS!

YOU LOVED ME.

N-NO! J-JOKER'S DAUGHTER--?!

I KNEW I WOULD *HUMBLE* YOU. THE PAST IS *NEVER FAR BEHIND*--

NOT FOR *ANYONE*.

I *TOLD* YOU, LIEBCHEN.

UNTIL THE DAY YOU DIE...

...ICH HALTE DICH.

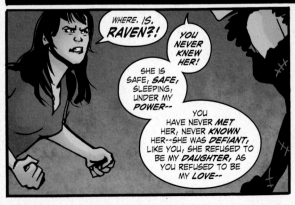

WHERE. IS. *RAVEN?!*

YOU NEVER KNEW HER!

SHE IS *SAFE, SAFE,* SLEEPING, UNDER MY *POWER*--

YOU HAVE NEVER *MET* HER, NEVER *KNOWN* HER--SHE WAS *DEFIANT,* LIKE YOU, SHE REFUSED TO BE MY *DAUGHTER,* AS YOU REFUSED TO BE MY *LOVE*--

SLAP

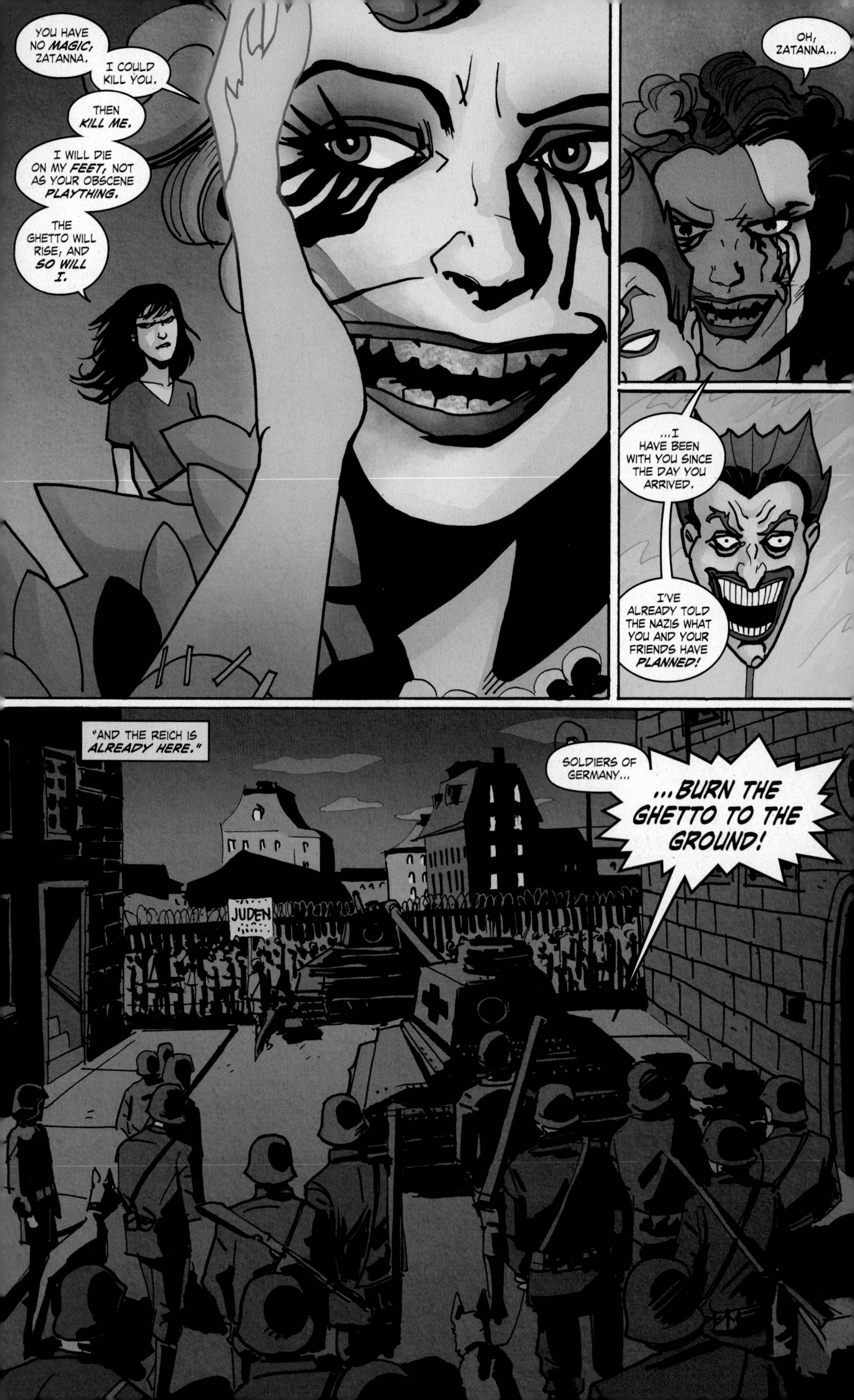
YOU HAVE NO MAGIC, ZATANNA.
I COULD KILL YOU.
THEN KILL ME.
I WILL DIE ON MY FEET, NOT AS YOUR OBSCENE PLAYTHING.
THE GHETTO WILL RISE, AND SO WILL I.
OH, ZATANNA...
...I HAVE BEEN WITH YOU SINCE THE DAY YOU ARRIVED.
I'VE ALREADY TOLD THE NAZIS WHAT YOU AND YOUR FRIENDS HAVE PLANNED!
"AND THE REICH IS ALREADY HERE."
SOLDIERS OF GERMANY...
...BURN THE GHETTO TO THE GROUND!
JUDEN

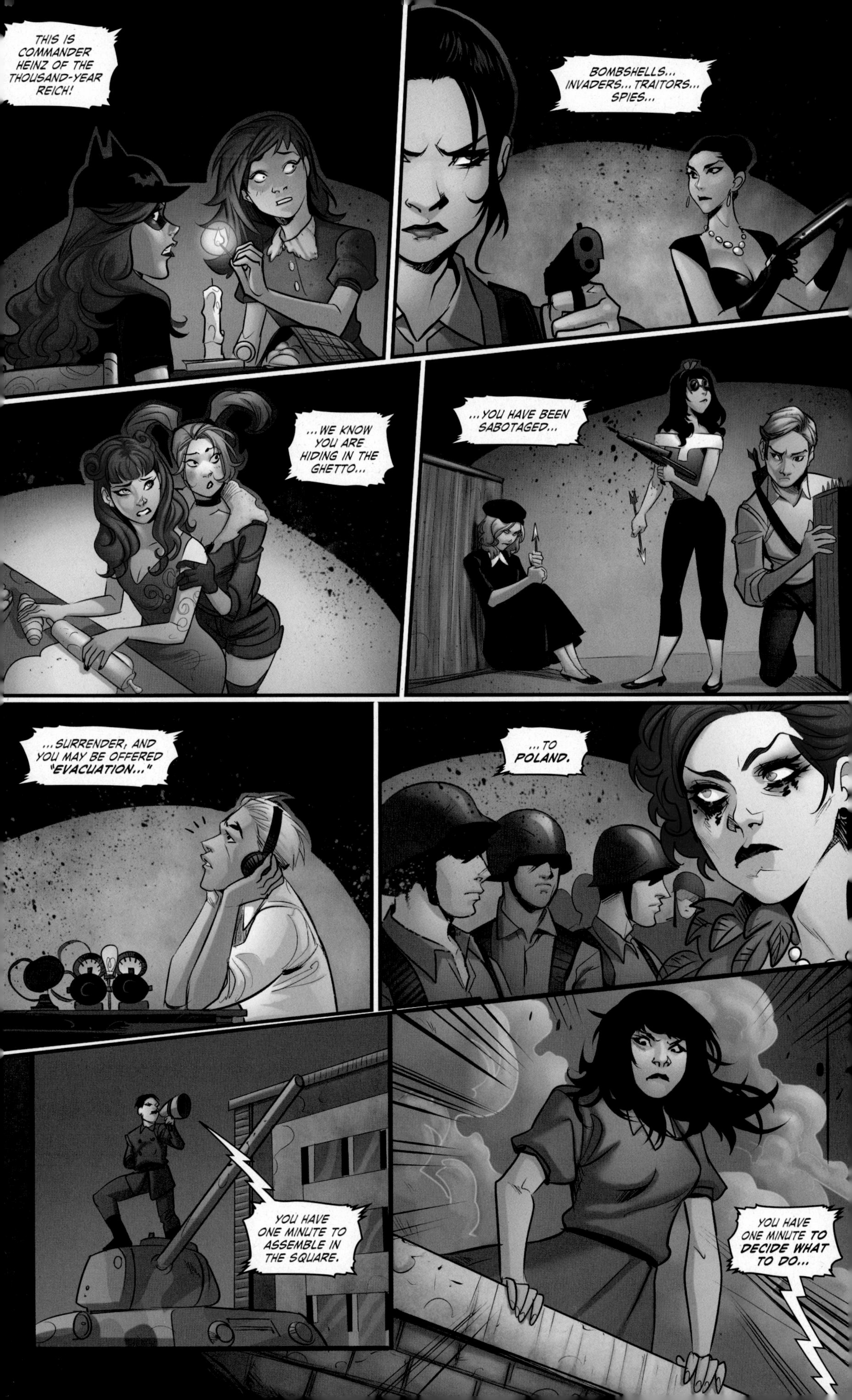
THIS IS COMMANDER HEINZ OF THE THOUSAND-YEAR REICH!
BOMBSHELLS... INVADERS... TRAITORS... SPIES...
...WE KNOW YOU ARE HIDING IN THE GHETTO...
...YOU HAVE BEEN SABOTAGED...
...SURRENDER, AND YOU MAY BE OFFERED "EVACUATION..."
...TO POLAND.
YOU HAVE ONE MINUTE TO ASSEMBLE IN THE SQUARE.
YOU HAVE ONE MINUTE TO DECIDE WHAT TO DO...

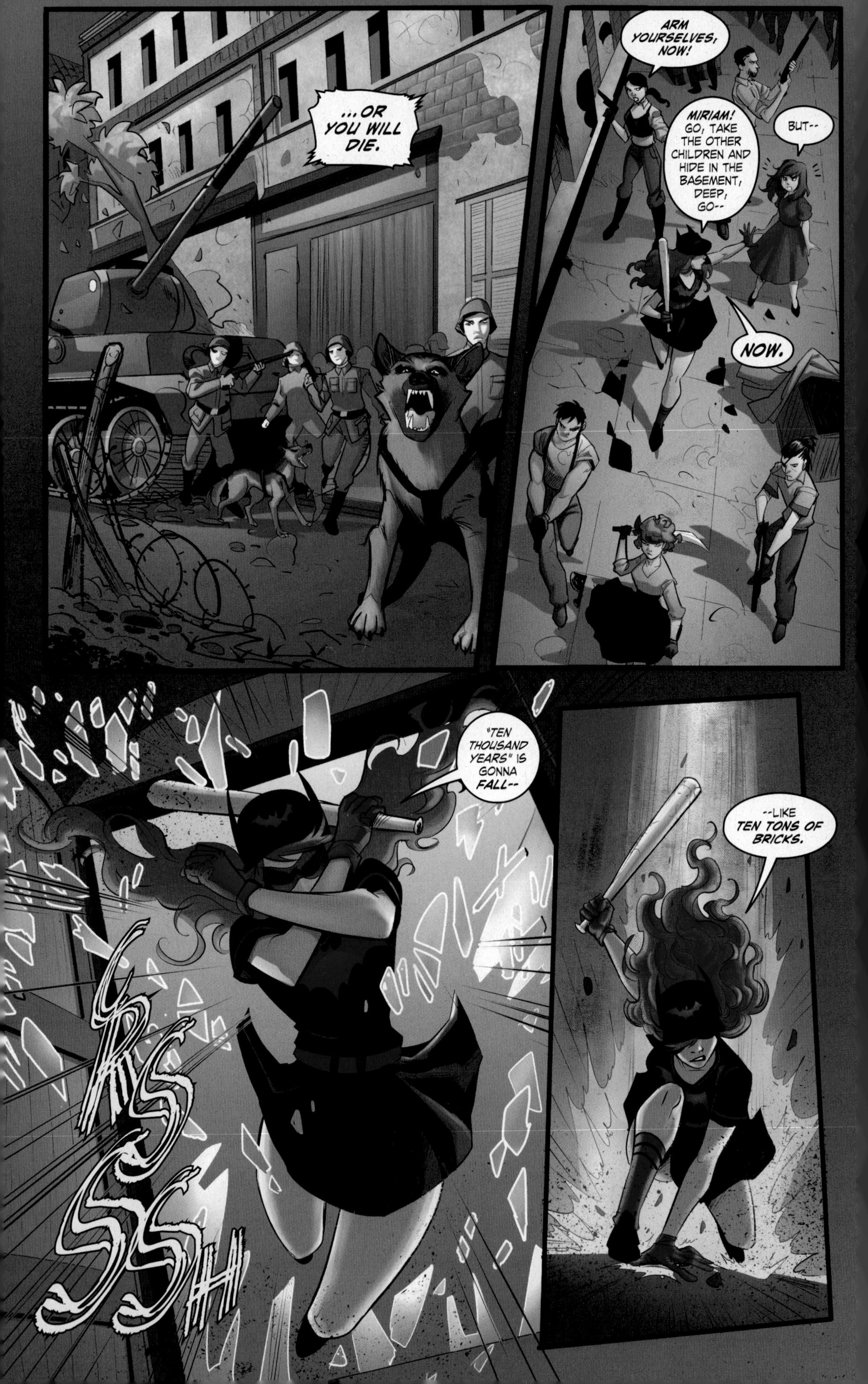
...OR YOU WILL DIE.
ARM YOURSELVES, NOW!
MIRIAM! GO, TAKE THE OTHER CHILDREN AND HIDE IN THE BASEMENT, DEEP, GO--
BUT--
NOW.
"TEN THOUSAND YEARS" IS GONNA FALL--
KRSSSSH
--LIKE TEN TONS OF BRICKS.

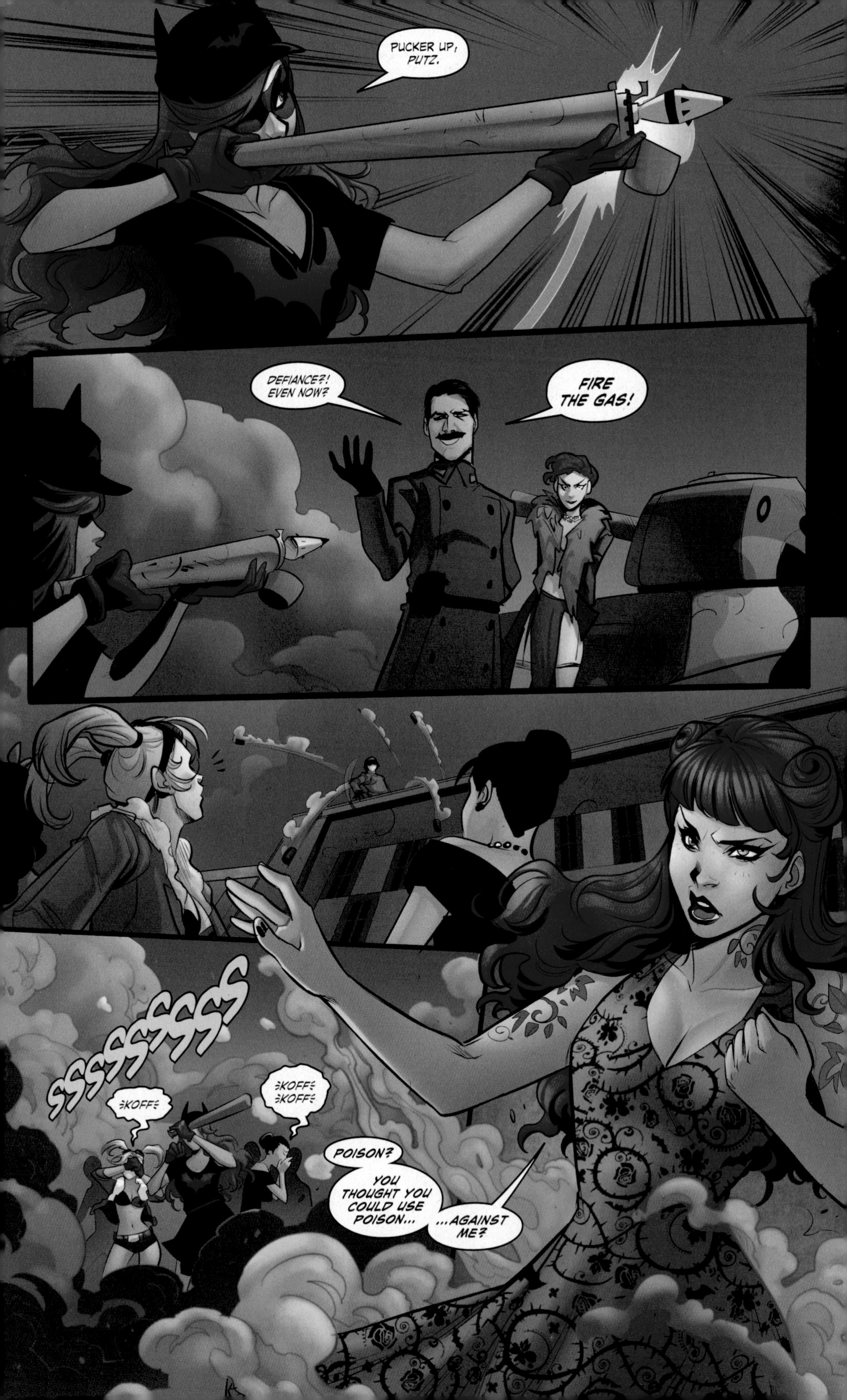
PUCKER UP, PUTZ.
DEFIANCE?! EVEN NOW?
FIRE THE GAS!
SSSSSSSSSS
KOFF
KOFF KOFF
POISON?
YOU THOUGHT YOU COULD USE POISON...
...AGAINST ME?

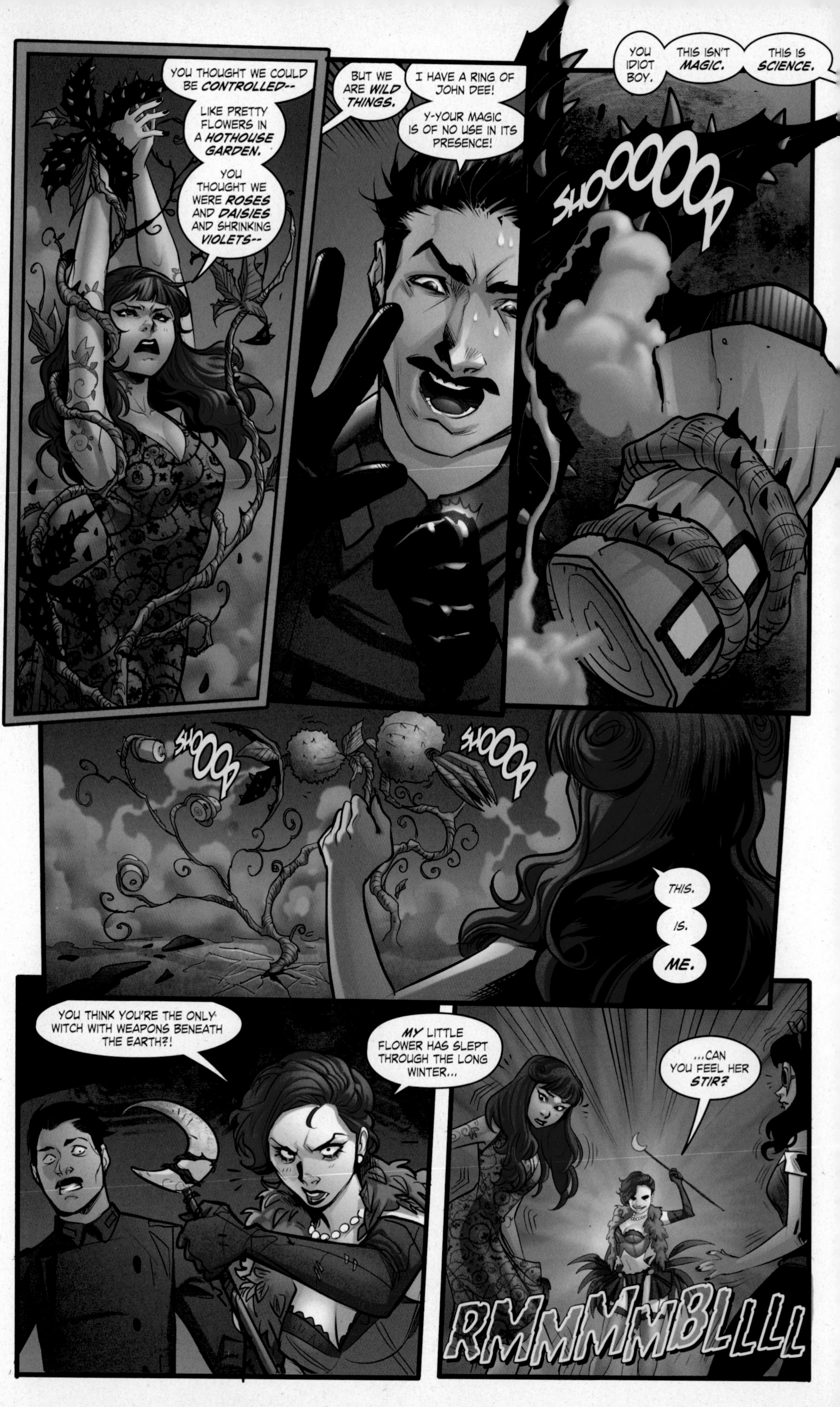
YOU THOUGHT WE COULD BE CONTROLLED--
LIKE PRETTY FLOWERS IN A HOTHOUSE GARDEN.
YOU THOUGHT WE WERE ROSES AND DAISIES AND SHRINKING VIOLETS--
BUT WE ARE WILD THINGS.
I HAVE A RING OF JOHN DEE!
Y-YOUR MAGIC IS OF NO USE IN ITS PRESENCE!
YOU IDIOT BOY.
THIS ISN'T MAGIC.
THIS IS SCIENCE.
SHOOOOOP
SHOOOP
SHOOOP
THIS.
IS.
ME.
YOU THINK YOU'RE THE ONLY WITCH WITH WEAPONS BENEATH THE EARTH?!
MY LITTLE FLOWER HAS SLEPT THROUGH THE LONG WINTER...
...CAN YOU FEEL HER STIR?
RMMMMMBLLLL

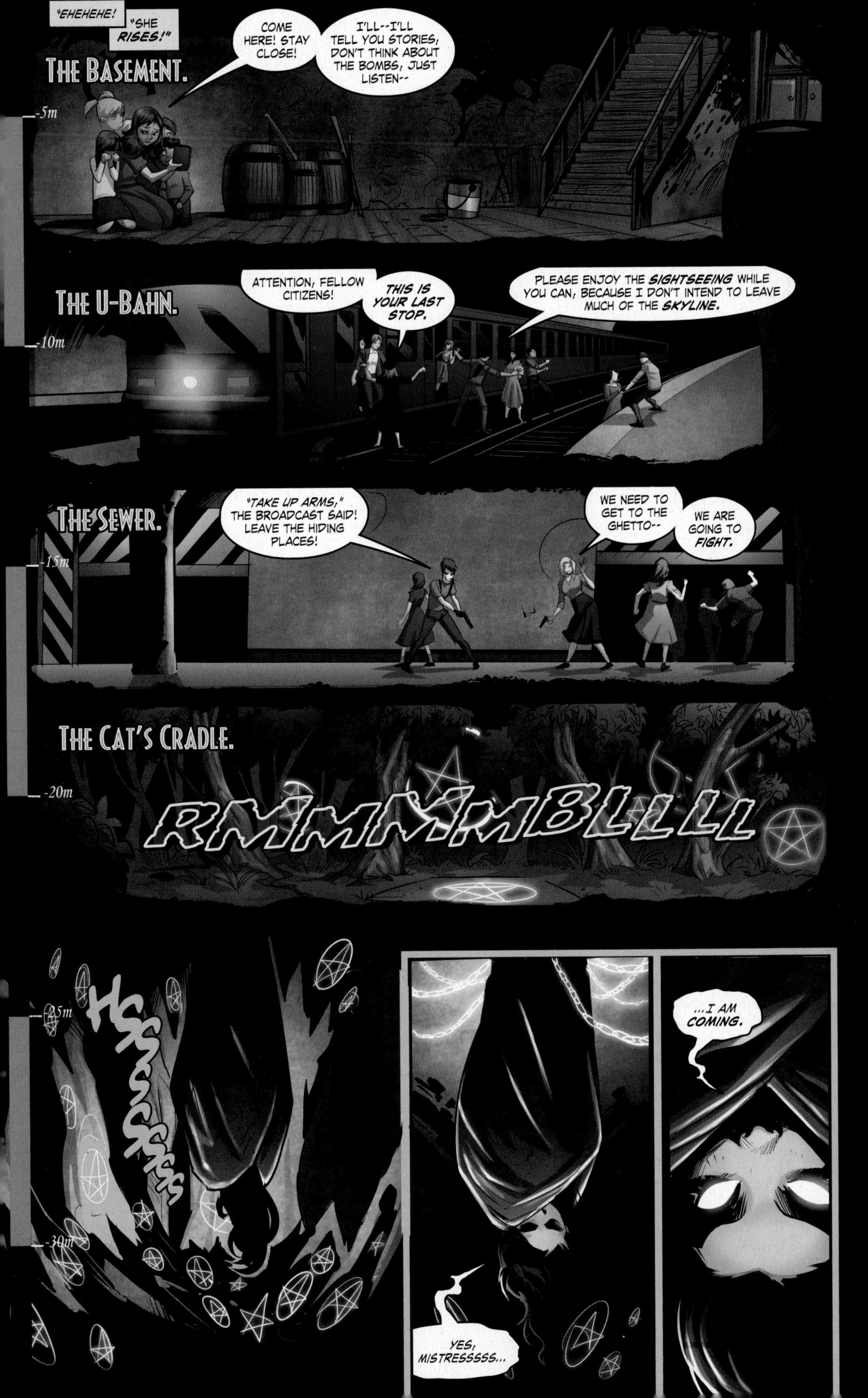
"EHEHEHE!
"SHE RISES!"
THE BASEMENT.
COME HERE! STAY CLOSE!
I'LL--I'LL TELL YOU STORIES, DON'T THINK ABOUT THE BOMBS, JUST LISTEN--
-5m
THE U-BAHN.
ATTENTION, FELLOW CITIZENS!
THIS IS YOUR LAST STOP.
PLEASE ENJOY THE SIGHTSEEING WHILE YOU CAN, BECAUSE I DON'T INTEND TO LEAVE MUCH OF THE SKYLINE.
-10m
THE SEWER.
"TAKE UP ARMS," THE BROADCAST SAID! LEAVE THE HIDING PLACES!
WE NEED TO GET TO THE GHETTO--
WE ARE GOING TO FIGHT.
-15m
THE CAT'S CRADLE.
-20m
RMMMMBLLLL
HSSSSSSSS
-25m
-30m
YES, MISTRESSSSS...
...I AM COMING.

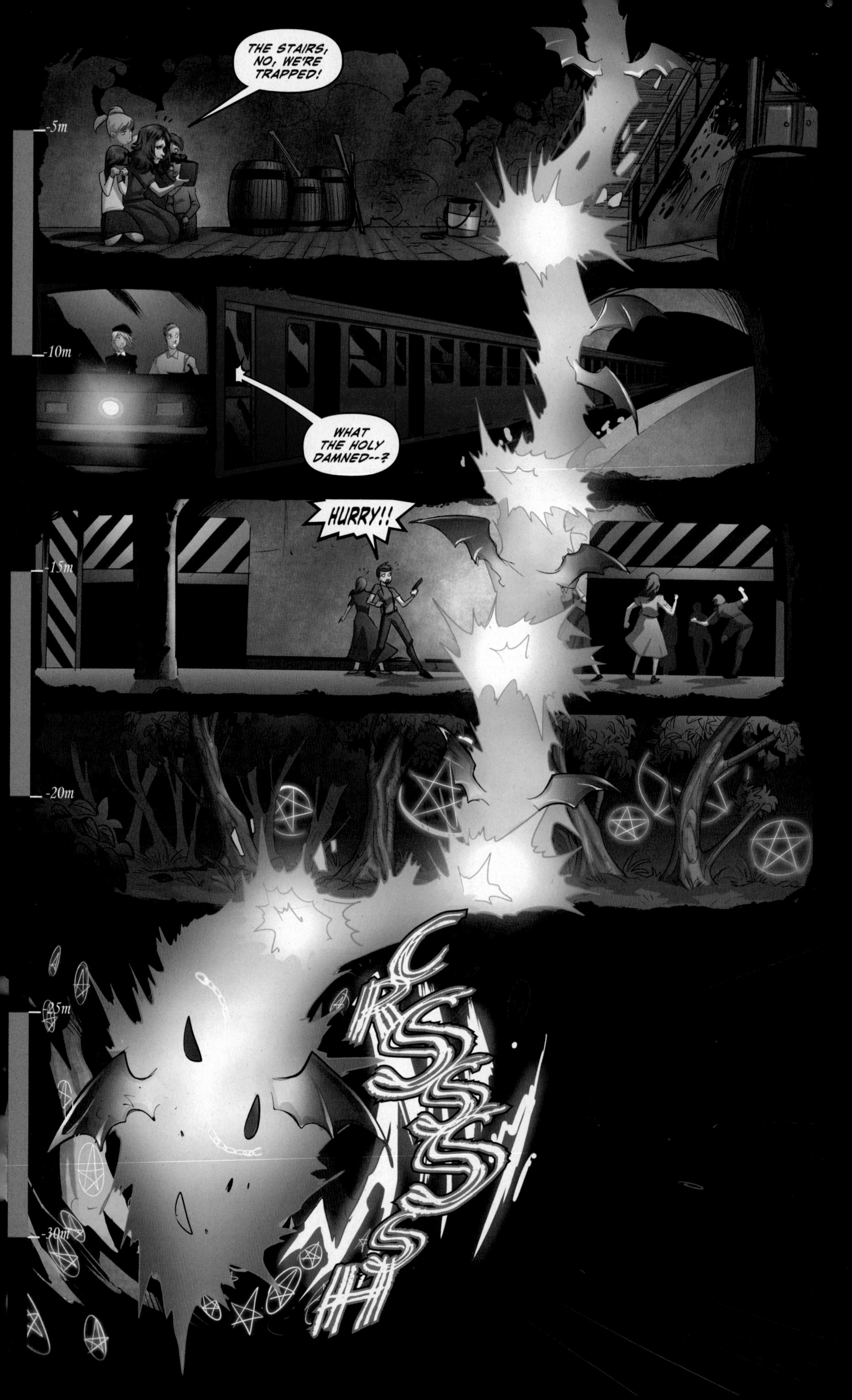

THE STAIRS, NO, WE'RE TRAPPED!
-5m
-10m
WHAT THE HOLY DAMNED--?
HURRY!!
-15m
-20m
-25m
-30m
CRSSSSSH

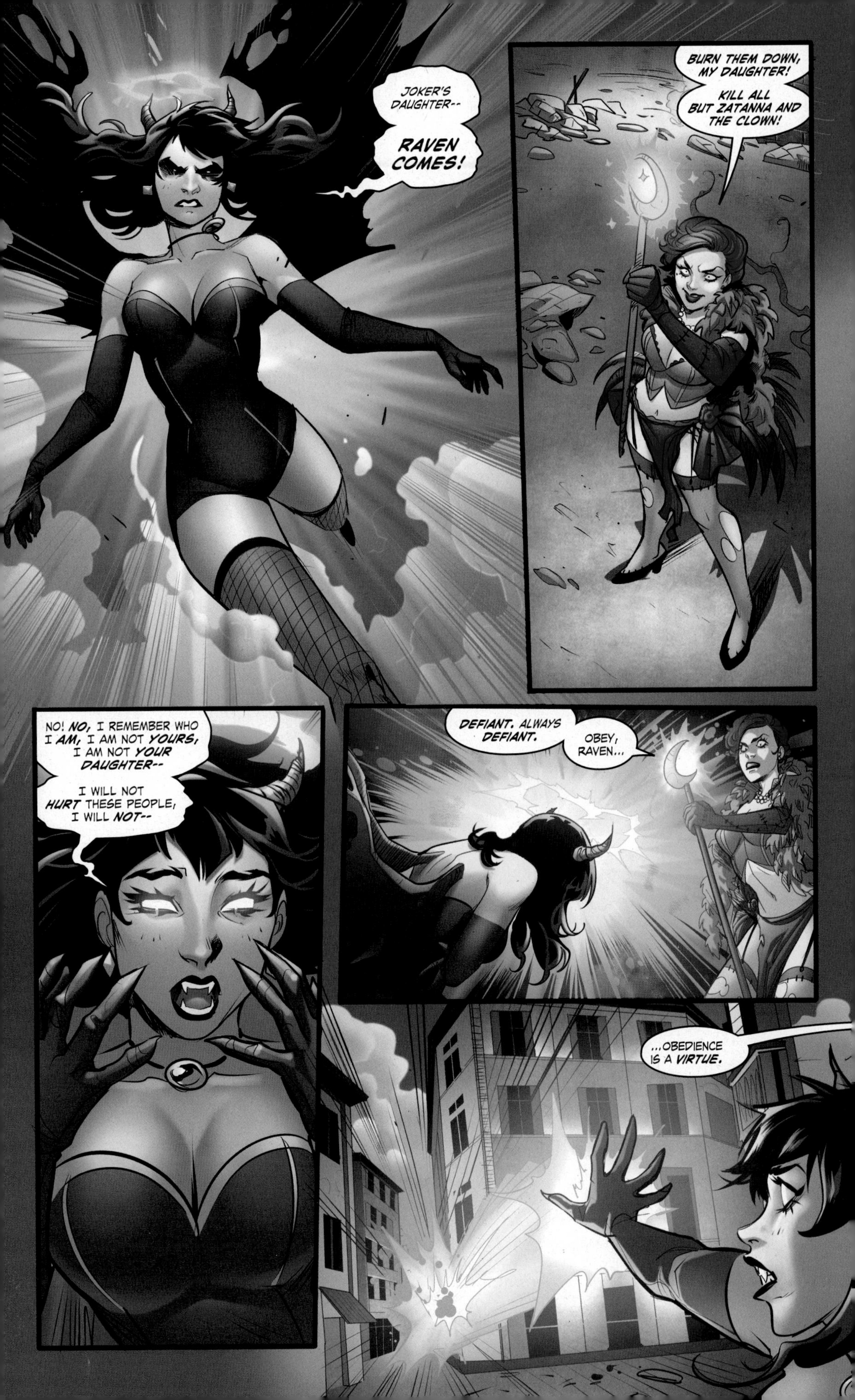
JOKER'S DAUGHTER--
RAVEN COMES!
BURN THEM DOWN, MY DAUGHTER!
KILL ALL BUT ZATANNA AND THE CLOWN!
NO! NO, I REMEMBER WHO I AM, I AM NOT YOURS, I AM NOT YOUR DAUGHTER--
I WILL NOT HURT THESE PEOPLE, I WILL NOT--
DEFIANT. ALWAYS DEFIANT.
OBEY, RAVEN...
...OBEDIENCE IS A VIRTUE.

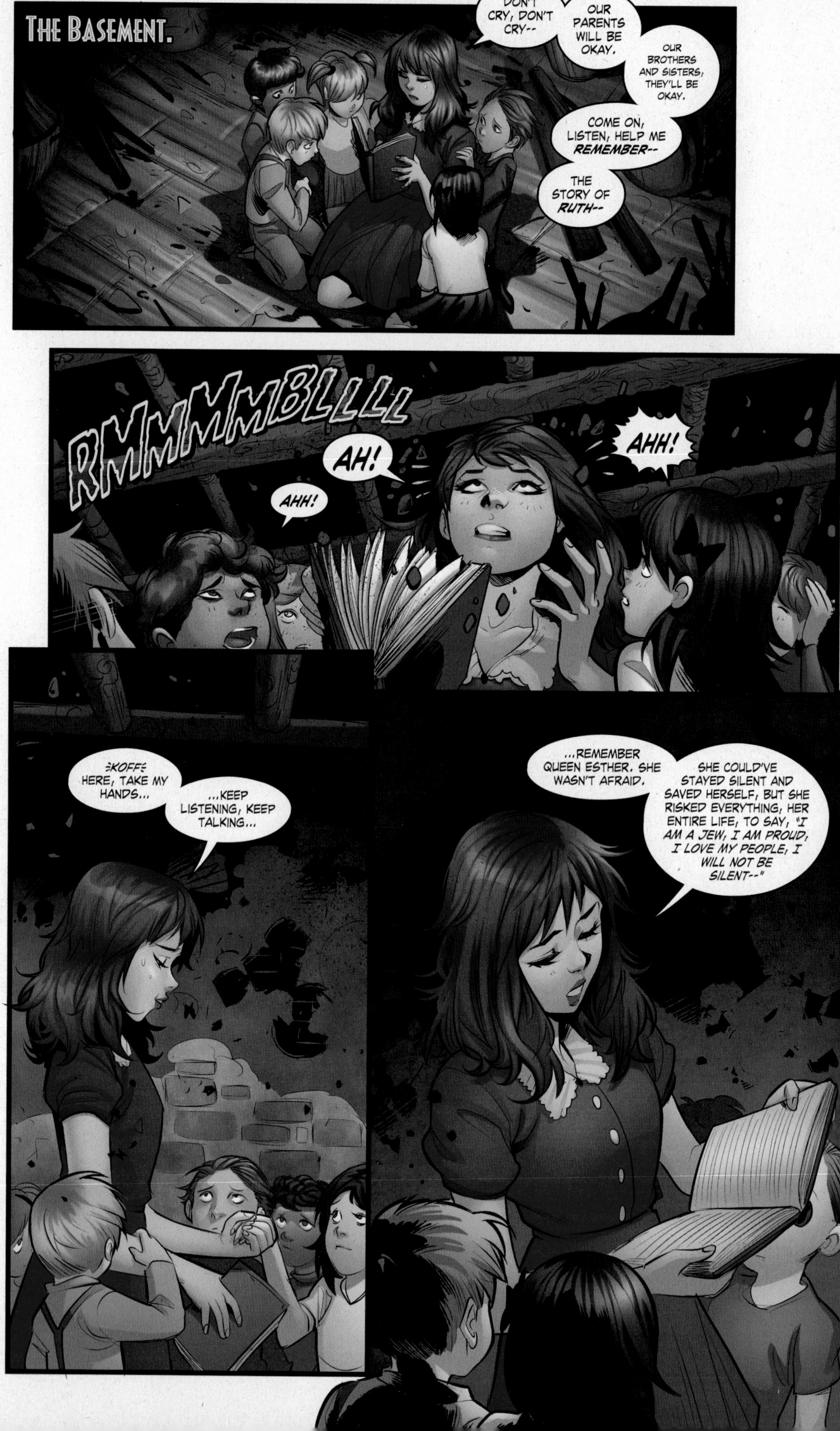

THE BASEMENT.
DON'T CRY, DON'T CRY--
OUR PARENTS WILL BE OKAY.
OUR BROTHERS AND SISTERS, THEY'LL BE OKAY.
COME ON, LISTEN, HELP ME *REMEMBER*--
THE STORY OF *RUTH*--
RMMMMBLLLL
AH!
AHH!
AHH!
KOFF
HERE, TAKE MY HANDS...
...KEEP LISTENING, KEEP TALKING...
...REMEMBER QUEEN ESTHER. SHE WASN'T AFRAID.
SHE COULD'VE STAYED SILENT AND SAVED HERSELF, BUT SHE RISKED EVERYTHING, HER ENTIRE LIFE, TO SAY, *"I AM A JEW, I AM PROUD, I LOVE MY PEOPLE, I WILL NOT BE SILENT--"*

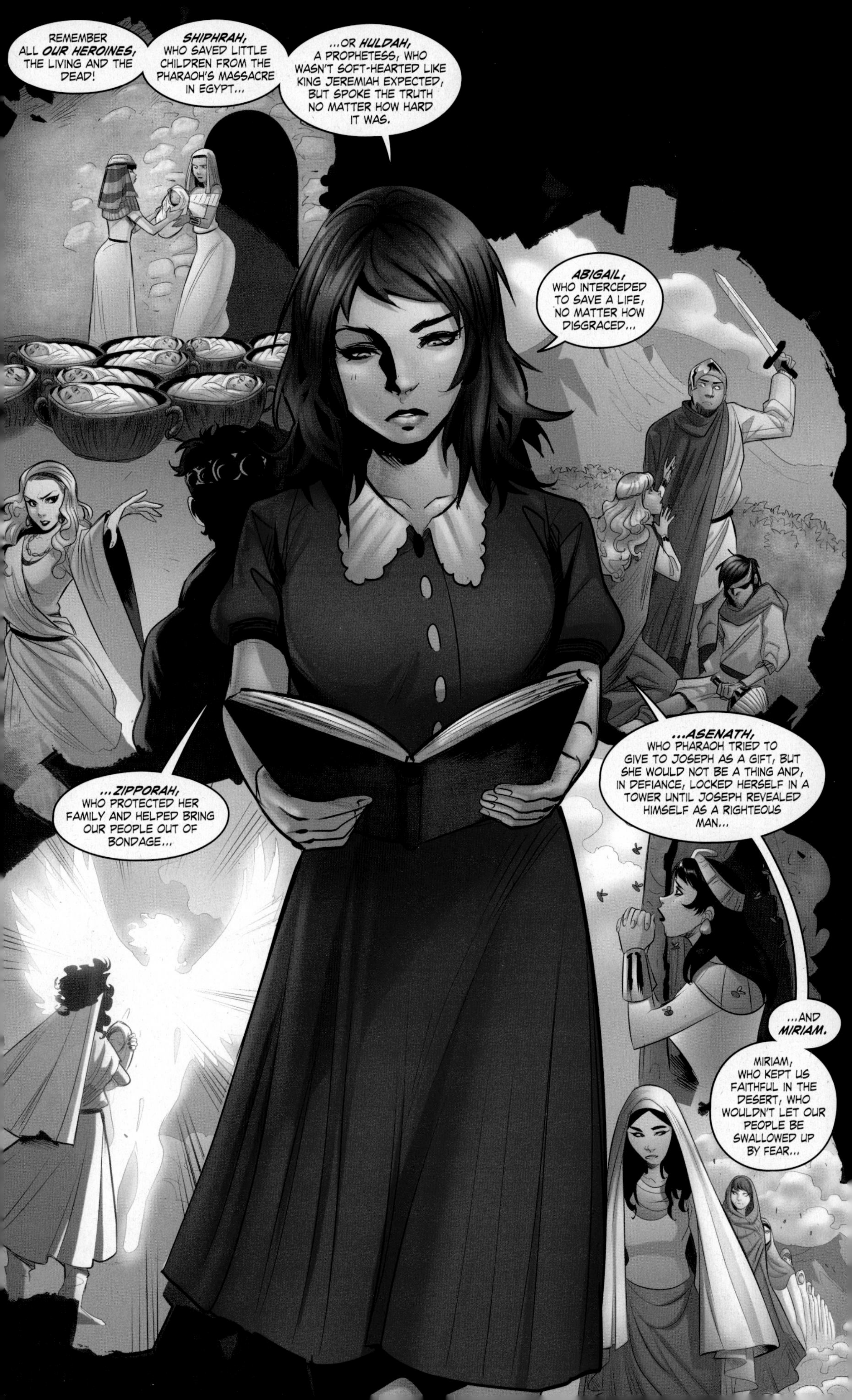
REMEMBER ALL OUR HEROINES, THE LIVING AND THE DEAD!
SHIPHRAH, WHO SAVED LITTLE CHILDREN FROM THE PHARAOH'S MASSACRE IN EGYPT...
...OR HULDAH, A PROPHETESS, WHO WASN'T SOFT-HEARTED LIKE KING JEREMIAH EXPECTED, BUT SPOKE THE TRUTH NO MATTER HOW HARD IT WAS.
ABIGAIL, WHO INTERCEDED TO SAVE A LIFE, NO MATTER HOW DISGRACED...
...ZIPPORAH, WHO PROTECTED HER FAMILY AND HELPED BRING OUR PEOPLE OUT OF BONDAGE...
...ASENATH, WHO PHARAOH TRIED TO GIVE TO JOSEPH AS A GIFT, BUT SHE WOULD NOT BE A THING AND, IN DEFIANCE, LOCKED HERSELF IN A TOWER UNTIL JOSEPH REVEALED HIMSELF AS A RIGHTEOUS MAN...
...AND MIRIAM.
MIRIAM, WHO KEPT US FAITHFUL IN THE DESERT, WHO WOULDN'T LET OUR PEOPLE BE SWALLOWED UP BY FEAR...

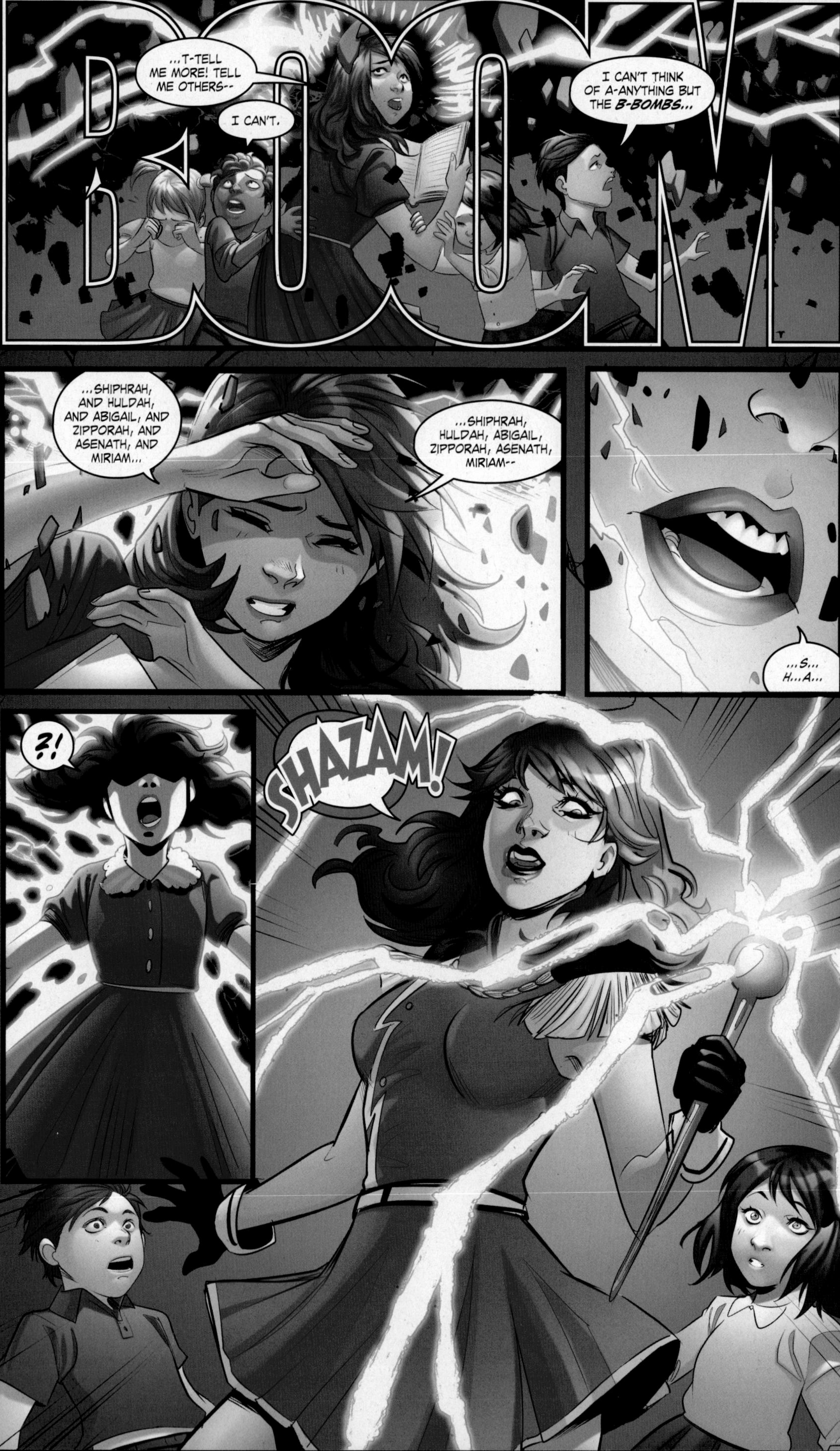
BOOM
...T-TELL ME MORE! TELL ME OTHERS--
I CAN'T.
I CAN'T THINK OF A-ANYTHING BUT THE B-BOMBS...
...SHIPHRAH, AND HULDAH, AND ABIGAIL, AND ZIPPORAH, AND ASENATH, AND MIRIAM...
...SHIPHRAH, HULDAH, ABIGAIL, ZIPPORAH, ASENATH, MIRIAM--
...S... H...A...
?!
SHAZAM!

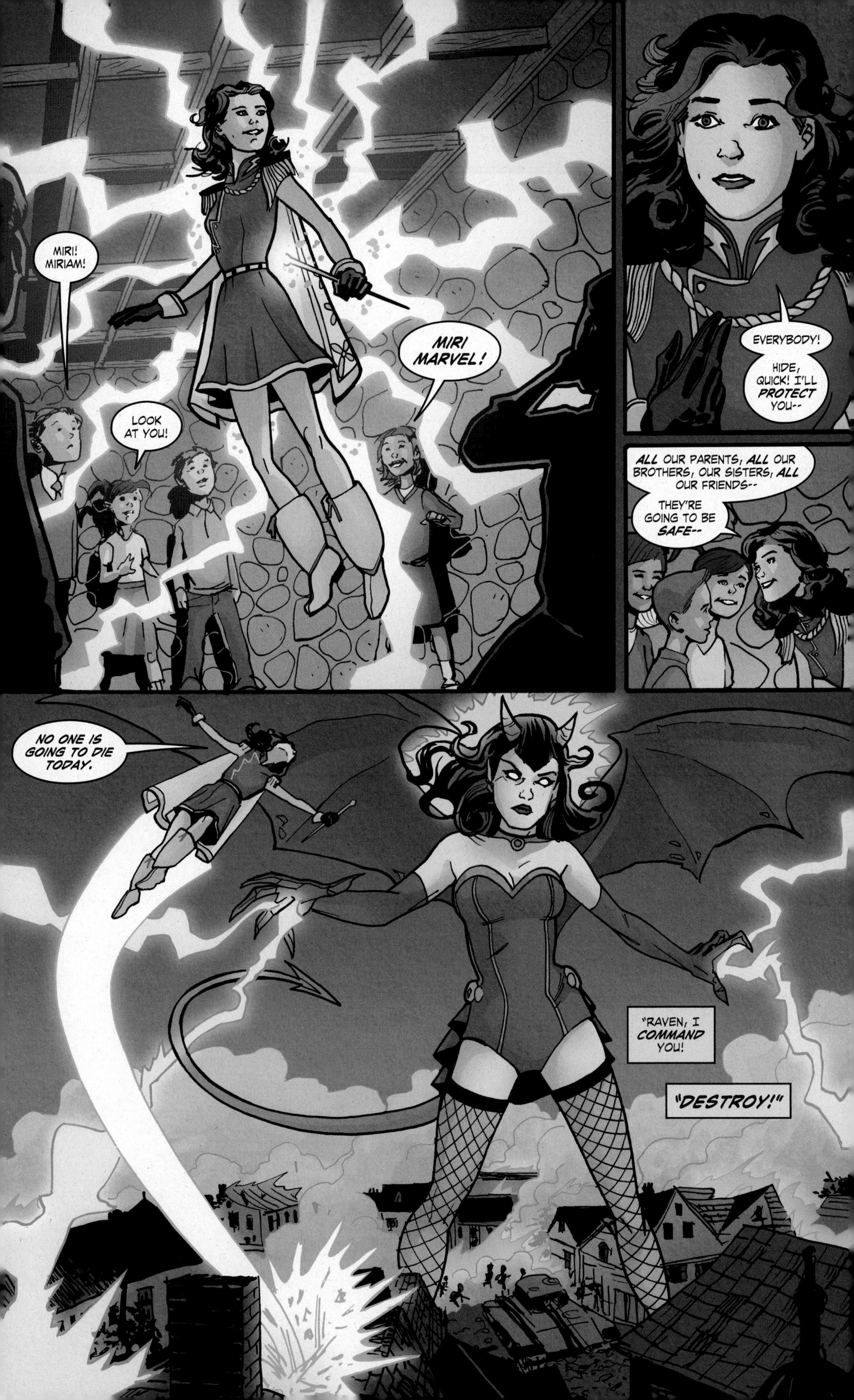

MIRI! MIRIAM!
LOOK AT YOU!
MIRI MARVEL!
EVERYBODY!
HIDE, QUICK! I'LL PROTECT YOU--
ALL OUR PARENTS, ALL OUR BROTHERS, OUR SISTERS, ALL OUR FRIENDS--
THEY'RE GOING TO BE SAFE--
NO ONE IS GOING TO DIE TODAY.
"RAVEN, I COMMAND YOU!
"DESTROY!"

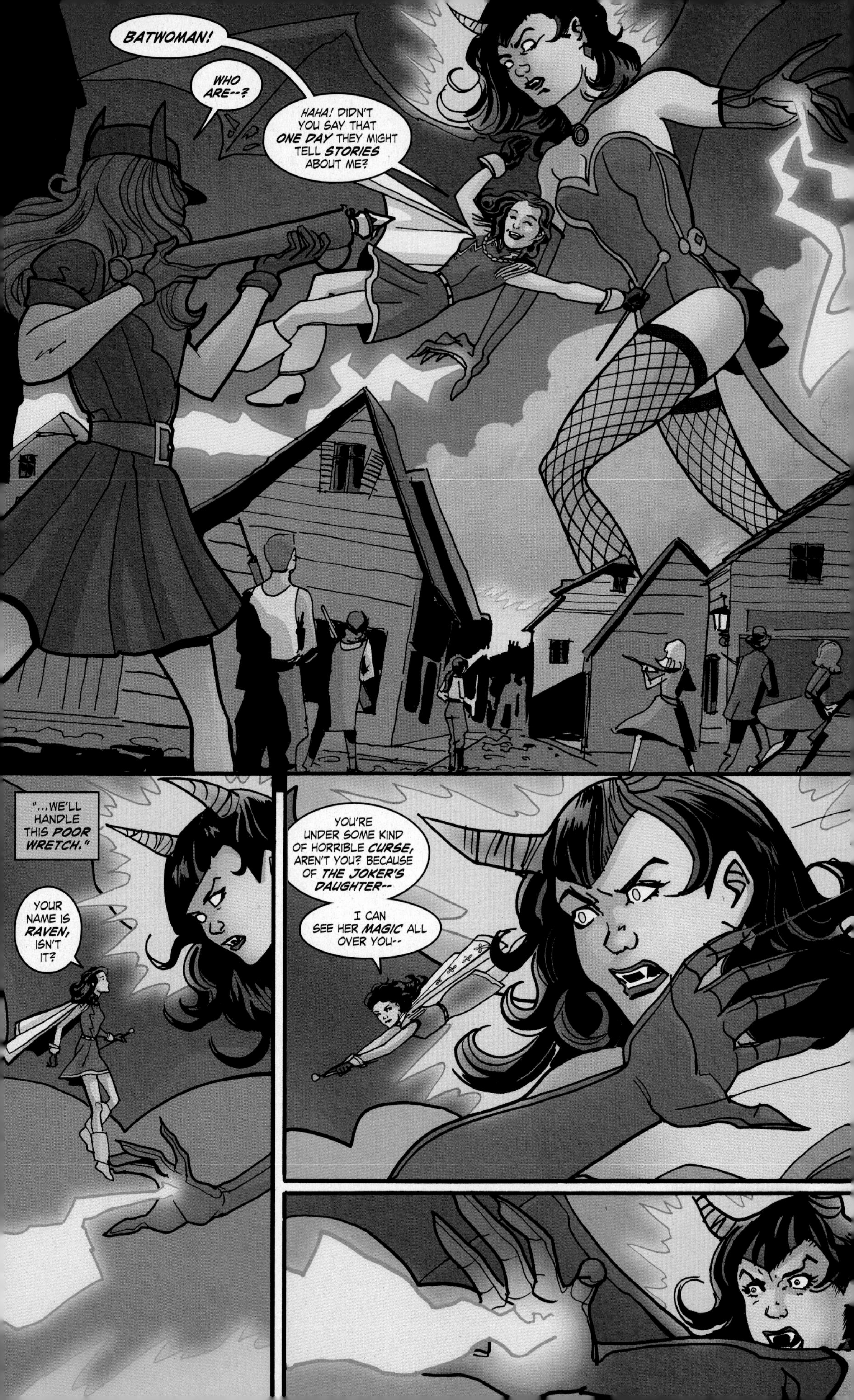

BATWOMAN!
WHO ARE--?
HAHA! DIDN'T YOU SAY THAT ONE DAY THEY MIGHT TELL STORIES ABOUT ME?
"...WE'LL HANDLE THIS POOR WRETCH."
YOUR NAME IS RAVEN, ISN'T IT?
YOU'RE UNDER SOME KIND OF HORRIBLE CURSE, AREN'T YOU? BECAUSE OF THE JOKER'S DAUGHTER--
I CAN SEE HER MAGIC ALL OVER YOU--

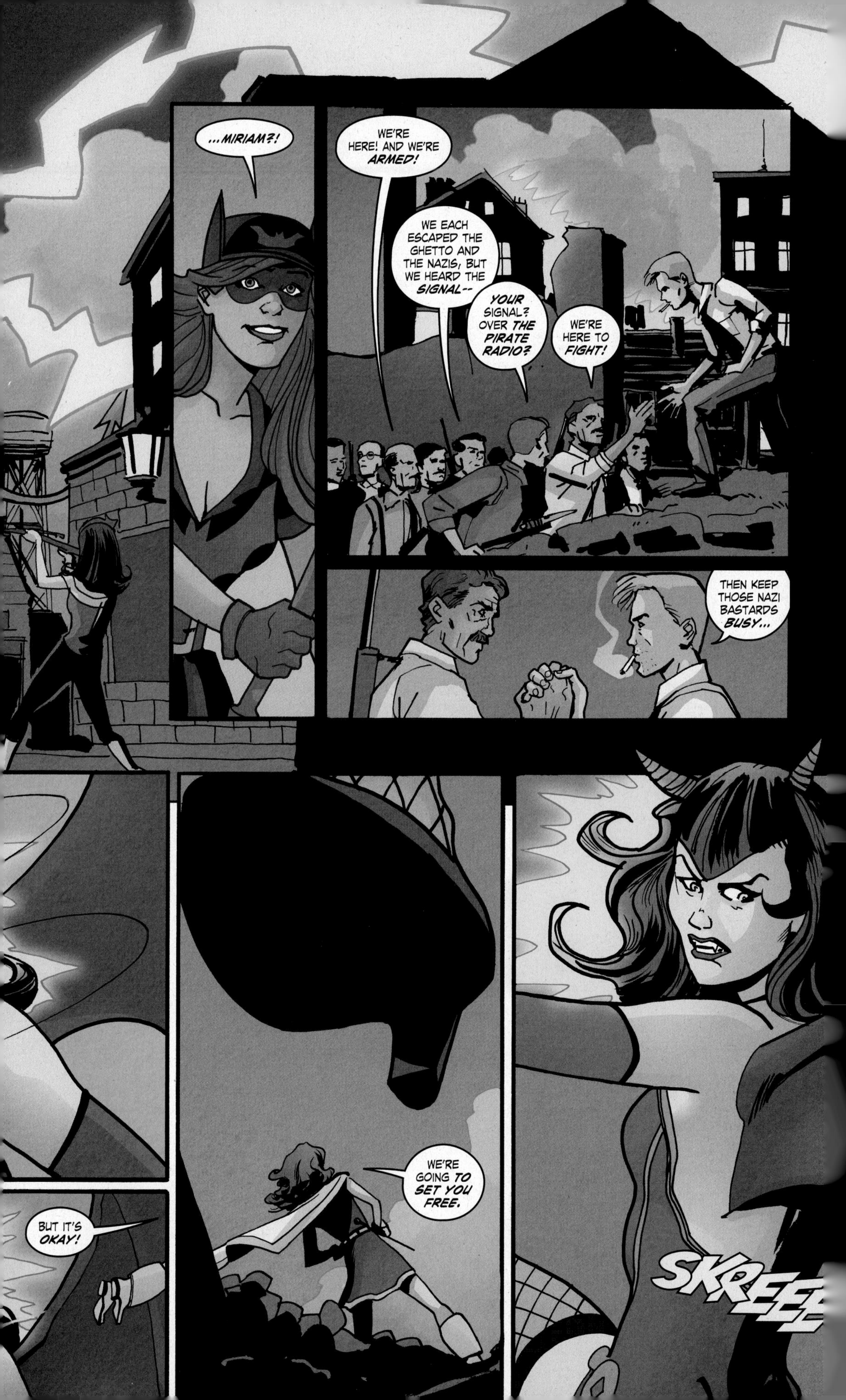
...MIRIAM?!
WE'RE HERE! AND WE'RE ARMED!
WE EACH ESCAPED THE GHETTO AND THE NAZIS, BUT WE HEARD THE SIGNAL--
YOUR SIGNAL? OVER THE PIRATE RADIO?
WE'RE HERE TO FIGHT!
THEN KEEP THOSE NAZI BASTARDS BUSY...
BUT IT'S OKAY!
WE'RE GOING TO SET YOU FREE.
SKREEE

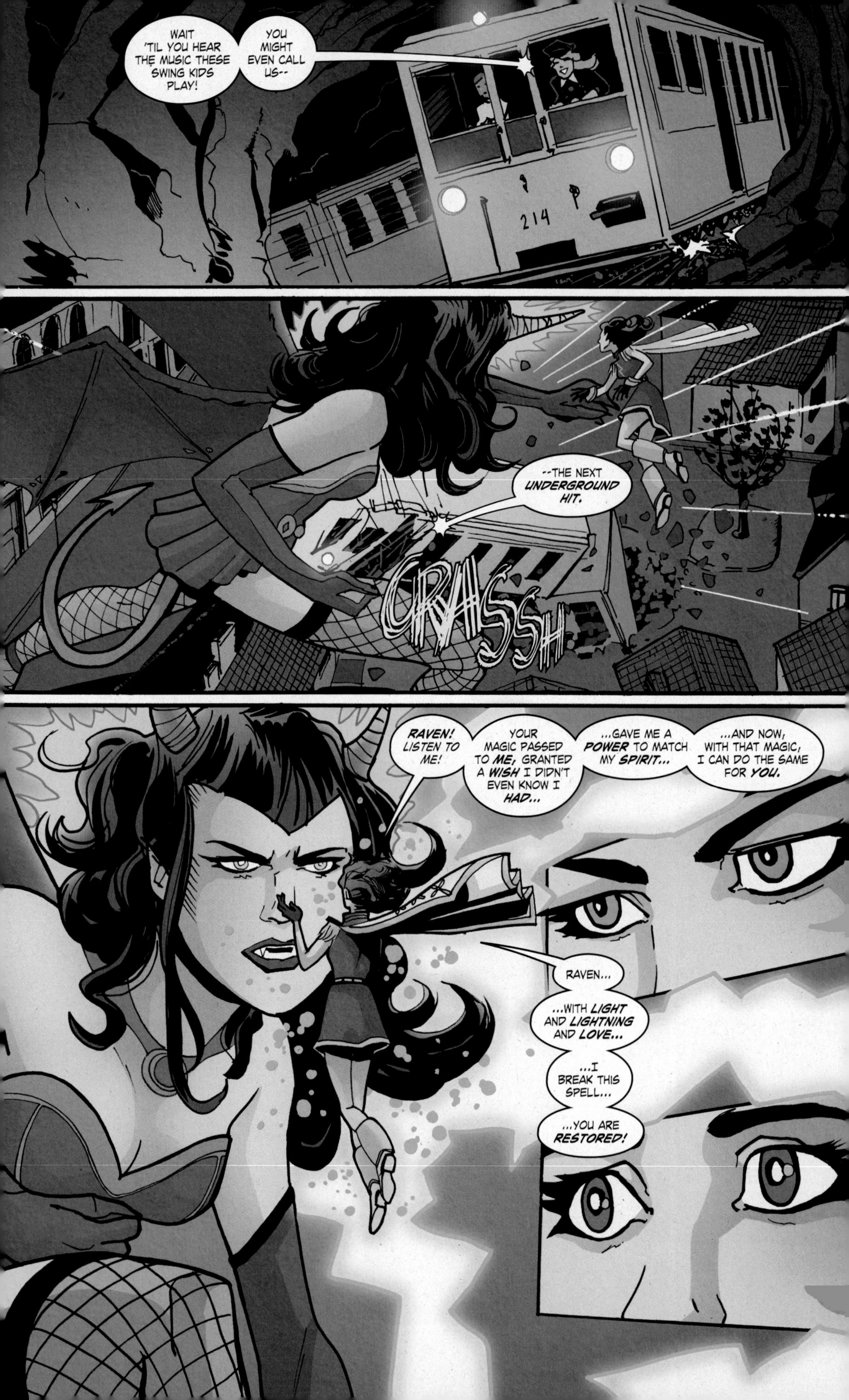
WAIT 'TIL YOU HEAR THE MUSIC THESE SWING KIDS PLAY!
YOU MIGHT EVEN CALL US--
--THE NEXT UNDERGROUND HIT.
CRASSSH
RAVEN! LISTEN TO ME!
YOUR MAGIC PASSED TO ME, GRANTED A WISH I DIDN'T EVEN KNOW I HAD...
...GAVE ME A POWER TO MATCH MY SPIRIT...
...AND NOW, WITH THAT MAGIC, I CAN DO THE SAME FOR YOU.
RAVEN...
...WITH LIGHT AND LIGHTNING AND LOVE...
...I BREAK THIS SPELL...
...YOU ARE RESTORED!

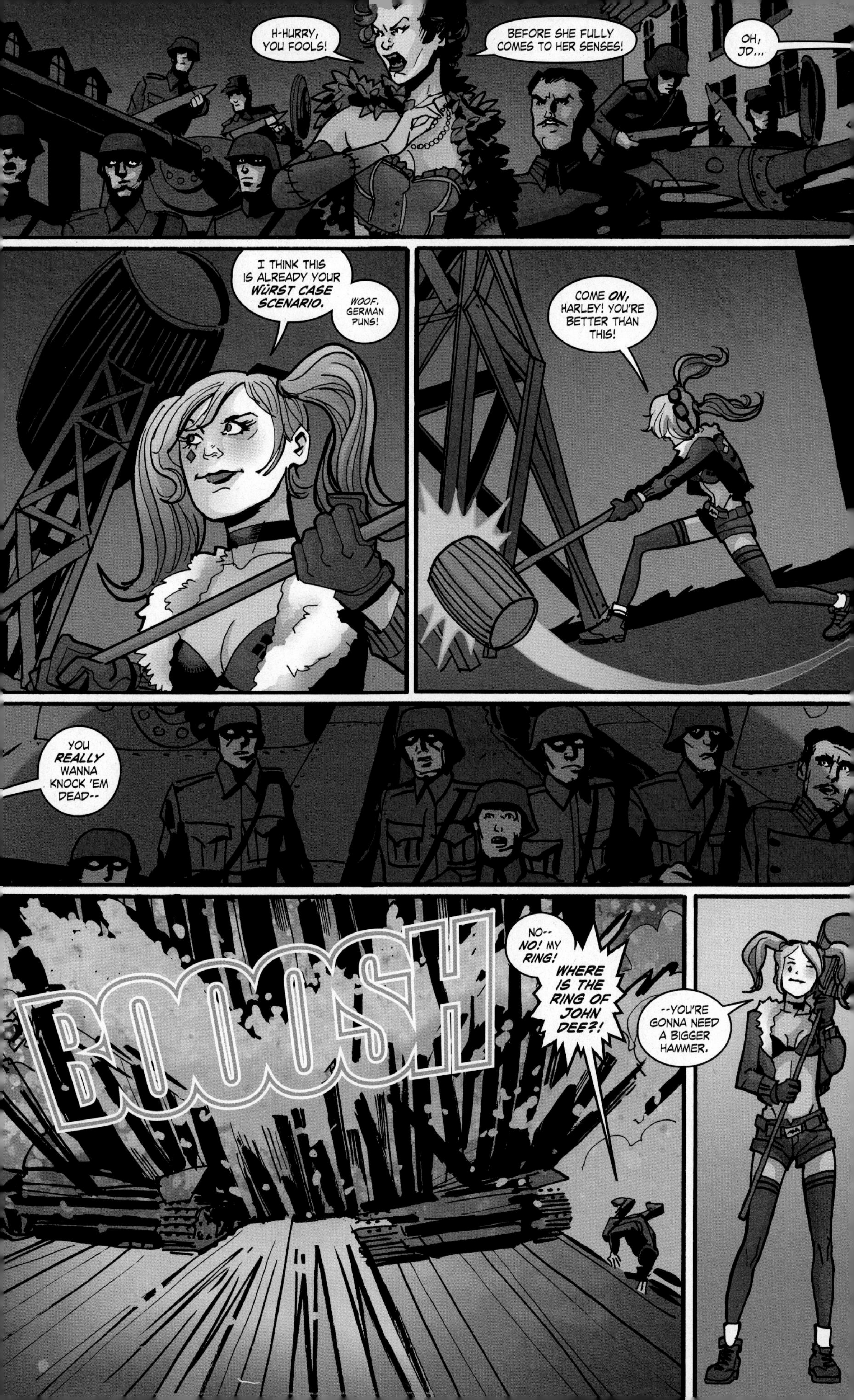
H-HURRY, YOU FOOLS!
BEFORE SHE FULLY COMES TO HER SENSES!
OH, JD...
I THINK THIS IS ALREADY YOUR WÜRST CASE SCENARIO.
WOOF. GERMAN PUNS!
COME ON, HARLEY! YOU'RE BETTER THAN THIS!
YOU REALLY WANNA KNOCK 'EM DEAD--
BOOOSH
NO-- NO! MY RING! WHERE IS THE RING OF JOHN DEE?!
--YOU'RE GONNA NEED A BIGGER HAMMER.

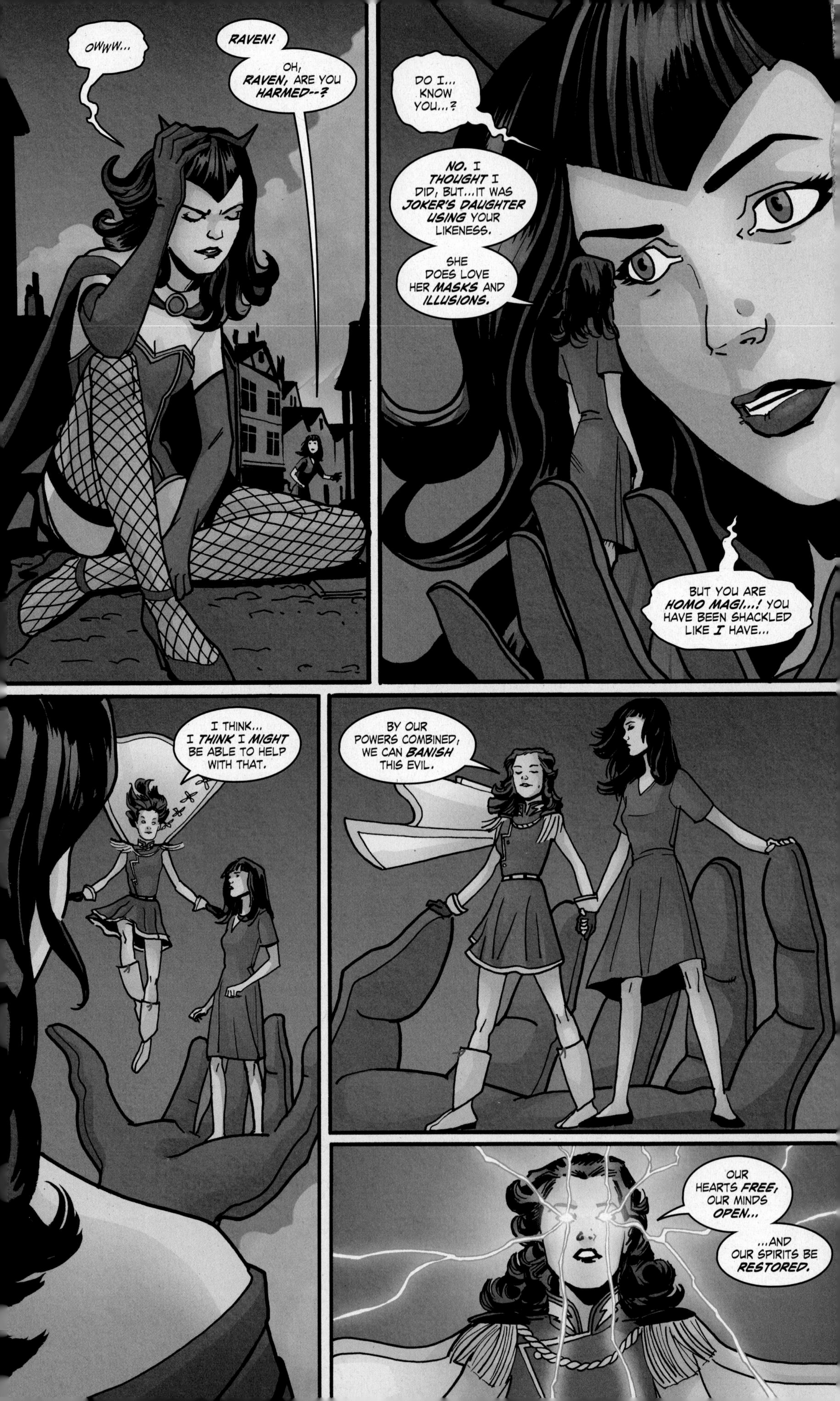
OWWW...
RAVEN!
OH, RAVEN, ARE YOU HARMED--?
DO I... KNOW YOU...?
NO. I THOUGHT I DID, BUT...IT WAS JOKER'S DAUGHTER USING YOUR LIKENESS.
SHE DOES LOVE HER MASKS AND ILLUSIONS.
BUT YOU ARE HOMO MAGI...! YOU HAVE BEEN SHACKLED LIKE I HAVE...
I THINK... I THINK I MIGHT BE ABLE TO HELP WITH THAT.
BY OUR POWERS COMBINED, WE CAN BANISH THIS EVIL.
OUR HEARTS FREE, OUR MINDS OPEN...
...AND OUR SPIRITS BE RESTORED.

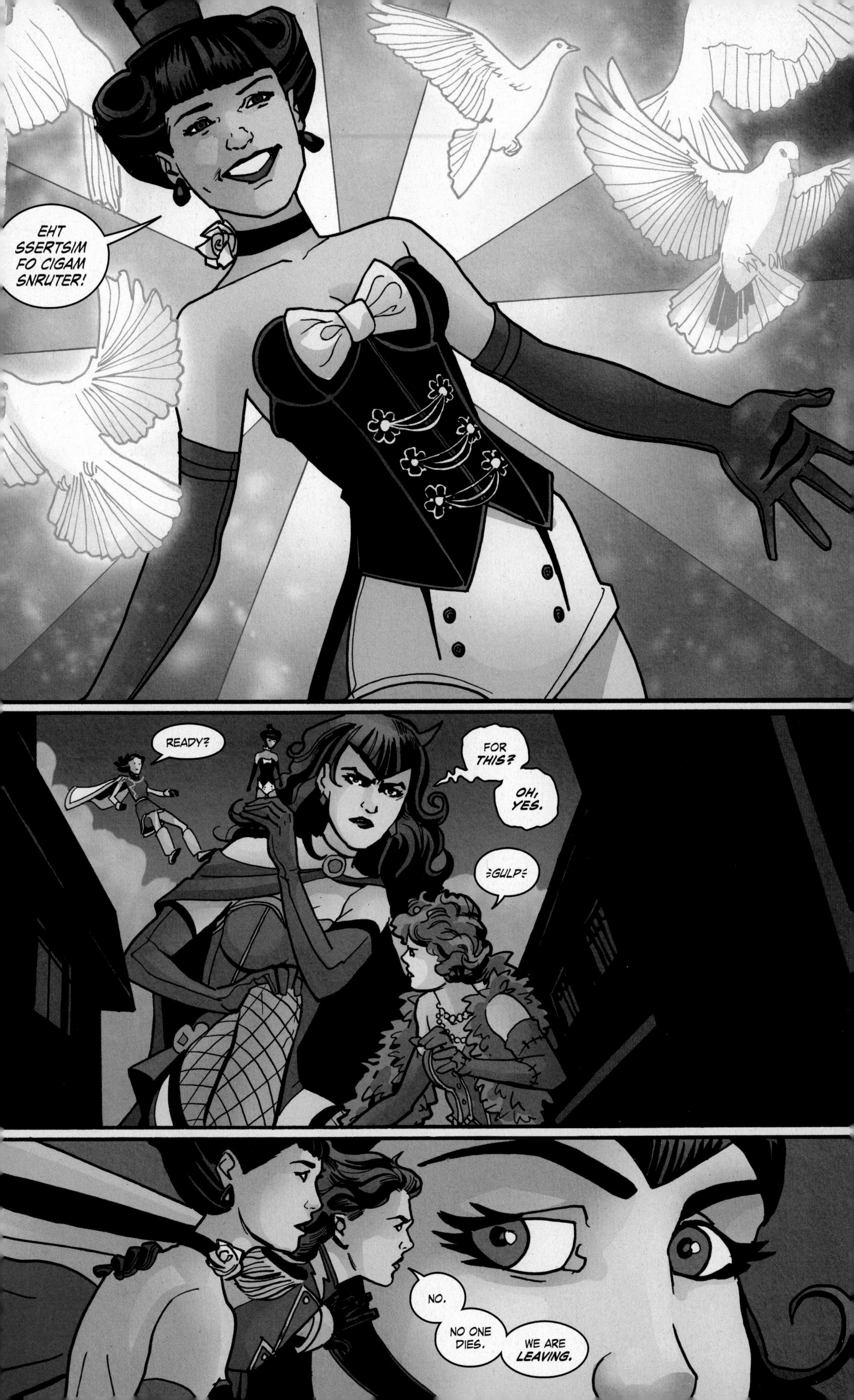
EHT SSERTSIM FO CIGAM SNRUTER!
READY?
FOR THIS?
OH, YES.
=GULP=
NO.
NO ONE DIES.
WE ARE LEAVING.

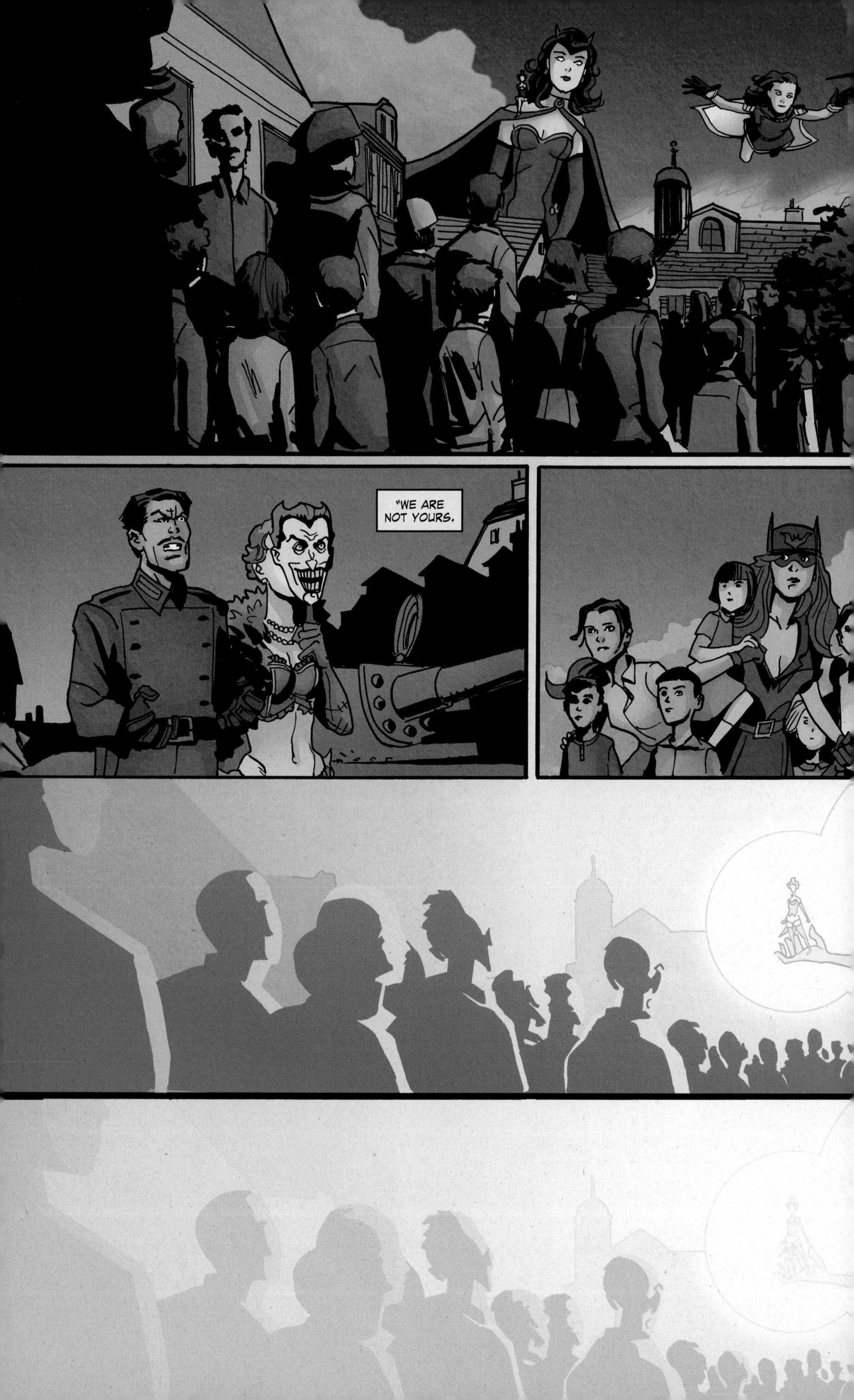
"WE ARE
NOT YOURS.

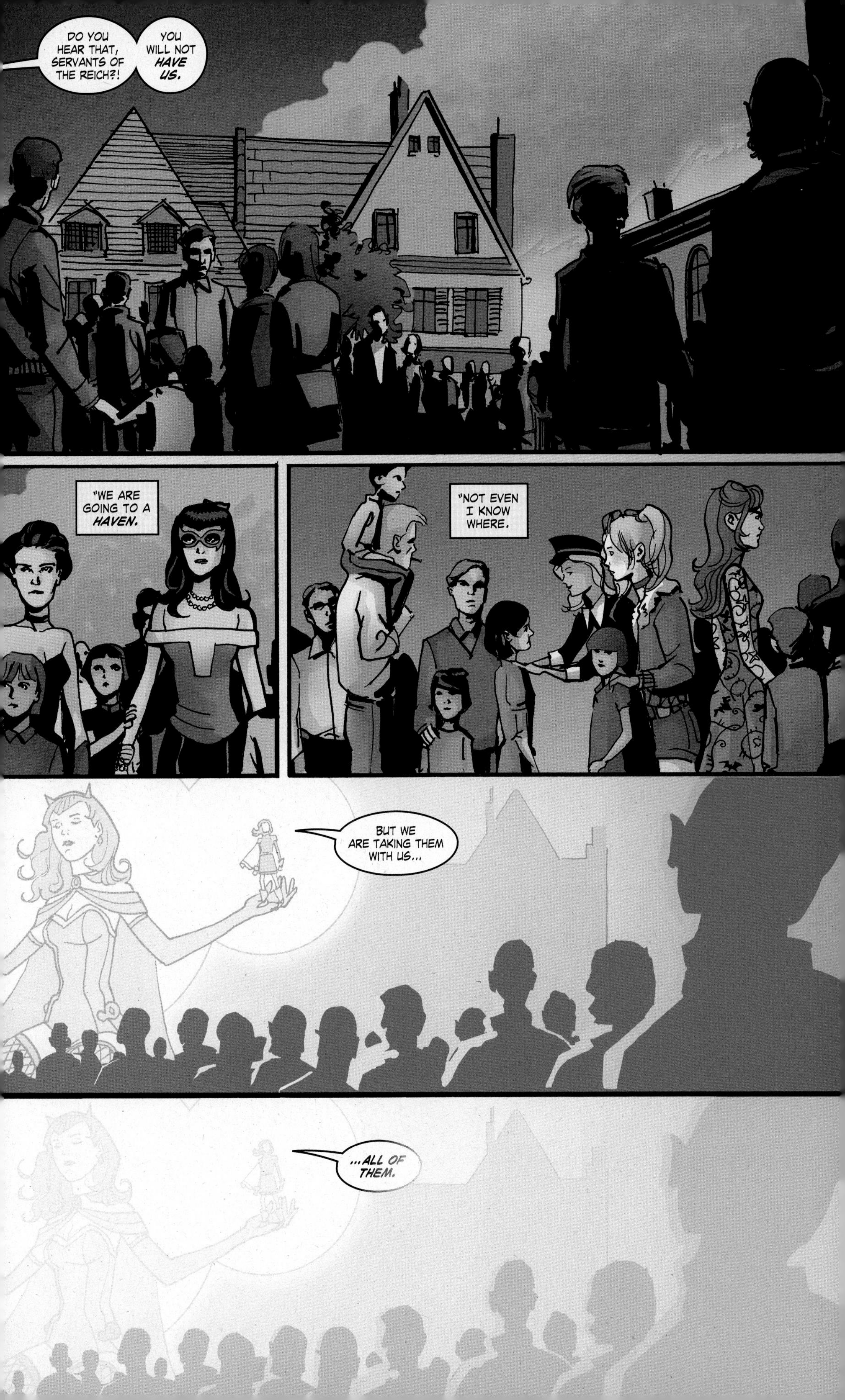
DO YOU HEAR THAT, SERVANTS OF THE REICH?!
YOU WILL NOT *HAVE US.*
"WE ARE GOING TO A *HAVEN.*
"NOT EVEN I KNOW WHERE.
BUT WE ARE TAKING THEM WITH US...
...*ALL OF THEM.*

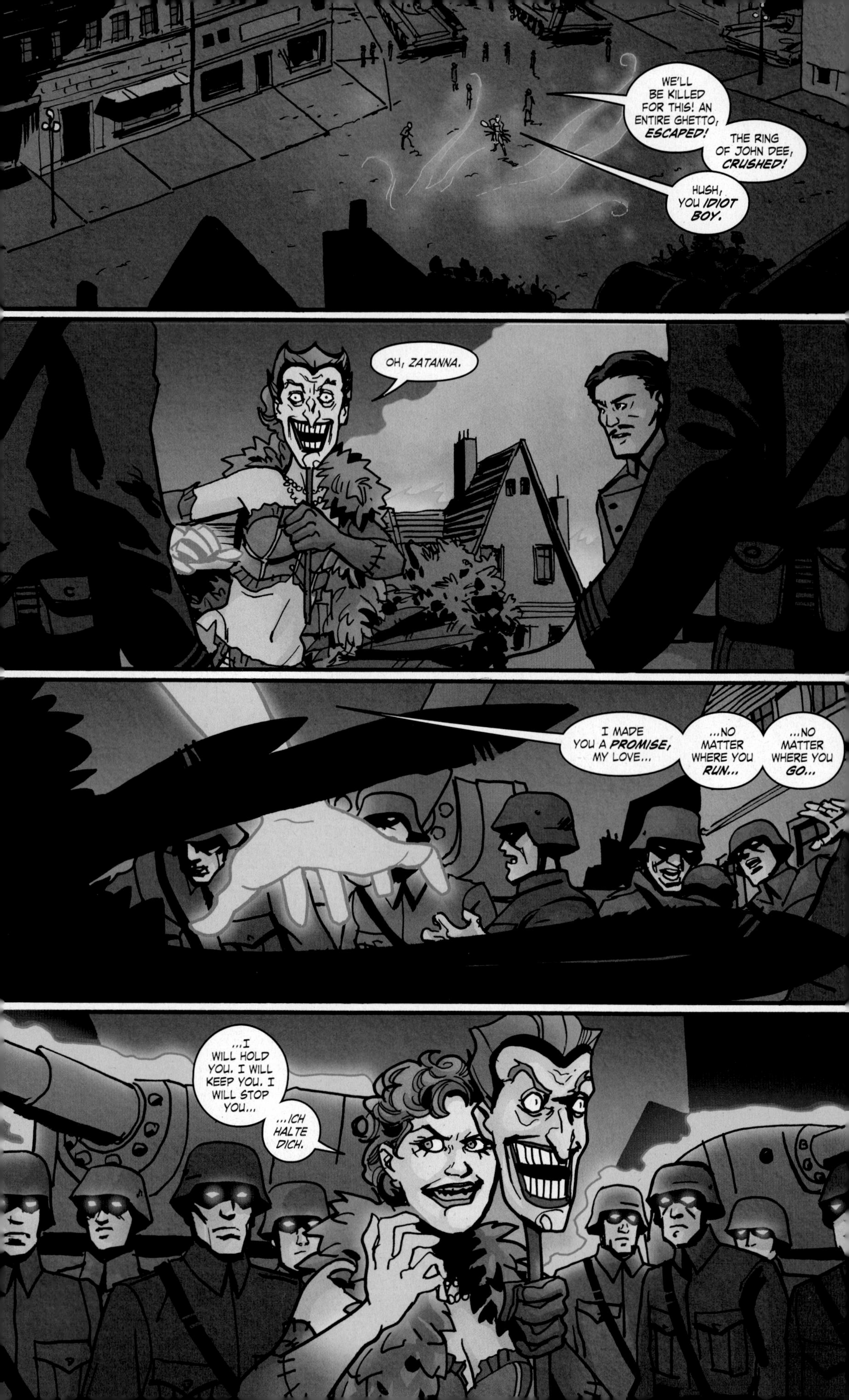

WE'LL BE KILLED FOR THIS! AN ENTIRE GHETTO, ESCAPED!
THE RING OF JOHN DEE, CRUSHED!
HUSH, YOU IDIOT BOY.
OH, ZATANNA.
I MADE YOU A PROMISE, MY LOVE...
...NO MATTER WHERE YOU RUN...
...NO MATTER WHERE YOU GO...
...I WILL HOLD YOU. I WILL KEEP YOU. I WILL STOP YOU...
...ICH HALTE DICH.

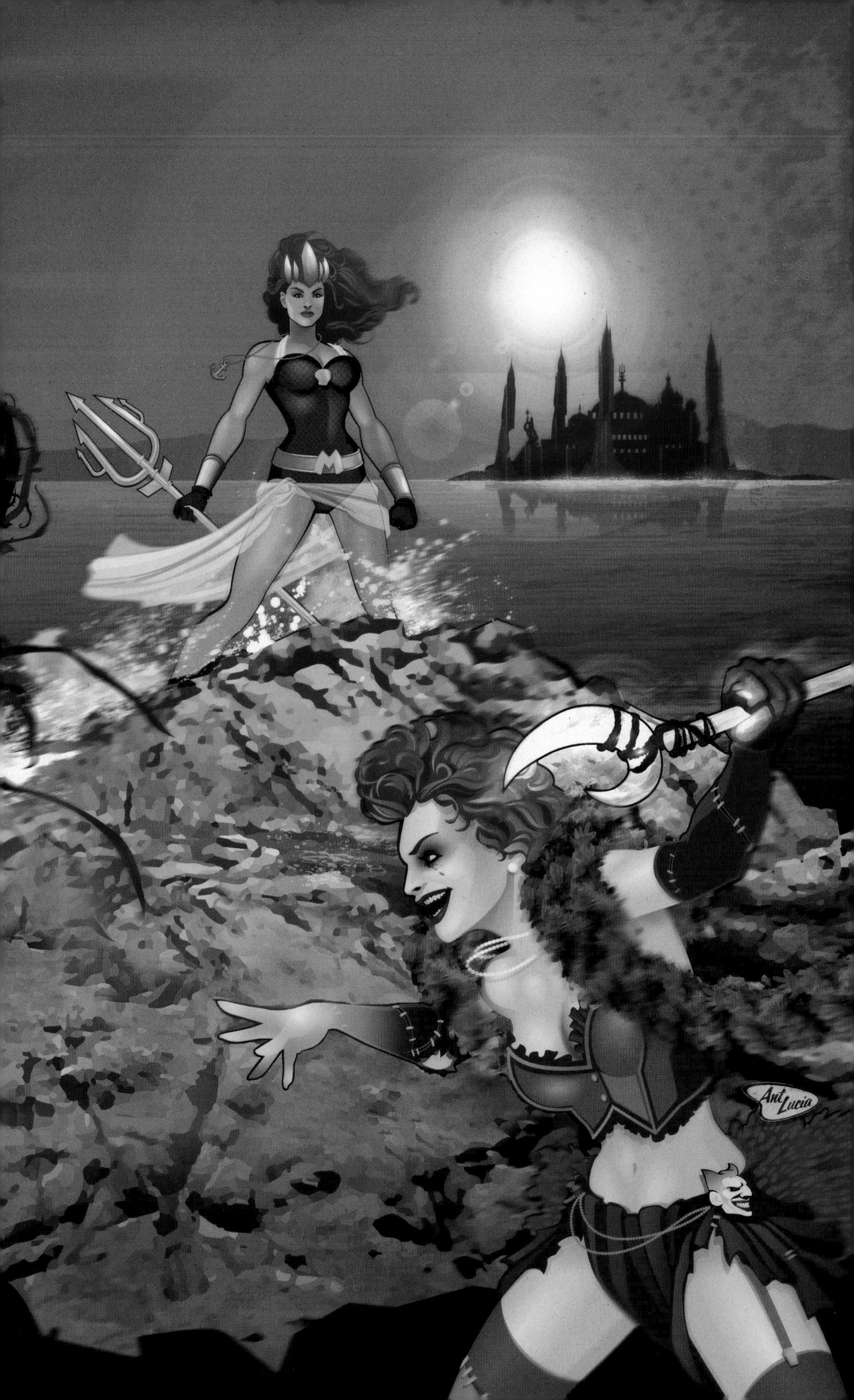
Ant Lucia

UPRISING
PART TWO

MARGUERITE BENNETT
Writer

LAURA BRAGA
MIRKA ANDOLFO
Artists

J. NANJAN
Colorist

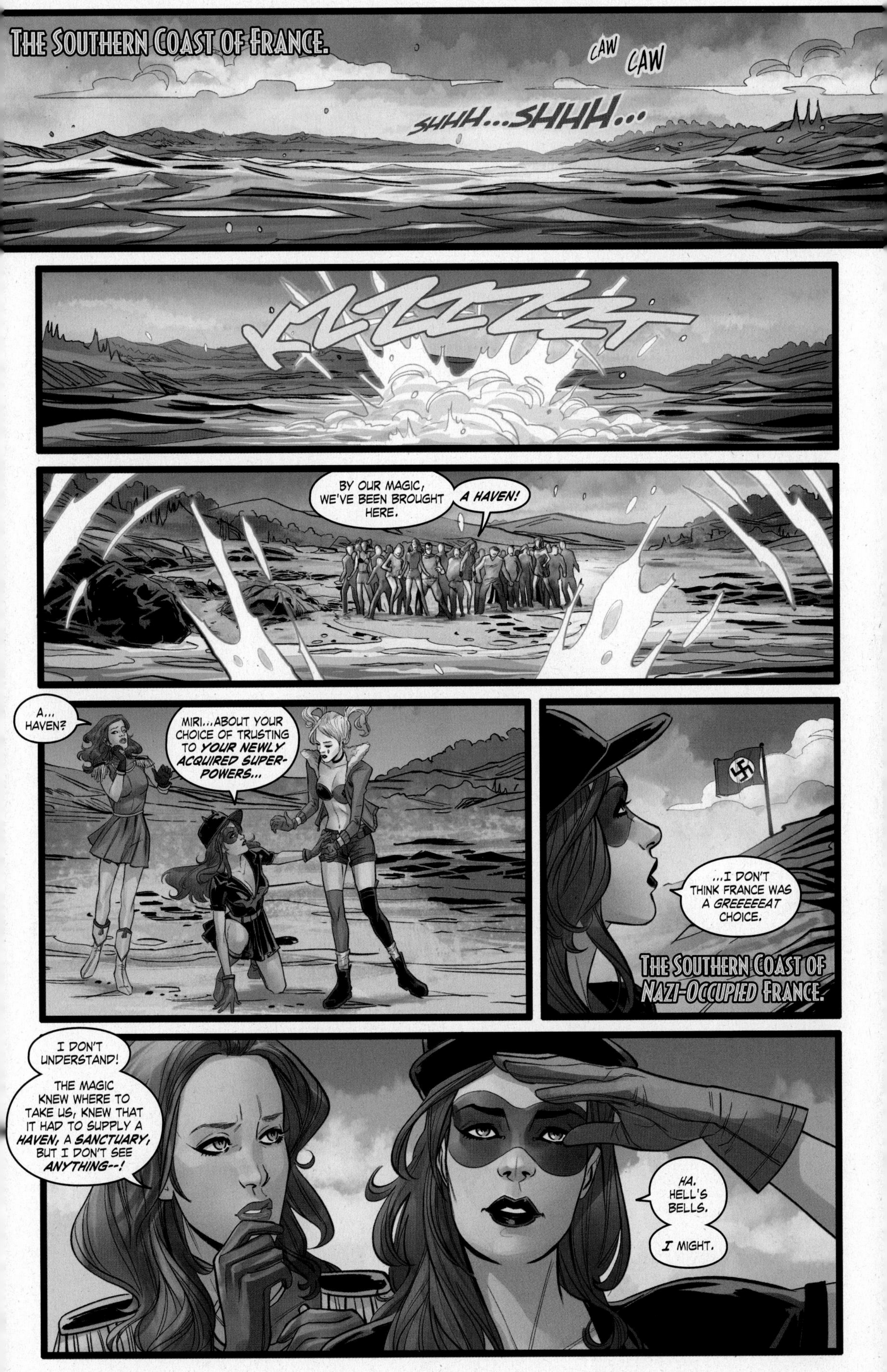
THE SOUTHERN COAST OF FRANCE.
CAW
CAW
SHHH...SHHH...
KZZZZT
BY OUR MAGIC, WE'VE BEEN BROUGHT HERE.
A HAVEN!
A... HAVEN?
MIRI...ABOUT YOUR CHOICE OF TRUSTING TO YOUR NEWLY ACQUIRED SUPER-POWERS...
...I DON'T THINK FRANCE WAS A GREEEEEAT CHOICE.
THE SOUTHERN COAST OF NAZI-OCCUPIED FRANCE.
I DON'T UNDERSTAND!
THE MAGIC KNEW WHERE TO TAKE US, KNEW THAT IT HAD TO SUPPLY A HAVEN, A SANCTUARY, BUT I DON'T SEE ANYTHING--!
HA. HELL'S BELLS.
I MIGHT.

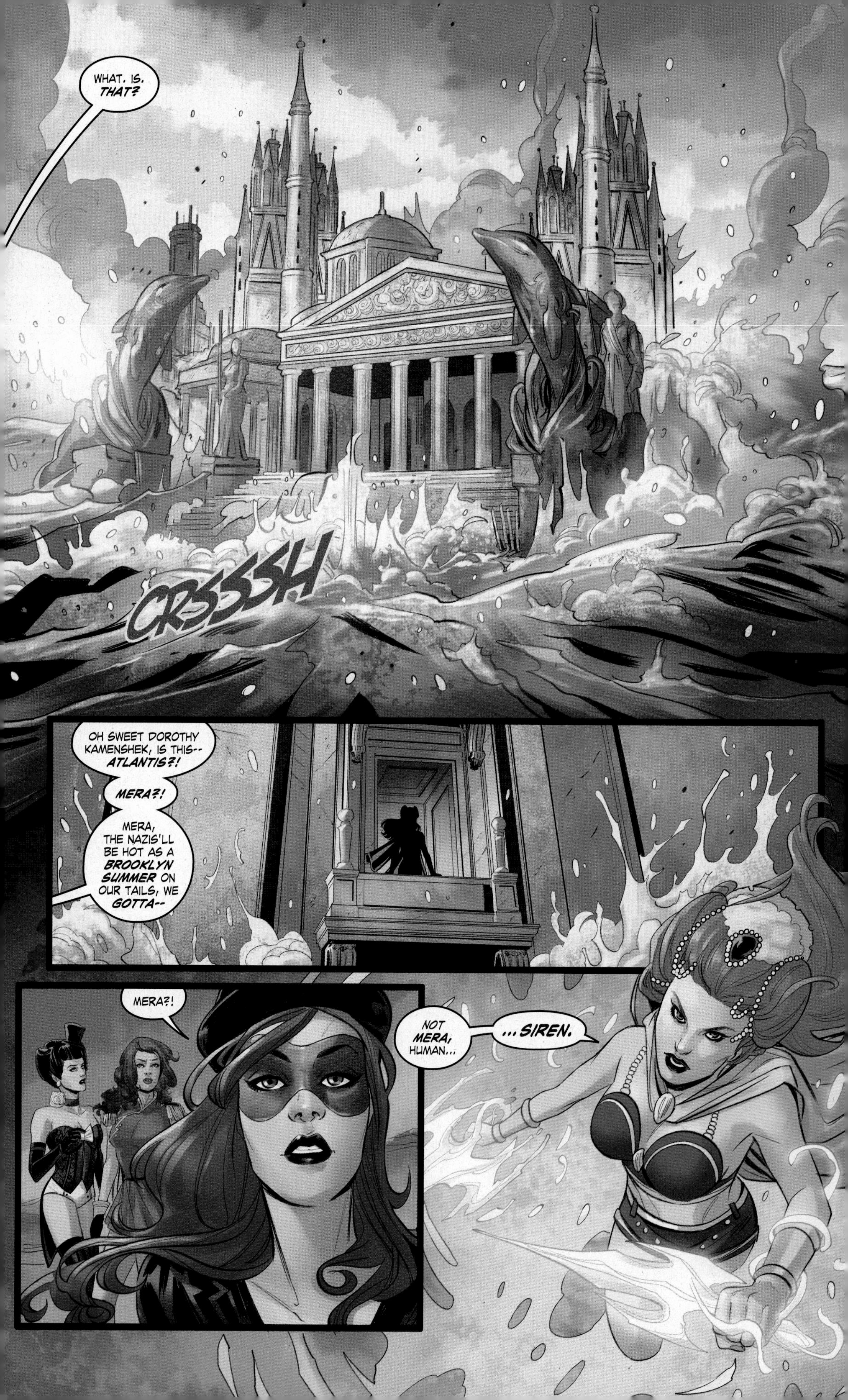
WHAT. IS. THAT?
CRSSSH
OH SWEET DOROTHY KAMENSHEK, IS THIS-- ATLANTIS?!
MERA?!
MERA, THE NAZIS'LL BE HOT AS A BROOKLYN SUMMER ON OUR TAILS, WE GOTTA--
MERA?!
NOT MERA, HUMAN...
...SIREN.

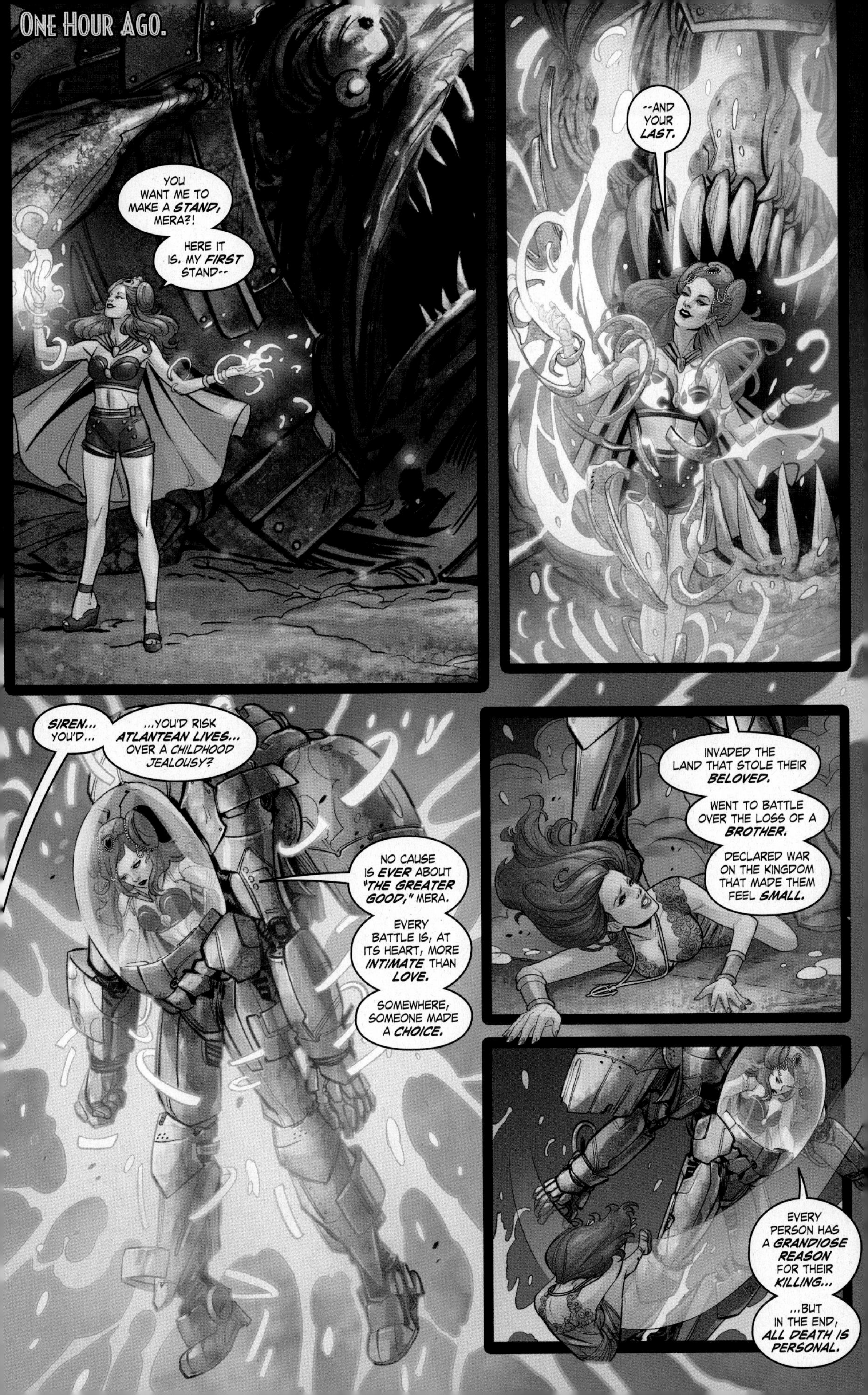
ONE HOUR AGO.
YOU WANT ME TO MAKE A STAND, MERA?!
HERE IT IS. MY FIRST STAND--
--AND YOUR LAST.
SIREN... YOU'D...
...YOU'D RISK ATLANTEAN LIVES... OVER A CHILDHOOD JEALOUSY?
NO CAUSE IS EVER ABOUT "THE GREATER GOOD," MERA.
EVERY BATTLE IS, AT ITS HEART, MORE INTIMATE THAN LOVE.
SOMEWHERE, SOMEONE MADE A CHOICE.
INVADED THE LAND THAT STOLE THEIR BELOVED.
WENT TO BATTLE OVER THE LOSS OF A BROTHER.
DECLARED WAR ON THE KINGDOM THAT MADE THEM FEEL SMALL.
EVERY PERSON HAS A GRANDIOSE REASON FOR THEIR KILLING...
...BUT IN THE END, ALL DEATH IS PERSONAL.

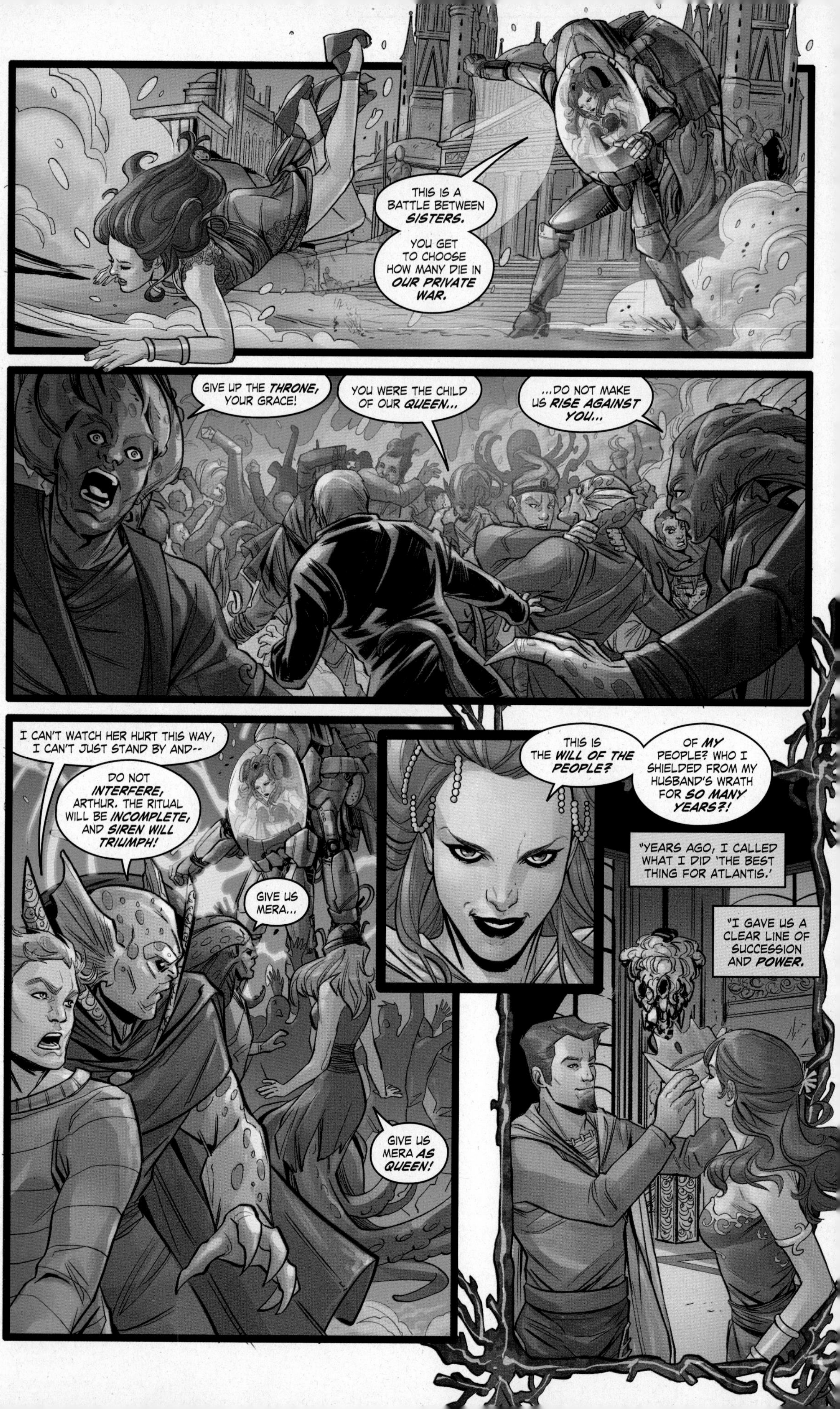
THIS IS A BATTLE BETWEEN SISTERS.
YOU GET TO CHOOSE HOW MANY DIE IN OUR PRIVATE WAR.
GIVE UP THE THRONE, YOUR GRACE!
YOU WERE THE CHILD OF OUR QUEEN...
...DO NOT MAKE US RISE AGAINST YOU...
I CAN'T WATCH HER HURT THIS WAY, I CAN'T JUST STAND BY AND--
DO NOT INTERFERE, ARTHUR. THE RITUAL WILL BE INCOMPLETE, AND SIREN WILL TRIUMPH!
GIVE US MERA...
GIVE US MERA AS QUEEN!
THIS IS THE WILL OF THE PEOPLE?
OF MY PEOPLE? WHO I SHIELDED FROM MY HUSBAND'S WRATH FOR SO MANY YEARS?!
"YEARS AGO, I CALLED WHAT I DID 'THE BEST THING FOR ATLANTIS.'
"I GAVE US A CLEAR LINE OF SUCCESSION AND POWER.

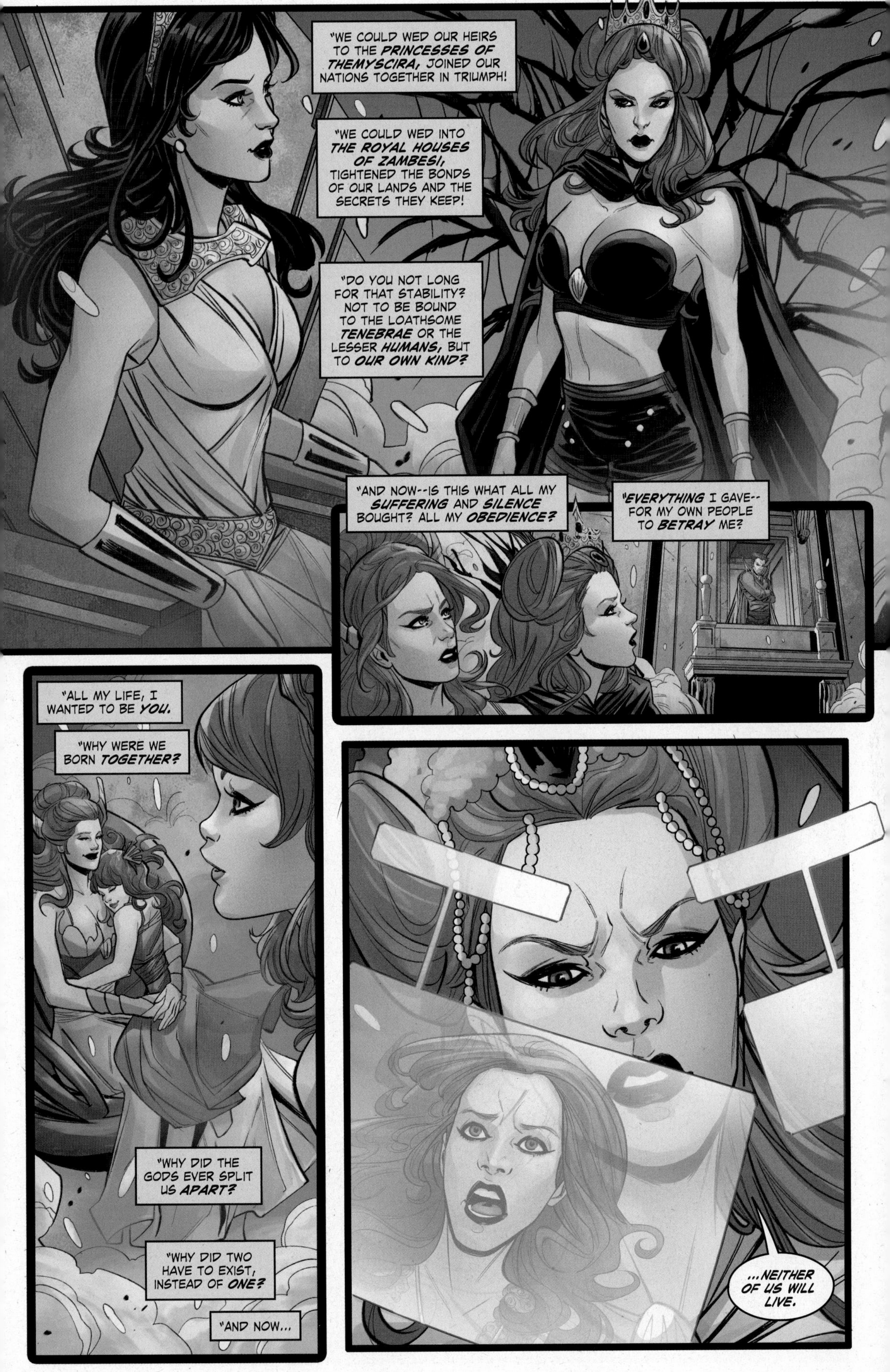
"WE COULD WED OUR HEIRS TO THE PRINCESSES OF THEMYSCIRA, JOINED OUR NATIONS TOGETHER IN TRIUMPH!
"WE COULD WED INTO THE ROYAL HOUSES OF ZAMBESI, TIGHTENED THE BONDS OF OUR LANDS AND THE SECRETS THEY KEEP!
"DO YOU NOT LONG FOR THAT STABILITY? NOT TO BE BOUND TO THE LOATHSOME TENEBRAE OR THE LESSER HUMANS, BUT TO OUR OWN KIND?
"AND NOW--IS THIS WHAT ALL MY SUFFERING AND SILENCE BOUGHT? ALL MY OBEDIENCE?
"EVERYTHING I GAVE--FOR MY OWN PEOPLE TO BETRAY ME?
"ALL MY LIFE, I WANTED TO BE YOU.
"WHY WERE WE BORN TOGETHER?
"WHY DID THE GODS EVER SPLIT US APART?
"WHY DID TWO HAVE TO EXIST, INSTEAD OF ONE?
"AND NOW...
...NEITHER OF US WILL LIVE.

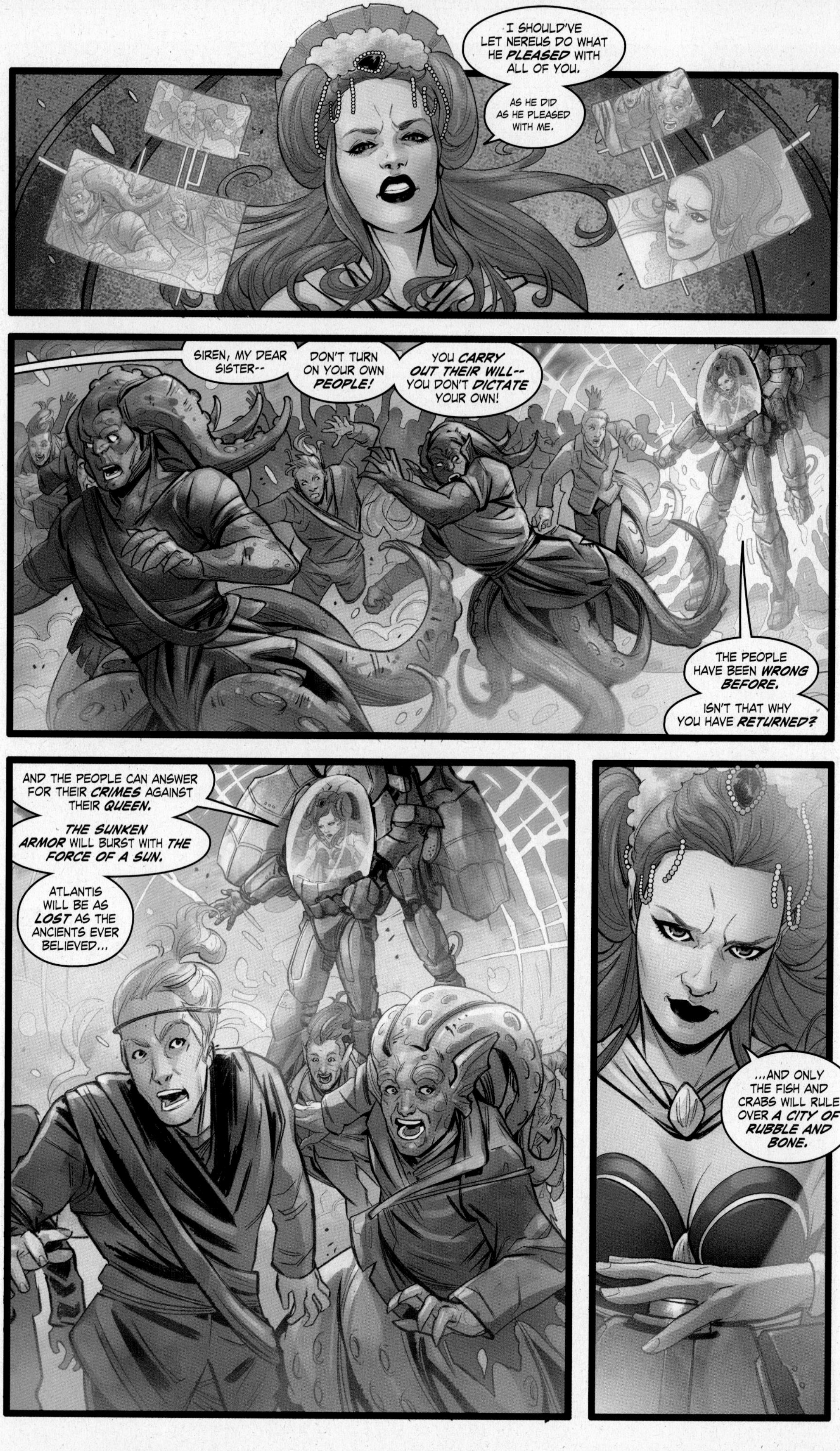

I SHOULD'VE LET NEREUS DO WHAT HE PLEASED WITH ALL OF YOU.
AS HE DID AS HE PLEASED WITH ME.
SIREN, MY DEAR SISTER--
DON'T TURN ON YOUR OWN PEOPLE!
YOU CARRY OUT THEIR WILL-- YOU DON'T DICTATE YOUR OWN!
THE PEOPLE HAVE BEEN WRONG BEFORE.
ISN'T THAT WHY YOU HAVE RETURNED?
AND THE PEOPLE CAN ANSWER FOR THEIR CRIMES AGAINST THEIR QUEEN.
THE SUNKEN ARMOR WILL BURST WITH THE FORCE OF A SUN.
ATLANTIS WILL BE AS LOST AS THE ANCIENTS EVER BELIEVED...
...AND ONLY THE FISH AND CRABS WILL RULE OVER A CITY OF RUBBLE AND BONE.

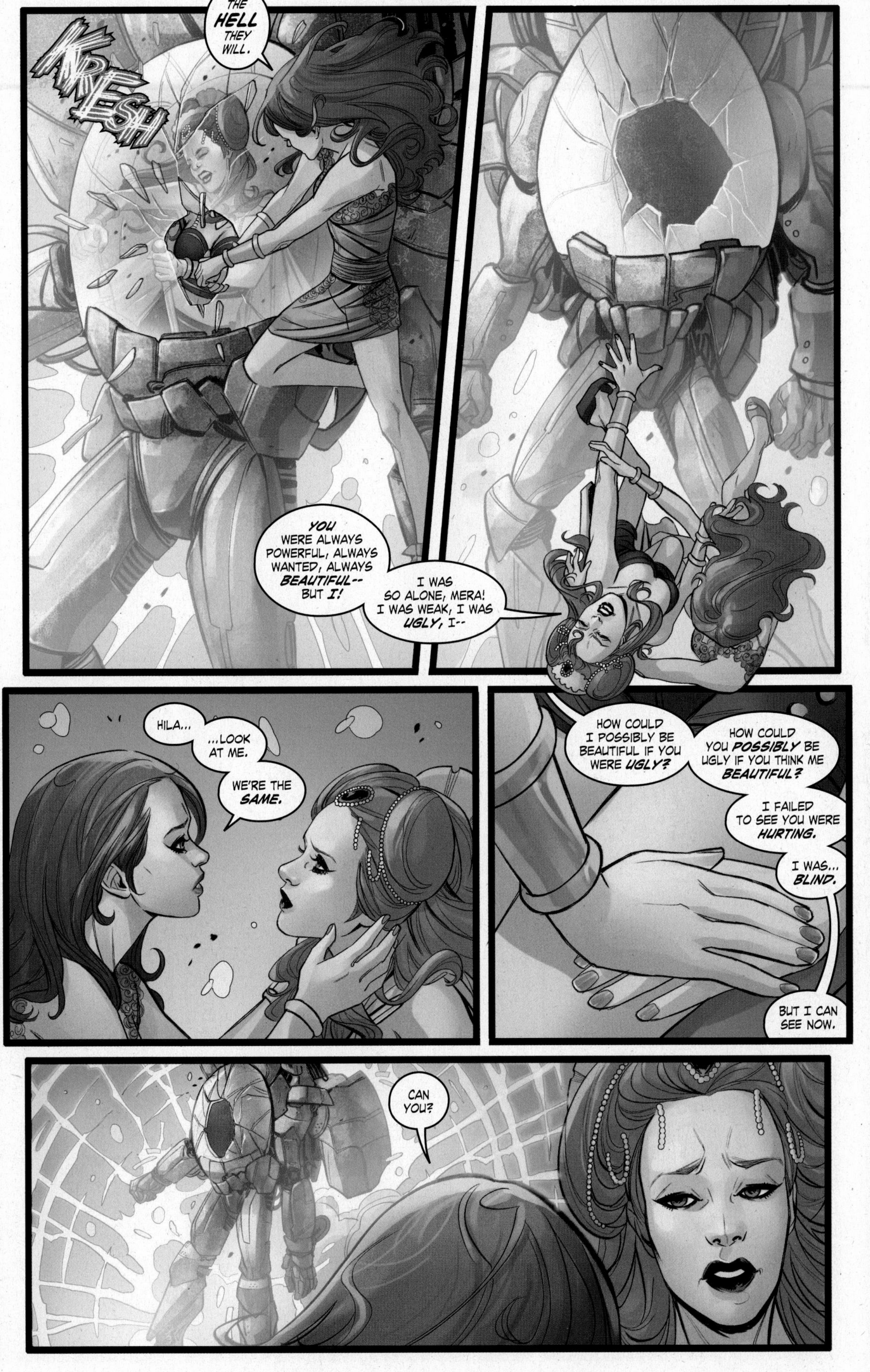
KRESH
THE HELL THEY WILL.
YOU WERE ALWAYS POWERFUL, ALWAYS WANTED, ALWAYS BEAUTIFUL-- BUT I!
I WAS SO ALONE, MERA! I WAS WEAK, I WAS UGLY, I--
HILA...
...LOOK AT ME.
WE'RE THE SAME.
HOW COULD I POSSIBLY BE BEAUTIFUL IF YOU WERE UGLY?
HOW COULD YOU POSSIBLY BE UGLY IF YOU THINK ME BEAUTIFUL?
I FAILED TO SEE YOU WERE HURTING.
I WAS... BLIND.
BUT I CAN SEE NOW.
CAN YOU?

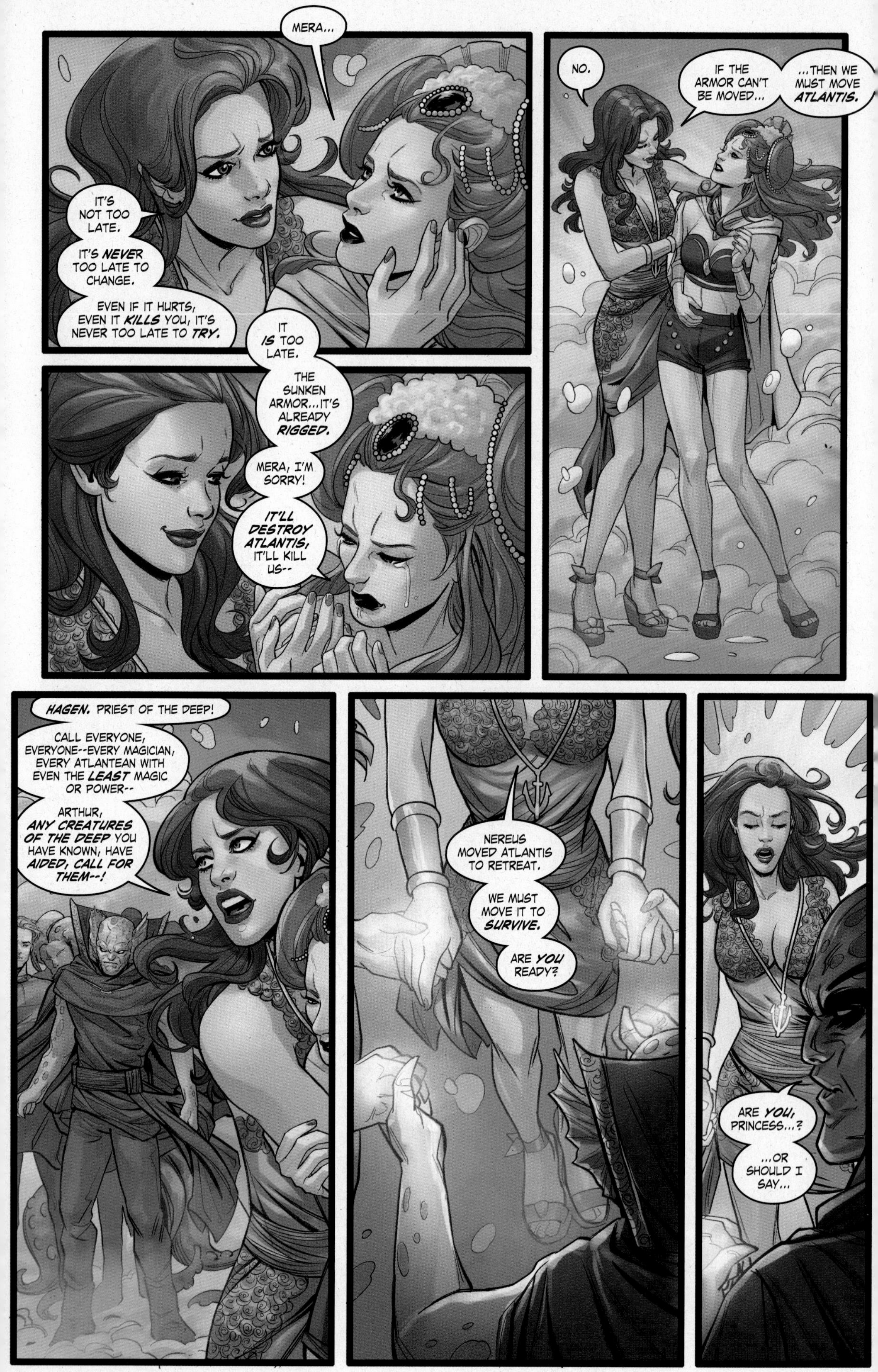
MERA...
IT'S NOT TOO LATE.
IT'S NEVER TOO LATE TO CHANGE.
EVEN IF IT HURTS, EVEN IT KILLS YOU, IT'S NEVER TOO LATE TO TRY.
IT IS TOO LATE.
THE SUNKEN ARMOR...IT'S ALREADY RIGGED.
MERA, I'M SORRY!
IT'LL DESTROY ATLANTIS, IT'LL KILL US--
NO.
IF THE ARMOR CAN'T BE MOVED...
...THEN WE MUST MOVE ATLANTIS.
HAGEN. PRIEST OF THE DEEP!
CALL EVERYONE, EVERYONE--EVERY MAGICIAN, EVERY ATLANTEAN WITH EVEN THE LEAST MAGIC OR POWER--
ARTHUR, ANY CREATURES OF THE DEEP YOU HAVE KNOWN, HAVE AIDED, CALL FOR THEM--!
NEREUS MOVED ATLANTIS TO RETREAT.
WE MUST MOVE IT TO SURVIVE.
ARE YOU READY?
ARE YOU, PRINCESS...?
...OR SHOULD I SAY...

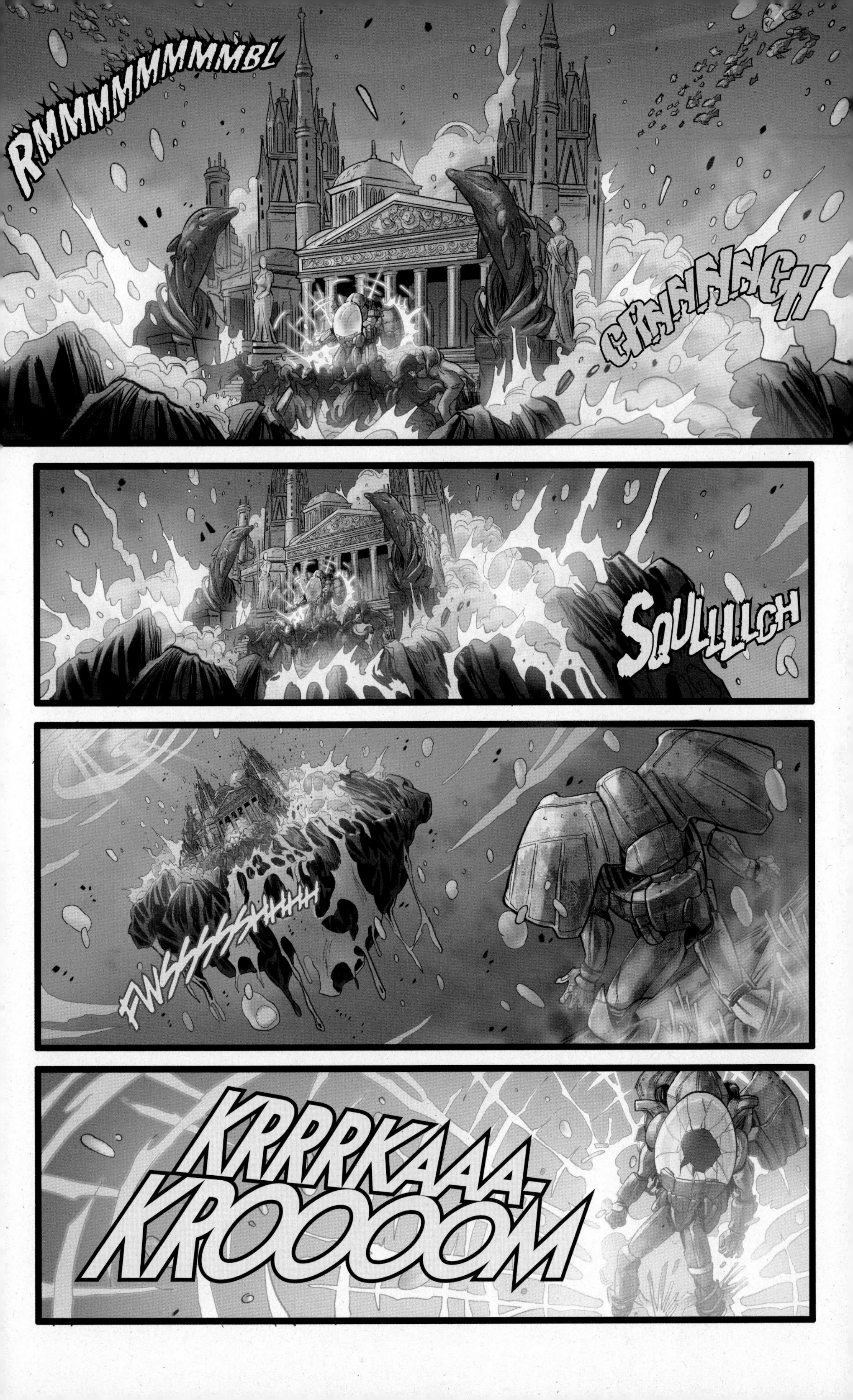
RMMMMMMMMMBL
GRNNNNCH
SQULLLLCH
FWSSSSSHHHH
KRRRKAAA-KROOOOOM

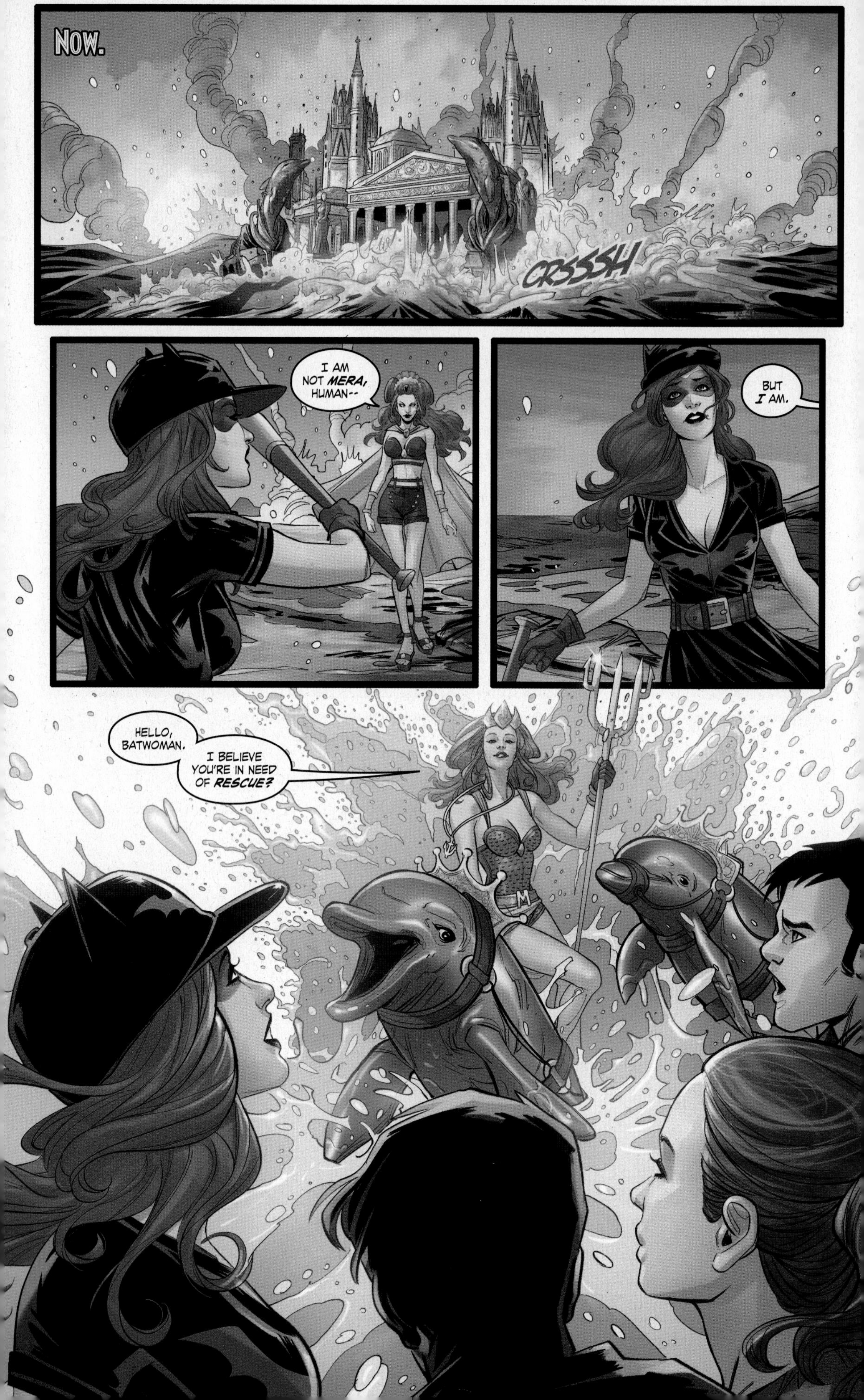
NOW.
CRSSSH
I AM NOT MERA, HUMAN--
BUT I AM.
HELLO, BATWOMAN.
I BELIEVE YOU'RE IN NEED OF RESCUE?

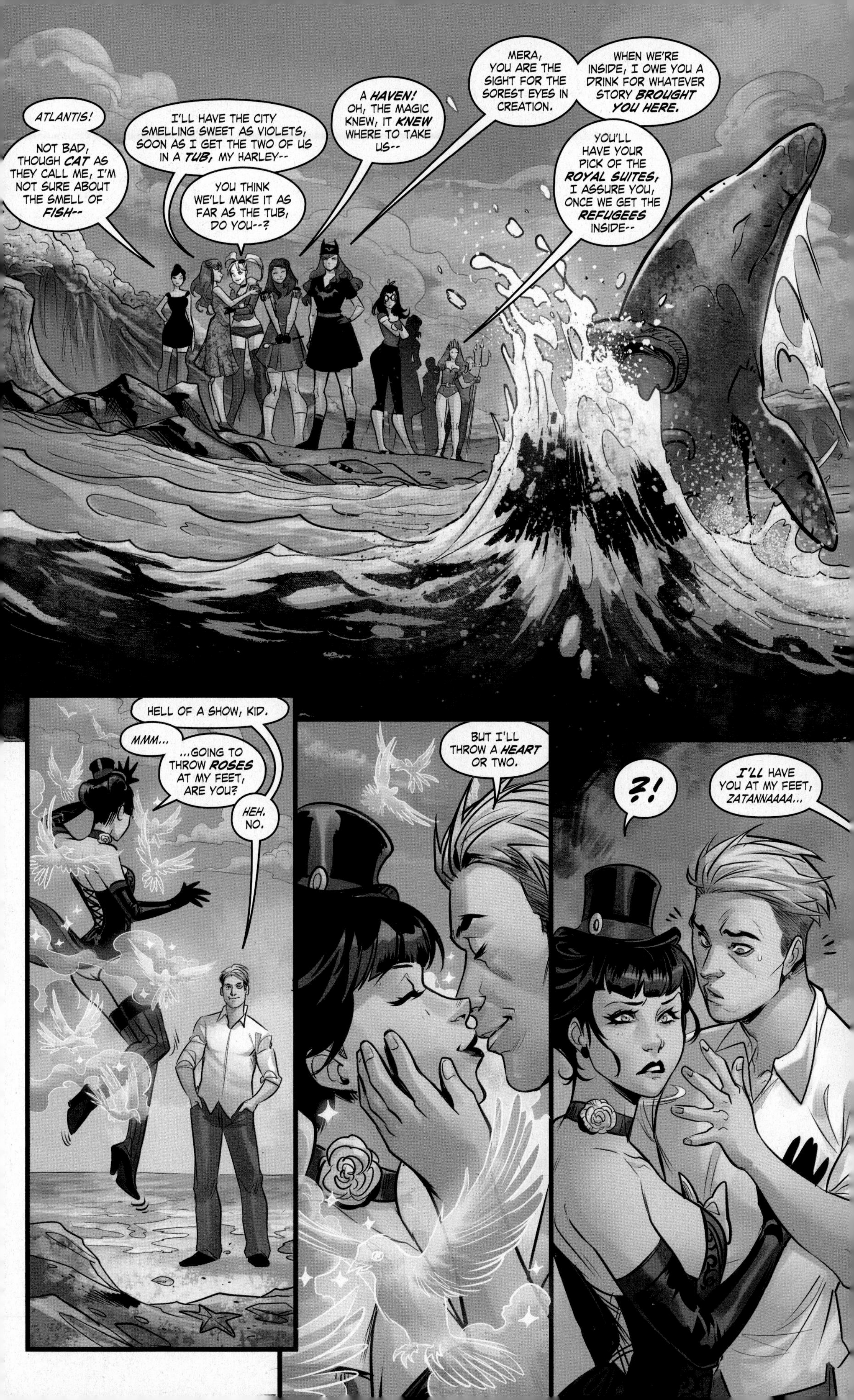
ATLANTIS!
NOT BAD, THOUGH CAT AS THEY CALL ME, I'M NOT SURE ABOUT THE SMELL OF FISH--
I'LL HAVE THE CITY SMELLING SWEET AS VIOLETS, SOON AS I GET THE TWO OF US IN A TUB, MY HARLEY--
YOU THINK WE'LL MAKE IT AS FAR AS THE TUB, DO YOU--?
A HAVEN! OH, THE MAGIC KNEW, IT KNEW WHERE TO TAKE US--
MERA, YOU ARE THE SIGHT FOR THE SOREST EYES IN CREATION.
WHEN WE'RE INSIDE, I OWE YOU A DRINK FOR WHATEVER STORY BROUGHT YOU HERE.
YOU'LL HAVE YOUR PICK OF THE ROYAL SUITES, I ASSURE YOU, ONCE WE GET THE REFUGEES INSIDE--
HELL OF A SHOW, KID.
MMM...
...GOING TO THROW ROSES AT MY FEET, ARE YOU?
HEH. NO.
BUT I'LL THROW A HEART OR TWO.
?!
I'LL HAVE YOU AT MY FEET, ZATANNAAAA...

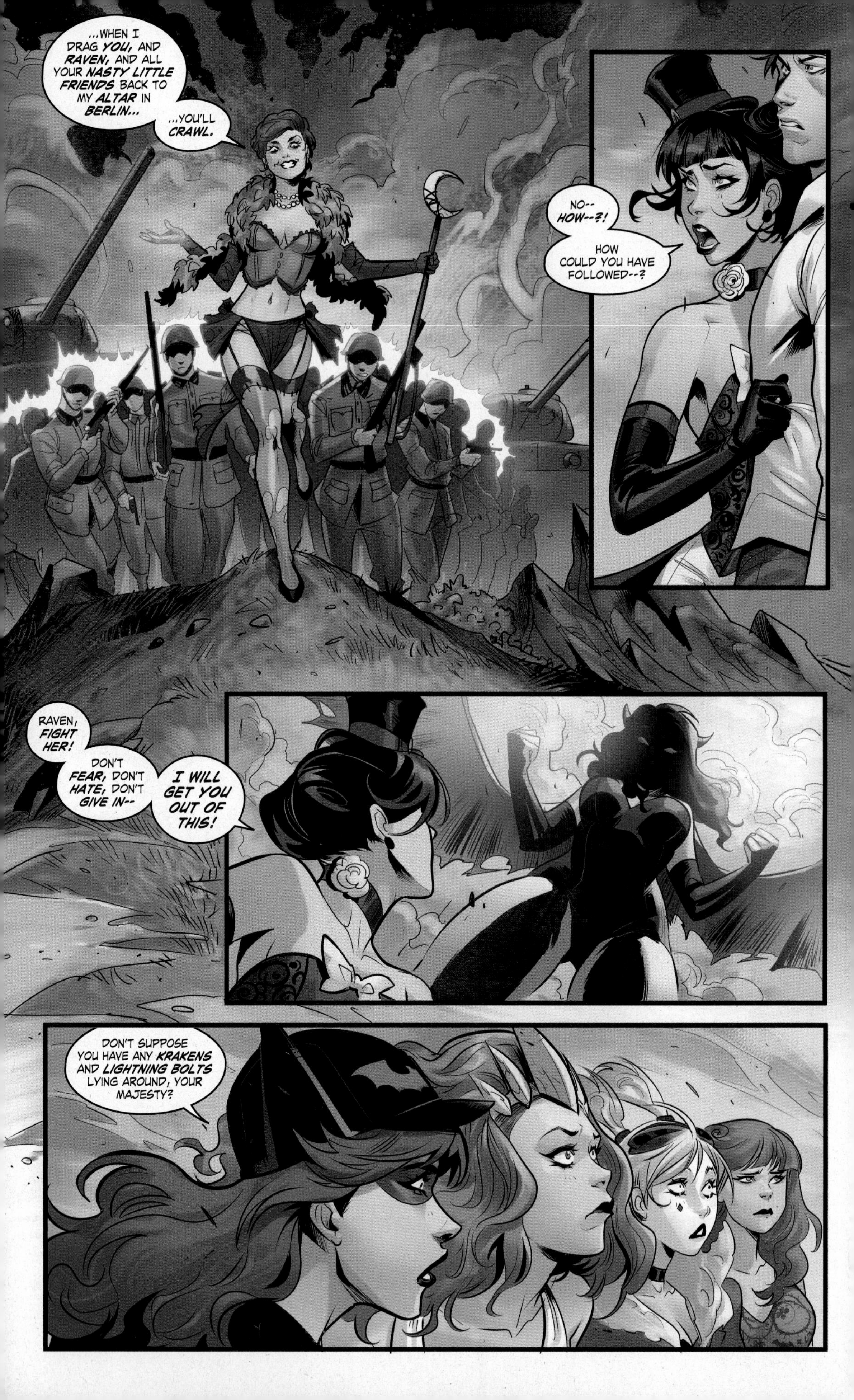
...WHEN I DRAG YOU, AND RAVEN, AND ALL YOUR NASTY LITTLE FRIENDS BACK TO MY ALTAR IN BERLIN...
...YOU'LL CRAWL.
NO-- HOW--?!
HOW COULD YOU HAVE FOLLOWED--?
RAVEN, FIGHT HER!
DON'T FEAR, DON'T HATE, DON'T GIVE IN--
I WILL GET YOU OUT OF THIS!
DON'T SUPPOSE YOU HAVE ANY KRAKENS AND LIGHTNING BOLTS LYING AROUND, YOUR MAJESTY?

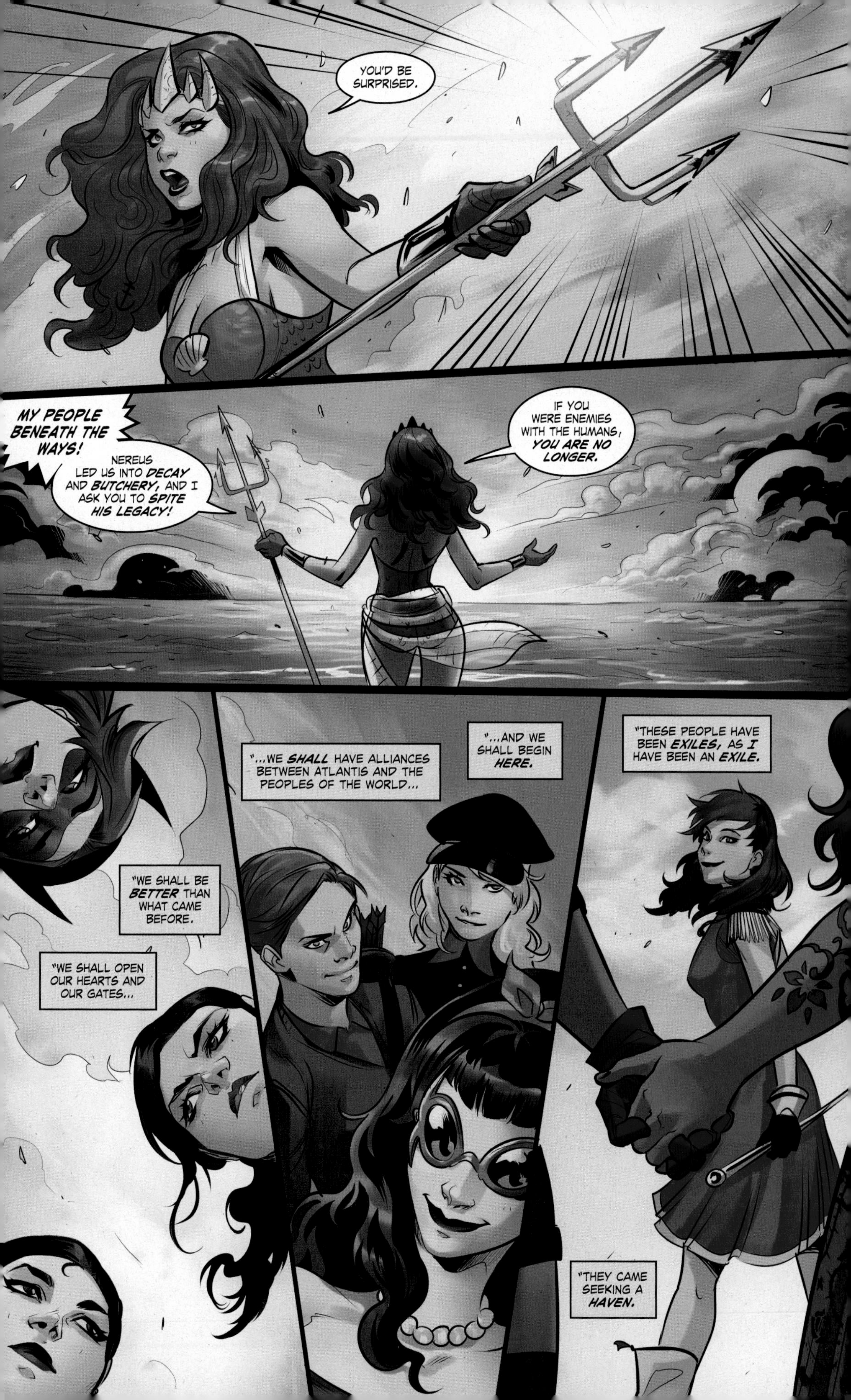
YOU'D BE SURPRISED.
MY PEOPLE BENEATH THE WAVES!
NEREUS LED US INTO DECAY AND BUTCHERY, AND I ASK YOU TO SPITE HIS LEGACY!
IF YOU WERE ENEMIES WITH THE HUMANS, YOU ARE NO LONGER.
"WE SHALL BE BETTER THAN WHAT CAME BEFORE.
"WE SHALL OPEN OUR HEARTS AND OUR GATES...
"...WE SHALL HAVE ALLIANCES BETWEEN ATLANTIS AND THE PEOPLES OF THE WORLD...
"...AND WE SHALL BEGIN HERE.
"THESE PEOPLE HAVE BEEN EXILES, AS I HAVE BEEN AN EXILE.
"THEY CAME SEEKING A HAVEN.

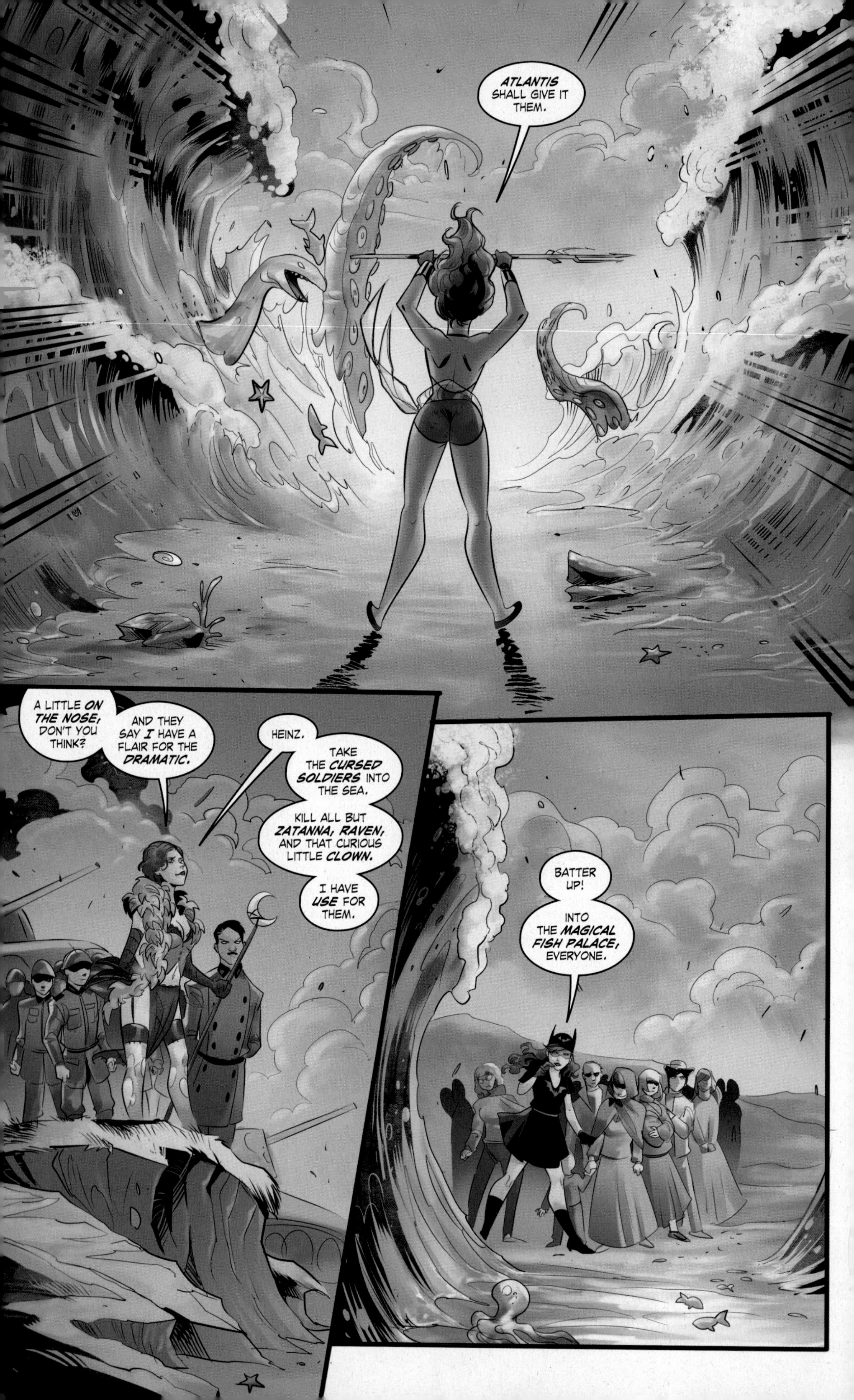
ATLANTIS SHALL GIVE IT THEM.
A LITTLE ON THE NOSE, DON'T YOU THINK?
AND THEY SAY I HAVE A FLAIR FOR THE DRAMATIC.
HEINZ.
TAKE THE CURSED SOLDIERS INTO THE SEA.
KILL ALL BUT ZATANNA, RAVEN, AND THAT CURIOUS LITTLE CLOWN.
I HAVE USE FOR THEM.
BATTER UP!
INTO THE MAGICAL FISH PALACE, EVERYONE.

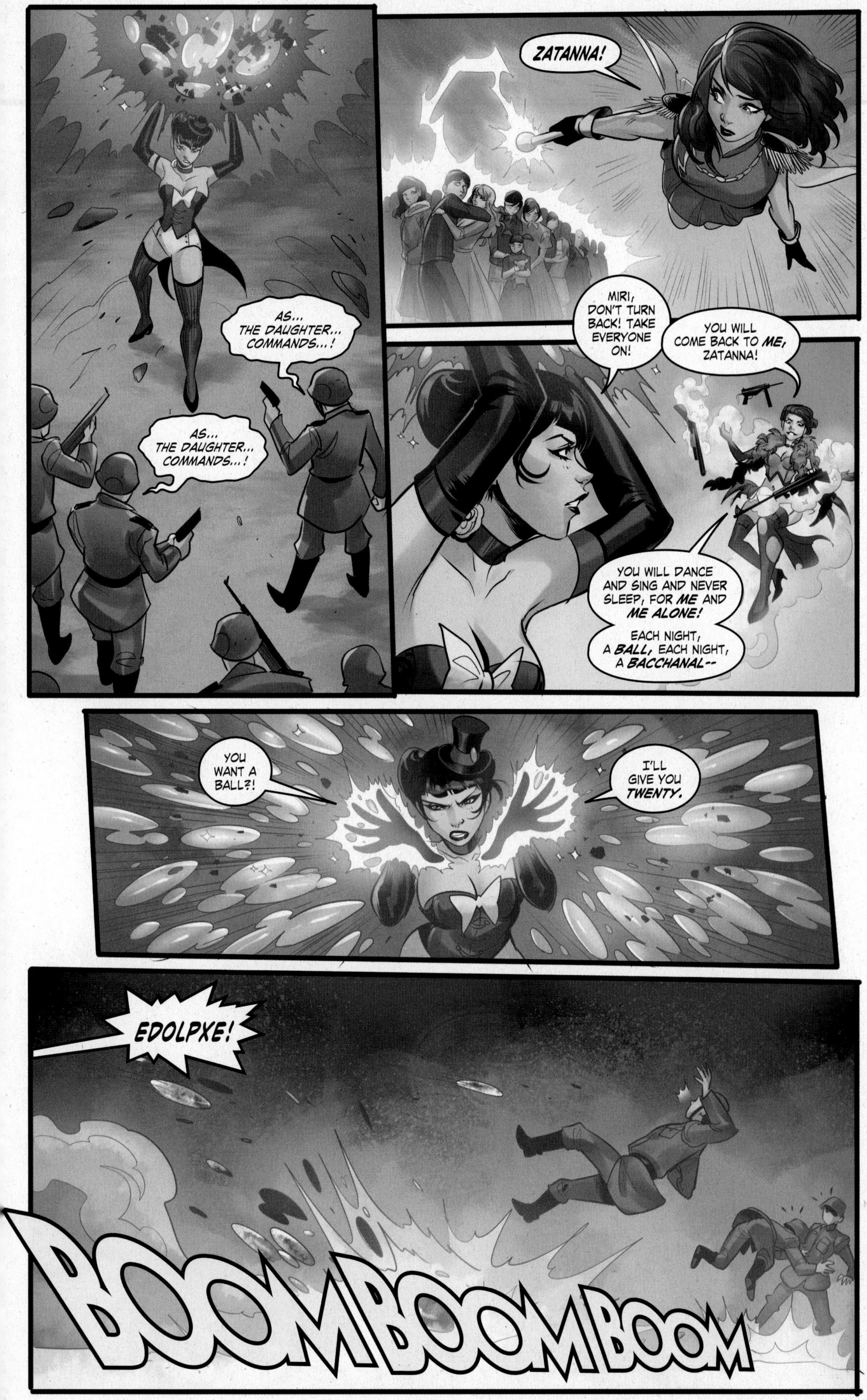
AS... THE DAUGHTER... COMMANDS...!
AS... THE DAUGHTER... COMMANDS...!
ZATANNA!
MIRI, DON'T TURN BACK! TAKE EVERYONE ON!
YOU WILL COME BACK TO ME, ZATANNA!
YOU WILL DANCE AND SING AND NEVER SLEEP, FOR ME AND ME ALONE!
EACH NIGHT, A BALL, EACH NIGHT, A BACCHANAL--
YOU WANT A BALL?!
I'LL GIVE YOU TWENTY.
EDOLPXE!
BOOMBOOMBOOM

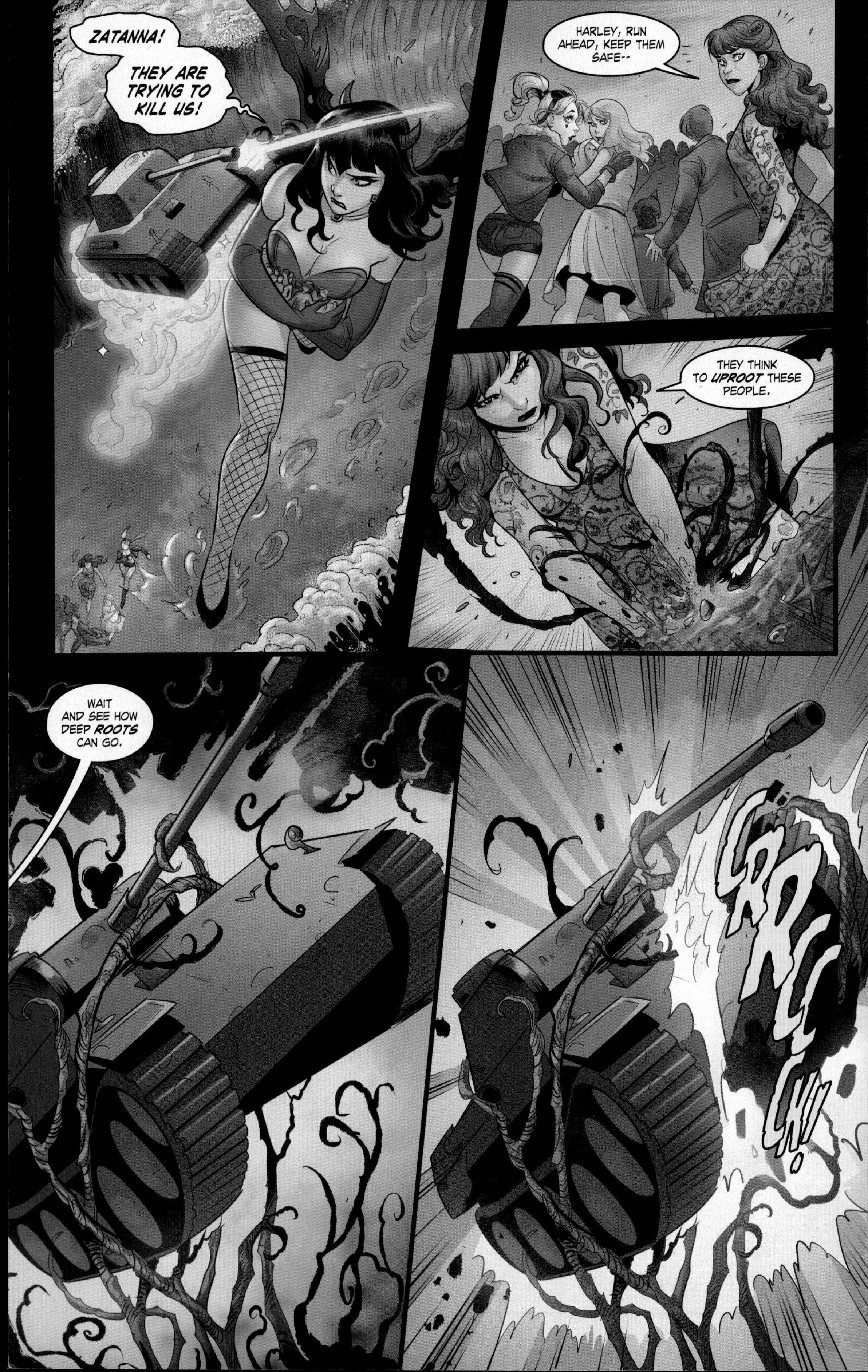
ZATANNA!
THEY ARE TRYING TO KILL US!
HARLEY, RUN AHEAD, KEEP THEM SAFE--
THEY THINK TO UPROOT THESE PEOPLE.
WAIT AND SEE HOW DEEP ROOTS CAN GO.
CRUNCH!

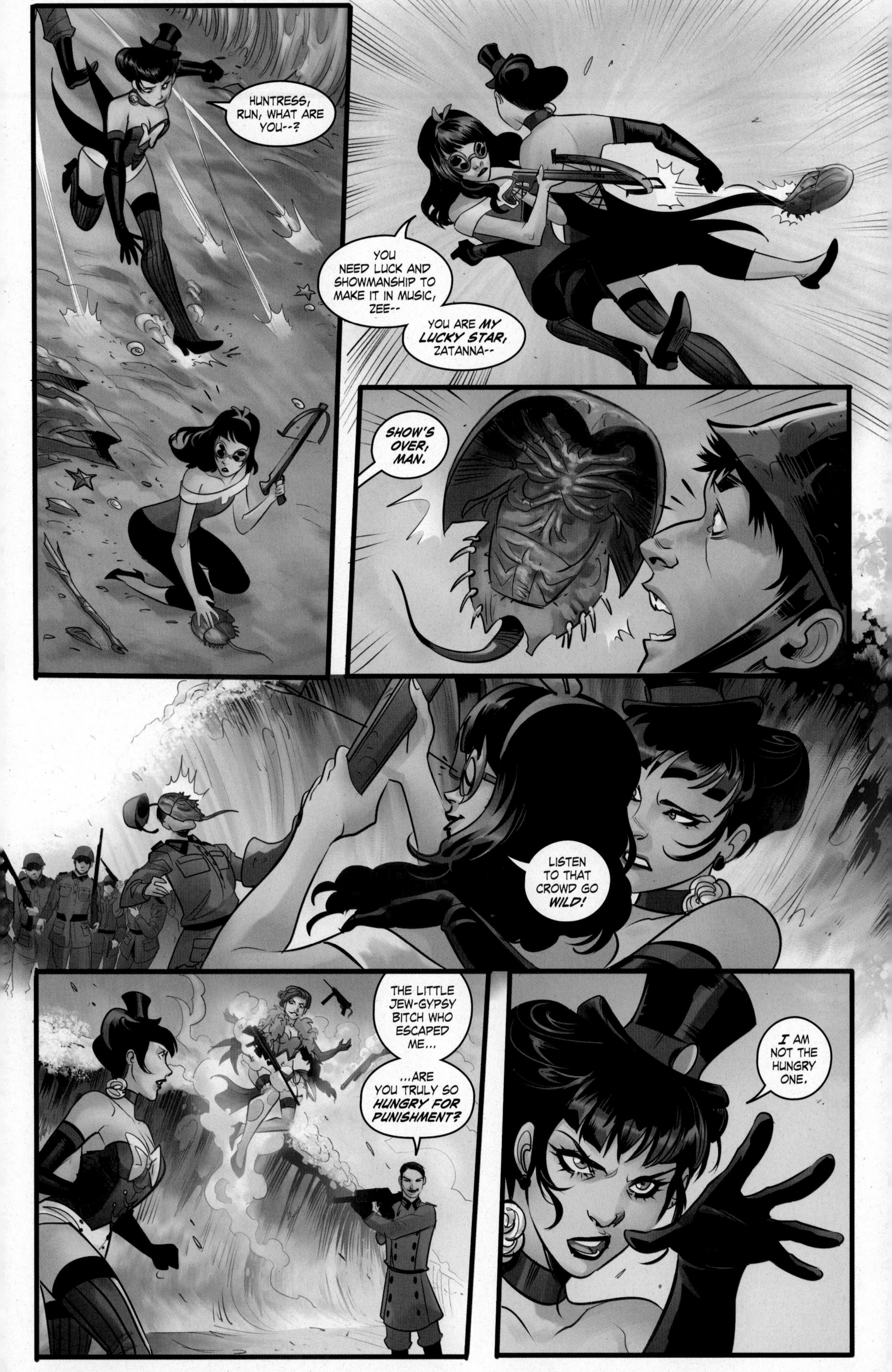
HUNTRESS, RUN, WHAT ARE YOU--?
YOU NEED LUCK AND SHOWMANSHIP TO MAKE IT IN MUSIC, ZEE--
YOU ARE *MY LUCKY STAR,* ZATANNA--
SHOW'S OVER, MAN.
LISTEN TO THAT CROWD GO *WILD!*
THE LITTLE JEW-GYPSY BITCH WHO ESCAPED ME...
...ARE YOU TRULY SO *HUNGRY FOR PUNISHMENT?*
I AM NOT THE HUNGRY ONE.

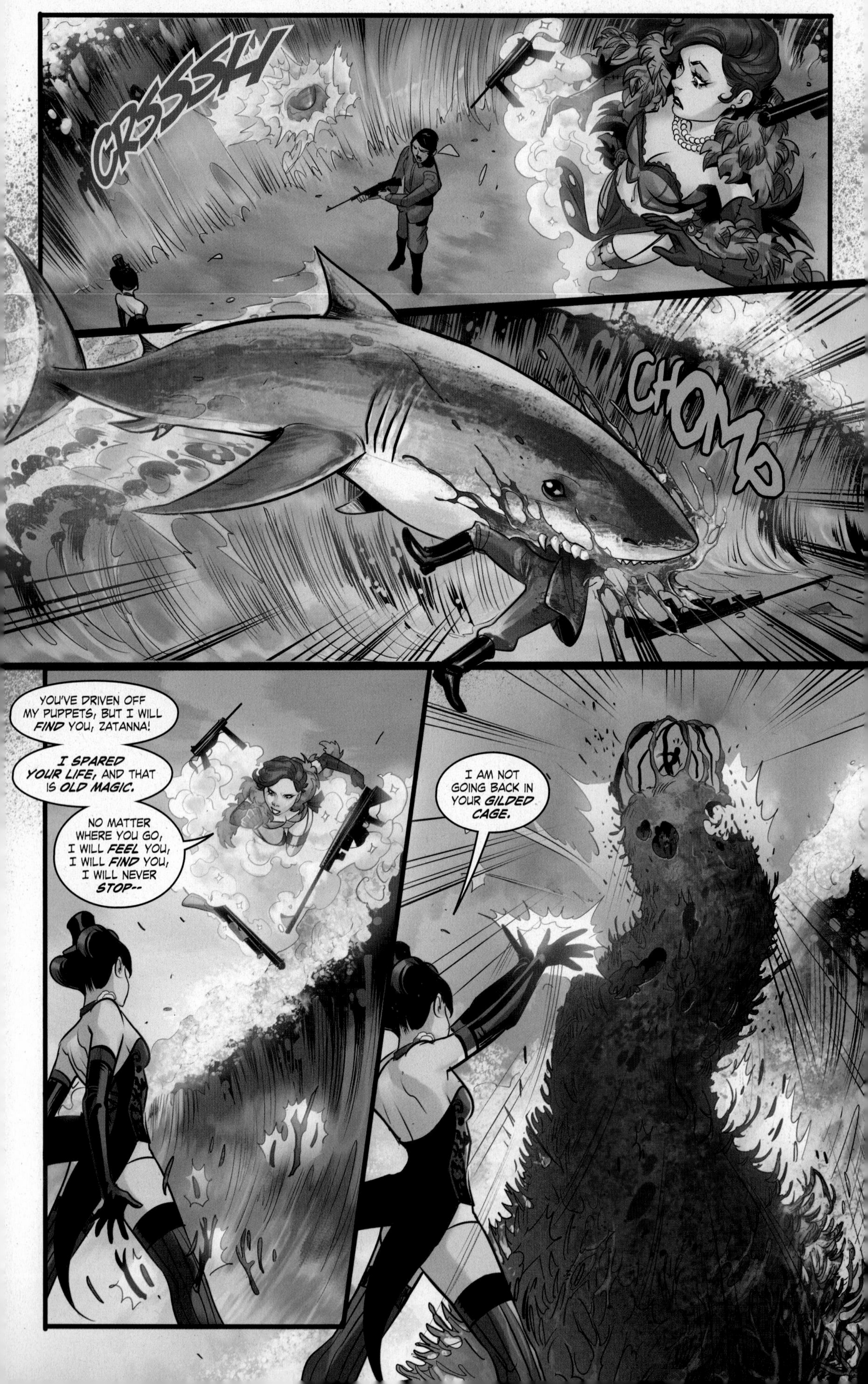
CRSSSH
CHOMP
YOU'VE DRIVEN OFF MY PUPPETS, BUT I WILL FIND YOU, ZATANNA!
I SPARED YOUR LIFE, AND THAT IS OLD MAGIC.
NO MATTER WHERE YOU GO, I WILL FEEL YOU, I WILL FIND YOU, I WILL NEVER STOP--
I AM NOT GOING BACK IN YOUR GILDED CAGE.

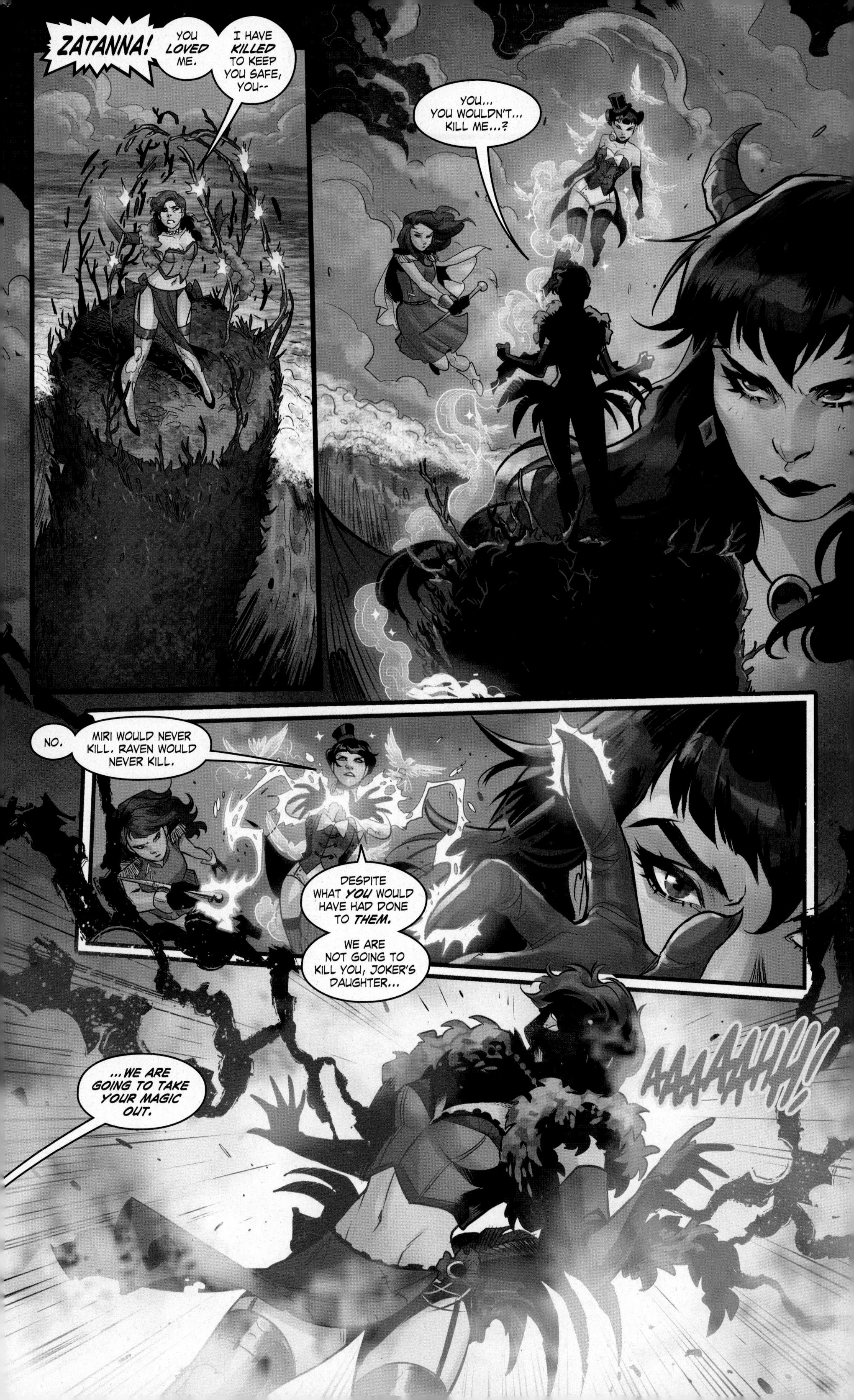
ZATANNA!
YOU LOVED ME.
I HAVE KILLED TO KEEP YOU SAFE, YOU--
YOU... YOU WOULDN'T... KILL ME...?
NO.
MIRI WOULD NEVER KILL. RAVEN WOULD NEVER KILL.
DESPITE WHAT YOU WOULD HAVE HAD DONE TO THEM.
WE ARE NOT GOING TO KILL YOU, JOKER'S DAUGHTER...
...WE ARE GOING TO TAKE YOUR MAGIC OUT.
AAAAAAHH!

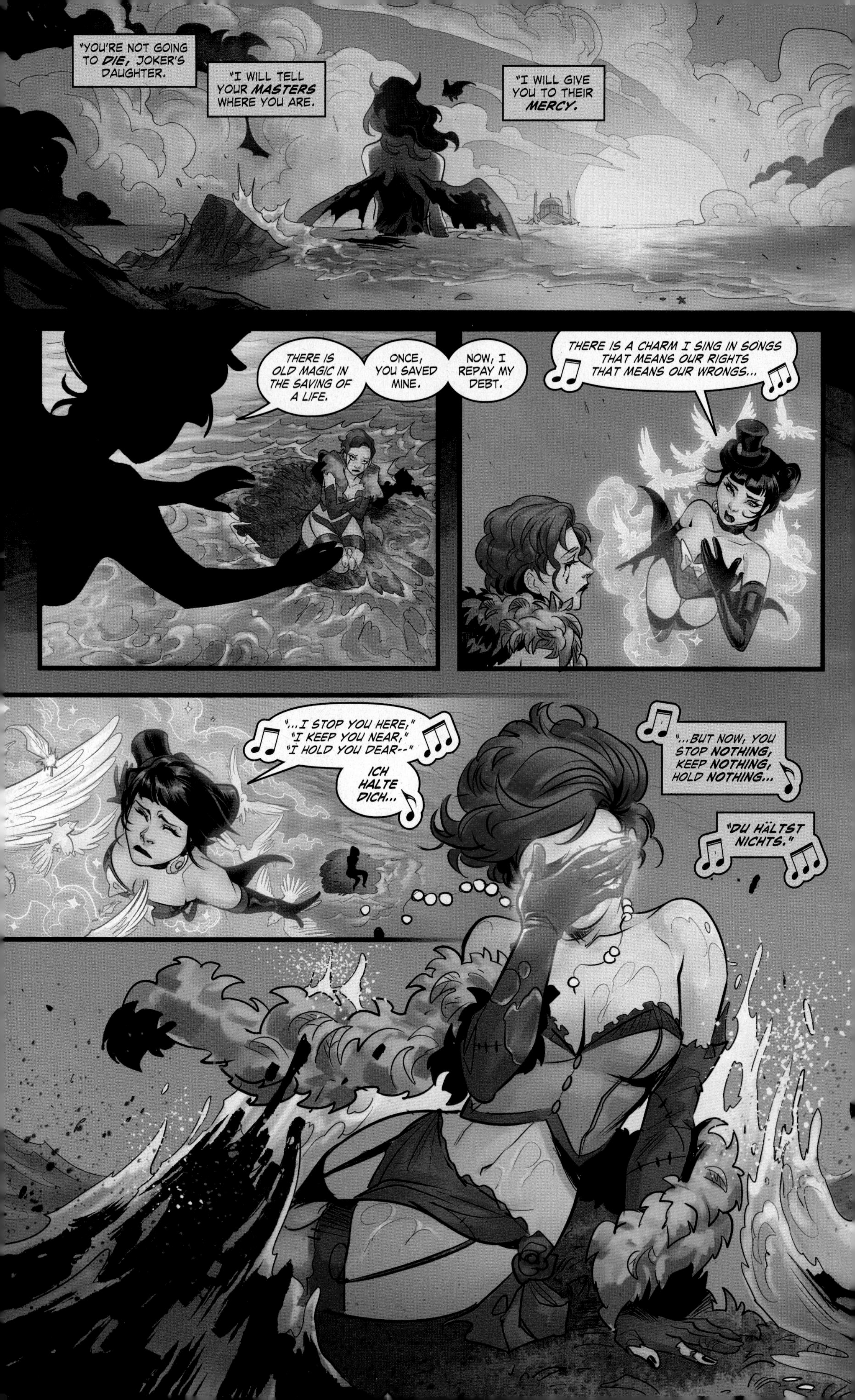
"YOU'RE NOT GOING TO DIE, JOKER'S DAUGHTER.
"I WILL TELL YOUR MASTERS WHERE YOU ARE.
"I WILL GIVE YOU TO THEIR MERCY.
THERE IS OLD MAGIC IN THE SAVING OF A LIFE.
ONCE, YOU SAVED MINE.
NOW, I REPAY MY DEBT.
THERE IS A CHARM I SING IN SONGS THAT MEANS OUR RIGHTS THAT MEANS OUR WRONGS...
"...I STOP YOU HERE," "I KEEP YOU NEAR," "I HOLD YOU DEAR--"
ICH HALTE DICH...
"...BUT NOW, YOU STOP NOTHING, KEEP NOTHING, HOLD NOTHING...
"DU HÄLTST NICHTS."

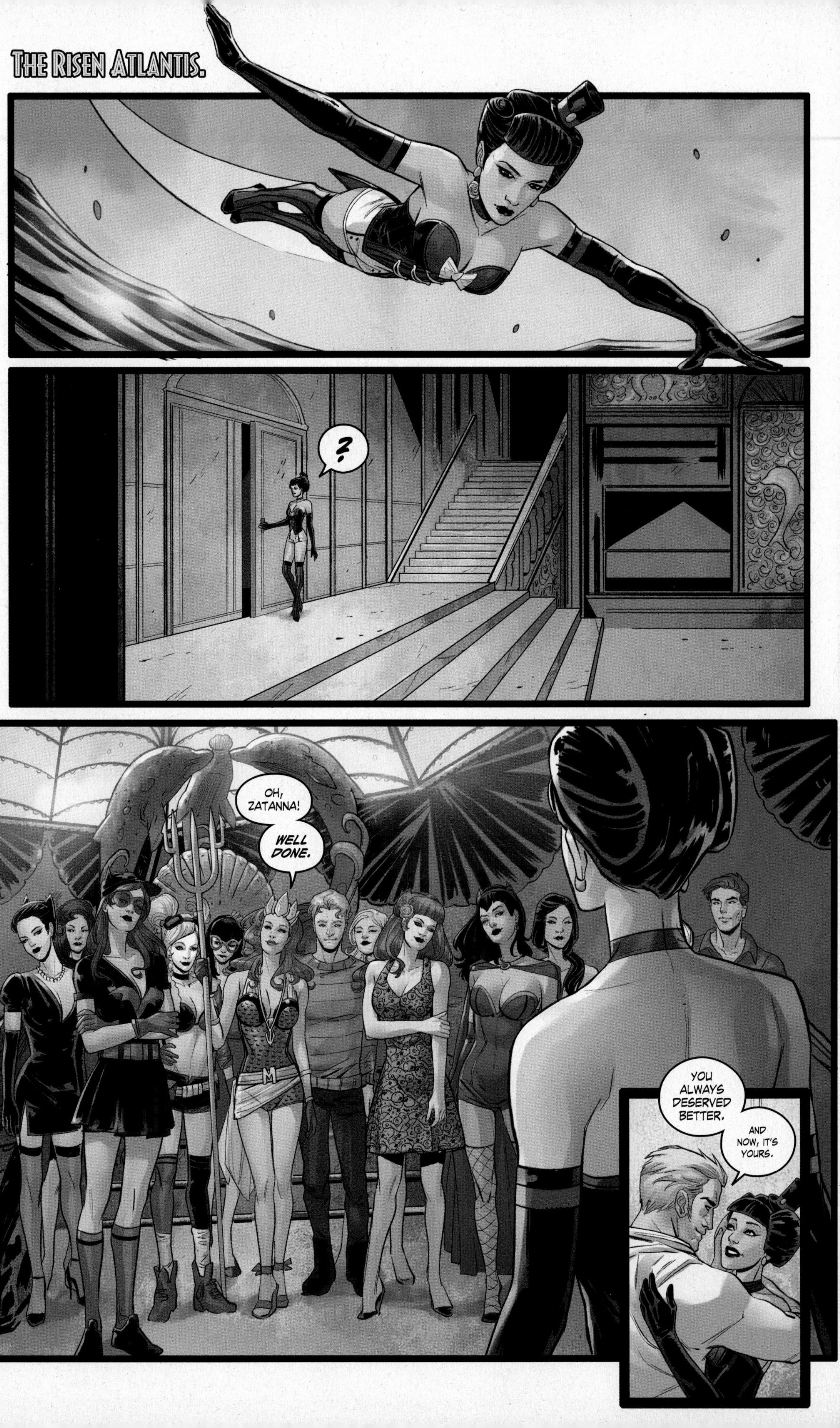
THE RISEN ATLANTIS.
?
OH, ZATANNA!
WELL DONE.
YOU ALWAYS DESERVED BETTER.
AND NOW, IT'S YOURS.

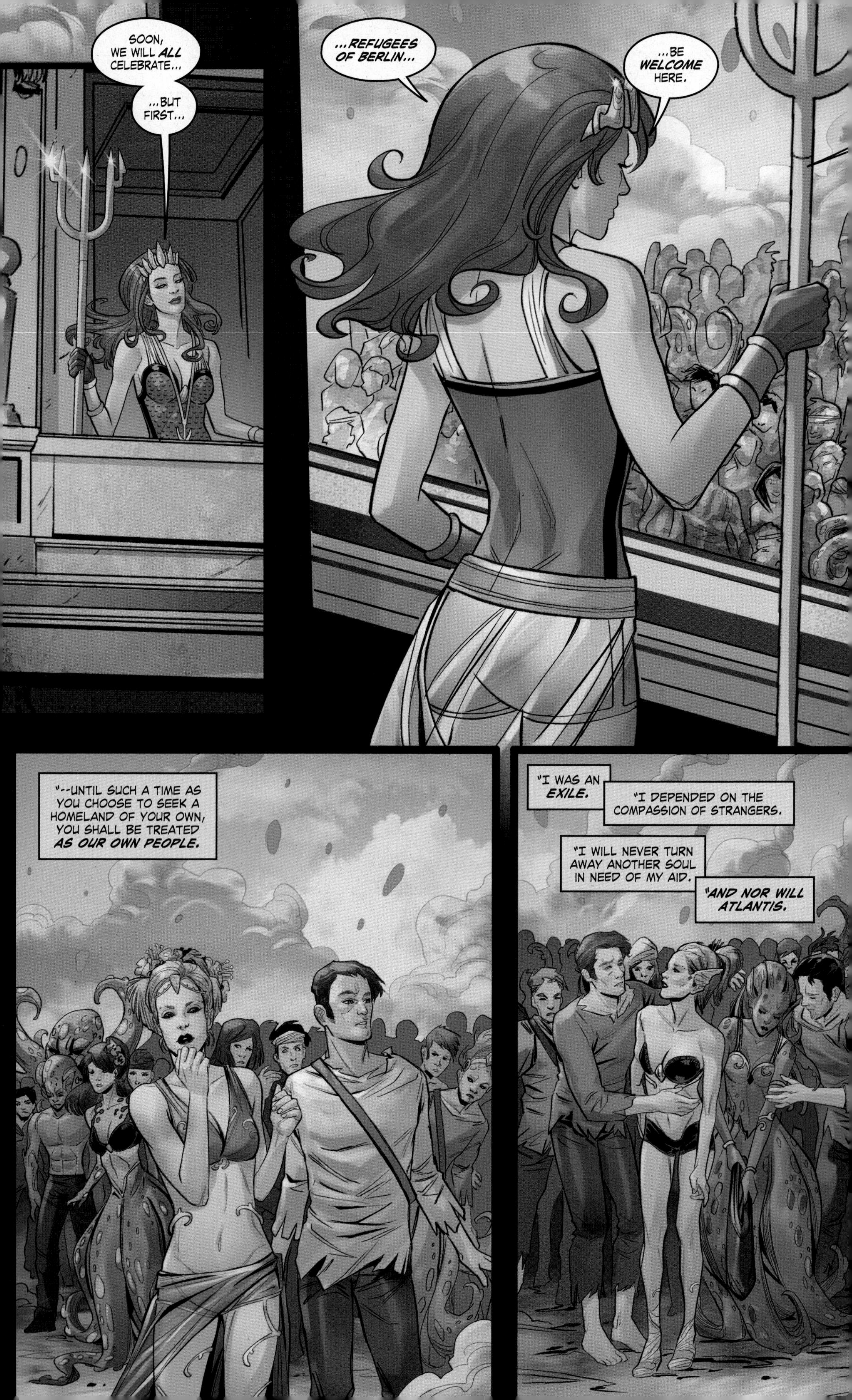
SOON, WE WILL ALL CELEBRATE...
...BUT FIRST...
...REFUGEES OF BERLIN...
...BE WELCOME HERE.
"--UNTIL SUCH A TIME AS YOU CHOOSE TO SEEK A HOMELAND OF YOUR OWN, YOU SHALL BE TREATED AS OUR OWN PEOPLE.
"I WAS AN EXILE.
"I DEPENDED ON THE COMPASSION OF STRANGERS.
"I WILL NEVER TURN AWAY ANOTHER SOUL IN NEED OF MY AID.
"AND NOR WILL ATLANTIS.

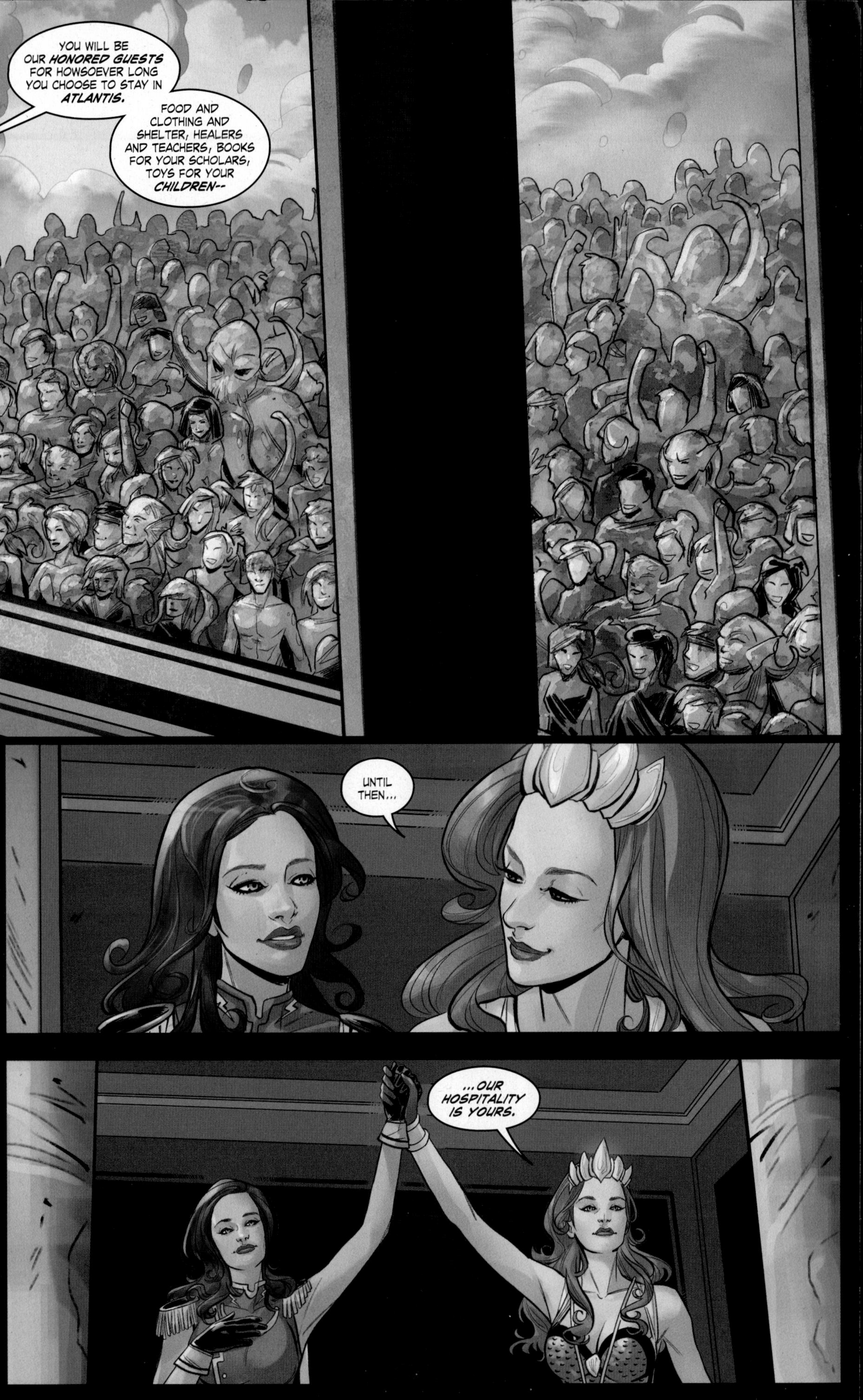
YOU WILL BE OUR HONORED GUESTS FOR HOWSOEVER LONG YOU CHOOSE TO STAY IN ATLANTIS.
FOOD AND CLOTHING AND SHELTER, HEALERS AND TEACHERS, BOOKS FOR YOUR SCHOLARS, TOYS FOR YOUR CHILDREN--
UNTIL THEN...
...OUR HOSPITALITY IS YOURS.

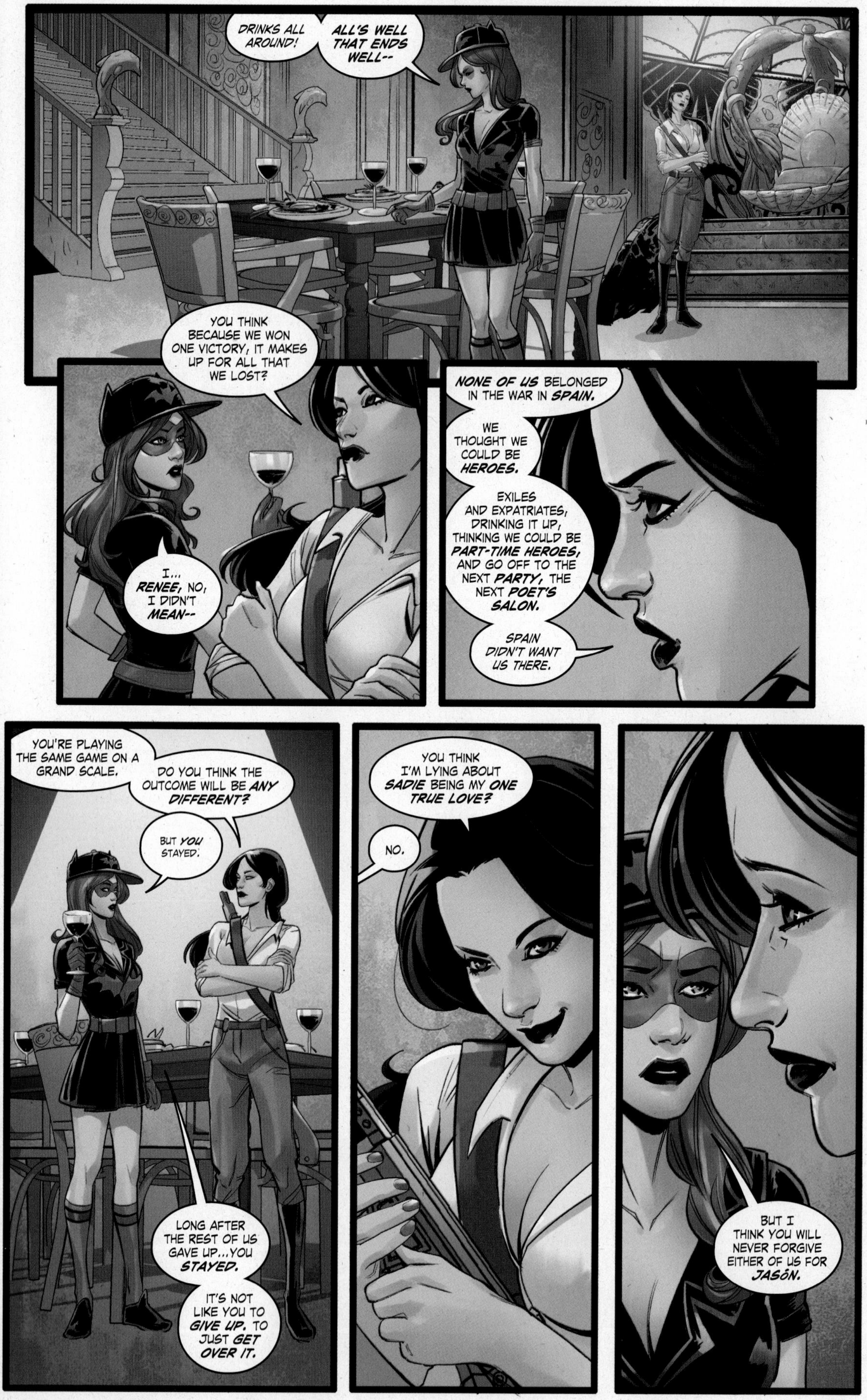

DRINKS ALL AROUND!
ALL'S WELL THAT ENDS WELL--
YOU THINK BECAUSE WE WON ONE VICTORY, IT MAKES UP FOR ALL THAT WE LOST?
I... RENEE, NO, I DIDN'T MEAN--
NONE OF US BELONGED IN THE WAR IN SPAIN.
WE THOUGHT WE COULD BE HEROES.
EXILES AND EXPATRIATES, DRINKING IT UP, THINKING WE COULD BE PART-TIME HEROES, AND GO OFF TO THE NEXT PARTY, THE NEXT POET'S SALON.
SPAIN DIDN'T WANT US THERE.
YOU'RE PLAYING THE SAME GAME ON A GRAND SCALE.
DO YOU THINK THE OUTCOME WILL BE ANY DIFFERENT?
BUT YOU STAYED.
LONG AFTER THE REST OF US GAVE UP...YOU STAYED.
IT'S NOT LIKE YOU TO GIVE UP. TO JUST GET OVER IT.
YOU THINK I'M LYING ABOUT SADIE BEING MY ONE TRUE LOVE?
NO.
BUT I THINK YOU WILL NEVER FORGIVE EITHER OF US FOR JASÓN.

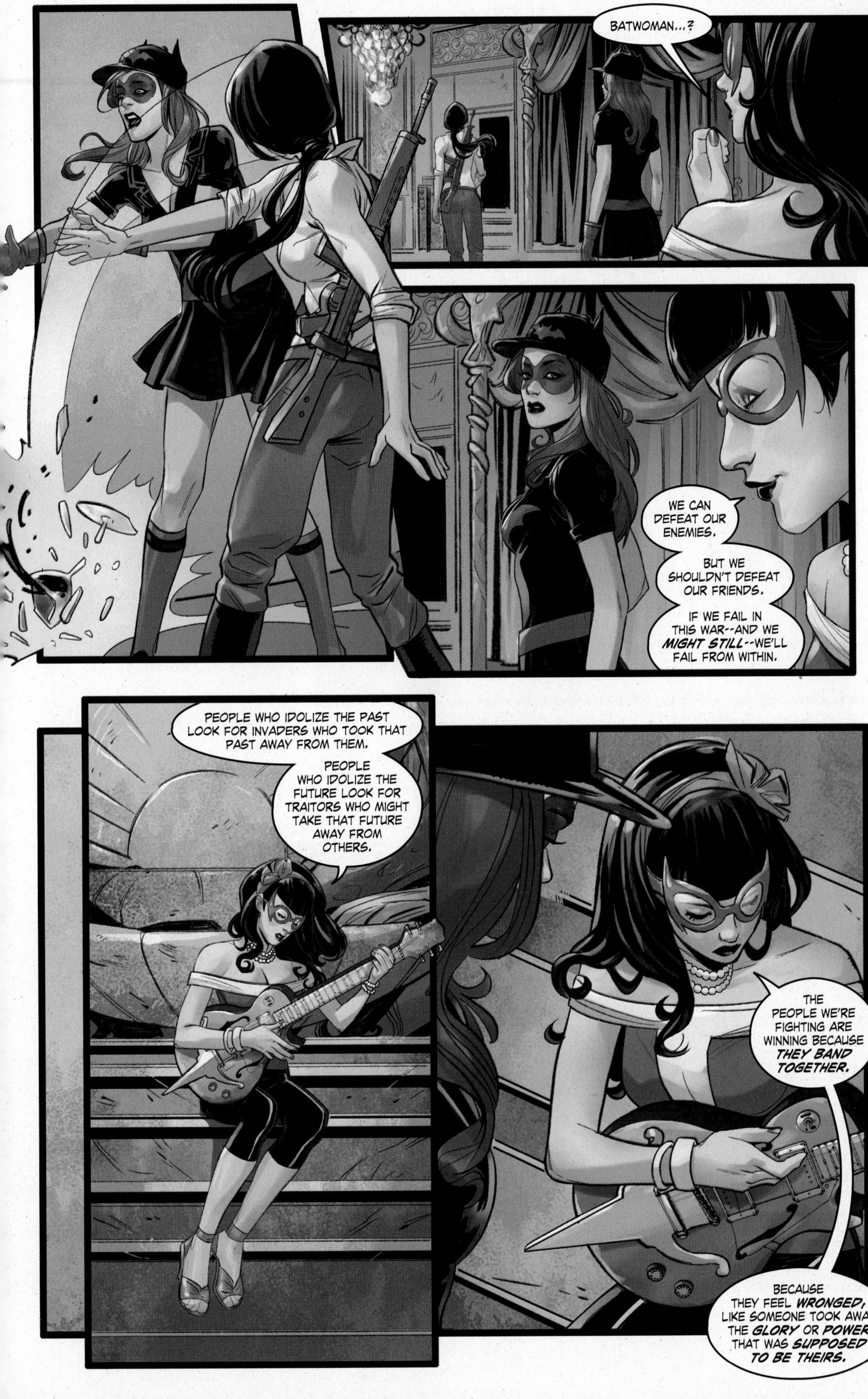
BATWOMAN...?
WE CAN DEFEAT OUR ENEMIES.
BUT WE SHOULDN'T DEFEAT OUR FRIENDS.
IF WE FAIL IN THIS WAR--AND WE MIGHT STILL--WE'LL FAIL FROM WITHIN.
PEOPLE WHO IDOLIZE THE PAST LOOK FOR INVADERS WHO TOOK THAT PAST AWAY FROM THEM.
PEOPLE WHO IDOLIZE THE FUTURE LOOK FOR TRAITORS WHO MIGHT TAKE THAT FUTURE AWAY FROM OTHERS.
THE PEOPLE WE'RE FIGHTING ARE WINNING BECAUSE THEY BAND TOGETHER.
BECAUSE THEY FEEL WRONGED, LIKE SOMEONE TOOK AWAY THE GLORY OR POWER THAT WAS SUPPOSED TO BE THEIRS.

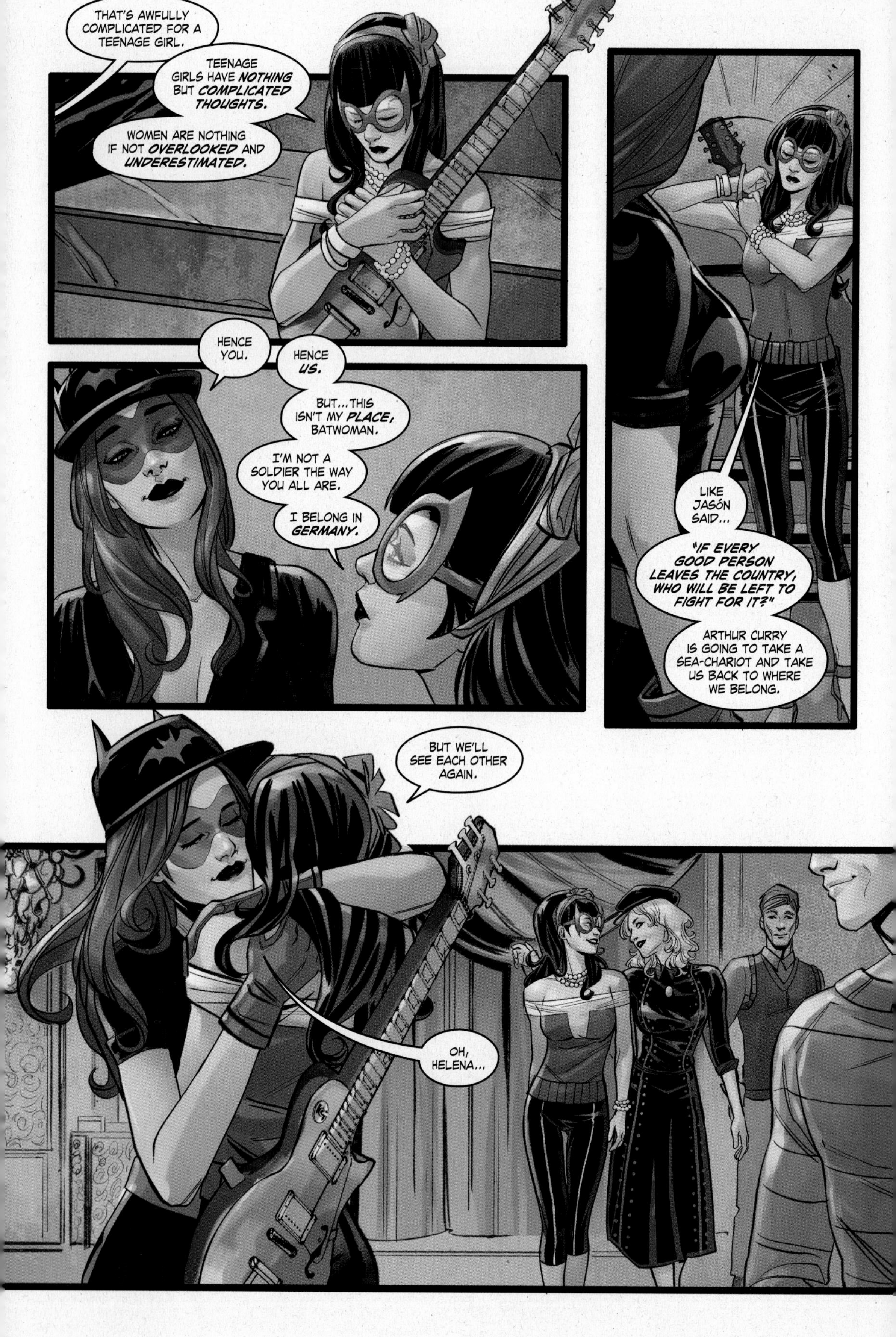

THAT'S AWFULLY COMPLICATED FOR A TEENAGE GIRL.
TEENAGE GIRLS HAVE *NOTHING* BUT *COMPLICATED THOUGHTS.*
WOMEN ARE NOTHING IF NOT *OVERLOOKED* AND *UNDERESTIMATED.*
HENCE YOU.
HENCE *US.*
BUT... THIS ISN'T MY *PLACE,* BATWOMAN.
I'M NOT A SOLDIER THE WAY YOU ALL ARE.
I BELONG IN *GERMANY.*
LIKE JASÓN SAID...
"IF EVERY GOOD PERSON LEAVES THE COUNTRY, WHO WILL BE LEFT TO FIGHT FOR IT?"
ARTHUR CURRY IS GOING TO TAKE A SEA-CHARIOT AND TAKE US BACK TO WHERE WE BELONG.
BUT WE'LL SEE EACH OTHER AGAIN.
OH, HELENA...

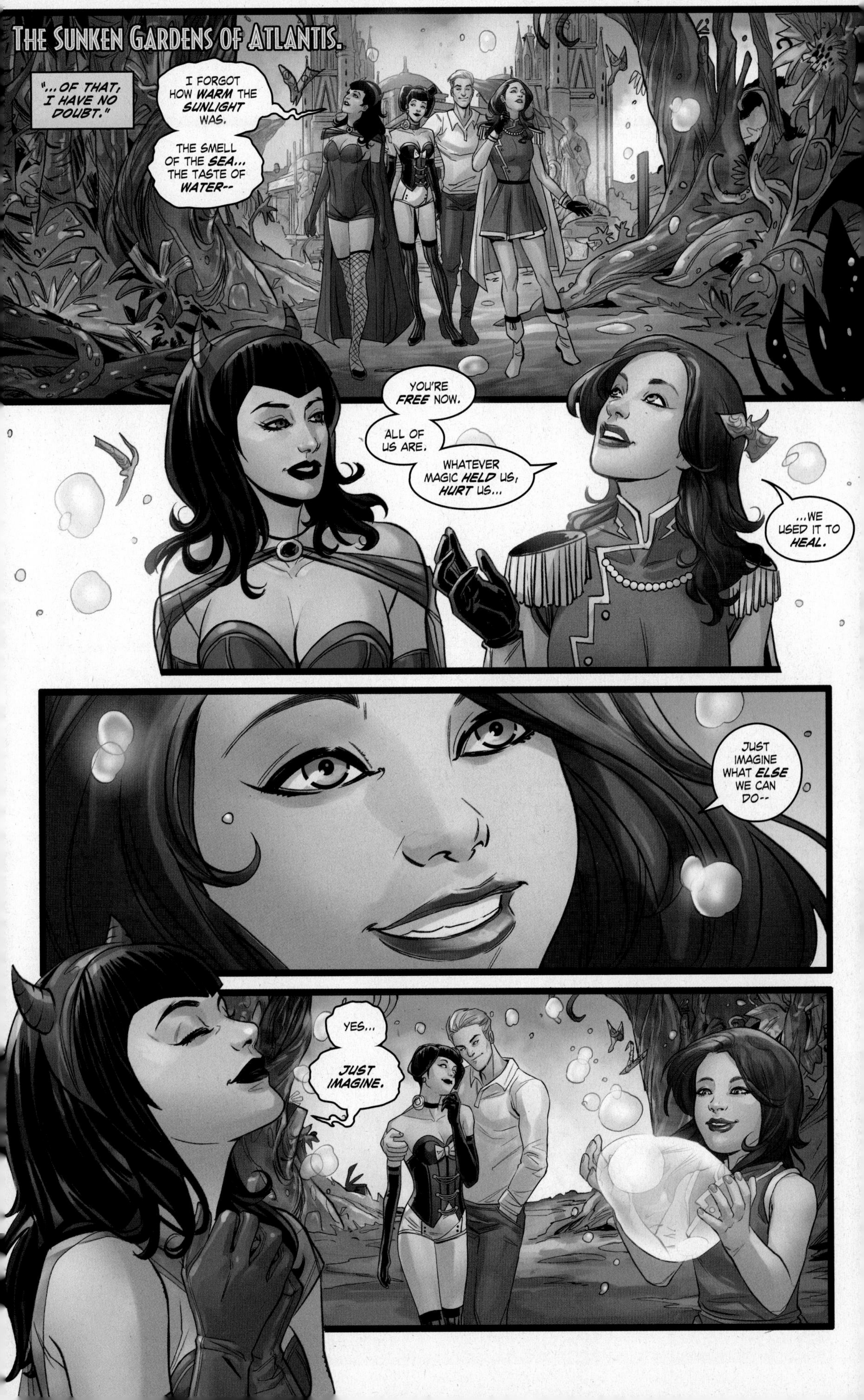
THE SUNKEN GARDENS OF ATLANTIS.
"...OF THAT, I HAVE NO DOUBT."
I FORGOT HOW WARM THE SUNLIGHT WAS.
THE SMELL OF THE SEA... THE TASTE OF WATER--
YOU'RE FREE NOW.
ALL OF US ARE.
WHATEVER MAGIC HELD US, HURT US...
...WE USED IT TO HEAL.
JUST IMAGINE WHAT ELSE WE CAN DO--
YES...
JUST IMAGINE.

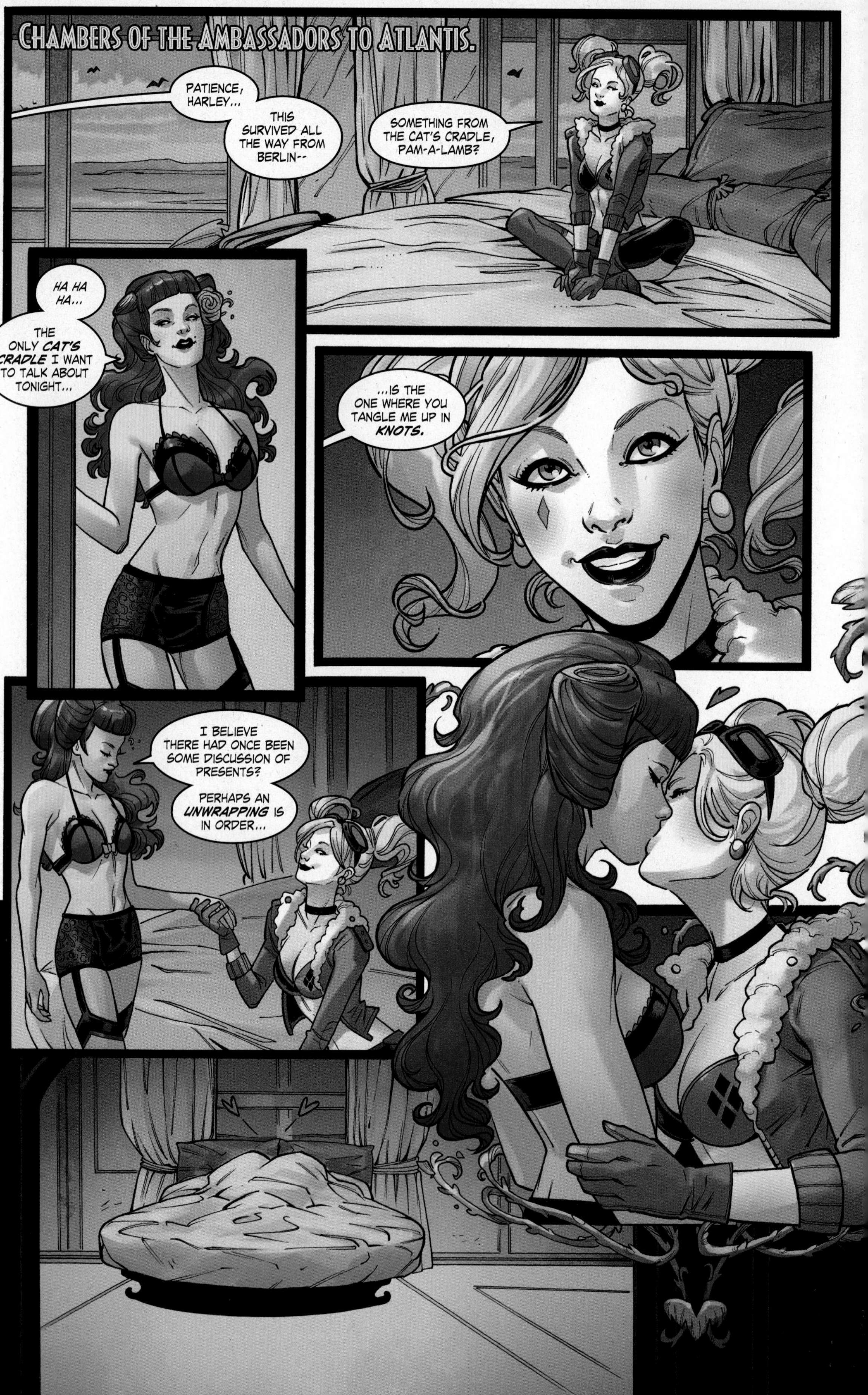
CHAMBERS OF THE AMBASSADORS TO ATLANTIS.
PATIENCE, HARLEY...
THIS SURVIVED ALL THE WAY FROM BERLIN--
SOMETHING FROM THE CAT'S CRADLE, PAM-A-LAMB?
HA HA HA...
THE ONLY CAT'S CRADLE I WANT TO TALK ABOUT TONIGHT...
...IS THE ONE WHERE YOU TANGLE ME UP IN KNOTS.
I BELIEVE THERE HAD ONCE BEEN SOME DISCUSSION OF PRESENTS?
PERHAPS AN UNWRAPPING IS IN ORDER...

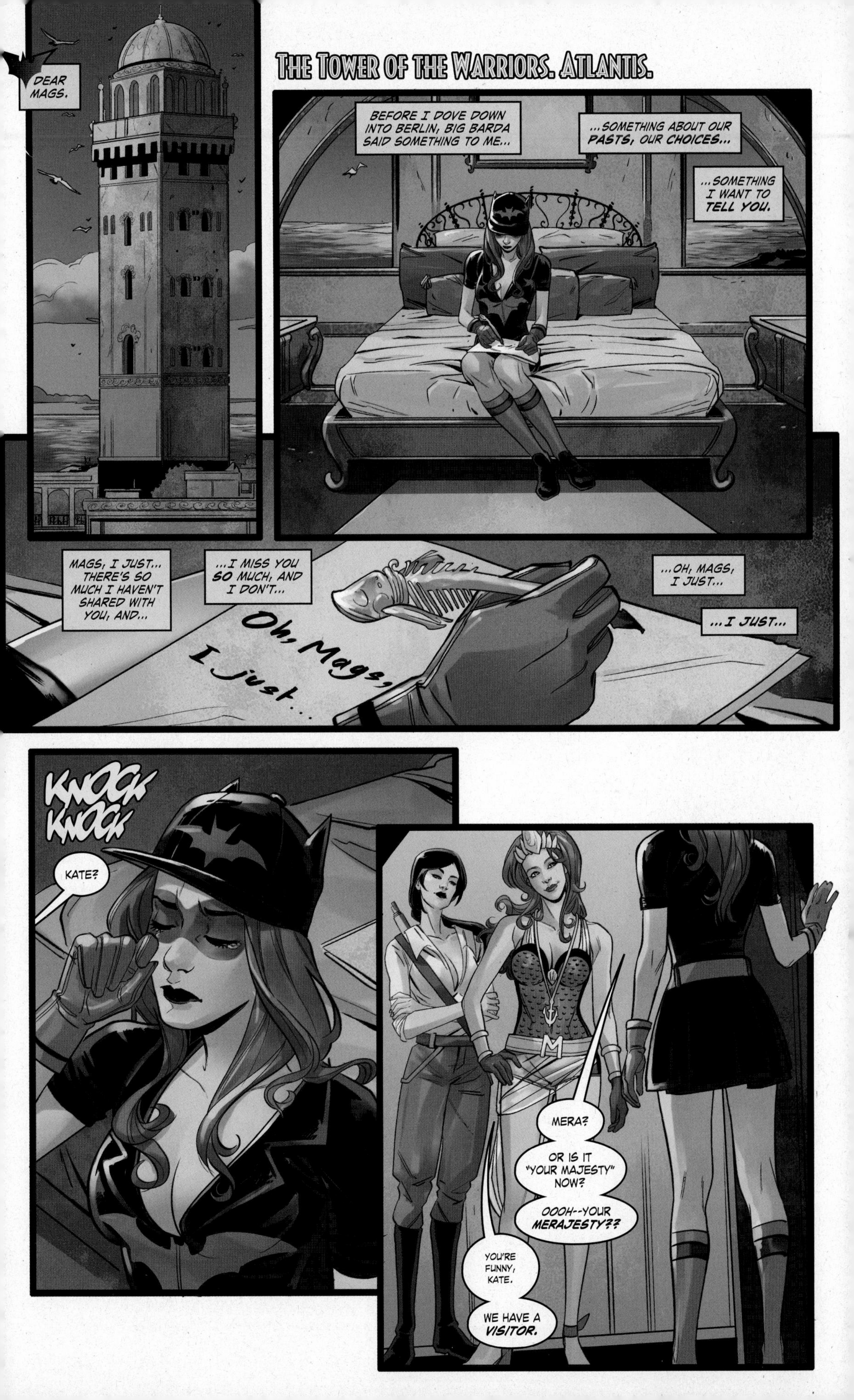
DEAR MAGS.
THE TOWER OF THE WARRIORS. ATLANTIS.
BEFORE I DOVE DOWN INTO BERLIN, BIG BARDA SAID SOMETHING TO ME...
...SOMETHING ABOUT OUR PASTS, OUR CHOICES...
...SOMETHING I WANT TO TELL YOU.
MAGS, I JUST... THERE'S SO MUCH I HAVEN'T SHARED WITH YOU, AND...
...I MISS YOU SO MUCH, AND I DON'T...
Oh, Mags, I just...
...OH, MAGS, I JUST...
...I JUST...
KNOCK KNOCK
KATE?
MERA?
OR IS IT "YOUR MAJESTY" NOW?
OOOH--YOUR MERAJESTY??
YOU'RE FUNNY, KATE.
WE HAVE A VISITOR.

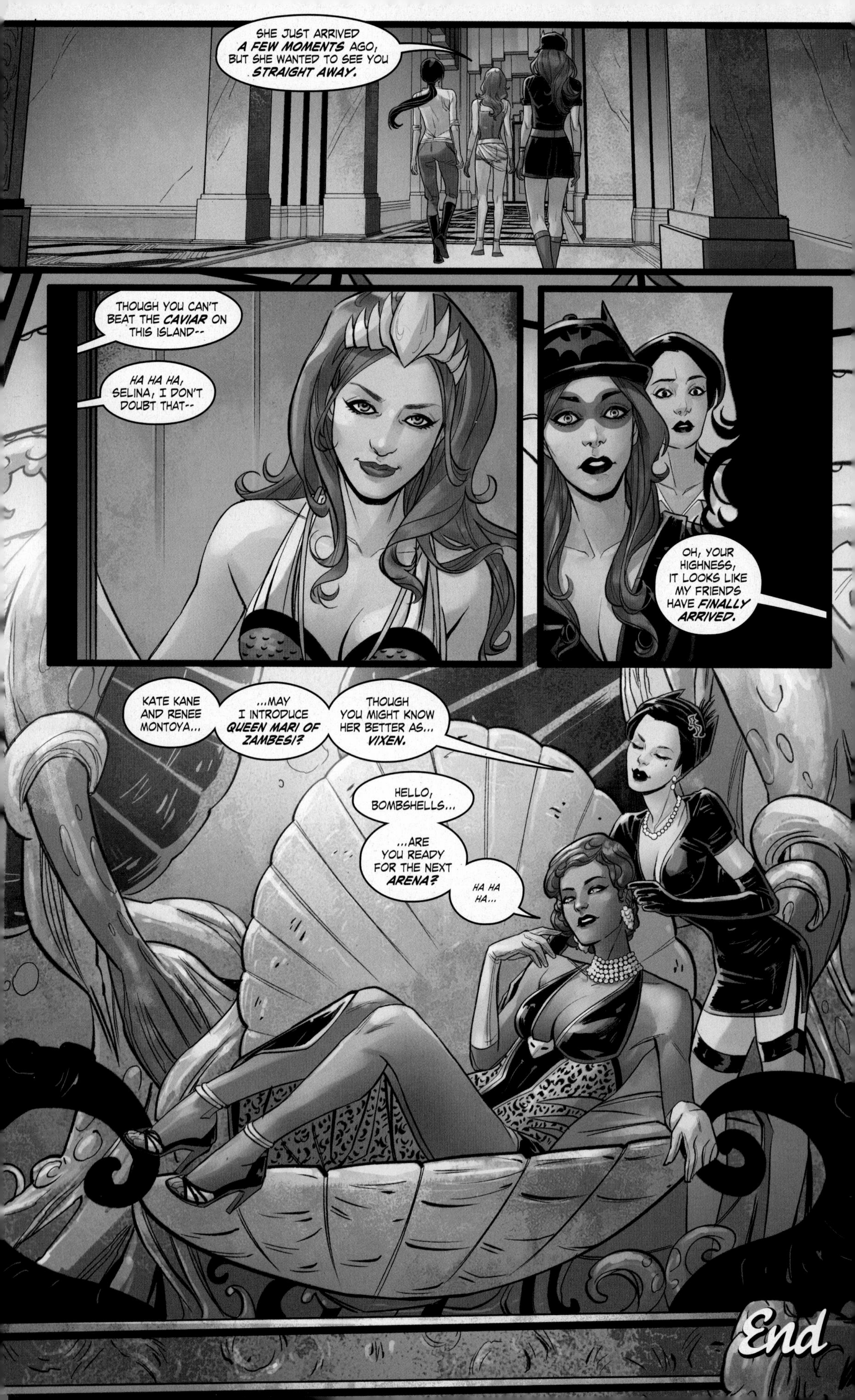
SHE JUST ARRIVED A FEW MOMENTS AGO, BUT SHE WANTED TO SEE YOU STRAIGHT AWAY.
THOUGH YOU CAN'T BEAT THE CAVIAR ON THIS ISLAND--
HA HA HA, SELINA, I DON'T DOUBT THAT--
OH, YOUR HIGHNESS, IT LOOKS LIKE MY FRIENDS HAVE FINALLY ARRIVED.
KATE KANE AND RENEE MONTOYA...
...MAY I INTRODUCE QUEEN MARI OF ZAMBESI?
THOUGH YOU MIGHT KNOW HER BETTER AS... VIXEN.
HELLO, BOMBSHELLS...
...ARE YOU READY FOR THE NEXT ARENA?
HA HA HA...
End

COVER LAYOUTS
BY ANT LUCIA

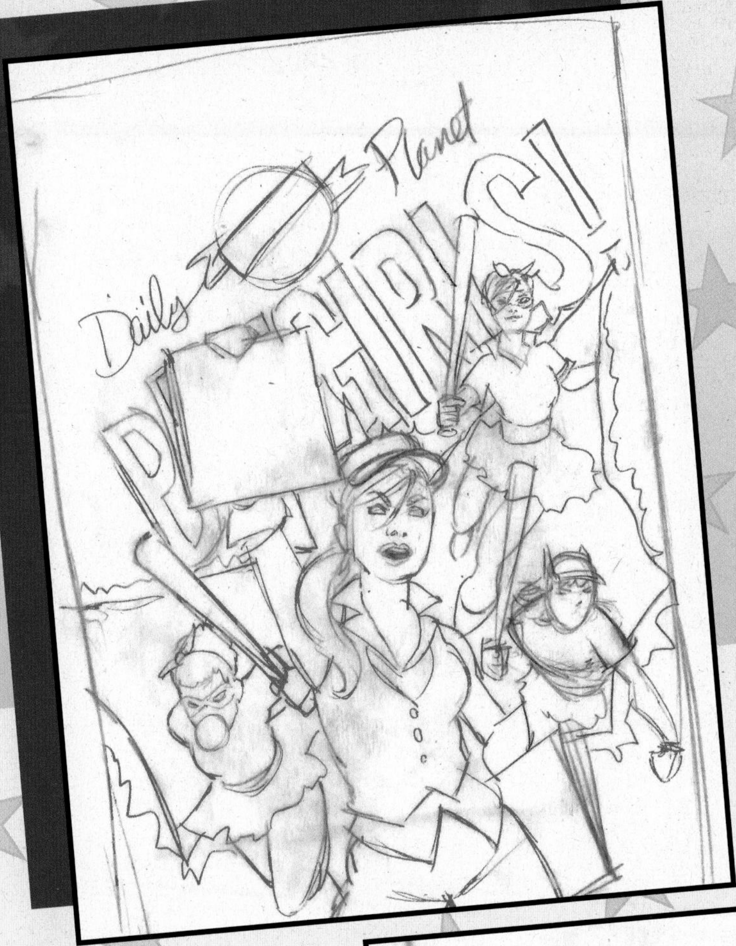

Daily Planet

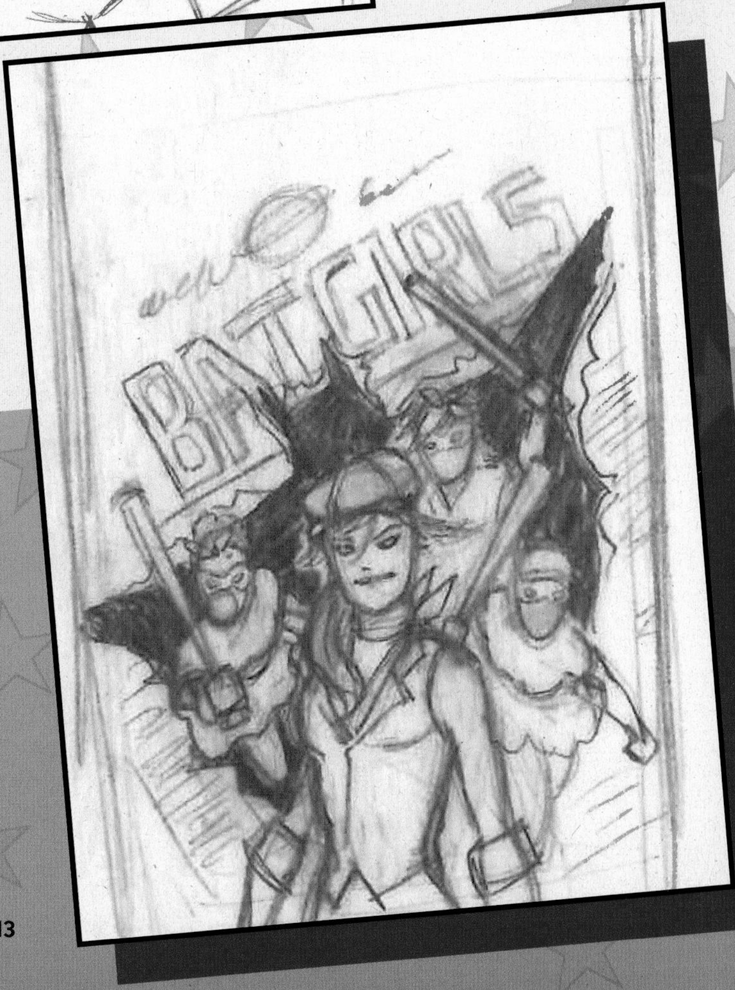

BATGIRLS

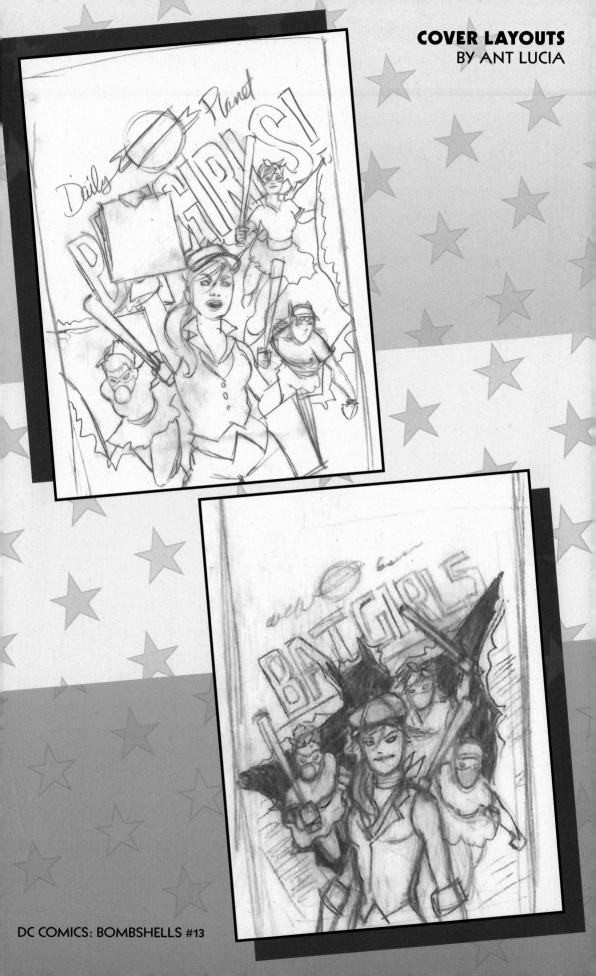

DC COMICS: BOMBSHELLS #15

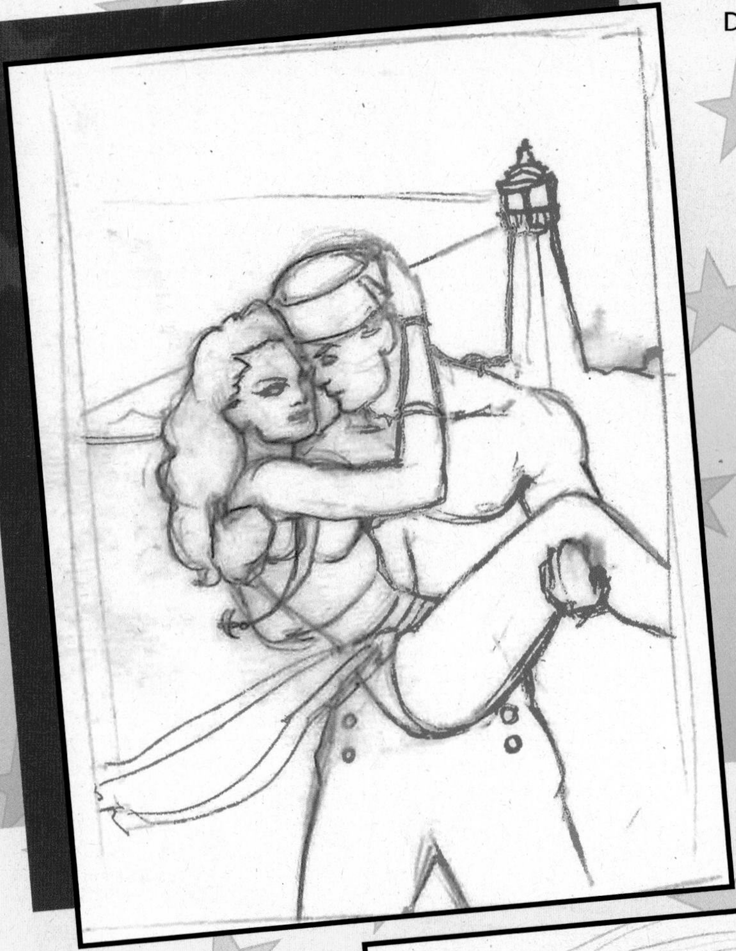

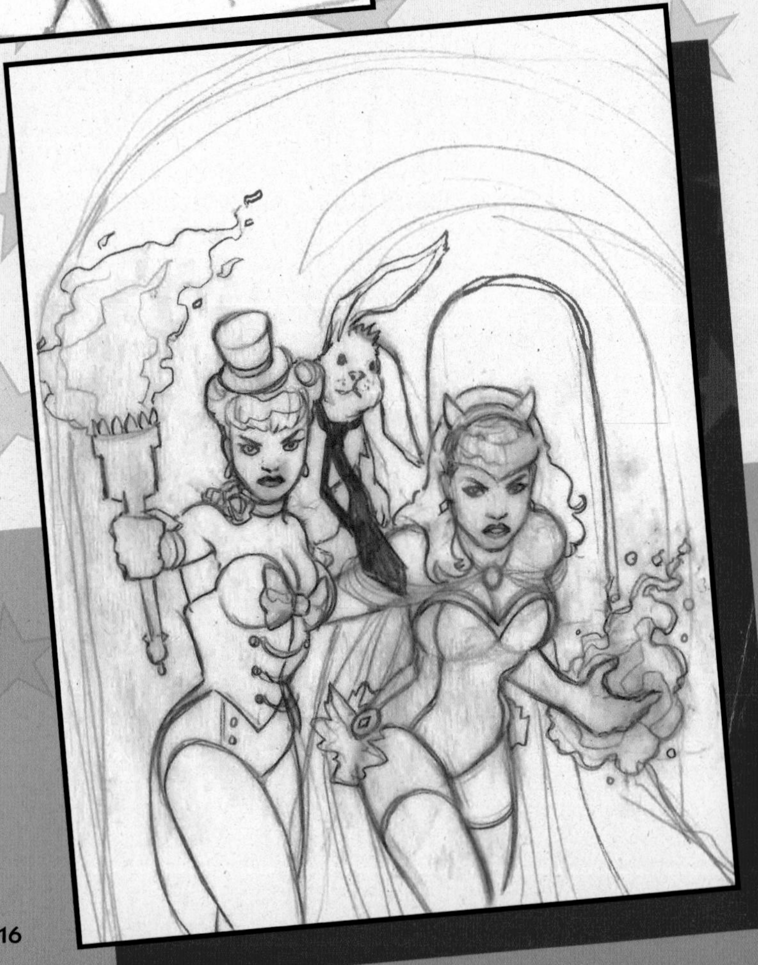

DC COMICS: BOMBSHELLS #16

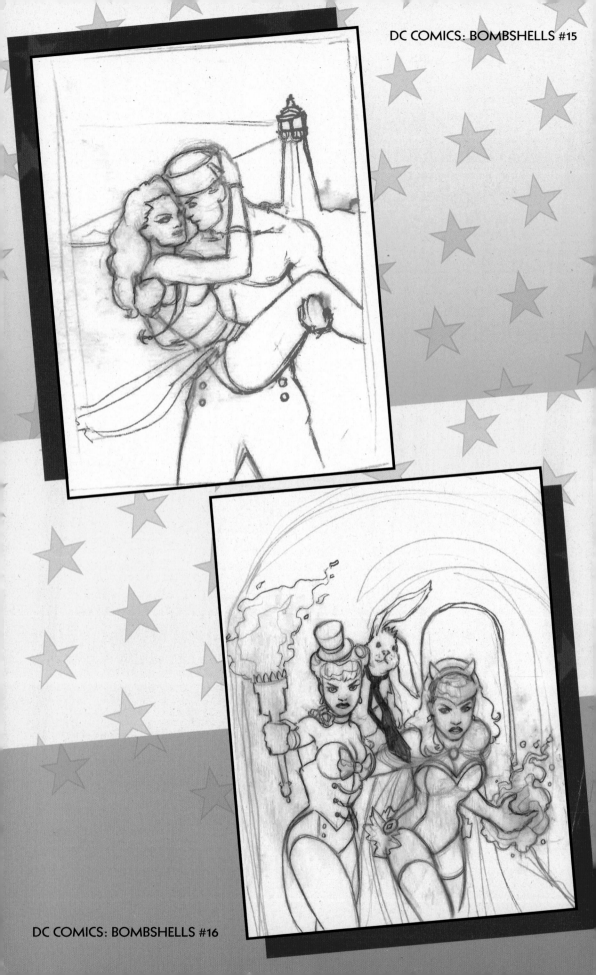

DC COMICS: BOMBSHELLS #17

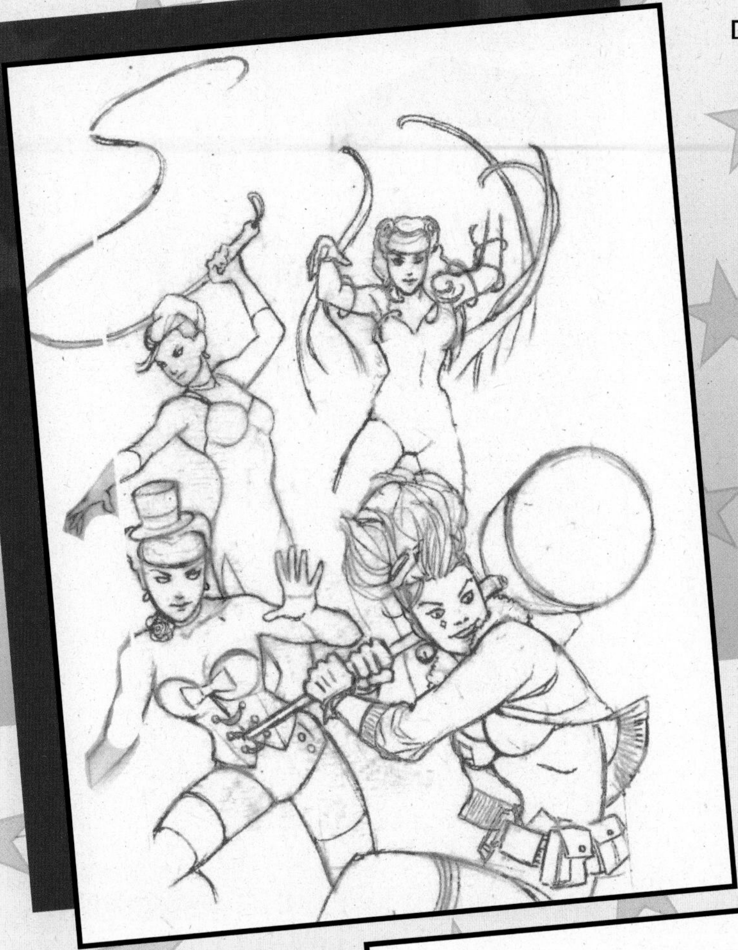

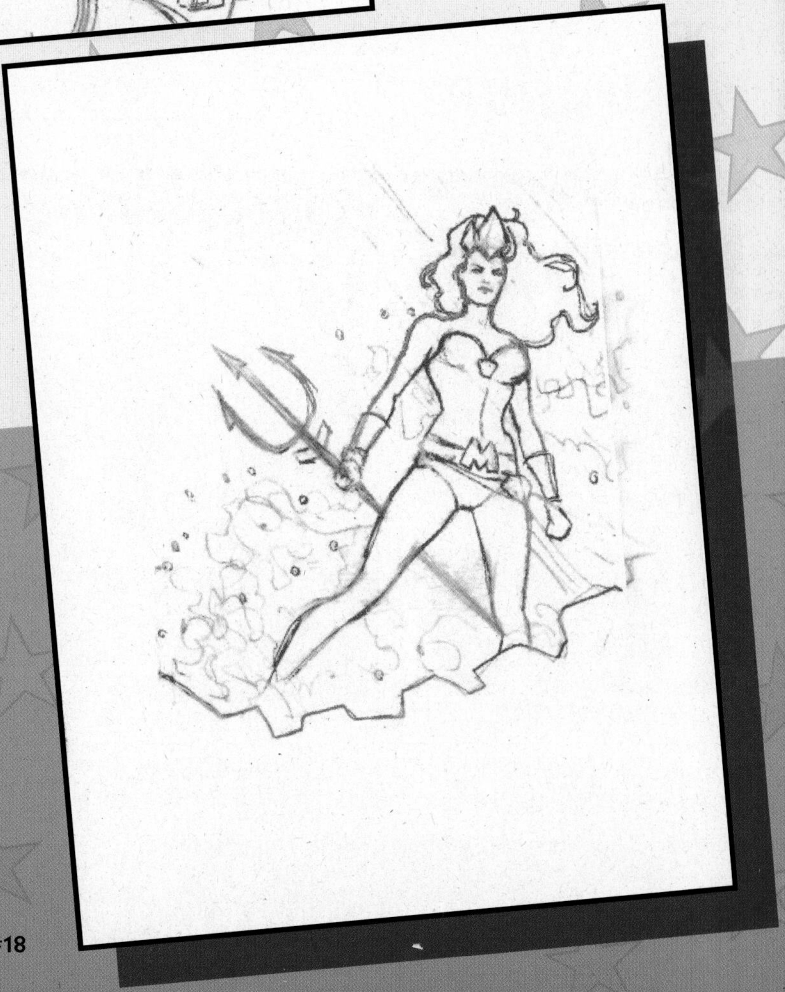

DC COMICS: BOMBSHELLS #18

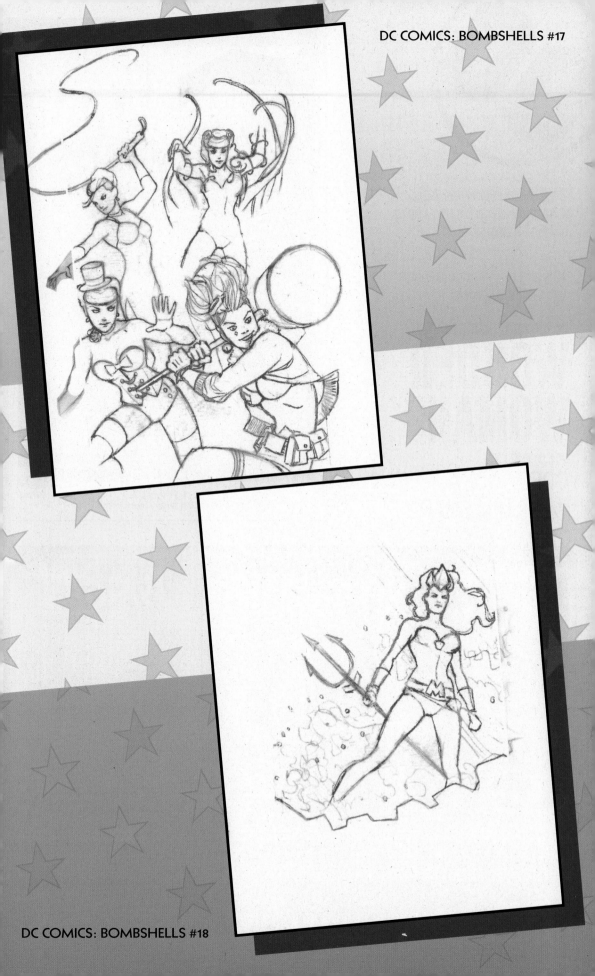

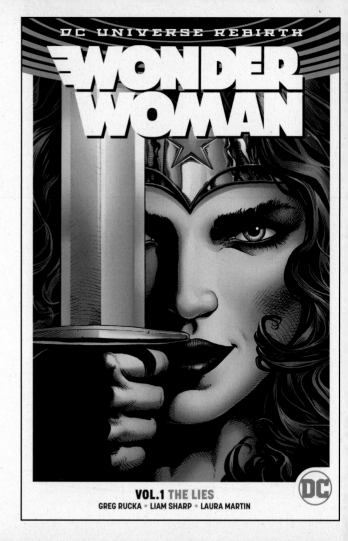